# COLLINS
## POCKET GUIDE

# BIRDS
## OF BRITAIN & EUROPE
### WITH NORTH AFRICA & THE MIDDLE EAST
HERMANN HEINZEL • RICHARD FITTER • JOHN PARSLOW

HarperCollins*Publishers*
77–85 Fulham Palace Road
London W6 8JB

03 02 01 00 99 98

12 11 10 9 8 7 6 5 4

First published 1972
Second Edition 1973
Third edition 1974
Reprinted 1976, 1977
Fourth edition 1979
Reprinted with revisions to the text 1984
Reprinted 1987, 1990, 1992
Completely redesigned, repainted, rewritten, revised and updated
edition 1995
Reprinted with text revisions 1997
Reprinted with text revisions 1998

ISBN 0 00 219894 0

Colour reproduction and film setting by
Saxon Photolitho Ltd, Norwich, UK
Printed & bound by Mondadori Editore, Milan, Italy

# Contents

**Passerines.** The following families, also called Songbirds or Perching Birds, belong to the large order Passeriformes. They are all land birds, mostly small, but including the crows (Corvidae). Most of the commoner and more familiar birds of the countryside and town parks and gardens are songbirds. Here they are all shown on a larger scale than the birds illustrated above.

# Introduction

## The Text

All the birds of Europe, North Africa and the Middle East are described in the text, species by species, arranged in their families. For the boundaries of this area, see p.14.

The **text** stresses the characters which are most important for identifying birds in the field, and especially those which are less obvious or which cannot be shown in the illustrations, for instance song, call notes, habits such as mode of flight, and habitat.

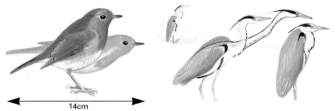

14cm

**Size** in centimetres (cm.), measured by length (L) from the tip of the bill to the tip of the tail, is given at the end of each description. If a bird, e.g. Grey Heron (p.48), is at rest, it may be hunched up and so not showing its full length. Wingspan in centimetres (WS), largely taken from *Birds of the Western Palaearctic*, though known to be less precise than the lengths, is given for certain larger species, mainly seabirds and birds of prey, where it may help in identification.

Reed Warbler (p.282). Song a continuous medley of 'churrs', 'chirrucs' and mimicked bird calls, usually uttered within a reed-bed.

Marsh Warbler (p.282). Song louder, jerkier, more musical, varied and mimetic than Reed Warbler, often from prominent perch and at night.

**Voice** is often one of the most important clues to a bird's identity, and in a few instances, such as Chiffchaff and Willow Warbler (p.296) and Reed and Marsh Warblers (p.282), is almost essential to certain identification in the field. Birds utter two main kinds of sound, song and call notes. **Song** is a specialised utterance, usually designed to establish and maintain a male bird's right to a breeding territory, which it will defend against other males of the same species; it may also help to attract females to the chosen territory. Song is therefore usually loud and fairly continuous, and is normally only heard before and during the breeding season, though some birds, e.g. Robin (p.258) and Wren (p.314) also sing again in the autumn, after the moult. Some songbirds also utter subsong, a quiet form of their normal song, apparently related to their learning efforts when young. **Call notes** on the other hand, can be heard all the year round and are the normal conversation of a bird: they express alarm, anger, warning or the need to maintain contact. Only a few larger birds, e.g. scoters (p.76), are silent outside the breeding season. The text continues the convention of reproducing bird calls and song, inevitably somewhat inexactly, in words designed to describe sounds that may have vowels but cannot have consonants. The scientifically more exact sonagrams are unintelligible to most laypersons.

**Habitat**, the type of country where a bird is usually found, where it feeds or roosts or makes its nest, is another vital clue to the identity of some species, such as Meadow Pipits (p.242) on moors and Rock Pipits (p.244) on rocky coasts, and Tawny Owls (p.212) in woods and Short-eared Owls (p.208) in open country. The very similar Marsh and Willow Tits (p.308), however, both breed in woods.

Most birds are rather conservative in their choice of breeding habitat, and may even be restricted by a shortage of nest sites, as the Corncrake (p.122) is all over Western Europe due to changes in farming practice and the Barn Owl (p.212) is in Britain due to the lack of holes in old barns and other buildings. On the other hand, man-made changes in habitat may encourage birds to spread. Thus the great increase in gravel workings, especially in Britain, means that Sand Martins (p.238) and Little Ringed Plovers (p.138) now breed in many lowland areas where they were formerly scarce or absent.

Grey Wagtail, 1st w     Yellow Wagtail

Although Ravens (p.326), for instance, rarely stray far from their breeding territory, most birds leave it after their young have flown, and may frequent quite different habitat. Thus Golden Plovers (p.140) breed on moors but winter on lowland grassland or on the coast, while Crossbills (p.352) and Waxwings (p.252) often forsake their northern conifer woods for southern town parks and gardens. The extreme examples of this movement are the annual migration to Africa of many European breeding birds, and the wintering at sea of the cliff-breeding auks (p.188) and Kittiwake (p.174).

Not all birds are resident or present in Britain or even in Europe throughout the year. Some migrate here in spring to breed, returning southwards to winter, perhaps in Africa. Others come here each autumn from places further north to spend the winter in what is to them a warmer climate or a better feeding ground. Thus a wagtail with yellow underparts seen in Britain in January is much more likely to be the resident Grey Wagtail (p.248) than the

The full distribution of the Swallow shows that it migrates south to winter in sub-Saharan Africa.

9

summer visitor Yellow Wagtail (p.248). A few species, passage migrants such as Curlew Sandpiper (p.144), normally visit Britain only in spring and autumn on their way to and from breeding grounds further north and wintering grounds further south. Less frequent visitors can be divided into those which appear in Britain annually in small numbers, e.g. Red-breasted Flycatcher (p.302) and those which occur only irregularly, perhaps at intervals of several years or even decades, such as those on the list of accidentals on pp.368-375.

## Some Acknowledgments

Apart from the personal field experience of the three authors, extending over a period of more than 70 years, the text, like all other such texts, depends on a common quarry of facts in the literature. When the now much revised text was first drafted, in the early 1970s, this quarry was basically Richard Fitter's *Pocket Guide to British Birds* (1952), illustrated by R A Richardson and the first of the modern field guides. This in turn, though based on some 30 years of personal observations, had been quarried mainly from *The Handbook of British Birds* (1938-43) by H F Witherby and others, then the latest in a long line of comprehensive books on British birds, together with the path-breaking *Songs of Wild Birds* (1936) by E M Nicholson and Ludwig Koch. A special word of homage is due to Bernard Tucker, pioneer author of the field characters sections of *The Handbook*.

The maps adjoining the text show the status and distribution of all breeding birds and regular visitors in the region, so that this is omitted from the text.

## Maps

These maps aim to show the general bird-watching reader the approximate distribution of every species found regularly in Europe, North Africa and the Middle East.

The various colours, shadings and symbols are explained in detail in the sample map below. The meaning of the colours is as follows:

**Green**: breeds, bird present for whole year

**Yellow**: breeds, present in summer only
**Blue**: present in winter only
**Blue Hatching**: bird occurs in spring and/or autumn migration, but does not usually breed or overwinter
**Blue Arrow**: shows the general direction of migration for birds that overfly an area, with either only a few alighting or birds alighting only in a few widely scattered localities.

Kestrel, p.108. Resident; about 50,000 pairs in Britain, thinning out to the west, and 10,000 pairs in Ireland.

Blackbird, p.272. Resident; about 4,400,000 pairs in Britain, mainly in the lowlands, and 1,800,000 pairs in Ireland.

Nightingale, p.256. Summer visitor; about 5,500 pairs in Britain; absent from Ireland.

Moussier's Redstart, p.262. A bird whose whole world range lies within the region.

Steller's Eider, p.74. A winter visitor, with only a marginal range in the region.

Several intractable problems face the compilers of small-scale maps such as these. For instance, they cannot show how common a bird is within its range – Kestrel and Blackbird both occur throughout Britain, but although their British ranges are similar, Blackbirds are always commoner than Kestrels; see the British Trust for Ornithology's *New Atlas of Breeding Birds in Britain and Ireland* (1993) for how this can be dealt with in larger maps. Small-scale maps also tend to exaggerate the occurrence of species within their range, since all birds have certain habitat preferences, but few as broad as Blackbird and Wren. A breeding bird may frequent only larger freshwater bodies, e.g Great Crested Grebe (p.26), or have altitudinal preferences linked with local climate or habitat. Some birds tend to be nomadic, breeding in different districts from year to year. Thus the Black-necked Grebe (p.26), which will only breed on still fresh water at a critical shallow depth, moves elsewhere when the water dries out during droughts. To ensure that the range of such very local, often colonial, breeding birds shows up on these maps, it has sometimes had to be deliberately exaggerated.

The mapping of wintering ranges is also difficult since these depend partly on the severity of the winter or, with birds that feed on berries or seeds, on a food supply that often fluctuates from year to year. Thus in a normal winter many thousands of Lapwings, both migrants from northern Europe and locally bred birds, are found throughout Britain, but in a severe one, such as 1985-86, they almost all depart for southern Europe. Scandinavian breeding birds such as Fieldfares may linger, even in the far north of Norway, through most of a mild winter, but in a normal cold one, or when food is short, none remain there.

Each map shows the full distribution of the species in the region. All maps do not always show the whole region, as with the map on the left for the Nightingale, which only occurs south of Scandinavia. With birds, such as Moussier's Redstart (left) and Steller's Eider (left), that have an even smaller range, the map shows only the area where the bird occurs, but with an identifiable adjacent geographic feature (Red Sea, Spain) to allow the distribution to be placed in context. Rare birds, when they do not breed in the area, do not have maps.

The information on which these maps are based has been derived from many sources. All current compilers of such maps are now indebted to the editors of the great *Handbook of the Birds of Europe, the Middle East and North Africa* (1977-1994). The first edition of our own book (1972) was also indebted to the editors of its predecessor *The Handbook of British Birds* (1938-1944); to G P Dementiev and N A Gladkov's *The Birds of the Soviet Union* (1951-1954); to P A D Hollom's maps in the Peterson *Field Guide to the Birds of Britain and Europe* (1954) and to

K H Voous's *Atlas of European Birds* (1960). More recently the British Trust for Ornithology has produced three atlases for Britain and Ireland, two for breeding birds (1976 and 1993) and one for wintering birds (1986). In France, L Yeatman edited the pioneer *Atlas des Oiseaux nicheurs de France* (1976) and his daughter D Yeatman-Berthelot followed with the *Atlas des Oiseaux de France en Hiver* (1991). In 1988 P A D Hollom produced further maps in *Birds of the Middle East and North Africa*.

The maps in this book owe much to the pioneering work of all these authors, perhaps most of all to Dementiev, Gladkov and Hollom. Fresh information is continuously becoming available from the great array of national bird atlases, check-lists and other ornithological books and journals produced in recent decades. The information from western Europe tends to be more complete, accurate and up-to-date than from elsewhere, simply because there are more ornithologists and bird-watchers and more publications there than elsewhere in the region.

Like all published information, these maps will start to become out of date on the day they go to press. The authors and publishers will welcome any information that will either bring them up to date or correct existing errors.

# The Illustrations

We have carefully designed these to show all significantly distinct plumages of all birds that breed in the region or occur there regularly. For many they also show typical flight and other attitudes. The main picture of each bird is in breeding plumage, i.e. its plumage from late winter to summer, though the ducks (pp.62-81) moult into breeding plumage in late autumn after starting to go into 'eclipse', as their moult plumage is called, about midsummer. Feather tips gradually wear away, so that most plumages get steadily duller the longer it is since the last moult. At first, when freshly moulted, they may look brighter than they appear in the plates, but just before the moult they may look duller and dowdier. For a few birds, e.g. Brambling (p.338), the process is reversed, brighter colours being revealed as the tips wear down, while others have three moults, the third being either partial, as when Black-headed Gulls (p.168) assume their brown hood in late winter, or complete, as in Ptarmigan (p.110). For the great majority of birds, we give every distinct plumage, breeding and winter, male and female, juvenile and immature when these are distinct enough. In a few groups, however, notably the waders and gulls, where there are many plumages, often only slightly different, we have not been able to do so. Juvenile plumage is the first feathered as distinct from downy plumage, and any other plumages that intervene between the juvenile and adult stages are called immature, as for instance with the birds of prey and gulls, many of which take several years to reach adult plumage. Some winter plumages may start to appear immediately at the end of the breeding season, in summer.

Where relevant, we also show important colour variations or morphs, both spread throughout the whole population as with the Cuckoo (p.202), Ruff (p.150) and Buzzard (p.94), or occurring in different regions, as with subspecies. We omit, however, most of the numerous instances of partial albinism, melanism or other colour forms that occur as freaks or sports.

The main birds on each page are painted to scale, but colour variants and subspecies, birds in flight and other behaviour sketches, birds shown for the sake of comparison and rare visitors are mostly shown on a smaller scale.

Besides the above sex symbols and plumage abbreviations, we also use the abbreviations opposite:

Family or group to which the birds on the plate belong.

Showing a typical large flock of the species.

Female in breeding plumage.

Male in breeding plumage.

Male in winter plumage.

English name of species. Capital letters indicate a species.

Typical habits or identification points.

In flight to show typical shape or features of wing or rump.

1st year, 2nd year, etc to indicate plumages in the 1st year etc after the juv plumage (in some larger species up to the 4th year) before the bird assumes adult plumage.

Subspecies name, when more than one shown.

Other plumages may be illustrated if theyre are important intermediary stages between breeding and non-breeding, summer winter etc.

♂ = male
♀ = female
juv = juvenile
imm = immature
br = breeding (summer)
nbr = non-breeding (winter)
Subspecies text on a plate is always in smaller type and summarises range and other details where space permits. For explanation of subspecies, see p.16.

Subspecies and various special identification characters, such as head shapes and patterns, are often shown on the left-hand pages.

**13**

# The Birds in the Book

We include all birds which either breed in, or visit regularly in the winter or on migration, any part of Europe; of North Africa and the Arabian Peninsula south to about 27°N; and of SW Asia and the Middle East, east to the Caspian Sea and about 52°E in Iran (see map on p.10). It thus includes virtually the whole of the Western Palaearctic Region, except for the bulk of the Arabian Peninsula and parts of the Sahara. It covers all the NE Atlantic islands (Azores, Canaries, Madeira, Faeroe, Iceland, Jan Mayen and Spitsbergen, but not the Cape Verde Is), all Morocco, Egypt and the Red Sea N of Hurghada, all Iraq, the Caucasus, the western shores of the Caspian Sea and the whole European part of the former USSR, including the foothills of the Urals. The breeding birds of East Greenland are also included, since they are all also European birds.

The term Levant is here used in the narrower sense to refer to the area between Turkey and Egypt at the east end of the Mediterranean, including Syria, Lebanon, Israel (Palestine) and Jordan; it originally referred to the whole east end of the Mediterranean.

A White-rumped Sandpiper (p.148), a rare but annual vagrant from North America to Europe, mostly July-October, between Dunlins and Curlew Sandpipers (p.144), from both of which it needs to be distinguished.

Birds which do not occur regularly present a problem, partly because bird-watching is now so intensive in western Europe that birds new to the European list of vagrants are added almost every year. Already a great many North American migrants have been recorded as vagrants in Europe, and within the next decade or two it seems likely that the majority of those that use either the east coast or the Mississippi flyway will have been identified at least once on the wrong side of the Atlantic. To avoid overloading the book with vagrant North American and also East Asian species, we have therefore provided only thumbnail sketches of the more infrequent of these accidentals, on pp.368-375. Those vagrants that have occurred most often, however, together with many waders and gulls, are included in the main text among their commoner relatives. Some vagrants too are clumped in the main text following the regular species, viz. the most frequent escaped waterfowl (pp.376-377), thrushes (pp.276-279) and North American and East Asian songbirds (pp.362-367).

# Birds in Britain and Ireland

Distribution, status and relative abundance in Britain (England, Wales, Scotland) and Ireland we indicate by the following symbols and letters, which end the text description of each bird.

● Rsmw

● Regular: widespread and common. Likely to be seen every year by most bird-watchers.
⊙ Regular: local or uncommon. Can be seen every year by visiting its favoured localities.
○ Regular: very local or rare. Usually in very small numbers, or restricted to very few localities.
- Vagrant or Escape (including deliberate release).

|  | Main status | Lesser status |
|---|---|---|
| Resident | R | r |
| Summer resident | S | s (breeds) |
| Migrant | M | m |
| Winter visitor | W | w |
| Annual Vagrant | A |  |
| Irregular Vagrant | V |  |
| Escape/Release | E |  |
| Has bred in Britain/Ireland (b) (not regularly now) | | |

Thus the Kestrel (p.108) is Rsmw = Widespread and common *Resident*, some also occurring as a *summer resident* that winters outside Britain/Ireland, as a *migrant* that breeds and winters outside Britain/Ireland, though passing through on migration, and as a *winter visitor* which breeds outside Britain/Ireland but spends the winter here. Other examples are the resident House Sparrow (p.334), which is just R, and the Blackbird (p.272), which is a common migrant and winter visitor, RmW.

# Classifying Birds

Scientists classify all animals, in a series of groupings, starting with 22 extant phyla and proceeding downwards through classes, orders, families (ending in -idae), subfamilies (ending in -inae) and genera (plural of genus) to the actual species, below which there are sometimes subspecies or races based on geographical variation. Birds belong to the phylum Chordata (backboned animals), along with the mammals, reptiles and fishes, and are themselves distinguished as the Class Aves. Within the Aves there are 27 orders of living birds, comprising some 8500 living or recently extinct species, new ones being still discovered every year.

Much the largest order of birds is the Passeriformes, loosely known as songbirds, perching birds or passerines, which includes more than half the known bird species and more than a third of the 154 bird families. They are all terrestrial and very diverse in shape and form, but generally adapted to perching in trees and often have a well-developed song. Here the Passeriformes start with the larks (p.230) and end with the buntings (p.360).

We use the family as the basic unit of classification, 74 families or just under half of all bird families, being represented in the bird fauna of the area. The beginning of all but the smallest families is indicated by a solid black circle ● beside the heading.

For the actual arrangement of birds in the text, we have adopted, with a few exceptions, mainly due to the need to fit birds on to plates, the order of families used in the *List of Recent Holarctic Bird Species*, by the Dutch ornithologist K H Voous (1977) and published in *Ibis*, Vols.115 and 119 (1973, 1977).

# Bird Names

The scientific name of an animal is part of the international language of science, enabling scientists and naturalists in one country to know what those in another are talking about. For instance 'Raven' might not mean anything to a Chinese ornithologist, but *Corvus corax* would. An animal's scientific name consists of two Latinised words, the name of the genus, which has a capital initial, followed by the name of the species, which does not. Where subspecies or geographical races are referred to, a third word is added to the name. Thus the Guillemot *Uria aalge* has a northern race *Uria aalge aalge* and a southern race *Uria aalge albionis*. For scientific names we have followed Voous (see p.15), except where later research has suggested changes. For English names we have followed our first edition as far as possible so as not to confuse readers used to familiar names, but for some non-European birds we use the new English names which the British Ornithologists' Union has suggested for world-wide use.

# How to Set about Identifying Birds

The basic rules and requirements for identifying birds are few and simple. The first necessity is to be patient. You cannot expect, especially when you first begin, to know what every bird is the first time you see it. You must have a reasonably good view, and for long enough, and regrettably birds go about their own affairs oblivious, or sometimes all too aware, of the bird-watcher eagerly trying to find out whether they are seeing a Whitethroat or a Lesser Whitethroat. The second necessity is to be quiet. You will certainly not see or hear many birds while you plunge noisily through the undergrowth, or chatter unheedingly to a friend. A knowledgeable friend can, however, be a great help in setting your footsteps on the right path, and especially in identifying the songs and calls of birds you cannot see. If you have no such friend, and even if you have, join a local bird-watching society or field club, most of which have field meetings for beginners. You can also visit one of the coastal bird observatories. The addresses of both societies and observatories can be found in *The Birdwatcher's Yearbook and Diary* (p.22). The full recipe for successful bird identification is thus patience, quietness, a reasonably sharp eye and ear, knowledgeable friends and a good bird book.

Although the common garden birds can readily be identified by attracting them within close range at a well-sited bird table, for general bird-watching a pair of binoculars is essential. The best magnifications for binoculars are 7x and 8x. Their most important quality is light-gathering power, measured by the figure that represents the diameter of the object-lens and is usually engraved after the magnification, e.g. 7 x 40 or 8 x 50. You get the key figure by dividing the magnification into the diameter, e.g. 7 into 40 goes 6 (or near enough) and any result between 4 and 7 is okay.

It is also helpful to memorise the names for the various parts of a bird on the pictures opposite. A beginner may find it hard to remember all these technical terms, but if you want a more experienced bird-watcher to identify a bird from your description, it makes it much easier if you can tell him or her you saw a white spot on the scapulars instead of just on the wing. So, once these are memorised, you can make more meaningful notes on what you have seen.

# Topography of a Bird

**Upperwing**

Primaries

Greater primary coverts

Median primary coverts

Alula
Carpal
Greater coverts
Median coverts
Lesser coverts

Secondaries

Tertials

Tail feathers

Rump

Upper tail coverts

Back

Nape

Tertials

Axillaries (armpit)

Underwing coverts ('wing lining')

**Underwing**

Inner web

Quill

Outer web

**Tail feather**

Crown stripe
Supercilium
Lateral crown stripe
Eye stripe
Lore
Ear coverts
Chin
Moustachial stripe

Border of supercilium
Supercilium
Nape
Scapulars
Tertials
Primaries
Secondaries
Greater coverts
Median coverts
Lesser coverts
Crown
Malar stripe
Submoustachial stripe
Moustachial stripe

**Primary feather**

Crown
Lore
Forehead
Bill
Chin
Throat
Side of neck
Breast
Wing bars
Alula
Primary coverts
Flanks
Belly
Ear coverts
Mantle
Scapulars
Tertials

Upper tail coverts
Tail feathers
Vent
Under tail coverts
Tibia ('thigh')
Tarsus
Outer tail feathers

17

# Important Identification Points

When you start bird-watching, it is often hard to tell the difference between birds of the same size, not just the traditional little brown birds, which may be warblers or sparrows or buntings, but large black ones (rooks and crows) and female ducks as well. So, in keeping your notes, bear in mind the following points to look for in seeking the identity of a new or doubtful bird:

1. Size, compared with some fairly common bird, and general shape. Among land birds, for instance, Blue Tit, House Sparrow, Starling, Lapwing, Rook and Pheasant are six well-known birds that you can compare with the sizes of other birds. On fresh water you might have Moorhen, Mallard and Mute Swan, and on the coast Ringed Plover, Black-headed Gull and Herring Gull.

2. General colour above and below. Thus a rook-sized bird that is grey with black head and wings can only be a Hooded Crow (p.324).

3. Any conspicuous marks or patches, their colour and position on the bird. An all-black bird, smaller than a Rook, with a grey patch on the nape must certainly be a Jackdaw (p.324).

4. Size and shape of bill, legs, wings, tail and neck. A black and white bird, nearly rook-sized, with a long tail is clearly a Magpie (p.322). A long-legged brown bird with a markedly down-curved bill, on the other hand, may be either a Curlew or a Whimbrel, or in some parts of the region could even be a Slender-billed Curlew (p.156).

5. Colour of bill, legs, feet and eyes. Bill colour separates the Chough and Alpine Chough (p.322), and eye colour distinguishes the Long-eared Owl (p.208) from the Short-eared Owl (p.208).

6. Actions and character of flight or gait, e.g. whether flight bounding, like a finch, woodpecker or Little Owl, or direct like a crow or wader, and whether the bird runs like a Starling or hops like a Blackbird. Some birds also have helpful mannerisms, such as the tail-wagging of wagtails, hovering of Kestrel and some other birds of prey, and plummet-diving of Gannet and sea terns. A small brown bird with a curved bill that creeps about tree trunks will be either a Treecreeper or a Short-toed Treecreeper (p.314).

7. Any call notes or song. Voice is one of the most helpful clues to a bird's identity. Some birds with very similar plumage, such as Chiffchaff and Willow Warbler (p.296) and Marsh and Willow Tits (p.308) can be distinguished much more readily by their calls than by sight. An experienced bird-watcher in woodland or scrub will detect more birds by ear than by eye.

8. Comparisons with any other birds that come to mind. For instance, a small falcon that "flies like a swift" may well prove to be a Hobby (p.108), and a small brown bird with a straight bill that behaves like a woodpecker is likely to be a Wryneck (p.228).

9. Date, time, place and weather are also important clues to a bird's identity. A wagtail with yellow underparts in southern England in November is much more likely to be a Grey Wagtail than a Yellow Wagtail (p.248), which as a summer visitor should by this time be in Africa. A brown owl beating over the heather at noon is more likely to be a Short-eared Owl (p.208) than a Tawny Owl (p.212), which rarely flies by day and then usually in or near broad-leaved woodland close to sunrise or dusk. In Britain a silent Reed Warbler need only to be checked to see if it is in fact a Marsh Warbler (p.282) if it is somewhere near the small area of overlap in southern England between these two very similar species. A small dark white-rumped bird seen over Lake Windermere is much more likely to be a House Martin (p.240) than a small petrel (p.28).

10. Habitat and general surroundings. A small red-tailed bird seen in oakwood in Gloucestershire is likely to be a Redstart (p.262), but one seen on an industrial site in East London is almost certainly a Black Redstart. However, odd individual birds can and do turn up in the most unlikely places. One can see a Peregrine in the centre of a large city, a Green Woodpecker on a treeless cliff slope, and a lost migrant bird almost anywhere.

11. Angle of vision, conditions of light, distance of bird from observer, and whether it was at rest, flying or swimming, should all be noted. A Magpie (p.322) flying towards you so that you cannot see its tail looks very odd indeed, and birds flying directly towards or away from the observer are often almost impossible to identify. When gulls are directly overhead, for instance, unless they cant to one side, it may be impossible to see the colour of their back and wings, which would reveal whether they are Herring Gulls or Lesser Blackbacks (p.172). In poor light or misty conditions all kinds of strange illusions may occur. Excellent advice on bird recording can be had from the handy little *Bird Recording Handbook* obtainable from the British Trust for Ornithology (p.22).

An unfamiliar 'rare bird' may well be an escape from captivity, like this siskin-like Himalayan Greenfinch *Carduelis spinoides*, behaving like a fully wild bird.

## ... and If You Do See a Rare Bird

Those lucky enough to find in Britain a bird that is rare in a particular county may like to report it to their county bird recorder. whose name and address may be found in the *Birdwatcher's Yearbook* (p.22), together with those of the Hon. Secretary of the Irish Rare Birds Committee. Birds rare in Britain as a whole may be reported to the Rarities Committee of *British Birds* (p.23), whose Secretary can supply a list of the species rare enough to be adjudicated by the Committee and the form in which records should be submitted, with criteria inevitably much stricter than those set out on p.18 for beginners.

## Attracting Birds

Many people would like to see more birds around their home and garden. You can always attract some of the commoner birds even if you live on an upper floor in the middle of a town, so long as there are some gardens, a park or a row of street trees nearby. There are two main ways of doing this: by feeding them and by encouraging them to breed in well-sited nestboxes. In winter many birds can be induced to approach the windows of a house by a suitably sited bird table, kept supplied with either commercial bird foods or the more old-fashioned household scraps, bits of fat and so forth. A container full of peanuts hung on a branch will bring the tits and with luck a Nuthatch too, as will the more traditional half coconut or old bone. By careful varying of the food supply, even such seemingly unlikely birds as Great Spotted Woodpecker can be tempted in. In really hard weather the feeding of birds by householders in northern and western Europe saves the lives of hundreds of thousands of birds and has led, for instance, to Great Tits wintering further north in Scandinavia.

Nestboxes are of two main types, those with a small hole, for tits, Pied Flycatcher, Redstart and Nuthatch

This nestbox can be used by tits and many other small birds, depending on the size of the entrance hole.

The open type of nestbox, suitable for Robins and Wrens among others, should not be used where Magpies are common, as they will rob it.

(which will plaster up the hole), and those with an open front for such ledge-builders as Robin, Wren and Spotted Flycatcher. Special boxes or ledges cater for Treecreeper, Tawny Owl, Swallow and House Martin, while Mallards can be induced to nest in wicker baskets.

Nestboxes, bird tables, nut containers and bird food can all be obtained from the Royal Society for the Protection of Birds and from the British Trust for Ornithology (p.22), which also publishes a small book on nestboxes. Commercial bird foods are widely advertised in bird journals, and together with peanuts are available in many shops. However, some peanuts in shops have been treated with substances toxic to birds, so care is necessary.

The entrance hole should always be at the top of the nestbox; all space above a low entrance hole is wasted.

# Where to Look for Birds

Another key to successful bird-watching is to know where to look for different species, which vary greatly from one habitat to another. In the farmed countryside, with its mixture of arable and grass fields, small ponds, houses with gardens and scattered broad-leaved woodlands, you can see a fair variety of birds during a morning's or afternoon's walk. If the patchwork of habitats also includes some wetlands, marshes, lakes or rivers, a total of 50-60 species in a few hours is by no means impossible, especially in late spring or early summer. Keen motorised bird-spotters or twitchers (the ones who travel to seek new species for their life lists) intent on their sport can knock up 100 or even 150 in a day, especially in such favoured regions as East Anglia, Dorset or Kent.

Habitats are most easily generally classified into land, waterside and open-water habitats.

**Land habitats** are a whole spectrum of overlapping habitats, often followed in sequence by the natural development of an area: from bare ground with increasing vegetation cover to dense woodland. In deserts, lack of rainfall allows only the sparsest vegetation, and leads to a characteristic assemblage that includes larks, wheatears and sandgrouse. Desert merges imperceptibly into semi-desert and grassy steppe, represented in settled Britain and western Europe by the artificially maintained chalk downs, grass moors and farmed grasslands. Here there are still some birds of open country, such as larks, pipits, partridges and Stone Curlew. In northern Europe the hill grasslands, maintained as such largely by sheep grazing, merge into the heather moors, with their special group of birds, including Willow/Red Grouse, Meadow Pipit, Skylark and Ring Ouzel.

Heather is a woody undershrub, so that heather moor is botanically a scrub formation. Taller scrub, the intermediate stage between grassland and woodland, is one of the region's most important bird habitats, favoured by many thrushes, warblers, finches and other songbirds. On acid soils it takes the form of heath. A mixture of patches or glades of open grassland, scrub and scattered trees provides birds with a wide range of ecological niches. This mixture is found especially in open woodlands and on wood edges, and in much of Europe also includes houses and gardens in villages, suburbs and towns. The characteristic garden birds are thus also those of open woodland and scrub: Blackbird, Song Thrush, Robin, Dunnock, Wren, Great and Blue Tits, Chaffinch and Greenfinch.

Scrub develops naturally into woodland, which is of two main kinds: *coniferous*, in a broad belt across northern Europe, called the taiga, and in a corresponding zone in the Alps and other mountains further south; and *broad-leaved*, mainly deciduous trees such as oak, ash and beech, occupying the central and southern lowlands of Europe and, of course, most of lowland Britain. Millennia of human destruction have made extensive woodland a rare habitat in Britain, Ireland, North Africa and the Middle East.

Coniferous woodland has a special assemblage of birds, including Goldcrest, Coal and Crested Tits and crossbills. Broad-leaved woodland, besides most of the familiar garden birds, holds many birds, such as Woodcock and Pied Flycatcher, which are rare or absent in gardens, even large country ones, and some, such as Black Stork and Lesser Spotted Eagle, which are never seen there at all.

Waterside habitats consist of both waterlogged swamps, fens and bogs, and the more open margins of lakes and rivers. The long-legged wading birds, herons, rails, snipes and sandpipers, are typical of the waterside, together with a few songbirds, such as the reed warblers. Lapwing and Golden Plover, on the other hand, breed in open country but resort to the waterside in winter. The Arctic and sub-Arctic tundra is the northern counterpart of the desert, but in winter is too cold for almost all birds, and in spring and summer is mostly waterlogged and so attracts waders and other waterside birds.

The waterside habitats by the sea consist mainly of cliffs, where many birds of the open sea nest, and saltmarshes and mudflats, where numerous waders feed along the shore.

The birds of open water, both sea and fresh water, must of course come to land to breed, though for grebes 'land' is a floating nest of waterweeds. However, grebes, divers, diving ducks, swans, auks, gannets, cormorants, petrels, phalaropes, terns and many gulls spend all or most of the rest of their lives on the water, some of them, such as grebes, Moorhen, Coot and most ducks, breeding by fresh water, and others, such as gannets, auks and phalaropes wintering far out at sea.

# Bird-watchers and Birds

The closer you are to a bird, the greater your responsibility not to disturb it. In Britain, if it is a rare nesting bird, it is actually illegal to disturb it. But a responsible bird-watcher should not worry whether a nesting bird is rare or not. He or she should not interfere in any way with any bird's routine for rearing its young, i.e. should not flush it off its nest, or prevent it from feeding its young. If you see a bird hanging around, either with food in its bill or showing vocal signs of distress, it has young nearby and you should move on at once, even if you have just started a picnic. Nor should you disturb birds once they have gone to roost. In very cold weather, it is especially important not to flush flocks resting either on the ground or on the water, for this makes them use up energy which they will find it hard to replace.

Take great care too in going on private land in pursuit of birds, especially if this involves approaching houses, entering parts of private grounds away from houses, or entering fields with grazing livestock.

For a more detailed birdwatchers' code of conduct, see the *Birdwatcher's Yearbook* (below).

# Bird Societies (for their journals, see below)

Army Ornithological Society

Birdlife International, Wellbrook Court, Girton Rd, Cambridge, CB3 0NA; the international organisation for bird protection, formerly the International Council for Bird Preservation

British Ornithologists' Club

British Ornithologists' Union, c/o Natural History Museum, Tring, Herts HP23 6AP

British Trust for Ornithology, National Centre for Ornithology, The Nunnery, Thetford, Norfolk IP24 2PU

Hawk and Owl Trust

International Council for Bird Preservation, see Birdlife International

Irish Wildbird Conservancy, Ruttledge House, 8 Longford Place, Monkstown, Co. Dublin

Ornithological Society of the Middle East

Royal Air Force Ornithological Society

Royal Naval Birdwatching Society

Royal Society for the Protection of Birds, the Lodge, Sandy, Beds, SG19 2DL : the largest bird society in Europe, with more than 850,000 members

Scottish Ornithologists' Club, 21 Regent Terrace, Edinburgh EH7 5BT

Seabird Group

Welsh Ornithological Society

Wildfowl and Wetlands Trust, New Grounds, Slimbridge, Gloucester GL2 7BT

Addresses are restricted to the principal societies because they change so often (out of 10 given in our 1984 edition, only three were unchanged in 1994). So for current addresses of the above and the names and addresses of the numerous county and other local bird societies and bird recorders, we refer you to *The Birdwatcher's Yearbook* and the Inquiries sections of the RSPB, BTO, and public libraries.

# Bird Journals

*Birding World*, Ticker's, High St, Cley next the Sea, Holt, Norfolk, NR25 7RR; especially for 'twitchers'; monthly, subscription only; runs the Bird Information Service and Birdline, one of several national and regional telephone and pager systems that provide almost constant updates of rare bird information throughout the country; others are advertised in bird journals.

*Birds*, magazine of the Royal Society for the Protection of Birds; quarterly.

*Bird Study* and *BTO News* thrice-yearly scientific journal and bi-monthly newsletter of the British Trust for Ornithology.

*Birdwatch*, P O Box 1786, London E17, 7JG; a monthly magazine, available from newsagents.

*Birdwatcher's Yearbook and Diary*, 25 Manor Park, Maids Moreton, Buckingham MK18 1QX.

*Birdwatching*, Bretton Court, Bretton Centre, Peterborough PE1 2TR; a monthly magazine, available from newsagents.

*British Birds*, Fountains, Park Lane, Blunham, Bedford, MK44 3NJ; the senior journal for serious bird-watchers, founded in 1907; monthly, subscription only.

*Ibis*, journal of the British Ornithologists' Union; quarterly; one of the world's most senior scientific ornithological journals.

*Irish Birds* and *IWC News*, annual journal and quarterly newsletter of the Irish Wildbird Conservancy.

*Scottish Bird News* and *Scottish Birds*, newsletter and journal of the Scottish Ornithological Society; both quarterly.

*Wildfowl* and *Wildfowl and Wetlands*: annual scientific journal and bi-annual magazine of the Wildfowl and Wetlands Trust.

*World Birdwatch*: quarterly magazine of Birdlife International.

## Abbreviations

| | |
|---|---|
| ♂ | Male |
| ♀ | Female |
| br | Breeding |
| cm | Centimetre |
| imm | Immature |
| juv | Juvenile |
| L | Length (see p.8) |
| nbr | Non-breeding |
| Sp | Species (sing.) |
| Spp | Species (plural) |
| Ssp | Subspecies (sing.) |
| Sspp | Subspecies (plural) |
| WS | Wing-span |

## Some Definitions

Albino: white morph

Eclipse: the moult in ducks

Jizz: characteristic appearance or attitude of a bird

Melanic: dark or black morph

Morph: a well-defined and genetically determined plumage variation, co-existing with the normal form in a bird population, e.g. the bridled form of the Guillemot (p.188)

Subspecies: see p.16

Taiga: coniferous forest

Twitcher: bird-watcher who chases after rare birds

**OSTRICH** *Struthio camelus* (Struthionidae): Unmistakable with its huge size and very long pinkish neck and flesh-coloured legs; flightless. Old males are black with white wing and tail feathers, females and juvs/imms are greyer brown. Ssp.*syriacus* formerly inhabited the region; the last known specimen, found near Maan, Jordan, in 1966 may have been washed down by flood water from Saudi Arabia. Releases in the Negev, Israel, are planned from a breeding programme for ssp.*camelus* (Sahara, Sahel) in Hai Bar Reserve. L males 210-275 cm, females 175-190 cm.

● DIVERS: *Gaviidae*. Short-tailed cigar-shape and legs being far back makes them fine divers but clumsy on land. In flight head and neck held straight out, slightly below plane of body, gives them a rather hump-backed look. Vocal mainly when breeding, with loud wailing or laughing calls. Sexes alike; in winter dark above, white below. Juvs less uniform above. In winter at sea inshore, rarely inland.

Of the six main groups of water birds that dive from the surface, divers overlap cormorants and sawbills in size, but are larger than grebes, diving ducks and auks. Most divers hold their head and bill at a shallower angle than cormorants.

**RED-THROATED DIVER** *Gavia stellata*. The smallest and slimmest diver, with faster wing-beats and legs hardly projecting in flight; swims with head and bill at 30° angle, emphasising uptilted effect due to angled lower mandible. In winter, face much whiter than other divers (dark eye standing out, especially in adult), crown and hind neck paler grey, back finely spotted with white, and rear flanks dark. When breeding has red neck patch (which can look black). Flight-note a quacking cackle. Breeds by small waters on moors and tundra, feeding on larger ones or sea. L 53-69 cm. ⊙RmW

**BLACK-THROATED DIVER** *Gavia arctica*. Between Great Northern and Red-throated, especially in size, stoutness of bill, projection of legs beyond tail in flight and speed of wing-beats; most distinctive in breeding plumage with grey head and black patch on grey neck. From bulkier Great Northern in winter differs in less peaked forehead, greyer head and neck, contrasting with dark back and clearly divided from the well-defined white patch at rear of flanks. From Red-throated in winter differs in its darker unspeckled back, larger white patch on rear flanks, and more extensive and contrasting dark area on head and neck, extending below the eye, and head and bill held almost level. Voice and habitat as Great Northern. L 58-73 cm. ⊙RW

**GREAT NORTHERN DIVER** *Gavia immer*. Larger and stouter than Black-throated; when breeding has all-black head and bill, distinctive greyish neck markings, stouter bill, more peaked forehead and heavier flight, feet projecting well beyond tail. In winter crown and hind neck darker than back; line between dark and white less clear-cut, white often extending above eye. Head and bill held almost level. Has loud, eerie, wailing cry; flight note a guttural 'kwuk-kwuk-kwuk'. Breeds by larger lakes, often on islands. L 69-91 cm. ⊙W(b)

**WHITE-BILLED DIVER** *Gavia adamsii*. Slightly larger and bulkier than much commoner Great Northern, differing mainly in yellowish-white bill (whitish-grey in winter Great Northern) and holding head at a 30° angle, emphasised by angled lower mandible. In winter necks of both the two largest divers may show a ghostly pattern of their breeding plumage, and White-billed usually has paler sides to its head and neck, with dark and white still less clearly divided and the eye conspicuous. L 76-91 cm. -A

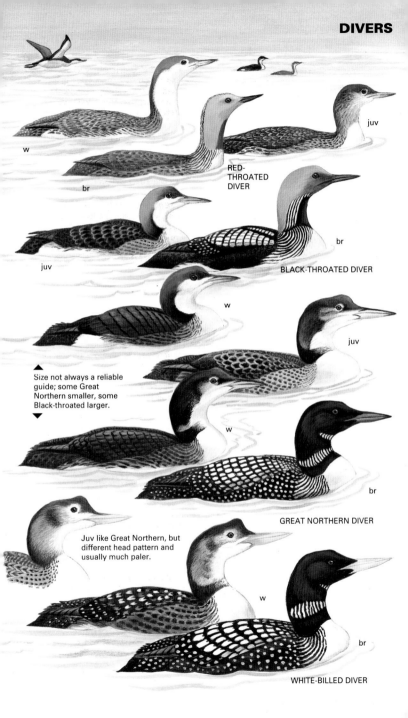

# DIVERS

w

RED-
THROATED
DIVER

juv

br

BLACK-THROATED DIVER

juv

br

w

▲
Size not always a reliable
guide; some Great
Northern smaller, some
Black-throated larger.
▼

juv

w

GREAT NORTHERN DIVER

br

Juv like Great Northern, but
different head pattern and
usually much paler.

w

br

WHITE-BILLED DIVER

● GREBES: *Podicipedidae*. Smaller than divers and with lobed toes, the larger species longer-necked and the smaller ones dumpier. Sexes alike. In winter dark above, white or pale below. Juvs striped on head and neck. In flight hold head and neck below level of body. Juvs have shrill, piping hunger call. Breed on fresh water, sometimes in colonies. In winter also in estuaries and coastal waters.

**GREAT CRESTED GREBE** *Podiceps cristatus*. Breeding adult unmistakable with dark double-horned crest and rufous tippets, used in mutual head-wagging and other striking courtship displays. In winter lack of these makes white cheeks conspicuous. White wing bar in flight. Bill pink. At rest often holds neck erect. Has an extensive range of barking, growling, crooning and clicking calls. L 46-51 cm. ●Rw

**RED-NECKED GREBE** *Podiceps grisegena*. Quite distinct when breeding, with chestnut neck, grey cheeks (darker in older birds), bright yellow base of bill and no ear-tufts. In winter differs from whiter and more graceful Great Crested in yellow of shorter bill, grey neck and lack of pale supercilium, the dark crown coming down below eye-level and shading off gradually into the white cheeks. At a distance more likely to be confused with smaller Black-necked than larger Great Crested. Very vocal when breeding, with loud, quacking, whinnying and braying calls. Winters mainly in coastal waters. L 40-50 cm.
⊙W(b)

**SLAVONIAN GREBE** *Podiceps auritus*. The largest and longest-necked of the three smaller, dumpier and shorter-billed European grebes, unmistakable when breeding for its chestnut neck and flanks and upward-pointing golden ear-tufts. In winter black of rather flat crown and hind-neck contrasts sharply at eye-level with white cheeks and fore-neck; white spot in front of eye. Bill straight, black with white tip and pink base. Calls varied like other grebes, often quite harsh. Winters mainly on coast. L 31-38 cm. ⊙rW

**BLACK-NECKED GREBE** *Podiceps nigricollis*. Slightly smaller and dumpier than Slavonian and differing always in angled lower mandible making bill appear tilted upwards; when breeding in black neck and fan-shaped golden-yellow ear-tufts; and in winter in greyish neck and much less contrast between black of more peaked head and white of cheeks, which merge gradually below eye-level. Calls generally less harsh than Slavonian. L 28-34 cm. ⊙sMw

**Pied-billed Grebe** *Podilymbus podiceps*. A transatlantic vagrant, one or two now almost annual and long-staying on fresh water in Britain. Stocky, relatively short-necked and large-headed, with a distinctive short, thick bill (dark-banded in summer) and whiter under tail-coverts than Little Grebe but hardly any white on wing. L 31-38 cm. -V

br

**LITTLE GREBE** *Tachybaptus ruficollis*. The smallest grebe of the region, distinctive when breeding for its chestnut cheeks and throat and white patch at base of bill. Rather dull brown in winter. Autumn juvs have some white on cheeks. Shows no white in flight. Song a whinnying trill; alarm note, 'whit, whit'. More frequent on rivers and less so in coastal waters than other grebes. L 25-29 cm. ●RW

# GREBES

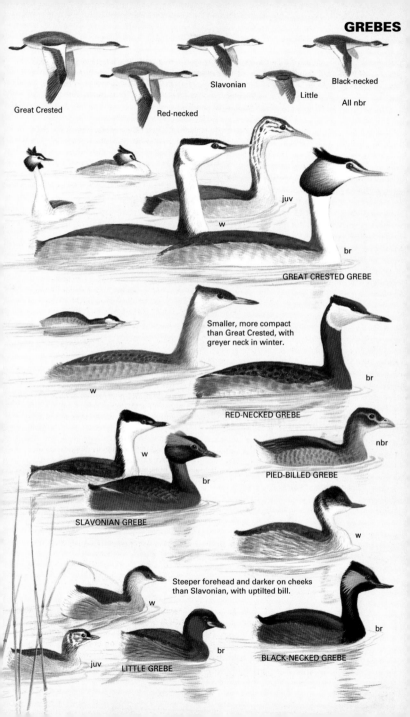

Great Crested

Red-necked

Slavonian

Little

Black-necked

All nbr

juv

w

br

**GREAT CRESTED GREBE**

Smaller, more compact than Great Crested, with greyer neck in winter.

w

br

**RED-NECKED GREBE**

nbr

**PIED-BILLED GREBE**

w

br

**SLAVONIAN GREBE**

w

Steeper forehead and darker on cheeks than Slavonian, with uptilted bill.

w

br

juv

**LITTLE GREBE**

br

**BLACK-NECKED GREBE**

● TROPICBIRDS: *Phaethontidae*. Largely white tropical seabirds whose long slender tail feathers give them a most distinctive flight outline.

Has bred Azores.

**RED-BILLED TROPICBIRD** *Phaethon aethereus*. Tail white, back barred dark, black band on primaries, eyestripe black and bill red. Juv has barred upperparts, black eyestripe and yellow bill. Flies with strong, pigeon-like beats, diving from a height. Shrill, rasping call often heard at sea. L 90-105, WS 99-106 cm.

● FRIGATEBIRDS: *Fregatidae*. Large, dark, piratical, ungainly, soar and flap lazily with long markedly crooked wings and long forked tail; bill long, hooked. Aka Man o' War Bird.

**Magnificent Frigatebird** *Fregata magnificens*. Vagrant from tropical seas. Male all-black with indistinct red throat-pouch; female has white breast and whitish collar at back of neck; imm has head, breast and belly white. Beware several other very similar potential vagrant species. L 95-110, WS 215-245 cm.                    -V

● ALBATROSSES *Diomedeidae*. The largest seabirds, noted for their great wingspan and sustained gliding flight; vagrants from S Atlantic.

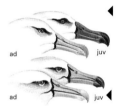

ad          juv

ad          juv

**Black-browed Albatross** *Diomedea melanophrys*. Back, wings, tail, eye-stripe and broad edge to underwing blackish; head and rest of underparts white; bill yellow with black tip. Imm greyer, especially on head; white band only develops gradually; bill blackish-grey, later horn-coloured. May summer at gannetries. L 80-95, WS 213-246 cm.                    -V

**Shy Albatross** *D. cauta* is somewhat larger than Black-browed with greyish head and underwing white only narrowly edged black. L 90-99, WS 220-256 cm. Cf. Yellow-nosed and Wandering Albatrosses (p.368).

● PETRELS, SHEARWATERS: *Procellariidae* (pp.28-32). Medium-sized, long-winged oceanic seabirds, superb gliders, with nostrils lying in two short tubes on the bill, and a strong musky smell. Colonial breeders. Shearwaters have a distinctive stiff-winged mode of flight, 'shearing' the waves, tilting from one wing-tip to the other.

**Capped Petrel** *Pterodroma hasitata*. Very rare vagrant from Caribbean, whose black crown contrasts strikingly with white forehead, nape, throat and underparts; upper tail coverts white. Aka Black-capped Petrel. L 41, WS 94 cm.                    -V

**ZINO'S PETREL** *Pterodroma madeira*. A rare gadfly petrel, Manx-shearwater-sized, but with distinct, more darting and undulating, flight. Upperparts grey, forehead pale, dark patch on ear coverts, partial grey chest-band, flanks heavily mottled grey, underwings dark and bill short, slender. c30 pairs breed Madeira, in mountains, where utters nocturnal wailing or tittering call. Aka Freira, 'Soft-plumaged Petrel' superspecies. L 32-33, WS 78-83 cm.

**FEA'S PETREL** *Pterodroma feae*. Slightly larger than Zino's Petrel, with more conspicuous white stripe over eye giving masked effect, and longer, stouter bill. c70 pairs breed in autumn on Bugio in Desertas. Aka Gon-gon, 'Soft-plumaged Petrel' superspecies. L 33-36, WS 84-91 cm.                    [-V]

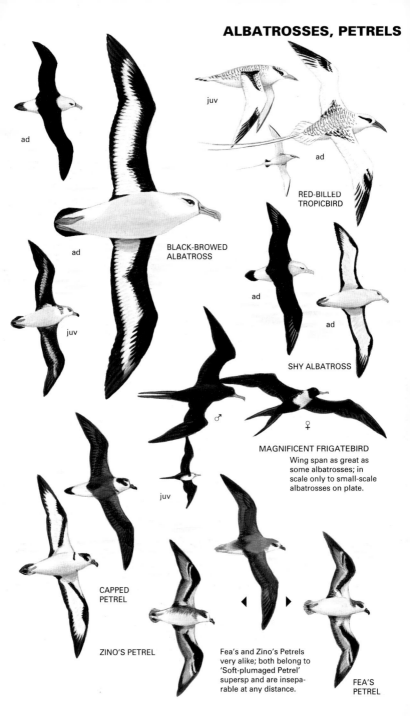

# ALBATROSSES, PETRELS

ad

juv

ad

**RED-BILLED
TROPICBIRD**

ad

**BLACK-BROWED
ALBATROSS**

ad

juv

ad

ad

**SHY ALBATROSS**

♂

♀

juv

**MAGNIFICENT FRIGATEBIRD**

Wing span as great as
some albatrosses; in
scale only to small-scale
albatrosses on plate.

**CAPPED
PETREL**

◀   ▶

**ZINO'S PETREL**

Fea's and Zino's Petrels
very alike; both belong to
'Soft-plumaged Petrel'
supersp and are insepa-
rable at any distance.

**FEA'S
PETREL**

**FULMAR** *Fulmarus glacialis*. A rather large, gull-like petrel, grey above, with head and underparts white, but grey in dark, mainly Arctic morph ('Blue Fulmar'). Differs from gulls in stiff-winged, shearwater-like flight, pale patch on primaries, thick neck, short bill and tubular nostrils. Guttural growls, grunts, chuckles and cackles, mainly at breeding sites. May defensively spit foul-smelling oil at intruders. Nests on sea cliffs, also old buildings, sometimes a few km inland; breeding season long. L 45-50, WS 102-112 cm. ●SR

**BULWER'S PETREL** *Bulweria bulwerii*. Like an outsize all-black Storm Petrel (p.34), with characteristic outline of long wings (pale diagonal bar on upperwing, cf. Leach's Petrel, p.34), and long tail, whose wedge-shape shows only briefly in buoyant, twisting flap-and-glide flight low over waves. Bill black, feet pink and black. Song, 'cheerful', 5-syllabic, also a barking call. L 26-28, WS 68-73 cm. -V

**Jouanin's Petrel** *B. fallax*. Rare vagrant from Indian Ocean. Slightly larger than Bulwer's, with no or obscurer wing panel, more weaving and banking flight, higher above waves, and (at close range) heavier head and bill. L 30, WS 75 cm.

**SOOTY SHEARWATER** *Puffinus griseus*. Large, all-dark except for variably pale centre of underwing; bill blackish, feet dark purplish pink. Darker and appreciably larger than Balearic Shearwater (p.32). Flight, with strong scything wing-beats, more like Great than Cory's. Regular autumn visitor from the southern oceans to the seas of the region; occasional inshore. L 40-51, WS 94-109 cm. ○M

**Flesh-footed Shearwater** *P. carneipes*. Rare vagrant from southern oceans. All-dark, differing from same-sized Sooty in dark-tipped pale bill, flesh-pink feet and whitish flash at base of underwing primaries. Aka Pale-footed Shearwater. L 43, WS 100 cm.

**GREAT SHEARWATER** *Puffinus gravis*. Large and distinctive, even at a distance, from the marked capped effect of its dark crown, sharply defined by white throat and neck. Dark bill, white patch at base of tail and greyish patch on belly less easily seen. Has typical low skimming shearwater flight and also soars. Harsh cries from squabbling birds around fishing fleets. Late summer and autumn visitor from S Atlantic at sea, sometimes inshore near headlands. L 43-51, WS 100-118 cm. ○M

**CORY'S SHEARWATER** *Calonectris diomedea*. Marginally the region's largest shearwater, brown to grey-brown above and white below; bill large, pale. Lacks Great's black and white head, and may have small white patch at base of tail. Much paler than Sooty and larger than Balearic Shearwater (p.32). Flight more often gliding (with bowed wings), soaring or even flapping than Great and Sooty, but depends on wind speed. Raucous coughing and wailing cries when breeding, on rocky islands and cliffs. L 45-56, WS 100-125 cm. ○M

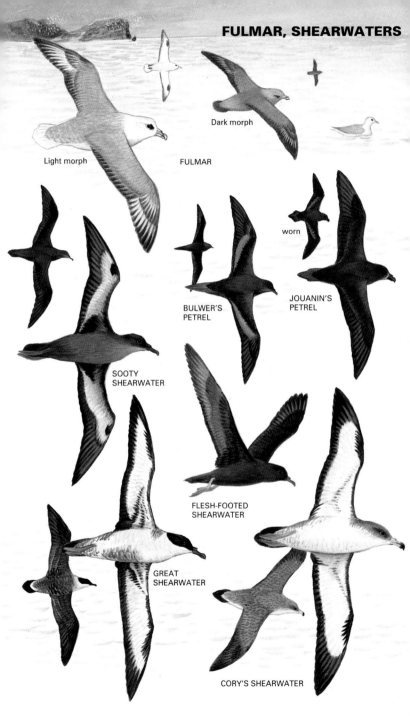

# FULMAR, SHEARWATERS

Dark morph

Light morph          FULMAR

BULWER'S
PETREL

worn

JOUANIN'S
PETREL

SOOTY
SHEARWATER

FLESH-FOOTED
SHEARWATER

GREAT
SHEARWATER

CORY'S SHEARWATER

**Manx Shearwater Group**. These medium-sized and smaller *Puffinus* species, have named the whole genus with their characteristic stiff-winged mode of flight, 'shearing' the waves, often appearing first black and then white as they tilt alternately from one wing-tip to the other, especially in strong winds. Unlike the larger shearwaters, they also have a fluttering flight. Never follow ships.

**MANX SHEARWATER** *Puffinus puffinus*. The commonest shearwater in the NW of the region, with sharp contrast of dark upperparts and white underparts; legs pink and bill black. Typical stiff-winged 'wave-shearing' shearwater flight is interspersed with more fluttering flight. Often fish in flocks. Very noisy at breeding places at night, with eerie loud cooing and strangled caterwauling cries. Breeds on marine islands, sometimes high up and well inland, flocks often assembling on nearby sea before dusk. L 30-35, WS 76-82 cm.                    ⊙S

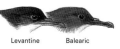

Levantine and Balearic

Levantine          Balearic

**LEVANTINE SHEARWATER** *Puffinis yelkouan*. Slightly longer-tailed and with much less contrasted plumage than same-sized Manx (of which sometimes considered a subspecies). Upperparts paler brown, and underparts paler brown to dull white, so appearing more contrasted than slightly larger Balearic Shearwater. Flight similarly combines shearing and fluttering flight, often more fluttering than Manx. Voice similar to Manx. Mediterranean and Black Seas only. L 30-35, WS 76-82 cm.

**BALEARIC SHEARWATER** *Puffinus mauretanicus*. Noticeably larger than Manx and Levantine Shearwaters (has been treated as a ssp of both). Less blackish than Manx and darker brown than Levantine, with brown under tail coverts and rest of underparts often dark enough to lead to confusion with the larger, longer-winged, stronger flying Sooty Shearwater (p.30), which does not have fluttering flight. Reaches Bay of Biscay and British seas mainly in autumn. L 32-38, WS 78-89 cm.        OM

boydi          baroli

**LITTLE SHEARWATER** *Puffinus assimilis*. Ssp.*baroli* is black and white like Manx, but smaller and rounder-winged than Manx (but hard to judge at sea) and best told by greater proportion of flapping or fluttering flight, lower over the water; at close range due to blue feet, shorter bill and whiter face due to black of crown not extending below eye. Breeds on rocky islands, Azores, Canaries, Desertas and Salvages, where less noisy than Manx. L 25-30, WS 58-67 cm.                    -V

Ssp.*boydi* from Cape Verde Is is a possible rare vagrant.

**PERSIAN SHEARWATER** *Puffinus persicus*. Intermediate between Levantine and Little in size, bill length and flight characteristics; brown above, white below, with much brown also on underwing, axillaries, flanks and under tail coverts; legs pink. Arabian seas only; in the Gulf throughout the year. (Often treated as a ssp of the pan-tropical Audubon's Shearwater *P. lherminieri* - itself sometimes treated as a ssp of Little Shearwater - whose black and white W Atlantic ssp.*lherminieri* is a potential vagrant to the region.) L 29-31, WS 62-69 cm.

Manx          Persian

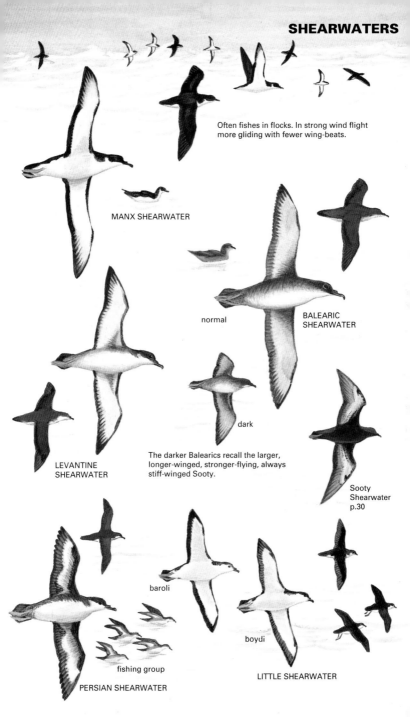

# SHEARWATERS

Often fishes in flocks. In strong wind flight more gliding with fewer wing-beats.

MANX SHEARWATER

normal

BALEARIC SHEARWATER

dark

LEVANTINE SHEARWATER

The darker Balearics recall the larger, longer-winged, stronger-flying, always stiff-winged Sooty.

Sooty Shearwater p.30

baroli

boydi

fishing group

PERSIAN SHEARWATER

LITTLE SHEARWATER

● STORM PETRELS: *Hydrobatidae*. Small, oceanic black petrels, mostly white-rumped, flying or fluttering low over surface; on land above ground only at night when breeding in holes on rocky coastal islands, or storm-wrecked. Sexes alike; bill short, black, tube-nosed. Most species may follow ships and appear to patter along surface with outspread wings.

**STORM PETREL** *Hydrobates pelagicus*. The region's smallest and commonest small petrel, not unlike a large, square-tailed House Martin (p.240); white rump contrasting with almost all-black plumage; upperwing with faint pale line; underwing with pale to white bar; feet black, not projecting beyond tail. Flight either direct or fluttering and batlike, interspersed with short glides. Prolonged nightjar-like churring song, interrupted by hiccuping 'chikka' notes. L 14-17, WS 36-39 cm.                ○S

**LEACH'S PETREL** *Oceanodroma leucorrhoa*. Larger, browner and longer-winged than Storm Petrel, and with pale band on upperwing, all-dark underwing and forked tail; grey centre to white rump may be either absent or hard to see. Best field mark is buoyant, bouncing, zigzag flight, with angled wings; seldom pattering; rarely follows ships. Song purring, call chattering. Most widespread late autumn. L 19-22, WS 45-48 cm.
○Sm

**MADEIRAN PETREL** *Oceanodroma castro*. Slightly shorter- and broader-winged than very similar Leach's; less conspicuous wing bar, more extensive all-white rump and slightly less forked tail are hard to see at sea. Best field mark is more shearwater-like flight, intermediate between erratic Leach's and bat-like Storm, with distinctive side-to-side, not up-and-down zigzags. Song resembles Storm; flight-note 'kair chuch-a-chuck chuck chuck'. Stays near breeding islands in winter. L 19-21, WS 42-45 cm.                -V

**Swinhoe's Petrel** *O. monorhis*. Leach's sized, all-dark, with a pale wing bar, no white rump, well forked tail and swooping, tern-like flight. Increasingly recorded vagrant from Indian Ocean. L 19-22, WS 44-46 cm.                -V

**WILSON'S PETREL** *Oceanites oceanicus*. Small, square-tailed, white-rumped, very dark brown, differing from smaller Storm and larger Leach's in its long, thin legs, with feet well beyond tail (yellow webs hard to see); wing bar more conspicuous than Storm's, less so than Leach's; and underwing usually dark. Flight often more gliding and tern-like than either, with wings not angled. Oceanic visitor from Antarctic, rare inshore. L 15-19, WS 38-42 cm.                -V

**FRIGATE PETREL** *Pelagodroma marina*. The region's only small petrel that is mainly grey above and white on face and below, and thus superficially like a same-sized winter phalarope (p.162). Flight wavering and erratic, often side-to-side, long legs extending well beyond square tail; webs orange. Calls include a cooing song. Aka White-faced Petrel. L 20-21, WS 41-43 cm.                -V

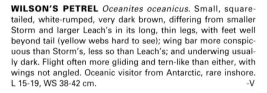
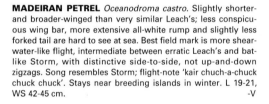

34

Underwing pattern variable;
pale band on upperwing
rarely visible.

STORM PETREL

LEACH'S
PETREL

MADEIRAN
PETREL

SWINHOE'S PETREL

WILSON'S
PETREL

FRIGATE
PETREL

juv

2 year

3 year

sub ad

ad

● **GANNETS/BOOBIES**: *Sulidae*. Large, cigar-shaped seabirds; tail wedge-shaped. Flight strong, flapping and gliding. Diving from both air and surface.

**GANNET** *Morus bassanus*. White with black wing tips, recognisable from afar when dives steeply into sea. At close range: yellow-buff head and neck, long stout bluish-white bill, blackish-brown legs and bare, blue-grey skin around grey eye. Sexes alike. Juv dark brown, speckled white, imm whitening over 3-4 years. Voice harsh. Colonies breed rocky coasts, marine islands; in winter on open sea. L 87-100, WS 165-180 cm.　　　　　　　　　　　　　　　　　●Smr

**Cape Gannet** *M. capensis*. Vagrant from S Atlantic, averaging smaller than Gannet, adult with tips and whole trailing edge of wing, tail, longer throat stripe and bare skin round eye black. L 84-89 cm.　　[-V]

Cape　　　　Masked

**Masked Booby** *Sula dactylatra*. Rare vagrant from tropical seas. Adult has white head, more black on secondaries than Cape Gannet, and tail dark chocolate brown. Imm like Brown Booby but with white collar. L 81-92, WS 152 cm.

**BROWN BOOBY** *Sula melanogaster*. Visitor from tropical seas, regular to Gulf of Elat/Aqaba from Red Sea colonies; smaller than Gannet, dark brown except for white breast and belly. Imm similar but paler, differing from imm Gannet in sharp, two-tone appearance. L 64-74, WS 132-150 cm.

● **PELICANS**: *Pelecanidae*. Very large, bill long with capacious throat pouch. Flight majestic, flapping, gliding and soaring, neck retracted, often in formation.

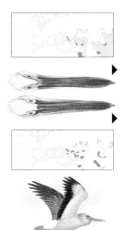

**WHITE PELICAN** *Pelecanus onocrotalus*. White, tinged pink and crested when breeding; wings broad, black-tipped above, trailing edge black below; tail very short; yellow patch on breast; eye red, pouch yellow, bare skin on face yellow or orange, legs pink or reddish. Imm pale brown, whitening over 3-4 years. Voice guttural. Colonial. Fresh and brackish lakes, marshes, shallow coastal waters. L 140-175, WS 270-360 cm.

**DALMATIAN PELICAN** *Pelecanus philippensis*. Somewhat larger than White Pelican, but has plumage greyer (never pink), no crest, eyes yellow, pouch orange and face-skin purple when breeding, and especially wholly white underwing and grey legs. L 160-180, WS 310-345 cm.

**Pink-backed Pelican** *P. rufescens*. Rare vagrant from tropical Africa, smaller than White Pelican and with whole plumage greyish-white tinged in breeding season with pink, especially on upperparts and belly; bill and pouch pink, face-skin speckled black. L 125-132, WS 265-290 cm.

36　　juv

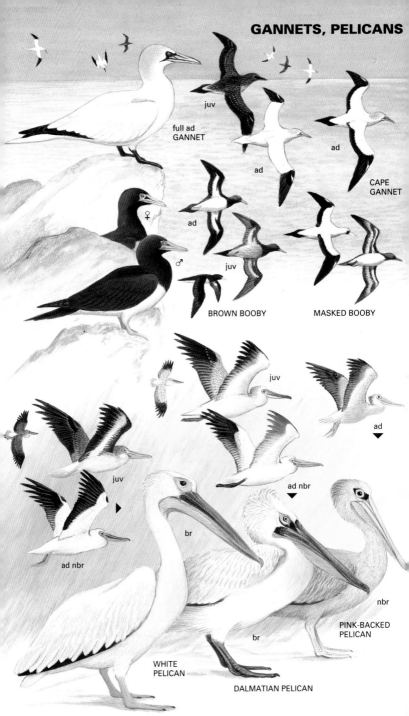

# GANNETS, PELICANS

full ad
GANNET

juv

ad

ad

CAPE
GANNET

♀

♂

ad

juv

BROWN BOOBY

MASKED BOOBY

juv

juv

ad

ad nbr

ad nbr

br

WHITE
PELICAN

br

DALMATIAN PELICAN

nbr

PINK-BACKED
PELICAN

● CORMORANTS:*Phalacrocoracidae*. Large, gregarious, blackish water birds, with long neck, longish stout hooked bill and wedge-shaped tail. Sexes alike. Imm brown, paler beneath, becoming adult over two years. Swim with head at marked upward angle; dive from surface; fly with regular wing-beats, usually low over water, often in V-formation, with neck held level; cf. Divers (p.24).

**SHAG** *Phalacrocorax aristotelis*. Smaller than Cormorant and with steeper forehead. All-dark except for yellow skin at base of narrower bill and around green eye; recurved crest distinctive in breeding season. Juv/imm have whitish chin and throat, and paler brown underparts. Rocky coasts, nesting on cliffs and stacks, occasionally wandering to muddy or sandy shores or inland. L 65-80, WS 90-105 cm.                    ●R

Ssp.*desmaresti* (Mediterranean, Black Sea) is slightly smaller and has bill longer, slenderer and yellow, facial skin more extensive and paler/brighter yellow, crest shorter and sometimes absent, and feet with yellow webs; juv with much whiter underparts. Ssp.*riggenbachi* (N W Africa) is similar but with bill like ssp.*aristotelis*.

br aristotelis        br desmarestii

*desmarestii* is smaller with longer bill, paler/brighter facial skin and shorter crest.

Double-crested Cormorant

Cormorant                                Shag

Shag holds head at an angle in flight. Double-crested Cormorant has (hard to see) distinctive kinked neck. Both have faster wing beats than Cormorant, whose neck is held level in flight.

**CORMORANT** *Phalacrocorax carbo*. The region's largest all-dark seabird, with white patch on face, yellow or orange-yellow throat pouch, green iris and when breeding white patch on each thigh. Many older birds, especially in C & S Europe and N W Africa, have head and neck mainly white when breeding. Juv/imm have whitish throat; underparts vary from whitish through speckled to dark. Calls guttural. Inshore coastal waters, lakes, reservoirs; breeds on cliffs and rocks and in trees. L 80-100, WS 130-160 cm.                    ●Rmw

Ssp.*carbo* (Atlantic) has plumage glossed purple; ssp.*sinensis* (C & S Europe) is slightly smaller and when breeding has plumage glossed green and head and neck tending to have more white; ssp.*maroccanus* (N W Africa) is similar but with white upper breast.

nbr carbo        nbr sinensis

Facial differences are mainly age-related.

**Double-crested Cormorant** *P. auritus*, a rare transatlantic vagrant, is between Shag and Cormorant in size, all ages and sexes with no feathers on centre of orange throat pouch and orange streak on upper lores. Imm brown, paler beneath, especially on neck and upper breast. L 76-91, WS 137 cm.                    -V

Loral stripe and pouch always orange

# CORMORANTS

nbr

ad

juv

2nd year

juv

smarestii

juv

aristotelis

Distinctive wing-spread posture looks as if wings held out to dry, but this is disputed.

SHAG

nbr

carbo

br

juv
dark

juv light

br

Juvs variable, most with white belly

Greener *sinensis* has whiter head when breeding than most older, more purple *carbo*.

br

br
maroccanus

juv

nbr

DOUBLE-CRESTED
CORMORANT

CORMORANT. Not all individuals of the two sspp. are as easy to separate as these.

**SOCOTRA CORMORANT** *Phalacrocorax nigrogularis*. Smaller and slimmer than Cormorant and more like Shag. All-dark, but when breeding has white tuft behind eye, white speckling on neck and fine whitish streaks on rump; bill blackish-grey, iris green. Juv/imm differ from Cormorant in slenderer greyish bill, whitish speckles on wings and dark spots on whitish underparts. Coastal, nesting on ground. L 77-84, WS 102-110 cm.

Breeding adult
has white plume
behind eye.

ad

imm

imm

Socotra Cormorant

Cormorant

Socotra distribution overlaps with both Cormorant and Pygmy Cormorant. Inland Pygmy is much smaller, Cormorant always larger and breeding adult has white on face and thighs. Socotra has more shag-like jizz, often flies in formation low over water.

**PYGMY CORMORANT** *Phalacrocorax pygmeus*. The region's smallest cormorant, smaller than a Mallard (p.64) and easily told by its short thick neck, roundish head and long tail; iris dark. In breeding season head and neck red-brown (sometimes black just before breeding) and plumage speckled paler. Fresh and brackish water with extensive reed-beds; often at quite small ponds, nesting in trees and reed-beds. L 45-55, WS 80-90 cm.

Breeding adult's
head dark, later
browner.

Breeding adult
blackish-green
with short crest
and white
plumes.

**LONG-TAILED CORMORANT** *Phalacrocorax africanus*. Formerly the region's second smallest cormorant (now extinct), short-necked and round-headed, Winter adult and juv brownish with white throat and paler underparts. Long extinct as breeder, but when breeding is black with silvery speckling on wing coverts, a small crest and, briefly, white plumes behind eye. Fresh and coastal waters. L 50-60, WS 80-90 cm.

● DARTERS: *Anhingidae*. Large birds of fresh and brackish water, like slender, longer-necked, long-tailed cormorants, with bill pointed, not hooked.

**DARTER** *Anhinga melanogaster*. Plumage black, streaked with white; male's head and neck black above (female's brown) chestnut below (pinkish-brown in female) with long white streak back from eye (obscurer in female); iris yellow. Often makes snake-like movements with neck, which has curious kink; hence aka Snake-bird. May swim with only head and neck above surface. Holds out wings like cormorants. Grunts at nest. Lakes, rivers and estuaries; nests colonially, in trees and bushes near water. L 85-97, WS 116-128 cm.

♂ ♀ br

# CORMORANTS, DARTER

juv

nbr

imm

Highly gregarious, often in flocks of several thousand; sometimes out at sea, but mostly in coastal waters.

SOCOTRA CORMORANT

late br

juv

nbr

In flight looks like a long-tailed Coot (p.126).

imm

nbr

PYGMY CORMORANT

juv

♂

LONG-TAILED CORMORANT

♀

DARTER

submerged fishing

♀

Perches with outspread wings like cormorants; often swims with only head above surface.

● HERONS, EGRETS and BITTERNS: *Ardeidae.* Wading birds, well adapted to feeding in shallow water by their long legs, neck and bill. Tail rather short. Wings broad and rounded, the larger species with a ponderously slow flight, when neck retracted (unlike storks, spoonbills, ibises and cranes; see p.50) and legs outstretched. Elongated head and wing plumes usually more conspicuous when breeding; for breeding-season colour changes, see, p.46. Sexes usually alike. Voice often loud and harsh or croaking. Mainly colonial nesting, usually in trees or reed-beds.

**BITTERN** *Botaurus stellaris.* A rather large brown heron, blotched, mottled and streaked with black; crown black, gape blue-green. Very skulking, so less often seen than heard uttering its penetrating low booming or mooing 'song', like a distant cow or foghorn. Stands hunched up like large domestic fowl, but looks very different in alert or alarm positions and striking crouched threat posture with wings outstretched. Flight call a harsh 'kwow' or 'kwah'. Extensive reed-beds, fens and swamps; not colonial, only feeding in the open in hard weather. L 70-80, WS 125-135 cm.                    ⊙RW

European

**American Bittern** *B. lentiginosus.* Slightly smaller transatlantic vagrant, most frequent Britain & Ireland, autumn/winter, also Iceland & Faeroe. rufous crown, pale yellow gape, diagnostic black wing-tips, no black blotches above and a black stripe down each side of neck, showing as a patch when neck retracted. Flies more readily than Bittern, looks less owl-like and feeds more often in the open. Voice similar, with a hoarse 'kok, kok, kok' flight call and a nasal 'haink', but trisyllabic boom-note, likened to an old-fashioned water pump, unlikely to be heard in Europe. L 60-75, WS 105-125 cm.          -V

American

Rounded, somewhat down-bent wings make Bittern look owl-like in flight, but has long bill, trailing legs and bunched feet. American Bittern flies more often showing diagnostic black wing-tips, and looks more heron-like.

**LITTLE BITTERN** *Ixobrychus minutus.* Much the smallest resident heron-like bird of the region, and the only one with a prominent whitish wing-patch, giving male in particular a strong dark/light contrast in flight. Female duller, browner, more streaked below; juv similar but also streaked above. 'Song' a low but far-carrying croak or bark; flight note 'quer'; alarm note 'gat' or 'gack'. Very skulking, though may climb about reeds, like a giant Great Reed Warbler (p.282); may also freeze upright, like Bittern. Densely vegetated swamps and freshwater margins. L 33-38, WS 52-58 cm.          -A(b)

♀

Little

**Least Bittern** *I. exilis*, a smaller transatlantic vagrant, male with less strikingly pale wing-patches and pale stripes on scapulars. Female differs especially in its chestnut, not blackish, back; juv/imm similar, but more streaked on back and breast. Even more skulking, and in thick vegetation can be mistaken for rail or even rodent. L 28-36, WS 40-45 cm.

♂          ♀

Least

# BITTERNS

Bittern rarely feeds in open except in hard weather. American does so more often, but always near cover ·

juv

ad

BITTERN

▲
Bittern's alert or frozen upright alarm position with neck stretched right out. Little Bittern has same habit.

ad

juv

AMERICAN BITTERN

juv

imm Night Heron p.44 for comparison

♀

LITTLE BITTERN
♂

♂

♀

A more russet form has all black marks rufous ·

LEAST BITTERN

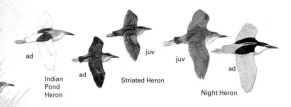

ad

ad

Indian
Pond
Heron

ad

juv

juv

Striated Heron

ad

Night Heron

Squacco
Heron

In flight white wings make both Squacco Heron and blunter-winged pond herons look almost as white as an egret. Striated Heron flies with bowed wing-beats. Night Heron flies mainly at dusk, with fast wing beats, often in lines.

**SQUACCO HERON** *Ardeola ralloides*. A small skulking brownish heron appearing largely white in flight. At rest is mainly tawny buff with wings, tail and belly white and vestigial crest (juv/imm more streaked); iris yellow, face-skin, bill and legs yellow-green. When breeding has crown and long crest streaked black, back plumes golden-buff, bill and face-skin bright blue and legs bright red. Call a high-pitched 'kerr'. Marshes, swampy riversides, nesting colonially in trees, often in heronries of other species. L 44-47, WS 80-92 cm.          -V

**INDIAN POND HERON** *Ardeola grayii*. Rare visitor to Gulf region from S Iran. Very like same-sized Squacco Heron when not breeding, but is less skulking, more blunt-winged in flight, has all underparts white and no vestigial crest; may have blue base to bill. When breeding looks very different: head and plumes unstreaked, back plumes darker, legs bright yellow. Aka Paddy-bird. L 42-45, WS 75-90 cm.

**STRIATED HERON** *Butorides striatus*. Crow-sized, dark, rather short-necked, short-winged and short-legged, with crested crown and upperparts very dark blue-green and face and neck grey or buff; legs yellow or orange. Juv browner, more streaked and speckled. Alarm call short, rather squawking, disyllabic. Mangroves and open tropical shores. L 40-48, WS 52-60 cm.

**Green Heron** *Butorides virescens*, a rare transatlantic vagrant, mainly to Britain, differs from Striated mainly in conspicuously chestnut face and neck. Formerly regarded as conspecific with Striated Heron and known as Green-backed Heron. L 46, WS 66 cm.          -V

◀ **NIGHT HERON** *Nycticorax nycticorax*. A small black, white and grey heron, habitual hunched attitude making it look compacter than its length suggests. Back and crown black with very long white crest plumes; bill black or partly green, eye red, face-skin blue, black or greenish, legs yellow or red. Juv/imm mainly brown, juv spotted white and resembling a small, boldly marked Bittern (p.42). Very broad-winged and dark/light contrasting in flight, with rather fast wing-beats, often flying in lines. Skulking and mainly nocturnal, most often seen flying at dusk, or hunched on secluded bough in densely vegetated swamp or marsh, fresh or salt, or even away from water. Call, a hoarse croak. Feral birds may occur in Scotland. Aka Black-crowned Night Heron. L 58-65, WS 105-112 cm.          -A

full br

Red colour appears only briefly, during courtship.

# SMALL HERONS

br

1st w

SQUACCO HERON

nbr

juv

1st br

br

juv

INDIAN POND HERON

ad

imm

juv        STRIATED HERON

ad

juv

GREEN HERON

ad

imm

juv

2nd year

juv
see also p. 42

NIGHT HERON

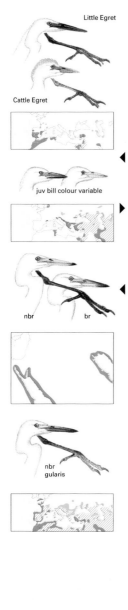

Little Egret

Cattle Egret

juv bill colour variable

nbr | br

nbr
gularis

COLOUR CHANGES WHEN BREEDING: During pair-formation, from courtship until egg-clutches are complete, the face-skin, bill and legs of many herons and egrets are more brightly coloured, especially more red or orange (these changes are shown in brackets below), and the yellow irises all turn red.

**CATTLE EGRET** *Bubulcus ibis*. Smaller and compacter than Little Egret, with shorter, stouter, yellow (orange-red) bill, and shorter, thicker neck with heavy jowl, always hunched at rest. Appears all-white both in flight and, except when breeding, at rest. When breeding has dark buff plumes on crown, breast and mantle. Face-skin yellow (bright red); legs dark green (dull red), with yellowish soles. Usually feeds in grassland near cattle or horses. Expanding its range. L 48-53, WS 90-96 cm.     -V

**GREAT WHITE EGRET** *Egretta alba*. Much the largest all-white egret; no visible crest, but long wing plumes in breeding season. Face-skin greenish (bright green), bill yellow (red/pink, later black, sometimes yellow at base); legs dark brown (black). Short black line behind eye separates from all other white herons and egrets, including rare white form of Grey Heron (p.48). Marshes, shallow fresh and brackish water, usually nesting in reed-beds. Aka Great White Heron. L 85-102, WS 140-170 cm.     -A

**Intermediate Egret** *E. intermedia*. A rare vagrant from the tropics, rather smaller than Great White Egret, with shorter all-yellow bill and face-skin yellow. Shorter legs protrude less far beyond tail in flight. Aka Yellow-billed Egret. L 65-72, WS105-115 cm.

**WESTERN REEF HERON** *Egretta gularis*. Almost exclusively coastal, having both dark and white forms, with confusing intermediates. Has crest, plumes, dark legs and yellow toes like the more graceful Little Egret, but bill stouter and either yellow or brownish. Dark forms only confusable with rare dark form of Little Egret, but very variable, from almost black to bluish-grey, with chin and throat white; imm grey-brown. Face-skin yellow-green (tinged orange). Aka Western Reef Egret. L 55-65, WS 86-104 cm.

White form dominant in slightly larger eastern ssp.*schistacea* breeding at heads of Red Sea and Gulf, but dark form predominates in western ssp.*gularis*, vagrant from tropical Africa.

**LITTLE EGRET** *Egretta garzetta*. A small all-white egret with black bill (brownish in juv) and legs and yellow feet, which show clearly in flight. When breeding has long drooping crest and long fuzzy wing plumes; blue-grey or blue-green lores briefly turn orange. Very rare slate-grey dark form has throat often dark and bill smaller. Cf. Cattle Egret, Intermediate Egret, Western Reef Heron. A harsh bark at nest. Marshes, shallow fresh and coastal waters, usually breeding in trees and near water. L 55-65, WS 88-95 cm.     ⊙Mw

# EGRETS

juv

br

CATTLE EGRET

nbr

br

nbr dark phase

GREAT
WHITE
EGRET

nbr

br white phase
schistacea
WESTERN REEF
HERON

juv

nbr

LITTLE EGRET

Purple Heron

Black-headed Heron

Great Blue Heron

Grey Heron

Goliath Heron

The larger herons fly with necks retracted (unlike storks, spoonbills, ibises and cranes), legs outstretched and ponderously slow flaps of broad rounded wings. Head points upwards in flying Grey Heron, downwards in flying Purple Heron

**GREY HERON** *Ardea cinerea*. The region's commonest large heron, mainly grey, with head and neck white and crest black (crown dark grey in uncrested juv/imm). Flight slow and heavy, with outer half of very rounded wings black, and head pointed upwards. Commonest call a harsh 'kraaaank'; other calls and castanet-like bill-snapping at nest. Feeds in marshes or shallow fresh or coastal water, even garden ponds; often stands hunched up. Nests in trees, less often in reed-beds or on cliffs. L 90-98, WS 175-195 cm. ●Rw

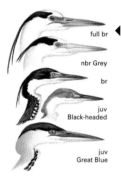

full br

nbr Grey

br

juv
Black-headed

juv
Great Blue

◄ Grey Heron's bill may flush deep orange when breeding. Occasional juvs are unusually dark. Rare albino adults are confusable with Great White Egret (p.46).

**Black-headed Heron** *A. melanocephala*, a rare vagrant to Israel from tropical Africa, has crown and hind neck black, and underwing white, not grey as in slightly larger Grey Heron. No rufous in plumage distinguishes from slightly smaller Purple Heron. L 92-96 cm.

**Great Blue Heron** *A. herodias*, a rare vagrant, the larger American counterpart of the Grey Heron, has neck tinged greyish-tawny, and thighs and leading edge of wing rufous. Juv duller than adult, with crown and back a greyer brown and chestnut on some wing coverts. The rare white morph has never been recorded in the region. L 91-137, WS 183 cm.

**GOLIATH HERON** *Ardea goliath*. Much the largest heron of the region, but a rare vagrant unless still breeds S Iraq. Like a giant plump Purple Heron, but with crown and plumes chestnut not black, distinguishing it also from Grey Heron, and heavier, slower flight. Loud, harsh, deep, hound-like baying call. Marshes, shallow water. L 135-150, WS 210-230 cm.

**PURPLE HERON** *Ardea purpurea*. Appreciably smaller, more rakish looking, with more snake-like neck, and much darker than Grey Heron, with longer and slenderer bill, black crown and belly, striped rufous neck and chestnut breast. Juv/imm sandy brown (cf. stouter Bittern, p.42), lacking most of black on crown and stripes on neck, paler and sandier than juv Grey; change to adult plumage may take up to five years, and some birds breed in sub-adult plumage. In faster flight, head points downwards, whole wing uniformly dark, legs projects further beyond tail, and neck bulge deeper, making an angle with breast. Shallow fresh water, usually skulking and nesting in reeds or marsh vegetation. L 78-90, WS 120-150 cm. -A

sub. ad Purple

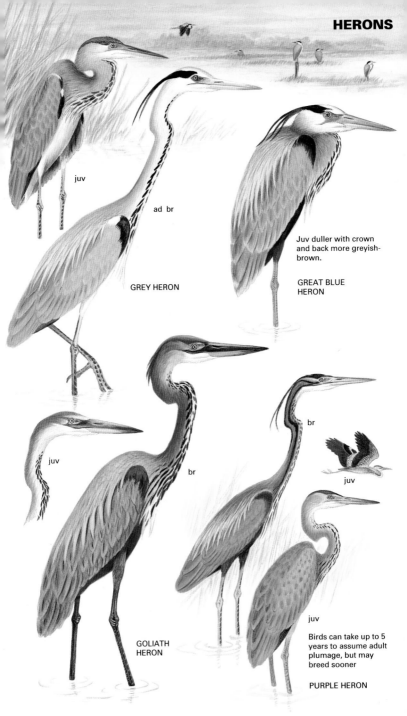

# HERONS

juv

ad br

GREY HERON

Juv duller with crown and back more greyish-brown.

GREAT BLUE HERON

juv

br

GOLIATH HERON

br

juv

juv

Birds can take up to 5 years to assume adult plumage, but may breed sooner

PURPLE HERON

● IBISES and SPOONBILL: *Threskiornithidae*. Ibises curlew-sized and spoonbills heron-sized wading birds, flying with neck outstretched, like curlews but unlike herons. Bill long and curved in ibises, straight and spoon-shaped at tip in Spoonbill. Sexes alike. Colonial nesters.

**SPOONBILL** *Platalea leucorodia*. The only large white heron-like bird with a long broad black bill, spoon-shaped at the tip, but cf escaped African Spoonbills *P. alba* with red face and legs. Yellowish breast-band, and in breeding plumage a long yellowish crest; legs black. Juv/imm have wing-tips blackish and pink bill and (at first) legs. Normally silent, but may grunt in breeding season. Shallow fresh and coastal waters, nesting in trees, bushes and reed-beds in marshy areas. L 80-90, WS 115-130 cm.                                                                          ○M

Curlew see p. 156

Bald Ibis

Sacred Ibis

Ibis flock

**GLOSSY IBIS** *Plegadis falcinellus*. Large, dark, comparatively short-legged, with a curved bill; superficially curlew-like, but with a very distinctive flight, the fast wing-beats interspersed with glides, and often flying in long lines. Plumage purplish-brown, appearing black at a distance, wings and tail glossed green, legs greenish-brown; juv with some white markings. Dark bill separates from red-billed escaped Puna Ibises *P.ridgwayi*. Call a harsh grating croak. Habitat as Spoonbill; often breeds in heron/egret/spoonbill colonies. L 55-65, WS 80-95 cm.          -V

**BALD IBIS** *Geronticus eremita*. Larger and shorter-legged than Glossy Ibis and with a bald red head, red bill and legs and neck-ruff of long, pointed, dark feathers, which wave in the wind and make the bird look somewhat shaggy. Call a rather high-pitched 'kay-kay'. Mainly semi-arid country, also grassland and shore in winter; nests on rocky cliffs and in caves. Almost extinct Turkey, rapidly decreasing Morocco. Aka Waldrapp. L 70-80, WS 125-135 cm.

2-3rd year

**SACRED IBIS** *Threskiornis aethiopica*. Unmistakable with its white plumage offset by black wing plumes, legs and bare head and neck. Juv/imm have head and neck partly feathered, above black with white bases, beneath, white; no wing plumes. Rather silent, but sometimes croaks. Margins of fresh and coastal water, marshes and cultivated land. Now breeds only S Iraq; formerly also Egypt. L 65-75, WS 112-124 cm.

# SPOONBILL, IBISES

br

feeding

nbr

Sexes alike, but
males larger with
longer bill and legs.

SPOONBILL

juv

nbr

juv

br

GLOSSY IBIS

BALD IBIS

juv

br

br

Imm has feathered
head, black above,
white below.

juv

SACRED IBIS

● STORKS: *Ciconiidae*. Large, long-legged, long-necked, with long stout bills. They fly, and often soar, with neck (unlike herons) and legs outstretched; gait stately.

**WHITE STORK** *Ciconia ciconia*. One of the region's largest land birds, differing from all other large white birds by combination of long red bill and legs, long neck, short tail and black wings with large white patch. Juv browner on black and red parts. Normally silent, but will hiss when annoyed and clatters mandibles together during courtship, while holding neck backwards in a U-bend. Farmland and open marshes; nests in trees or in W Europe (where decreasing) on buildings, usually on special platforms. Large flocks on migration. L 100-115, WS 155-165 cm.                                                              -A

**BLACK STORK** *Ciconia nigra*. All-black (glossed green and purple) with lower underparts white; bill red and legs brighter red. Juv similar but brownish. More vocal than White Stork, chief call being 'he lee, he lee'. A shy forest bird, nesting in trees and feeding at freshwater margins and in open marshy areas in well-wooded country; on migration in more open country. L 95-100, WS 145-155 cm.                                                              -A

**Yellow-billed Stork** *Mycteria ibis*. Rare vagrant from tropical Africa to N W Africa and Middle East, with yellow bill, bare red face-patch, pink on back and wings and black tail. Juv brownish on head, neck, upperparts; imm like adult, but no pink on upperparts. Fresh and coastal waters. Aka Wood Ibis. L 95-105, WS 150-165 cm.

**Marabou** *Leptoptilus crumeniferus*. Rare vagrant from tropical Africa to Israel, massive and unmistakable, dark above, white below, with huge bill and largely bare head and neck, from which a large air-filled pouch hangs. Flies heavily and soars, with neck retracted; stands hunched. Shallow fresh water, open country. L 115-130, WS 225-255 cm.

● FLAMINGOS: *Phoenicopteridae*. Very large, pink-and-white wading birds, with uniquely curved stout bill. Flying with neck and legs outstretched, often in formation.

**GREATER FLAMINGO** *Phoenicopterus ruber*. Easily told by its remarkable 'Roman nose' black and red bill, specially adapted to sieving food from shallow water, and by red legs; also in flight by striking red-and-black contrast of wings. Sexes alike. Juv grey-brown; imm white. Noisy and highly gregarious, uttering loud goose-like honking cries in flight. Extensive shallow lakes or lagoons of salt or soda water, where it builds conical heaps of mud on which to lay its eggs. L 125-145, WS 140-165 cm.                                                              -E

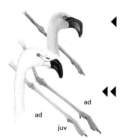

**Lesser Flamingo** *Phoeniconaias minor*. Rare vagrant from tropical Africa to Mediterranean, the smallest flamingo, markedly smaller, stockier, darker and brighter pink than Greater Flamingo, and with redder and even more down-curved bill. L 80-90, WS 95-100 cm.

**Chilean Flamingo** *Phoenicopterus chilensis*. Increasingly frequent escape, which has nested in the region. Differs from Greater Flamingo in black and white bill and grey-green to pale blue legs with red joints and toes. L 105 cm.                                                              -E(b)

ad

ad

juv

juv

ad

WHITE STORK

ad

juv

juv

BLACK STORK

nbr

YELLOW-BILLED
STORK

When breeding
more pink on
wing and face
deeper red.

imm

juv

chick

chick

Males mostly
larger, some
strikingly larger.

GREATER FLAMINGO

● SWANS, GEESE and DUCKS: *Anatidae*. Long-necked, web-footed water birds; bill flattened and blunt, except for sawbills (p.80). Downy young leave nest soon after hatching. Two main subfamilies: swans and geese, Anserinae (pp.54-61), and ducks, Anatinae (pp.62-81). Many exotic species escape. *SWANS: Cygnus*. The largest waterfowl, adults all white, legs black; sexes alike. Juvs (cygnets) grey-brown, whitening over their first year, with a pink bill; usually with adults in winter.

**WHOOPER SWAN** *Cygnus cygnus*. Adult's bill yellow and black without a knob, the yellow extending towards the black tip at an acute angle; cf. smaller and shorter-necked Bewick's Swan. Juv greyer, less brown, than juv Mute. Gait and flight similar to Mute Swan, but holds neck upright at rest and wings make only normal swishing sound in flight. Frequently utters a loud, clanging or bugling, somewhat goose-like 'ahg-ha', especially in flight. Breeds south of tundra. Gregarious in winter. L 145-160, WS 218-243 cm. ⊙W(b)

Bewick's

Stained Whoopers

Swans with rusty-coloured marks on head and neck have been feeding in water stained with iron compounds or algae. They can also become discoloured from feeding in ordinary soil.

**BEWICK'S SWAN** *Cygnus columbianus bewickii*. Smaller, shorter-necked and more goose-shaped than Whooper, yellow on bill very variable, but extends less far down bill and ends bluntly. Calls 'hoo, hoo' a higher-pitched and more musical honk than Whooper. Breeds in marshy and swampy tundra; gregarious in winter. Aka Tundra Swan. L 115-127, WS 180-211 cm. ⊙W

**Whistling Swan** *C.c. columbianus*, a slightly larger rare vagrant from N America, has bill all-black or sometimes (like a few Bewick's) with small yellow patch near eye. Beware Bewick's with soil on bill. L 120-150, WS 115-140 cm. -V

**MUTE SWAN** *Cygnus olor*. The commonest swan, adult's bill orange with black knob, cygnet's pinkish with no knob. Rare variety, Polish Swan, has white cygnets. Gait ungainly, waddling; swims gracefully, neck curved and tail slightly erect. May fly with loud 'hompa, hompa' wing-throbbing, otherwise largely silent. May breed colonially; non-breeders often flock. Still and slow-moving fresh water, often in towns, swamps, estuaries. L 145-160, WS 208-238 cm. ●R

**Black Swan** *Cygnus atratus* from Australia, a frequent escape, the only blackish water bird of its size, has white flight feathers and a white band near tip of red bill. L 120-140, WS 160-200 cm. -E

Black swan

stained

**Snow Goose** *Anser caerulescens*. A N American 'grey goose' (p.56), rare visitor, frequent escape: two forms: (i) all-white with black wing-tips, unlike swans and albino grey geese, but cf. much smaller and shorter-billed Ross's Goose *A. rossii* (p.369); (ii) 'Blue Goose', with bluish grey-brown back and wings, white head and neck and underparts of either colour or a mixture; cf. hybrids (p.58). Pink legs and bill, showing 'grin-gap' unlike Ross's; both dark in juv. L 165-180, WS 132-165 cm. -AE

54

# SWANS, GEESE

WHOOPER SWAN

juv

ad

BEWICK'S SWAN

juv

ad

All swans fly heavily.

MUTE SWAN

juv

ad

white

blue juv

BLACK SWAN

blue

white juv

white phase

blue phase ad

SNOW GOOSE

● **GEESE:** *Anserini.* Large, thickset, long-necked, gregarious birds; sexes alike. Flight fast, direct, with rather laboured wing-beats and loud cries, usually in V-formation. *GREY GEESE: Anser.* Plumage grey-brown, except Snow Goose (p.54); under tail coverts white. In winter on farmland, marshes, estuaries.

Greylag          Bean          Pinkfoot

Check bill and leg colour, bill shape and calls. In flight, note Greylag's very pale forewing, Bean's dark head, neck and forewing, and Pinkfoot's dark head and neck and pale forewing.

**GREYLAG** *Anser anser.* One of the two larger grey geese, with heavy flight and gait, large head, rather thick neck, and distinctive pale grey forewing, pink legs and large orange bill. May have a few small black spots on belly (cf. Whitefront, p.58). Flight call a clangorous 'aahng-ung-ung'; hisses when annoyed; both like farmyard goose, its domestic derivative. Breeds on moors and marshes and by fresh water. Aka Greylag Goose. L 75-90, WS 147-180 cm.          ●RW

Ssp.*anser* described above; paler ssp.*rubrirostris* with pink bill breeds in E Europe and Iraq. Some of numerous feral populations have hybridised with other geese, e.g. in Belgium, Britain.

**BEAN GOOSE** *Anser fabalis.* Another large grey goose, much darker, especially on head, neck and forewing, than Greylag; markedly larger than Pinkfoot, with longer neck and larger bill. Legs orange; bill blackish, orange-yellow or rarely pink. Flight calls like Pinkfoot, but lower-pitched and less frequent. L 66-84, WS 142-175 cm.          ○W

Forest-breeding ssp.*fabalis* has bill much less bulky than Greylag, orange-yellow and blackish; smaller, tundra-breeding ssp.*rossicus* has bill shorter, thicker-based, blackish, with narrow orange band near tip.

Pinkfoot

Bean          Whitefront

Exceptionally Greylag, Bean and Pinkfoot may have narrow band of white at base of bill, but never as broad as in adult Whitefront (p.58), whose band is also variable.

**PINKFOOT**. *Anser brachyrhynchus.* A distinctive smaller grey goose, warmer brown, with small dark rounded head, shortish dark neck, pale forewing, pink legs and short pink-tipped blackish bill (rarely bill and legs can be orange); cf. Bean. Flocks very vocal, with a rather shrill medley of 'wink, wink' and 'ung, ung' calls', the highest-pitched of the four commoner grey geese. Breeds on tundra, sometimes on cliff ledges. Aka Pink-footed Goose. L 60-75, WS 135-170 cm.          ⊙W

56

# GREY GEESE

juv

juv

ad

rubrirostis

ad

anser

GREYLAG

ad from a hybrid population

juv

ad

ad
showing
different
bill
pattern.

BEAN GOOSE

fabalis

ad

rossicus

ad

juv

PINKFOOT

In winter geese feed in flocks usually composed of family parties, juvs almost always feeding close to parents. Flocks may be of more than one species, and odd individuals often occur, e.g. Bean, Red-breasted and Lesser Whitefront in flocks of Whitefronts.

**WHITEFRONT** *Anser albifrons*. Adult is easiest northern grey goose to identify, with conspicuous broad white forehead (cf. note on p.56) and heavily and variably barred underparts. Legs orange; bill pink. Juv more uniform grey-brown, lacking white on face and differing from same-sized Pinkfoot in its less contrasted head and neck, darker forewing, all-pink bill, and orange legs. Calls a babble of yelping 'kow-yow' and 'kow-lyow' sounds, like excited puppies; almost as high as Pinkfoot in pitch. Breeds on marshy tundra. L 65-78, WS 130-165 cm.  ⊙W

Ssp. *flavirostris* (Greenland, wintering Britain and Ireland) has a longer, heavier orange-yellow bill and usually more black on belly.

**LESSER WHITEFRONT** *Anser erythropus*. The smallest grey goose, like Whitefront, with pink bill and orange legs, but white on adult's forehead reaches much further towards crown, bill much smaller, and narrow yellow eye-ring diagnostic. Juv lacks white forehead and (initially) eye-ring. Call higher-pitched. In W Europe vagrants in Whitefront flocks often detectable by faster feeding rate. Breeds drier tundra, towards forest. L 53-66, WS 120-135 cm.  -VE

**Bar-headed Goose** *A. indicus*. An Asian 'grey goose', and a frequent escape. Paler grey than other grey geese, and easily told by two black bars on adult's white crown; bill and legs orange-yellow. L 71-76, WS 142-167 cm.  -E

*Goose Hybrids*. Both grey and black geese readily hybridise, especially in captivity, and puzzling specimens in wild flocks often turn out to be such hybrids, either natural or escapes. Cf. especially 1, Greylag x Canada, with whitish faces, often seen where feral flocks of both species occur, and 2, Whitefront x Bean Goose (p.56); 3, Whitefront for comparison. Snow x Whitefront could be mistaken for an escaped Emperor Goose *A. canagicus* (p.376).

58

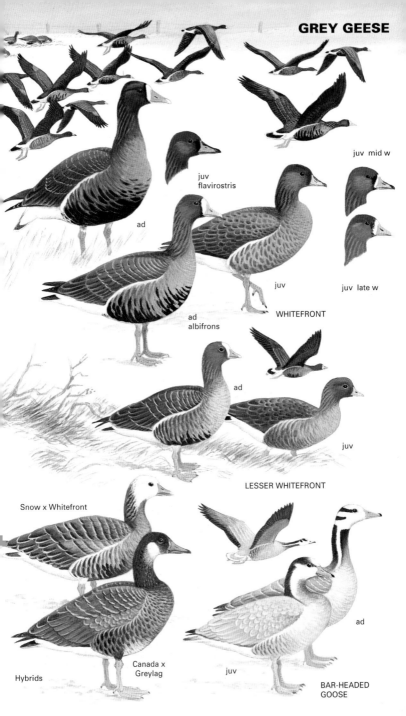

# GREY GEESE

juv
flavirostris

juv mid w

ad

juv late w

juv

ad
albifrons

WHITEFRONT

ad

juv

LESSER WHITEFRONT

Snow x Whitefront

Hybrids

Canada x
Greylag

juv

ad

BAR-HEADED
GOOSE

● BLACK GEESE *Branta*. Relatively small (except Canada), with crown and neck black (except Red-breasted); sexes alike. The three native species are mainly winter visitors to the region. Usually in flocks.

**BRENT GOOSE** *Branta bernicla*. The only goose with an all-black head, and the smallest and darkest of the three black-necked geese, though with a white patch on each side of the neck. Upper breast black; back, rump and wings dark grey-brown; tail coverts white. Imm at rest has conspicuous white lines on wing coverts and no white neck-patch. Call a croaking 'ruk, gruk, grunk'. Breeds on Arctic sea-shores and islands and on marshy tundra, wintering on estuaries and adjacent farmland. L 56-61, WS 110-120 cm.                        ⊙W

**Dark-bellied** *B.b. bernicla* (Siberia) has underparts slate-grey. **Pale-bellied** *B.b. hrota* (Franz Josef Land, Spitsbergen, Greenland; wintering in Ireland) has underparts pale grey-brown to white. N American/E Siberian **Black Brant** *B.b. nigricans*, with even blacker underparts and white flash on flanks is a vagrant.

**BARNACLE GOOSE** *Branta leucopsis*. The only black-necked goose with whole face white; crown, nape and neck black, with rest of plumage mainly grey, more or less barred black and white. Juv duller, with greyer face. Call, 'ark', like gruff yapping of small terrier. Breeds Arctic coasts and Gotland (Baltic); winters on coastal flats, marshes, grassland. Rare inland, except as escape; cf. smaller races of Canada Goose. L 58-70, WS 132-145 cm.                        ⊙WE

**CANADA GOOSE** *Branta canadensis*. A well-established introduction from N America, much larger than the other black-necked geese, with a longer neck and browner plumage than Barnacle, and white on head confined to cheeks and throat. Call a loud double trumpeting 'ker-honk'. Rivers, lakes, ponds and adjacent grassland and marshes inland (where a large black-necked goose will almost certainly be Canada); in winter also on coastal flats and marshes. L 90-100, WS 160-175 cm.            ●R

A few apparently genuine transatlantic vagrant Canada Geese appear fairly regularly in Ireland and W Scotland among flocks of Barnacles and Whitefronts (p.58) from Greenland. Some of these belong to races appreciably smaller and darker than the population naturalised in Europe. Occasional feral Barnacle x Canada hybrids closely resemble these small dark birds.

pale
small

aberrant

**RED-BREASTED GOOSE** *Branta ruficollis*. The smallest and most strikingly coloured of the true geese, with foreneck, breast and cheek-patch chestnut-red, separated from black upper and underparts by white lines, with a broad white line on flanks conspicuous at a distance. Juv duller, with smaller or no chestnut cheek-patch. Calls high-pitched, rather musical, disyllabic, e.g. 'kee-kwa', 'kik-wit', 'ti-che'. Winters in steppes and marshes in S W Asia and S E Europe; in W Europe a vagrant in flocks of other geese or an escape. L 53-56, WS 116-135 cm.                        -VE

# BLACK GEESE

ad hrota

ad
bernicla

**BRENT GOOSE**

juv

ad

nigricans

ad

juv

**BARNACLE GOOSE**

canadensis

interior

**CANADA GOOSE**

juv

ad

**RED-BREASTED GOOSE**

minima

● DUCKS: *Anatinae* (pp.62-81). Most ducks are smaller than swans and geese, with shorter necks and legs. In eclipse (moult), midsummer-autumn, drakes resemble ducks.

**SHELDUCK** *Tadorna tadorna*. Large, goose-like in flight and gait; looking white and black, but head dark green and breast-band chestnut; bill and legs pink. Sexes alike, breeding drake with knob on bill; in eclipse paler and browner. Juv has forehead, cheeks and underparts white, bill and legs greyish. Drake has whistling flight-note, duck a laughing quack, 'ak-ak-ak'. A burrow nester: in W dunes, estuaries, sandy and muddy seashores, locally inland; in E by brackish and fresh inland seas and lakes. Large flocks moult on mudflats, e.g. at mouth of Elbe. L 58-71, WS 110-133 cm.　　　　　　　　　　　●Rw

**RUDDY SHELDUCK** *Tadorna ferruginea*. Large, rather goose-like in flight and gait; deep buff-brown, with paler head, black wing-tips and tail and conspicuous white wing-patch in flight; bill and legs black. Drake has narrow black collar; duck's head paler. Call a loud, nasal, clanging, greylag-like 'aang, aang'. Inland freshwater shores, in steppes, deserts, mountains; decreasing. L 61-67, WS 121-145 cm.　　　　　　　　-VE

**EGYPTIAN GOOSE** *Alopochen aegyptiacus*. Slightly larger, paler, longer-necked and longer-legged than Ruddy Shelduck, with an even more upright, goose-like stance; also shows conspicuous white shoulder patches in flight. Adult has dark patch round each eye and on lower breast; bill and legs pink. Sexes alike. Male has loud husky call; female quacks or honks. Rivers, lakes, marshes; perches in trees. Vagrant N Africa; introduced Britain. L 63-73, WS 134-154 cm.　　　　　　　　⊙R

Also resident Netherlands/Belgium.

♂
♀

**Cotton Teal** *Nettapus coromandelianus*, a rare vagrant from India, is the smallest duck: male white with black crown and breast band and green upperparts; female greyer. Aka Indian Pygmy Goose. L 31-38 cm.

**MANDARIN DUCK** *Aix galericulata*. Crested drake has striking plumage, with wing-fans and cheek-plumes orange-chestnut. Duck mainly grey-brown, with narrow but variable white 'spectacle' round eye, extending back as a thin line; feathering at base of dark bill straight. Eclipse drake and juv similar, with red bill. Flight note of drake a sharp little whistle, 'wrrick'; of duck a plaintive 'ack'. By fresh water in wooded areas. Introduced from China. L 41-49 cm.　　　　　　　　　　⊙R

**Wood Duck** *Aix sponsa*. Drake unmistakable, but duck, eclipse drake and juv best separated from Mandarin by large white patch round eye, extending back as a shorter, thicker spur, and by indented feather-line at base of bill. Duck's call a loud 'oo-eek'. Habitat similar. Introduced from N America (also vagrant to Azores), but unlike Mandarin not fully established. Aka Carolina Duck. L 47 cm.　　　-E

**Fulvous Whistling Duck** *Dendrocygna bicolor*. Rare vagrant from tropical Africa. Strikingly upright, long-legged and long-necked; tawny brown with dark crown, hindneck and back, white rump and creamy flank-stripe. Sexes alike, juv darker. Flight slow, with legs beyond tail. Call a loud, whistling 'pe-chee'. L 51 cm.

# SHELDUCKS

juv

♂ eclipse

♀ variable

♂ br

SHELDUCK

eclipse

♂ br    ♀

Juv like duck but still duller, greyer, less brown.

RUDDY SHELDUCK

juv

EGYPTIAN GOOSE

Ad brown; also pale grey phase

♀

♂ br

COTTON TEAL

♂ clipse

♀

♂ br

MANDARIN DUCK

♀

♂ br

WOOD DUCK

**Dabbling Ducks**: *Anas*. pp.64-69. Normally feed on the surface or by up-ending, rarely diving except when young or unable to fly. Both sexes have a coloured wing-patch (speculum), important for identifying the brown ducks and juvs. Flight fast, direct.

**MALLARD** *Anas platyrhynchos*. The largest dabbling duck, the commonest and most widespread duck of the region; the origin of the farmyard duck. Drake has unique combination of green head (shot with purple towards the moult), narrow white collar and dark purple-brown breast; bill always yellow. Speculum blue; bill of duck greenish, of juv reddish. Full and partial albinos, due to interbreeding with domesticated stock, frequent in and near towns. Familiar loud harsh quack uttered by duck only; drake has a softer 'queek'. Still and slow-moving fresh water and marshes; in winter also on estuaries and seashores. L 51-62, WS 81-98 cm.                ●Rw

**American Black Duck** *A. rubripes*. A N American vagrant, liable to hybridise with Mallard on both sides of Atlantic. Both sexes resemble very dark female Mallard, with pale face and foreneck, violet-purple speculum and white underwing, which is conspicuous in flight. Duck quacks like Mallard; drake has low croak. L 58 cm.        -V (b)

**GADWALL** *Anas strepera*. Drake mainly grey, with chestnut wing coverts and contrasting black tail coverts. Duck resembles small greyish duck Mallard. Both sexes have steeper forehead, and in flight show white belly and black and white speculum. Bill shorter and less stout than Mallard; of drake grey, of duck dark horn edged orange, of juv yellow. Drake has deep nasal croak, 'nhek'; duck's quack higher-pitched than duck Mallard's. Lowland fresh waters, inland brackish waters, marshes. L 46-56 cm.                ●RsW

**WIGEON** *Anas penelope*. Drake has distinctive buff forehead and crown, contrasting with chestnut head and neck, also white blaze along grey flanks and black tail coverts; in flight shows conspicuous white forewing even at a distance. Duck smaller and slenderer than duck Mallard (cf. duck Pintail, p.68), either greyish or more rufous. Both sexes have rather peaked forehead, short bill, green speculum, pointed tail and white belly. Juv like duck but duller, drakes may lack white wing patch for first year. Often flies fast in flocks. Far-carrying 'whee-oo' call reveals drake even at a distance or in fog; duck has purring note. Breeds by fresh water on moors and tundra, and in coastal marshes; in winter on lakes, reservoirs, estuaries and shallow coastal waters, also grazes on nearby grassland. L 45-51 cm.                ●rmW

♀ Wigeon grey form.

**AMERICAN WIGEON** *Anas americana*. A rare transatlantic visitor and escape. Drake differs from Wigeon especially in white forehead and crown, green patch behind eye, and pinkish-grey flanks, but duck/juv hard to tell unless greyer head and neck and white axillaries and underwing can be seen, and in some spring ducks the contrasting pale edges of the dark tertials. Escaped hybrids of Wigeon with S American Chiloe Wigeon *A. sibilatrix* (p.377) can be very confusing. L 45-56 cm.        -AE

# DABBLING DUCKS

Partially albino and other aberrant park Mallards.

♂ br

♂ eclipse

♀

MALLARD

Mallards often cross with domestic ducks and when seen away from parks can be confused with other ducks. e.g. imm eiders

♂

AMERICAN BLACK DUCK

♂ eclipse

♂ br

♀

♂

♀

GADWALL

♂ eclipse

♀

♂ br

WIGEON

♂

♀

imm duller on head, back and flanks; shoulders grey.

♂ eclipse

♀

♂ br

♂

♀

AMERICAN WIGEON

Eclipse drake Teal darker than duck and has obscurer dark eye-

1st year br ♂ Falcated

♀ Cinnamon    Blue-winged

1st year br ♂    eclipse ♂

Baikal

Eclipse drake has darker crown and retains brighter wing colours than duck.

*A. sibilatrix* (p.377) can be very confusing. L 45-56 cm.         -AE

**TEAL** *Anas crecca*. The region's smallest breeding duck, often flying, fast and wader-like, in compact flocks. Drake has chestnut head with distinctive broad buff-edged green stripe; at rest can be picked out at a distance by horizontal white line above wing and yellow patches under tail. Duck resembles diminutive duck Mallard, but has black and green speculum, pale patches at tail base, white belly, and grey bill and legs. Juv like duck but bill pinkish. Call of drake a distinctive tinkling or whistling 'crrick, crrick', of duck a short, high-pitched quack; courting parties in spring utter a chorus of bell-like notes. Breeds by still and slow-moving fresh water with dense fringe of vegetation and in marshes, fens and bogs. In winter on fresh water and shallow coastal waters, especially estuaries. L 34-38 cm. ●RmW

**Green-winged Teal** *A.c. carolinensis*. A rare but annual transatlantic visitor. Drake has vertical instead of horizontal white line at side of breast, and buffish edging only below green face stripe. Duck virtually identical to duck Teal.                                         -A

**Falcated Teal** *Anas falcata*. Rare vagrant from E Asia, also an escape. Drake easily recognised by long crest and elongated wing feathers; broad green stripe on red-purple head not edged paler. Duck not unlike female Gadwall (p.64), but distinguished by short crest, grey forewing, black and green speculum and blackish bill and legs. Usually on fresh water, often with Wigeon. L 48-54.         -E

**GARGANEY** *Anas querquedula*. The region's second smallest breeding duck, larger and longer-bodied than Teal and with steeper forehead making head more angular. Drake unmistakable with conspicuous broad white stripe above eye; both sexes have blue-grey forewing, duller in duck and greyer than Shoveler (p.68) and Blue-winged Teal. Duck/juv have striped face patterns and pale spot at base of longer and wider bill, and lack the white at the base of Teal's tail. Speculum all-green; bill of drake dark grey, of duck olive-grey; legs and feet grey. In spring drake has curious crackling note, like a single match rattling in a matchbox; duck has a low quack. Shallow fresh water in lowlands, with much low cover. L 37-41 cm.                                         ☉Sm

**Blue-winged Teal** *Anas discors*. A rare transatlantic visitor, with forewing bluer-grey than wing, drake easily told by conspicuous white crescent on face. Duck has bluer forewing than duck Garganey, also much plainer face with pale loral spot and conspicuous whitish eye-ring, blackish bill and yellow legs; very like richer brown escaped duck Cinnamon Teal *A. cyanoptera*, which has longer, more spoon-shaped bill. Drake has a whistling 'peep' and a soft lisping 'tseef, tseef, tseef'; duck a soft, teal-like quack. L 37-41 cm.                                         -AE

**Baikal Teal** *Anas formosa*. Rare vagrant from Siberia, also an escape. Drake has unique green, cream and black head pattern, together with elongated fan of wing feathers and vertical white mark between breast and flanks. Duck resembles large duck Teal, with conspicuous pale spot at base of bill, and dark eyestripe surmounted by a broken pale line. Drake often repeats a curious clucking 'proop' or 'wot-wot'; duck has a harsh quack.

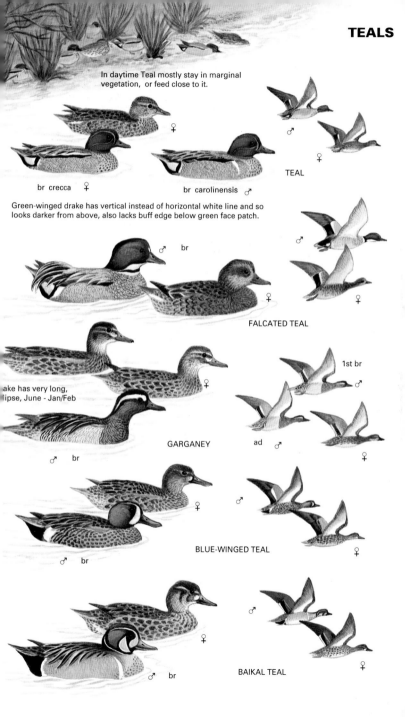

In daytime Teal mostly stay in marginal vegetation, or feed close to it.

♀

♂

♀

**TEAL**

br crecca ♀

br carolinensis ♂

Green-winged drake has vertical instead of horizontal white line and so looks darker from above, also lacks buff edge below green face patch.

♂ br

♀

♂

♀

**FALCATED TEAL**

♀

ake has very long, lipse, June - Jan/Feb

**GARGANEY**

1st br ♂

ad ♂

♀

♂ br

♀

♂

**BLUE-WINGED TEAL**

♂ br

♀

♂

♀

**BAIKAL TEAL**

♂ br

♀

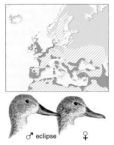

♂ eclipse ♀

Bill of eclipse drake paler than duck and with black base and tip

Bill from above and from side.

ad          juv

Bill of adult pink, of juv grey.

♂          ♀

Duck has rounder head due to smaller crest.

**PINTAIL** *Anas acuta*. An elegant duck with long, slender neck, the drake with greatly elongated central tail feathers, and striking combination of dark head and throat with white breast and neck stripe. Only other white-breasted dabbling duck is short-necked, heavy-billed Shoveler, and only the maritime drake Long-tailed Duck (p.78) has such a long tail. Duck like duck Wigeon (p.64), but paler and sandier with more pointed tail, slenderer neck and narrower wings. Speculum bronzy, bill slender and blue-grey, legs grey. Flies fast. Drake has weak, low, nasal, moorhen-like 'gseee' and in courtship a rather musical croak; duck's call a rather hoarse quack. Freshwater and brackish pools and marshes on moors and tundra and in coniferous forest; in winter also flooded meadows, estuaries and coastal marshes. L 51-66 cm.          ●rmW

**SHOVELER** *Anas clypeata*. Both sexes recognisable by heavy shovel-shaped bill producing characteristic head-down attitude on the water, also by blue-grey forewing in flight. Drake has striking plumage of dark green head (blackish in poor light), white breast and chestnut flanks, and is the only common dabbling duck with a yellow eye. Duck is like heavy-billed duck Mallard (p.64), but with green speculum. Drake's call a gruff 'took, took', duck's a double quack. Inland and coastal fresh and brackish waters and marshes in lowlands, especially with plenty of vegetation and shallow muddy water. In winter mainly on shallow fresh water, also deeper fresh waters and estuaries. L 49-52 cm.          ●rsMw

**Cape Teal** *A. capensis*. Rare vagrant to S of region from tropical Africa. Both sexes are pale grey-brown and speckled, with a slightly upturned bill and a conspicuous U-shaped white border to the black and bright green speculum. Duck and juv browner on head. Eyes of adults vary from pale brown through yellow and orange to red; of juv dark. L 44-48 cm.          -E

**MARBLED TEAL** *Marmaronetta angustirostris*. A pale grey-brown, speckled duck with a dark smudge around and behind eye contrasting with pale lower face, longish head, shaggy nape, pale wings and tail, and pink bill. Long neck and long narrow wings make it look like a small Pintail in flight. Sexes alike. Juv duller, greyer, with browner head markings and grey bill. The region's only dabbling duck with no obvious speculum. Drake has weak nasal squeak, duck a double whistle. Well-vegetated fresh or brackish water, marshes; in winter on more open waters, even temporary desert pools. L 39-42 cm. -E

**RED-CRESTED POCHARD** *Netta rufina*. Drake is the region's only red-billed and red-legged diving duck, also with crested chestnut-red head and long broad white wing bar in flight. Duck is only uniformly brownish duck to combine broad wing bar, pale (as distinct from white) cheeks, and pink-tipped bill. Up-ends as well as dives to feed. Drake has a hard, wheezing note, duck a harsh 'kurr'. Fresh or brackish lakes and lagoons, usually reed-fringed, and marshes. Frequently escapes and hybridises. L 53-57 cm.          -AE(b)

# DABBLING DUCKS

♂ eclipse

♂ br

♀

♀

PINTAIL

♂ eclipse

♂ supplementary

♀

♂ br

SHOVELER

CAPE TEAL

juv

Sexes very similar.

MARBLED TEAL

♂ eclipse

♀

♀

♂

juv

♂ br

RED-CRESTED POCHARD

Pochards *Aythya* often dive and swim submerged. Shorter-necked and more compact than most dabblers, with legs set further back. Flight direct, with rapid wing-beats.

**TUFTED DUCK** *Aythya fuligula*. Drake has strongly contrasting white flanks and black upperparts, and is the only waterfowl with a drooping black crest. Short-crested, brownish duck may have narrow white band on face at base of bill (cf. Scaup) or whitish under tail coverts (cf. Ferruginous Duck). Juv as duck. Bill blue-grey, eye yellow. White wing bar in flight. Still and slow-moving fresh water, in breeding season with vegetated margins; in winter often on bare-banked reservoirs, occasionally on coastal waters. L 40-47 cm.  ●RW

**Ring-necked Duck** *A. collaris*. Rare transatlantic vagrant; rear crown more peaked than Tufted, bold white ring near bill tip, grey wing bar in flight. Drake has vertical white band between black breast and grey flanks, and narrow ring near base of bill. Duck has pale eye-ring, often with a pale eye-stripe, and pale face near bill. L 37-46 cm.  -A

**Lesser Scaup** *A. affinis*. Rare transatlantic vagrant, similar to Scaup, but smaller and rather darker-backed, with peaked rear crown, dull purple gloss and shorter white wing bar. Cf. Hybrids, p.72. L 38-45 cm.  -V

**SCAUP** *Aythya marila*. Differs from smaller Tufted Duck especially in larger, more rounded head, drake's grey back and large white patch at base of duck's bill, much broader than white band of some duck Tufted; imms lack this band and are best told by head shape. Differs from same-sized drake Pochard in black head (glossed mainly green) neck and breast, and from both sexes in white wing bar in flight. Breeds in tundra and coniferous forest (taiga); in winter mainly on estuaries and coastal waters. L 42-51 cm.  ⊙rmW(b)

**POCHARD** *Aythya ferina*. Drake is the region's only common waterfowl to combine whole head and neck chestnut with grey upperparts; cf non-diving drake Wigeon (p.64), which has buff crown and white forewing. Duck brown in front, grey-brown behind. Both have blue-grey bill, black at tip and base, and show no pale wing bar in flight. As in all *Aythya*, juv resembles duck and drakes have a low, often wheezy whistle, ducks a harsh, growling 'kurrr, kurrr'. Habitat as Tufted Duck, but also breeds on brackish lakes. L 42-49 cm.  ●rmW

**FERRUGINOUS DUCK** *Aythya nyroca*. Drake like a small chestnut Tufted with Pochard head-shape and white eye; duck duller, browner, never with white at bill base. Both sexes differ from duck Tufted and Pochard in sharp contrast of white under tail coverts (Tufted may show this, but much less contrasted) and darker bill; also by more conspicuous white wing bar and white belly in flight. Lowland fresh or brackish still and slow-moving waters, often lurking in fringing vegetation; also marshes, reedbeds. Aka White-eyed Pochard. L 38-42 cm.  -AE

# POCHARDS

Mallard
for size
comparison.

TUFTED DUCK ♀ br ♂

RING-NECKED DUCK ♀ ♂ br

LESSER SCAUP ♂ br

SCAUP ♀ ♂ br

POCHARD ♀ ♂ br ♂ eclipse

FERRUGINOUS DUCK ♀ ♂ br

Ring-necked Duck

Tufted Duck

Lesser Scaup

Scaup

Baer's Pochard

Ferruginous Duck

Redhead

Pochard

*AYTHYA HYBRIDS.* Numerous hybrids have arisen in the diving duck genus *Aythya*, including hybrids with Red-crested Pochard *Netta rufina* (p.68), largely as a result of escapes from wildfowl collections. Hence any unusual *Aythya* must be scrutinised with especial care. The parents of many individual hybrids, especially females, can often only be guessed – or remain unknown. Described here are mostly the commoner drakes. The known or probable male parent is named first.

**Ring-necked Duck type.** Tufted Duck x either Pochard (grey-backed) or Ring-necked Duck (black-backed). Head peaked with short crest, red-brown; bill with white band (as in Ring-necked Duck) next to black tip and no white band but sometimes faint white line at base; flanks slightly vermiculated.

**Tufted Duck type.** Pochard x Tufted Duck. Crest between Tufted Duck and Lesser Scaup type, head purplish-black with green sheen. Black at tip of bill extends in a crescent up the sides.

**Lesser Scaup type.** The classic drake *Aythya* hybrid, Tufted Duck x Pochard, shortly crested and differing from Lesser Scaup in rear crown less peaked and with strong *brownish*-purple gloss, forehead less steep, back much more finely vermiculated, and bill more pointed and with black at tip extending in a crescent up the sides, also usually dark at base; eye orange-yellow. Wing bar whiter than Lesser Scaup but less so than Tufted Duck.

**Scaup type.** Tufted Duck x Scaup. Head peaked with short crest and both purple and green sheen; bill tip broad with slightly more black (sometimes fan-shaped) and back more finely vermiculated than Scaup or Lesser Scaup.

**Baer's Pochard type.** Tufted Duck x Ferruginous Duck. Head with short crest, dark coppery-red, glossed green; black at bill tip fan-shaped; some black at base; eye pale yellow. (True Baer's Pochard *A. baeri* from Far East, not yet seen wild in the region.) Other hybrids between these species resemble dull imm Ferruginous Ducks.

**New Zealand Scaup type.** Hybrids thought to be Ring-necked Duck x New Zealand Scaup *A. novaeseelandiae*, presumably escaped from wildfowl collections, have been seen in England and France. One was shorter than a Ring-necked, with flanks dull chestnut, head with a violet sheen, and a pale spot or band near the bill tip. This type could also be a dark form of Ferruginous Duck x either Tufted Duck or Ring-necked Duck.

**Ferruginous Duck type** (Paget's Pochard). Pochard x Ferruginous Duck. Head rich coppery-chestnut. Black at bill tip extends in a crescent up the sides; basal two-thirds of bill dusky; eye orange.

**Redhead type.** Some drake-Pochard-like Ferruginous Duck x Pochard and Pochard x Tufted Duck hybrids resemble a small **Redhead** *A. americana* (one occurrence as vagrant/escape in Britain), the former with forehead slightly steeper than Pochard and blue-grey of bill not as sharply demarcated from basal black, the latter similar but often with short crest, purple gloss to head and black at tip of bill often a crescent up the sides; both hybrids usually orange-eyed (yellow in Redhead).

# AYTHYA HYBRIDS

In winter Pochards often flock together, but sometimes with other species, which may lead to interspecific courtship, and so to hybrid offspring.

In winter flocks search for birds with unusual features, which may be either vagrants from America or hybrids that can mimic these vagrants.

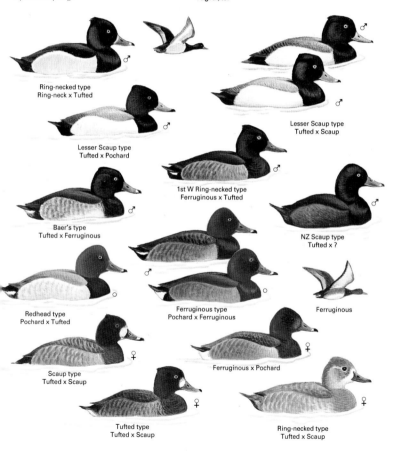

Ring-necked type
Ring-neck x Tufted

Lesser Scaup type
Tufted x Pochard

Baer's type
Tufted x Ferruginous

Redhead type
Pochard x Tufted

Scaup type
Tufted x Scaup

Tufted type
Tufted x Scaup

Lesser Scaup type
Tufted x Scaup

1st W Ring-necked type
Ferruginous x Tufted

NZ Scaup type
Tufted x ?

Ferruginous type
Pochard x Ferruginous

Ferruginous

Ferruginous x Pochard

Ring-necked type
Tufted x Scaup

The most frequent duck hybrids are due to interbreeding in the *Aythya* group, but other hybrids also occur, e.g. Pochard x Red-crested Pochard (p.68), Tufted x Red-crested Pochard and Mallard x Pintail (p.64).

With suspected hybrids, check especially colour of eyes, flanks and under tail coverts, head gloss and bill-tip pattern. Drakes are less difficult than the more variable ducks.

**Eiders**: *Somateria*. Large, heavily built sea ducks, expert divers; rare inland. Drakes strikingly patterned; ducks mottled brown; no speculum. Bill continues in almost straight line from forehead (except drake King Eider); feathering descends well down the upper mandible. Females in flight show faint line on wing. Both sexes more vocal than other ducks.

**EIDER** *Somateria mollissima*. Adult drake and drake Spectacled Eider are only waterfowl white above and black below, so that such birds paired with brown ones at sea most likely to be eiders. Crown and tail black, nape pale green and breast pink. In flight forewing largely white with black tip and trailing edge. Imm and eclipse drakes have mixtures of black and white, often very confusing in the field, but head usually dark and underparts black. Duck has distinctive heavy build, straight forehead, frontal lobes of bill almost reaching eyes, and breast barred. Drake's low crooning courtship note, 'ah-oo' or 'coo-roo-uh', accented on second syllable; duck grunts or croaks. Rocky and sandy coasts. L 50-71 cm. ●RW

1          2

3

Drakes: 2, ssp.*faeroensis* (Orkney, Shetland, Faeroe) is smaller than typical 1, ssp.*mollissima*, with darker grey bill and shorter frontal lobes; female barred darker; drake 3, ssp.*borealis* (Iceland, Spitsbergen) has bright yellow bill.

**KING EIDER** *Somateria spectabilis*. Very distinctive drake is the only waterfowl that appears white in front and black behind. Also has more rounded, pale grey head than drake Eider; steep, swollen forehead with orange frontal lobes and red bill; and in flight white on wing contrasting with black back. Imms/eclipse drakes have mixtures of dark and white plumage, but head generally blackish. Duck very like duck Eider, but more rufous with flank markings crescentic, more convex forehead, and more feathering on slightly shorter bill, the frontal lobes not reaching so far back. Voice as Eider, but drake's coo trisyllabic with accent at end. Arctic coastlines and fresh water in tundra; in winter only in coastal waters. L 47-63 cm.     -A

**Hybrid Eider x King Eider**. The two species sometimes interbreed in Iceland and elsewhere, but young are rarely produced.

**SPECTACLED EIDER** *Somateria fischeri*. Winter vagrant to Arctic coasts, markedly smaller (and duck darker) than Eider. Has distinctive large white (drake) or pale (duck) spectacle round eye; upper portion of shorter bill all feathered. Drake white above and black below, including lower breast; rest of head green. Flight pattern similar to Eider. Rarely vocal. L 52-57.

**STELLER'S EIDER** *Polysticta stelleri*. Much smaller than other eiders and with more rounded head, shorter blue-grey bill and purple speculum. Drake uniquely combines white head, black and white upperparts and rufous underparts; also has two green patches on head and flight pattern like Eider. Dark brown duck and eclipse drake have white wing bar. Drake has low croon, duck a harsh quack; both make whistling sound in flight like Goldeneye (p.78). Numerous throughout year N Norway, often close inshore (may breed occasionally); a few winter in Baltic; elsewhere a rare visitor. L 43-47 cm.     -V

# EIDERS

1st br ♂

♂ br

1st w ♂

w

♀ grey

♂ eclipse

aut ♂

♂

♀

eclipse

♀ eclipse

eclipse

♂ br

♀ br

EIDER

1st s

♀

♂ eclipse

♂

♀

♂ br

KING EIDER

♂ eclipse

♀

SPECTACLED EIDER

♂

♀

♂ br

♀

♂

♀

♂

STELLER'S EIDER

♀

♂ eclipse

♂

**Sea Ducks** (pp.76-79). A group of diving ducks, including scoters, goldeneyes and Harlequin and Long-tailed Ducks (p.78), as well as Scaup (p.70), that breed by fresh water but winter mainly in coastal waters.

Long-tailed    Harlequin

**HARLEQUIN DUCK** *Histrionicus histrionicus*. A small sea duck, very rare in Europe except Iceland. Drake has unique pattern of blue, white, chestnut and black, but at a distance just looks dark, when short bill and white on head may be best clues. Duck brown with three pale spots on face and no wing-bar, smaller and shorter-billed than scoters and with much less white on belly than imm Long-tailed Duck (p.78). Buoyant on water, often in surf and rough seas, and with tail cocked up. Drake has a low descending whistle, ending in a trill, and duck a harsh croak. Breeds on fast streams, often near waterfalls, wintering at sea near rocky coasts. L 38-45 cm.                    -V

1st w

Black Scoter

**COMMON SCOTER** *Melanitta nigra*. Drake is only waterfowl with all-black plumage. Duck and juv/imm all-brown, except for pale lower face and upper neck, which separate them from duck Red-crested Pochard (p.68) (white wing bar), and shorter-billed Long-tailed Duck (much whiter underparts). Both sexes have blackish bill swollen at base and blackish legs, but drake has black knob and orange-yellow patch on upper mandible. Drake often rests with relatively pointed tail cocked up. Drake has low cooing or whistling notes in courtship; duck has a harsh growling cackle. Breeds in tundra, moorland and taiga; in winter often flies in lines and masses in dense rafts offshore; many non-breeders summer well S of breeding range. L 44-54 cm.                    ●rMW

**Black Scoter** *M.(n.) americana*, a rare N American vagrant, has larger knob and bill yellow with black tip.                    -V

**VELVET SCOTER** *Melanitta fusca*. White wing bar, especially noticeable in flight, and red feet distinguish both sexes from smaller Common Scoter. Drake also has small white patch behind eye and orange-yellow sides to (not patch on) bill. Duck and imm have two pale patches on face. Breeds in the Eurasian taiga (coniferous forest), less often on tundra than Common Scoter; in winter mainly in small parties or with Common Scoters or eiders. L 51-58 cm.                    ☉mW

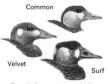

Common

Velvet

Surf

Female face pattern and bill
shape of scoters.

**SURF SCOTER** *Melanitta perspicillata*. Rare transatlantic visitor to coastal waters of N W Europe, differing from other scoters especially in large eider-like bill, parti-coloured with a red patch in drake, and greenish in duck. Drake also has a white patch on both forehead and nape; duck and imm usually have two pale patches on face and duck also sometimes one on nape, but these may be obscure or even absent. No wing bar; legs orange. L 45-56 cm.                    -A

**SEA DUCKS**

♂

♂

br ♂

♀

HARLEQUIN DUCK

♂ eclipse

1st s

♂ 1st w

americana

♀ nigra

br ♂

americana

♂ br

COMMON SCOTER

♀

br ♂

VELVET SCOTER

♂ 1st spring

juv

br ♂

♀

SURF SCOTER

**GOLDENEYE** *Bucephala clangula*. A diving duck best told by strikingly peaked, almost triangular shape of head, together with broad white wing bars, white neck and yellow eye. Drake's head black, glossed green, with large round white spot in front of eye; head of duck/juv chocolate-brown, slightly less peaked and with no spot. In spring drake has insistent 'speer, speer' and harsh 'quee-reek', and duck a guttural 'kurr'. In flight looks large-headed and short-necked and wings make a loud singing note. Breeds by fresh water in forests, usually coniferous, using tree holes and nestboxes; in winter on both fresh and coastal waters. L 42-50 cm.  ●rmW

**BARROW'S GOLDENEYE** *Bucephala islandica*. Very rarely seen away from Iceland. Both sexes differ from Goldeneye in rounder, almost bulbous head. Drake appears darker, due to large white spots on closed wing (Goldeneye looks barred) and has larger crescentic spot on purple-glossed head. Calls and flight-noise similar to Goldeneye. Breeds by freshwater lakes, nesting in cavities in cliffs, rocks, walls and ruined buildings; in winter also on inshore coastal waters. L 42-53 cm.  -VE

**Bufflehead** *B. albeola*. Rare transatlantic vagrant, whose white wing-patches make it look like a small Goldeneye in flight, but with less triangular head. Drake has rear half of head conspicuously white, duck a much smaller white patch behind eye; cf longer-billed Hooded Merganser (p.80). Drake has a rolling guttural note and duck a repeated 'guk, guk'. L 32-39 cm.  -VE

Buffleheads rise steeply from the water.

**LONG-TAILED DUCK** *Clangula hyemalis*. No other duck of the region has so many distinct plumages, but in all of them neat appearance, very short bill and lack of wing bar are distinctive. Adult drake has long tail (cf. Pintail, p.68), plume-like scapulars and pink bill-tip; duck and juv/imm have shorter and pointed tail and grey bill. Noisy drake in spring has loud musical call, 'ardelow-ar-ardelow' or 'ow, ow, owal-ow'; duck has soft quack. Has a distinctive swinging flight, not raising downcurved wings much above level of body. Breeds by fresh or salt water on tundra and Arctic coasts, and on mountains in Scandinavia; scarce inland in winter. L 40-47 cm.  ⊙W(b)

♂ 1st w

♀ autumn

juv

♂ eclipse

♂ autumn

♀ 1st winter

Adult drake in spring is dark on head, neck, breast and upperparts, white only on face and below; in winter mainly white, with blackish cheek-patch, breast-band, wings, rump and tail. Adult duck in spring like drake but with white parts greyish and dark cheek-patch; in winter whiter on head, neck and underparts. Imm drake like duck but has pink on bill; juv has distinctive white patch at base of bill.

78

# SEA DUCKS

♀

♂ br

♂ eclipse

♀

♂ br

♀

♂ eclipse

♂ br

GOLDENEYE

♀

♂ br

♀

BARROW'S GOLDENEYE

1st y. ♀

♂

♀

BUFFLEHEAD

♂ eclipse

♂ br

♀

♀ br

♂ summer

♂ w

♂ w

♀ w

LONG-TAILED DUCK

**Sawbills**: *Mergus*. Diving ducks, with narrow saw-edged bills and crested heads. Duck and juv/imm (redheads) have chestnut head and nape, with white chin.

**GOOSANDER** *Mergus merganser*. The largest sawbill. Drake has dark green head, rather bulbous due to obscure crest, long red bill, and white breast and flanks sometimes tinged pink. Redheads have full, lumpy or shaggy crest on back of head, and sharply defined white chin. In fast direct whistling flight cigar-shaped, holding head and neck straight out (cf. grebes, p.26), and showing broad white wing-patch (cf. divers, p.24). Upland and forest lakes and fast streams/rivers, less often sheltered coasts, nesting in tree and other holes; in winter on fresh water or estuaries. L 58-66 cm. ●RW

**RED-BREASTED MERGANSER** *Mergus serrator*. Appreciably smaller than Goosander, drake has conspicuous crest, pale chestnut breast and grey flanks. Redheads harder to separate; Merganser has markedly thinner bill, more gingery head and wispier crest higher up on nape, white of chin and separation of red-brown neck from breast less sharply defined, and upperparts, breast and flanks browner. Whistling flight similar. More frequent on coasts when breeding, nesting on ground; in winter regular on estuaries and sea, uncommon on fresh water. L 52-58 cm. ●RW

**SMEW** *Mergellus albellus*. Drake is the region's whitest small waterfowl, varied at rest by only a few black markings, but in flight looks more evenly black and white. Redheads have top of head and nape chestnut, with conspicuously white cheeks, and dive often, like grebes. Smaller lakes, ponds, slow-moving streams and rivers in taiga, nesting in tree-holes; in winter on fresh water and estuaries. L 38-44 cm. ⊙W

**Hooded Merganser** *Lophodytes cucullatus*. Rare transatlantic vagrant. Drake unmistakable; smaller drake Bufflehead (p.78) has head less rounded and lacks the two black stripes on pale rufous flanks; when crest lowered drake shows less white and resembles diminutive Red-breasted Merganser redhead. Duck like browner, longer-billed duck Smew, but whole head rufous. L 42-50 cm. -VE

**Stiff-tails**: *Oxyura*. Dumpy little large-headed, short-necked diving ducks; often swim with long tail cocked up, and may submerge all except head like grebes. Drakes cluck and squeak.

**WHITE-HEADED DUCK** *Oxyura leucocephala*. Drake greyish-rufous with chestnut-rufous breast, white head, black crown and neck and blue bill, swollen at base; in winter has more black on crown with grey bill. Duck greyer with brown crown, white cheeks (with a broad brown line) and neck and bill like drake but greyer. Juv like duck but paler. Shallow, often reed-fringed, fresh and brackish pools; dives often, flying reluctantly. L 43-48 cm. -E

**RUDDY DUCK** *Oxyura jamaicensis*. Introduced from N America, rapid spread may be checked by culling to prevent it hybridising with larger White-headed Duck, which has distinctive swollen base to bill. Drake Ruddy more uniformly rufous-chestnut, with much more black and less white on head, and under tail coverts white; duller in winter. Duck/juv Ruddy best told by bill base, but often have crown less dark and brown band on duller white cheek narrower. Fresh water inland; dives often; cannot walk on land. L 35-43, ⊙R

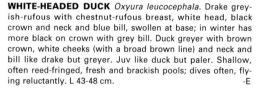

# SAWBILLS, STIFF-TAILS

GOOSANDER

RED-BREASTED MERGANSER

SMEW

HOODED MERGANSER

WHITE-HEADED DUCK

RUDDY DUCK

● DIURNAL BIRDS OF PREY: *Falconiformes*. pp.82-109. The diurnal birds of prey or raptors are medium to large, long-winged and adapted to flesh-eating by hooked bills and powerful talons; nostrils in swollen fleshy cere at base of bill. Sexes usually alike, but females larger than males. Imm plumages often confusing. Flight powerful, often soaring. Two families: *Accipitridae* (osprey, eagles, kites, buzzards, hawks, harriers, Old World vultures) and *Falconidae* (falcons); for distinctions between families see p.102. 'Hawk' is often loosely used for all smaller birds of prey, not just for the genus *Accipiter*.

**OSPREY** *Pandion haliaetus*. White head and underparts, long, angled wings with black patches at angles, and habit of plunging from air to fish are most distinctive. Differs from small eagles with pale underparts in wing-shape and from Marsh Harrier (p.90) in white underparts. Call a shrill cheeping, like a young gamebird. Flight slow and flapping when hunting over water; also glides, soars and hovers, with gull-like bowed wings. Often perches on dead tree or post. Wooded or moorland country with lakes or rivers, nesting on trees or small rocky islets; in winter at larger fresh, brackish or inshore salt waters. L 55-58, WS 145-170 cm.　　　　　●Sm

**WHITE-TAILED EAGLE** *Haliaeetus albicilla*. Enormous, with vulture-like long, broad, parallel-edged wings, neck, head and massive bill jutting as far out in front as tail does behind. From *Aquila* eagles (pp.96-99), differs in wedge-shaped (not square) tail and only half-feathered legs. Adult also differs from imm *Aquila* in all-white tail, while imm differs from adult Golden (p.96) in mottled white base of brown tail. Adult's head may be very pale, almost white; bill and cere yellow. Calls barking or yapping. Flight ponderous, heron-like, often low over water; may soar or swoop. Rocky coasts; lakes, rivers in wild country; nest on cliff, steep bank, tree. Aka Sea Eagle. L 70-90, WS 200-240 cm.　　　　　　　　　-VE(b)

Recently re-introduced Scotland

**Bald Eagle** *H. leucocephalus*. Rare vagrant or escape, adult with pure white head, neck and tail. Imm all-dark at first, becomes white over 4-5 years; very like imm White-tailed; differs from adult Golden (p.96) in diffused white on underwing, larger head, heavier bill, more wedge-shaped tail, unfeathered legs. L 75-108, WS 180-230 cm.　　　　-E/V

juv

ad

**PALLAS'S FISH EAGLE** *Haliaeetus leucoryphus*. Less bulky than White-tailed, with bill and cere blue-grey, head always pale, and adult's dark-tipped white tail very conspicuous in flight. Imm dark brown, with diffuse white on underwing and base of tail mottled white. Chief call a barking 'kvok, kvok, kvok'; rather silent in winter. Lakes, rivers, swamps, inland seas, scarcely overlapping White-tailed; nest in tree, on ledge or ground. L 76-84, WS 200-250 cm.

ad　　　　　　WS 190-240 cm　　　　　　juv

2nd year

**African Fish Eagle** *H. vocifer*. Rare vagrant from tropical Africa, shorter-tailed than other eagles, adult distinctively white, chestnut and black, white extending on to breast and back. Imm brownish above, whitish below, streaked darker. Has loud, wild, far-carrying call. L 74-84, WS 190-240 cm.

# OSPREY, SEA EAGLES

juv

ad

ad ♂

ad ♀

OSPREY

WS 145-170 cm

juv

3-4th year

ad

WS 200-240 cm

WHITE-TAILED EAGLE

ad

juv

ad

1st year

2nd year

WS 180-230 cm
Bald Eagle

juv

imm

ad

ad

WS 200-250 cm

PALLAS'S FISH EAGLE

**Kites:** *Milvus*. Large raptors, longer-winged and longer-tailed than buzzards (p.94), with forked tails which they twist from side to side in flight. Frequently feed on carrion and on refuse dumps. Nest in trees.

**BLACK KITE** *Milvus migrans*. A large, dark, pale-headed raptor, whose shallow tail-fork is often hard to see in flight. Flies more buoyantly than buzzards, but less so than Red Kite and harriers (p.90); soars less than buzzards and flaps more, with wings less angled than Red Kite. Cf. Marsh Harrier (p.90), which glides with wings canted slightly upwards. Noisy, with a high-pitched squealing cry. Often in loose parties. Open and farmed country, villages, towns, often over water. L 55-60, WS 160-180 cm.                                                                 -A

Larger ssp.*aegyptius* is browner above and more rufous below, with darker head, yellow bill, whiter underwing patches (cf. Red Kite) and barred tail. Egypt, frequent in towns and on Red Sea coast.

Recently re-introduced England and Scotland.

**RED KITE** *Milvus milvus*. The region's only large bird with a deeply forked tail, noticeable even at rest. Plumage much more rufous, head paler and tail more forked than Black Kite, and with conspicuous pale bar on upperwing and large whitish panel near tip of underwing. Calls a shrill, buzzard-like mew and a loud squealing whistle like Black Kite. Flight more buoyant and harrier-like than buzzards and Black Kite; also soars, often with markedly angled wings. Woodland, mainly deciduous, and areas with scattered trees. L 60-66, WS 175-195 cm.                                                                 ⊙RE

**BLACK-WINGED KITE** *Elaneus caeruleus*. A smallish grey and white, rather large-headed raptor, easily told by its black shoulders and frequent hovering; tail square. Imms are browner. Wings canted up and angled when gliding. Rather silent, but has weak whistling calls. Often perches on poles and wires and may fly at dusk. Open country with scattered trees and woods, often near water. Nest in tree. Aka Black-shouldered Kite. L 31-35, W 75-87 cm.

**SHORT-TOED EAGLE** *Circaetus gallicus*. A medium-large, long-winged raptor, appearing almost all-white below at any distance; cf. smaller and narrower-winged Osprey (p.82), which has black patch at carpal joint, and much smaller pale Buzzard (p.94), which has black (not pale) primary tips. Head rather rounded, often almost owl-like; wings blunt-tipped, tail 3-barred. Calls mewing, buzzard-like, 'piee-ou'. Soars and glides on level or slightly raised wings; often hovers. Open country with scattered woods and trees, in both hills and plains. Nest usually on top of low tree. In S Europe eats many snakes, so aka Snake Eagle. L 62-67, W 185-195 cm.

# KITES
# SHORT-TOED
# EAGLE

ad

ad

juv

BLACK KITE

juv

ad

ad

RED KITE

ad

juv

BLACK-WINGED
KITE

dark

light

hovering

dark

light

SHORT-TOED
EAGLE

**Vultures**: pp. 86-89. Large, generally brown-plumaged and short-tailed, raptors, their long, broad, blunt-tipped wings, with a span of 1.5-3 m, highly adapted to soaring. Often with a neck ruff; legs usually not feathered below 'knee'. Sexes alike. Gregarious carrion-feeders of open country. Movements sluggish, but soar at great heights, watching for carcasses and for other vultures flying towards carcasses. Once sighted, they quickly fly down to it, so that large numbers assemble.

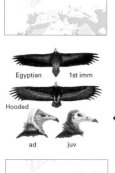

Egyptian   1st imm

Hooded

ad   juv

**EGYPTIAN VULTURE** *Neophron percnopterus*. Much the smallest breeding vulture of the region; adult has distinctive white wings with black tip and trailing edge, tail wedge-shaped and longer than most larger vultures, bare yellow skin on head and throat, shaggy ruff and noticeably slender bill, so that head looks narrow and pointed in flight. Imm dark brown with greyish face-skin, whitening over five years; soars or glides with wings level or bowed. Open country, in hills and plains, a village scavenger in the East and N Africa. Nests on rock ledges. L 60-70, WS 155-180 cm.                           -V

**Hooded Vulture** *Necrosyrtes monachus*. A possible vagrant from tropical Africa (once, S Morocco) is like a large imm Egyptian, but has a shorter tail, rounded not wedge-shaped. L 86 cm.

**LAMMERGEIER** *Gypaetus barbatus*. One of the region's largest vultures, whose long, narrow, angled, pointed wings and long diamond-shaped tail make it look in flight more like a giant Gyrfalcon (p.104) than a typical vulture. Mainly dark above with warm buff underparts; head white with conspicuous black band through eye, terminating in beard-like tuft of bristles (hence aka Bearded Vulture); legs fully feathered. Imm all dark with paler mottlings, underparts gradually becoming paler over five years, but not rufous till adult. Display call a high-pitched 'quee-er'. More active than typical vultures. Not gregarious within the region, and adult does not join other vultures at carcasses. Has unusual habit of splitting bones by dropping them from a height on to a hard surface, so as to eat the marrow. High and usually remote mountains, nesting on rock ledges. L 100-115, WS 266-282 cm.

**LAPPET-FACED VULTURE** *Torgos tracheliotos*. The region's rarest and marginally largest breeding vulture. A typical large, broad-winged, brown vulture, distinguished at close range by massive bill and bare cream, grey, brown or pink skin on head, often with small, loose folded lappets, pink on nape and grey on throat. In flight pale creamy-brown thighs are distinctive. May utter various growling, grunting or yelping sounds. Open plains, savannas and semi-deserts, with scattered trees, in which it nests. L 95-105, WS 255-290 cm.

A few individuals of ssp.*negevensis* remain in Israel. Ssp.*nubicus*, always with larger, often red throat lappets, paler underparts and thighs and a distinctive pale line along the leading edge of the adult's wing, formerly bred, now vagrant N W Africa.

Israel   N W Africa

# VULTURES

Vultures feeding at a carcass.

juv

ad

ad        WS 155-180 cm        imm

EGYPTIAN VULTURE

juv

imm

ad        WS 250-266 cm

LAMMERGEIER

juv

1st year

ad

ad        N W Africa

juv        Israel

ad        WS 255-290 cm

LAPPET-FACED VULTURE

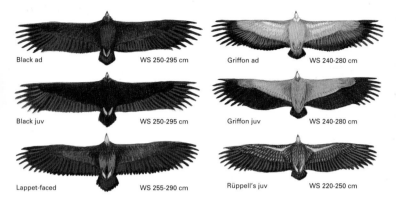

| | |
|---|---|
| Black ad — WS 250-295 cm | Griffon ad — WS 240-280 cm |
| Black juv — WS 250-295 cm | Griffon juv — WS 240-280 cm |
| Lappet-faced — WS 255-290 cm | Rüppell's juv — WS 220-250 cm |

In flight Black Vulture appears more rectangular-winged than Lappet-faced, and has diagnostic yellow legs.

In flight imm Griffon much paler beneath than adult. Rüppell's darker and shorter-winged.

imm    juv

♂

♀

♂

**BLACK VULTURE** *Aegypius monachus*. One of the region's largest vultures, all-dark except for paler wing-tips; imm paler beneath. Skin on head and neck blue-grey with black down (cf. slightly larger Lappet-faced); ruff black; legs (unlike all other vultures of region) sometimes yellow. In flight shows more wedge-shaped tail than Griffon (cf. longer-necked White-tailed Eagle, p.82) and always soars with straight wings. Various croaking, hissing and mewing notes. Less gregarious than most vultures, but will join and dominate Griffons at carcasses. Mainly open country, often in mountains, nesting in trees. Now rare in Europe. Aka Cinereous or Monk Vulture. L 100-110, WS 250-295 cm.                                                      -E

**GRIFFON VULTURE** *Gyps fulvus*. The region's most frequent larger vulture and the only pale-coloured one, mainly warm buff, with markedly contrasting dark wing and tail feathers; imm darker and more rufous above, paler below. Head and neck covered with white down; ruff creamy-white, not easily seen in field. Often soars at great height, with wings canted slightly upwards and a broad pale bar beneath; tail squarer than Black Vulture. Calls grunting, hissing or whistling. Rocky mountainous country, breeding on cliff ledges and usually roosting on rocks or crags. Takes precedence over Egyptian Vulture at carcasses, but gives way to Black Vulture. L 95-105, WS 240-280 cm.                                                      -V

**Rüppell's Vulture** *G. rüppellii*. Vagrant to Egypt from tropical Africa; much darker and somewhat shorter-winged than slightly larger Griffon, and with noticeably white-speckled wing coverts and underparts and three conspicuous broken horizontal white bars on dark underwing. Imm paler and more uniformly brown with white band along leading edge of wing and more diffuse mottling on underwing. Voice loud, harsh. L 85-95, WS 220-250 cm.

**Bateleur** *Teratopius ecaudatus*. Rare vagrant to Israel/Iraq from tropical Africa; large-headed and with tail so short that flight outline unmistakable. Male black with back, rump and tail rufous, underwing white and large pale patch on upperwing; female's wings brown and grey; bill black, yellow and red, with feet, cere and bare skin round eye all red. Imm warm brown with paler head and underparts. L 80-85, WS 170-180 cm.

# VULTURES

juv

ad

**BLACK VULTURE**

juv

ad

ad

**GRIFFON VULTURE**

WS 220-250 cm    ad

juv

WS 170-180 cm    imm

**RÜPPELL'S VULTURE**

♂

♀

**BATELEUR**

**Harriers:** *Circus*. Slim, medium-sized raptors with long, rather narrow wings and tail, wings rather pointed, long legs, and a slight ruff often making the face rounded and owl-like. Except Marsh, males are pale grey and smaller than females, while brown females/imms have white rump and barred tail, hence called ringtails. Glide low over ground to hunt; soar and glide with wings usually canted upwards. Nest on ground.

**MARSH HARRIER** *Circus aeruginosus*. The region's largest and most buzzard-like harrier, with broader, more rounded wings and heavier flight than the others. Males largely brown, grey only on wings and tail. Females/imms have unbarred tail and pale head. Darker imms and occasional melanistic individuals can be told from Black Kite (p.84) by lack of pale wing bar and forked tail, and from other all-dark raptors, e.g. dark Honey Buzzards (p.94) and Booted Eagle (p.96), by tail length and upwardly canted wings when soaring or gliding. Main calls similar to Hen Harrier, but chattering calls as threat or when mobbing, and wailing calls during display. Marshes, swamps, reed-beds, rice fields. L 48-56, WS 115-130 cm.          ⊙Srm

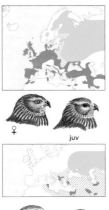

**HEN HARRIER** *Circus cyaneus*. Male uniformly pale grey except for black wing-tips, dark trailing edge of underwing, prominent white rump and white underparts. Ringtails brown (juv exceptionally with rufous underparts), with conspicuously barred tail, white rump, obscure facial pattern and ruff extending as blackish line across throat. Cf. smaller, narrower-winged Pallid and Montagu's Harriers. Main calls a chattering 'ke-ke-ke' or 'kek-kek-kek' both during aerial courtship display and as a threat or when mobbing, and squeals or wails, especially from female when breeding. Moors, heaths, steppes, open woodland, marshes, reed-beds, dunes. Name refers to former habit of preying on domestic fowls. L 44-52, WS 100-120 cm  ⊙RmW

♀          juv

**PALLID HARRIER** *Circus macrourus*. The region's smallest harrier, narrower-winged than both stouter Hen Harrier and only slightly larger Montagu's. Male paler and more uniformly grey than both, almost gull-like, with whiter head and breast, less black on wing-tips and no dark edge of underwing or white on rump. Ringtails even more alike, but only Pallid has striking face pattern of whitish cheeks and collar, offset by dark stripe through eye, and blackish crescent behind eye. Juv has rufous underparts like juv Montagu's. Open grassy plains, savannas, steppes. L 40-48, WS 95-120 cm.                         -V

♀          juv

**MONTAGU'S HARRIER** *Circus pygargus*. Appreciably slenderer and narrower-winged than Hen Harrier, males differing from both Hen and Pallid especially in dark bar on secondaries and rufous streaks on flanks and underwing. Female/imm best separated from Hen and Pallid by whitish cheeks and dark crescent behind eye, but only obscure dark eye-stripe and no whitish collar or dark ruff. Juv has dark rufous-buff underparts. A melanic form occurs. Call somewhat higher-pitched than Hen Harrier. Grassy steppes, coastal marshes, fens, reed-beds, dunes and young plantations. L 43-47, WS 105-120 cm.   ⊙Sm

♀          juv

# HARRIERS

juv

juv

♂

♀

juv

♂

♀

old

MARSH HARRIER

♂

♀

juv

♂

♂

♀

HEN HARRIER

juv

♂

juv

♀

♂

♂

♀

PALLID HARRIER

imm ♂

juv

juv

♂

♀

♂

♀

MONTAGU'S HARRIER

Hawks: *Accipiter*. The world's largest raptor genus comprises the true hawks, recognised by their combination of long tail and rather short, broad, rounded wings. Females larger than males. Flight fast, dashing, regularly hunting birds in woods and scrub. Nest in trees.

**SPARROWHAWK** *Accipiter nisus*. Rather short, broad, blunt wings, especially of female, distinguish blue-grey to slate-grey adult from the smaller falcons (p.108); wings of much smaller male more pointed and nearer shape of soaring female Kestrel or Merlin. Barred underparts also distinctive, with barring and cheeks more rufous in male; square-ended tail broadly barred; eyes yellow. Female has more white on head. Juv/imm brown above with irregular barring below. Typical flight patterns include: quick dash along hedge, up and over to pounce on prey; fast, low flight through wood or in the open; soaring, often in circular glide with a few wing-flaps from time to time; and steep downward plummet with closed wings. Chief call a chatter, based on 'kek', 'kew', 'kyow' or 'kiv'. Wooded country, villages, suburbs. Plucking posts, with feathers and prey remains on the ground, reveal presence. L 28-38, WS 55-70 cm. ●Rmw

**SHIKRA** *Accipiter badius*. Slightly smaller than Levant Sparrowhawk, with much less black on blunter wing-tips, paler cheeks and tail and dark vertical throat stripe. Male pale grey, female browner; juv's wing-tips blunter than juv Levant. Call 'kwik, kwik'. Flight as Sparrowhawk. Open woodland. L 30-36, WS 60-70 cm.

**LEVANT SPARROWHAWK** *Accipiter brevipes*. Has longer, more pointed wings than Sparrowhawk, white underparts contrasting strongly with black wing-tips; central tail feathers not barred; eyes red-brown, Male larger than male Sparrowhawk, with grey cheeks, and stronger contrast between paler upperparts and black wing-tips; female grey above. Juv dark grey-brown with rows of spots on strikingly white underparts. Call a distinctive, high-pitched 'kewick-kewick'. Woodland. Migrates in large flocks. L 33-38, WS 65-75 cm.

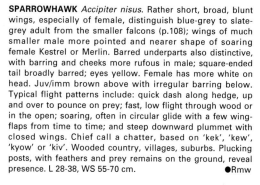

**GOSHAWK** *Accipiter gentilis*. Female is a buzzard-sized Sparrowhawk, with relatively longer, broader wings and slightly shorter tail. Male perhaps confusable with large female Sparrowhawk, but is much bulkier with tail broader and more rounded at tip. From below both sexes are pale greyish, often with a large white patch at vent; both have a dark head and usually a white supercilium. Juv browner with dark streaking on underparts and underwing coverts. Has fast, low hunting flight; soars with frequent flaps. Calls a shrill 'ca-ca-ca-ca' and 'quek-quek-quek-quek' and, from female, a screaming 'hi-aa, hi-aa'. Forests. L 48-62, WS 135-165 cm. ○RE

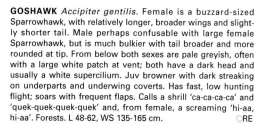

Ssp.*buteoides* (N Sweden to N Russia) is larger and paler, some almost white; ssp.*arrigonii* (Corsica, Sardinia) is smaller and, especially females, very dark-capped and heavily barred below; ssp.*atricapillus* (vagrant from N America) is larger with bluish upperparts and dark cap.

buteoides

Now rare Morocco.
Vagrant Spain, Israel.

**DARK CHANTING GOSHAWK** *Melierax metabates*. Adult all-grey, except for black tips to broad, blunt wings, and dark, white-tipped tail; rump and underparts barred; both legs and base of bill orange-yellow. Flight harrier-like, quartering the ground; often perches in distinctive horizontal position on tree or post. Chanting call a series of fluty piping notes. Open, dry bush country. L 38-48, WS 95-110 cm.

# HAWKS

juv

♀

♀

♀

♂

SPARROWHAWK

♀

juv

♀

♂

♂

♀

SHIKRA

LEVANT SPARROWHAWK

juv

♀

ad

ad

buteoides

GOSHAWK

juv

gentilis

juv

Hen Harrier
p.90

rigonii

juv

juv

ad

ad

DARK CHANTING GOSHAWK

Buzzard colour phases - each individual is different.

**Buzzards**: *Buteo/Pernis*. Large, short-necked, broad-winged raptors, much smaller than longer-necked *Aquila* eagles (pp.96-98) and overlapping Bonelli's/Booted Eagles (p.96) and longer-tailed kites (p.84) and Marsh Harrier (p.90). Note underwing patterns, tail bars.

**BUZZARD** *Buteo buteo*. Plumage exceptionally variable, from dark brown to white; underwing with dark patch at angle and often large pale patch near tip; tail finely and often faintly barred, with obscure dark band at tip. Sexes and juv alike. Glides with wings straight; often soars with wings slightly crooked at carpal joint and sometimes canted upwards, harrier-like; may hover. Call a high-pitched, almost gull-like 'peeeiooo'. Forests, wooded areas, farmland with trees, in winter in more open country. L 51-57, WS 113-128 cm.                    ●R

**ROUGH-LEGGED BUZZARD** *Buteo lagopus*. Unbarred white tail with broad dark bar at tip best distinction from Buzzard, together with more conspicuous black patch at angle of very pale, often white, underwing, and often paler head and broad brown breast-band. At close range feathered legs separate it from other same-sized raptors, except smaller eagles. Hovers more than other buzzards. Call louder and less shrill than Buzzard. Open country, tundra, moors, dunes, marshes. L 50-60, WS 120-150 cm.                    ○W

**LONG-LEGGED BUZZARD** *Buteo rufinus*. Slightly larger, longer-winged and longer-tailed than Buzzard and Steppe Buzzard, usually rufous, especially on underwing, with pale breast, contrasting with dark belly; outer half of underwing white; and tail uniform, barred in juv. Melanic form occurs. Flight and voice as Buzzard, but soars with inner half of wing canted up and outer half level. Plains, semi-deserts, mountains, other open country. L 50-65, WS 126-148 cm.

Ssp.*cirtensis* (N Africa) is smaller, with more Buzzard-like proportions, and usually paler.

**HONEY BUZZARD** *Pernis apivorus*. Has longer, narrower wings and tail, longer neck, smaller, 'pigeon-like', head and weaker bill than Buzzard, from which (and from other same-sized brown raptors) best told by three bands on pale tail, two at base and one at tip, as well as three dark bars across pale underwing. Glides with slightly down-curved wings, soars with flat wings; hovers, especially in display flight. Normal flight calls, usually disyllabic, higher-pitched and less mewing than Buzzard's; other calls at or near nest. Forested country, mainly deciduous; shy, but more often on ground than Buzzard, with habit of robbing bees' and wasps' nests. L 52-60, WS 135-150 cm.                    ○Sm

Honey Buzzard colour phases.

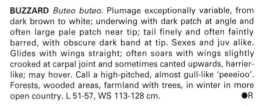

# BUZZARDS

ad typical
very variable

BUZZARD

Steppe Buzzard ssp. *vulpinus* (E Europe)
usually rufous, especially on underwing
and almost unbarred tail.

ad

ROUGH-LEGGED BUZZARD

ad red

ensis

ad typical
rufinus

juv

ad ▶

ad dark

ad

ad

LONG-LEGGED BUZZARD

ad ♂

♀

♀

HONEY BUZZARD

**Eagles:** *Hieraeetus* and *Aquila*. Large birds of prey with feathered legs (but cf. Short-toed Eagle, p.84), and broad wings and tail; cf. *Haliaeetus* eagles (p.82). Adult plumage assumed over 2-3 years. Flight rather heavy; soaring with outspread and often upturned primaries and so appearing blunt-winged. Wild mountainous or wooded country; nest on ledge or in tree.

Highly sedentary, but imms tend to wander in autumn.

**BONELLI'S EAGLE** *Hieraeetus fasciatus*. Relatively long, narrow wings, long tail and long neck give it the flight outline of a large Honey Buzzard (p.94); appreciably smaller than Golden Eagle. Best distinguished by white underparts, contrasted with dark band on underwing and dark tip to tail (cf. pale phase Booted Eagle), and white back contrasted with dark wings and upperparts. Imm variable, usually browner, with pale chestnut underparts; cf. Booted Eagle. Glides and soars with wings horizontal. Chief call a rather musical 'kluee-kluee-kluee'. Wooded, often rocky, mountains; in winter in more open country. L 65-72, WS 150-180 cm.

Migrates S in September, returning in March; resident on Minorca.

**BOOTED EAGLE** *Hieraeetus pennatus*. Buzzard-sized, with flight outline like Black Kite (p.84). Three colour forms, all with blackish primaries and trailing edge of wing, above and below, and unbarred square tail. Pale form, commoner in Europe, has rufous mantle and forewings, white underparts and strikingly black-and-white underwing (cf. larger Bonelli's Eagle). Rufous form, mainly in Middle East, has rufous underparts and dark brown band on underwing. Dark form rich dark brown with pale tail. Imm still more rufous, paler than juv Bonelli's. Glides with angled wings slightly down-curved; soars with flat wings. Call a melodic, rolling whistle. Forests, mainly in hills; in winter in more open country. L 45-53 cm, WS 100-121 cm.

Adults sedentary, but in N some imms move S in autumn.

**GOLDEN EAGLE** *Aquila chrysaetos*. A large eagle, adult tawny brown, sometimes with pale head; wings distinctly narrower at base, the flight feathers paler than the wing coverts and body. Imm has distinctive combination of white base of tail and conspicuous white patch on each spread wing. Tail longer than other *Aquila* eagles (p.98) and square, not wedge-shaped as in *Haliaeetus* (p.82). Flight majestic but graceful, both soaring and gliding with wings slightly canted upwards (unlike all other *Aquila* eagles) and head noticeably projecting, often staying on wing for hours at a time. Has a buzzard-like 'twee-o' and a barking call. Mainly in mountains, often treeless, but in E of region also lowland forests and extensive wetlands. L 75-88, WS 204-220 cm.                                                                       ⊙R

Sedentary in W; in E imms migrate S, but not far, returning late February or March.

**IMPERIAL EAGLE** *Aquila heliaca*. Longest-necked of the larger eagles, best told by white shoulders and sides of mantle, and pale crown, nape and base of tail, which become whiter with age. Imm yellower-brown with darker tail and primaries, no white on underwing and streaked underparts; cf. Steppe Eagle (p.98). Has a barking 'owk-owk-owk'. Lowland forests, wooded foothills, plains, steppes and marshes with scattered trees. L 72-83, WS 190-210 cm.

Ssp.*adalberti* (Spain, Portugal) has the white shoulders and sides of mantle joined together and leading edge of inner forewing also conspicuously white. Imm more rufous and less streaked.

# EAGLES

**BONELLI'S EAGLE**

juv

ad

sub ad

juv

ad

ad

Buzzard

Booted

ad dark

ad pale

juv

pale

dark

**BOOTED EAGLE**

ad

ad

juv

sub ad

juv

**GOLDEN EAGLE**

juv

ad

ad

juv

adalberti

ad

heliaca

heliaca

**IMPERIAL EAGLE**

Rare in Europe W of Russia; birds seen away from breeding areas usually imms.

**SPOTTED EAGLE** *Aquila clanga*. Large dark, broad-winged and short-tailed, flight outline recalling appreciably larger and somewhat longer-necked but wedge-tailed White-tailed (p.82). Slightly larger and darker than Lesser Spotted; slimmer and squarertailed than same-sized Steppe; and broader-winged and shortertailed than both. Adult uniformly dark above, except for pale crescent at base of tail, underwing coverts darker than primaries; juv/imm blacker, conspicuous pale spots and bars on upperparts, whiter V at base of tail. Rare pale form all creamy buff or pale rufous, except for darker primaries and secondaries, and extremely like similar plumage of Tawny. Holds wings straight in flight, tips slightly drooped when soaring and gliding. Call a barking 'kyak, kyak, kyak', like yapping of small dog. Lowland forests, often near lakes, rivers, marshes; in open country only on migration. L 65-72, WS 155-182 cm.                   -V

**LESSER SPOTTED EAGLE** *Aquila pomarina*. Slimmer than slightly larger Spotted Eagle, and with narrower wings and less conspicuous whitish crescent at base of longer tail; secondaries paler and more narrowly barred than Spotted and Tawny. Adult has underwing coverts diagnostically paler than primaries; imm has buff nape patch and is less conspicuously spotted above. Flight like Spotted, but wings usually held with carpal joint slightly crooked. Call higher-pitched and less resonant than Spotted. Habitat similar, but more often away from water. L 60-65 cm, WS 134-159 cm.

**STEPPE EAGLE** *Aquila nipalensis*. Large, broad-winged, dark brown, sometimes varying to very pale brown, upperparts usually completely uniform, no white markings, but pale forms may show striking contrast between dark flight feathers and rest of plumage; cf. Tawny. Juv/imm can also be very pale, but more often often resemble paler and rather blotchy adults; imm especially may be darker, and both have white upper tail coverts and pale double wing bar, upperparts have scaly appearance at rest, and diagnostic pale band on underwing. In soaring wings slightly crooked at elbow and shortish tail is noticeable. Open grassland (steppes), often treeless or bushy. L 65-77, WS 172-260 cm.

**TAWNY EAGLE** *Aquila rapax*. Very similar to larger Steppe Eagle. Adults may be buff or rufous (never tawny, as in sub-Saharan Africa), but are often paler and greyer-brown than Steppe. Pale yellow gape reaches back only as far as front of eye; behind it in Steppe. Imms also often paler than imm Steppe, both imm and juv have obscurer pale wing bars above, and diagnostically no pale band on underwing. Flight attitude and habitat both similar to Steppe. L 65-77, WS 172-260 cm.

Very rare in NW Africa, but widespread in Africa S of the Sahara.

**VERREAUX'S EAGLE** *Aquila verreauxi*. Adult deep black with large white patch from centre of lower back to rump, pale patch above and below on each wing conspicuous in flight and showing as shoulder patch at rest (cf. brown Imperial Eagle, p.96) and pale wing-tips in flight. Juv/imm brown and scaly, like a large Steppe Eagle, with pale crown. More graceful flight than most large eagles, the wings distinctivly narrowing towards the base from a broad tip; outer primaries well splayed out when gliding. Various yelping, barking or crow-like calls. Rocky hills. Aka Black Eagle. L 80-95, WS 225-245 cm.

# EAGLES

juv pale

ad dark

ad

juv

juv

juv dark

SPOTTED EAGLE

ad

juv

ad

juv

LESSER SPOTTED
EAGLE

juv

ad

ad

juv

STEPPE EAGLE

ad

juv

ad

TAWNY EAGLE

juv

ad

ad

juv

juv

VERREAUX'S EAGLE

BIRDS OF PREY IN FLIGHT. Flying raptors are most likely to be seen from below when soaring overhead, especially at such well known migration points as Falsterbo in Sweden, the Pyrenean and Alpine passes, and Elat in Israel, when the date and whether birds are flying singly or in flocks are important. Note especially the barring and other patterns of the undersides of wings and tail. The shapes of flying birds of prey vary greatly according to what the bird is doing, as shown below for Buzzard (p.94).

Soaring with tail open.　　Soaring with tail closed.　　Gliding with slightly angled wings.　　Fast gliding with markedly angled wings.

**Honey Buzzard** (p.94) has some flight shapes like Buzzard, but plumages vary widely between individuals, though basic tail pattern is the same, except in juvs.

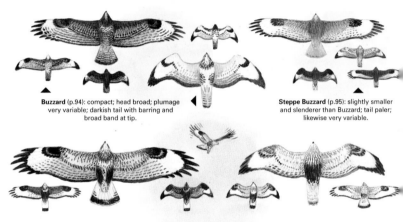

**Buzzard** (p.94): compact; head broad; plumage very variable; darkish tail with barring and broad band at tip.

**Steppe Buzzard** (p.95): slightly smaller and slenderer than Buzzard; tail paler; likewise very variable.

**Rough-legged Buzzard** (p.94): slightly larger and longer-winged than Buzzard, with tail unbarred but black at tip, and black patch at carpal joint of paler underwing.

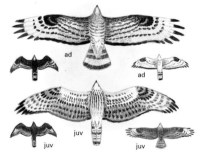 

**Honey Buzzard** (p.94): slenderer and longer-tailed than Buzzard, with pigeon-like head and double broad dark bar near tail base. Often in large flocks on migration.

**Long-legged Buzzard**: p.94): appreciably larger than similar Steppe Buzzard; tail of adult unbarred, of juv barred; like other buzzards, may hover.

100

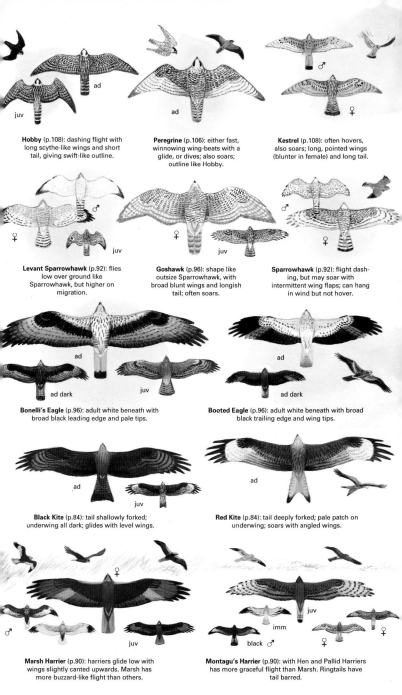

**Hobby** (p.108): dashing flight with long scythe-like wings and short tail, giving swift-like outline.

**Peregrine** (p.106): either fast, winnowing wing-beats with a glide, or dives; also soars; outline like Hobby.

**Kestrel** (p.108): often hovers, also soars; long, pointed wings (blunter in female) and long tail.

**Levant Sparrowhawk** (p.92): flies low over ground like Sparrowhawk, but higher on migration.

**Goshawk** (p.96): shape like outsize Sparrowhawk, with broad blunt wings and longish tail; often soars.

**Sparrowhawk** (p.92): flight dashing, but may soar with intermittent wing flaps; can hang in wind but not hover.

**Bonelli's Eagle** (p.96): adult white beneath with broad black leading edge and pale tips.

**Booted Eagle** (p.96): adult white beneath with broad black trailing edge and wing tips.

**Black Kite** (p.84): tail shallowly forked; underwing all dark; glides with level wings.

**Red Kite** (p.84): tail deeply forked; pale patch on underwing; soars with angled wings.

**Marsh Harrier** (p.90): harriers glide low with wings slightly canted upwards. Marsh has more buzzard-like flight than others.

**Montagu's Harrier** (p.90): with Hen and Pallid Harriers has more graceful flight than Marsh. Ringtails have tail barred.

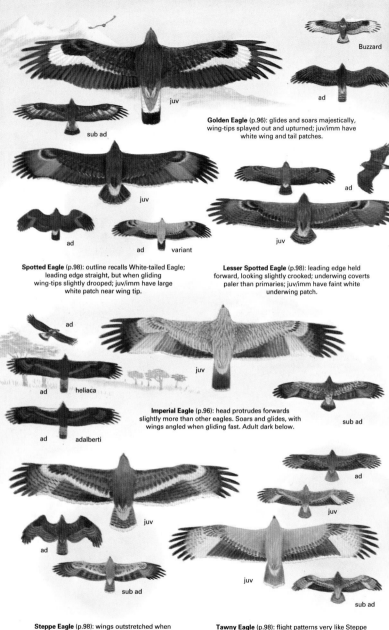

**Buzzard**

**Golden Eagle** (p.96): glides and soars majestically, wing-tips splayed out and upturned; juv/imm have white wing and tail patches.

sub ad

juv

**Spotted Eagle** (p.98): outline recalls White-tailed Eagle; leading edge straight, but when gliding wing-tips slightly drooped; juv/imm have large white patch near wing tip.

ad

ad    variant

juv

**Lesser Spotted Eagle** (p.98): leading edge held forward, looking slightly crooked; underwing coverts paler than primaries; juv/imm have faint white underwing patch.

ad

juv

**Imperial Eagle** (p.96): head protrudes forwards slightly more than other eagles. Soars and glides, with wings angled when gliding fast. Adult dark below.

ad    heliaca

ad    adalberti

juv

sub ad

**Steppe Eagle** (p.98): wings outstretched when soaring, but varyingly crooked when gliding. Juv/imms show white line on underwing with dark trailing edges and tips.

juv

ad

sub ad

**Tawny Eagle** (p.98): flight patterns very like Steppe Eagle, but juv/imms lack the diagnostic pale line on the underwing. Attacks other raptors piratically.

ad

juv

juv

sub ad

**White-tailed Eagle** (p.82): massively broad wings with wedge-shaped, not square, tail distinguish it from other large eagles; soars and dives.

sub ad

juv

ad

**Griffon Vulture** (p.88): broad parallel-sided wings distinguish vultures from eagles; trailing edge, tips and tail black; leading edge pale.

juv

ad

**Lammergeier** (p.86): Long narrow angled and pointed wings and remarkable long diamond-shaped tail distinguish it from all eagles and vultures.

juv

ad

Honey Buzzard

ad

sub ad

juv

**Egyptian Vulture** (p.86): adult has distinctive pattern of leading edge and wedge-shaped tail white, and trailing edge black.

ad

ad     very variable     ad

**Short-toed Eagle** (p.84): only large raptor except smaller Osprey with underparts all white except for black wing and tail tips. Glides with angled wings, soars and hovers.

♀

♂

Honey Buzzard

**Osprey** (p.82): differs from Short-toed Eagle especially in black patch on each carpal joint and habit of diving from the air to catch fish; flight rather slow and flapping.

103

● FALCONS: *Falconidae*. Diurnal raptors with long, pointed wings, sharing with the owls (p.204) several marked behaviour differences from the Accipitridae (p.92): they build no nest of their own; they kill their prey by biting and severing the back of the neck; they hold their food in one claw; the young hiss when afraid or threatening; and they bob their heads when curious. Females often much larger than males. When alarmed or displaying, utter high-pitched chattering calls.

**GYRFALCON** *Falco rusticolus*. The largest true falcon, larger and stouter than Peregrine (p.106), but with longer tail and slightly blunter and broader-based wings. Plumage very variable, from almost white with a few dark flecks to almost uniform dark grey; imm mainly brown. Flight slower than Peregrine; calls louder, harsher, lower-pitched. Cliffed and rocky coasts, mountains, coniferous forest edge. L 50-60, WS 130-160 cm.                                             ○W

Gyr          Peregrine

Most frequent form of Gyr is like pale Peregrine, but with no (or only a faint) moustachial streak, and contrast between pale primaries and darker underwing coverts. Some dark-phase birds have rather peregrine-like head and cheeks whitish and unmarked. Greenland and Iceland Falcons (not now recognised as separate sspp.) are larger, with the whitest forms (which migrate SE in winter) most frequent in N Greenland, Iceland birds mainly grey, and European mainland birds darker grey.

**SAKER** *Falco cherrug*. Broader-winged and longer-tailed than Peregrine (p.106), and with brown upperparts and contrasting dark primaries. Also differs from Peregrine and Lanner, both usually slightly smaller, in pale head with crown feathers black tipped rufous, often obscure moustachial stripe, and spotted not barred tail. Smaller than Gyrfalcon, with similar underwing pattern, but range does not overlap. Fairly variable, and can be very pale. Imm more streaked. Sometimes hovers. Open country, high plateaus, steppes, plains, semi-deserts, with scattered trees. L 45-55, WS 102-126 cm.                            -E

cherrug

Ssp.*cherrug* (C & SE Europe, W Asia) has underparts not barred; ssp.*milvipes* (C Asia, vagrant to region) has rufous bars on upperparts, and some barring also on underparts.

**LANNER** *Falco biarmicus*. Intermediate in size between Saker and Peregrine (p.106). European breeding birds have longer tail and longer, blunter wings, than Peregrine, with browner upperparts, pinkish underparts, rufous or buff crown and much narrower moustachial stripe; crown cream or pale rufous with blackish streaks. Some dark-phase birds have rather peregrine-like head and cheeks whitish without any markings. Slightly larger Saker is stouter and still browner, with contrasting dark primaries, paler crown and obscure moustachial stripe. Deserts and open country, usually nesting on cliffs or rocky outcrops, sometimes in ruins. L 34-50, WS 90-115 cm.              -E

♀

erlangeri                              ♂

tanypterus

Ssp.*feldeggi* (Italy to Turkey) described above; ssp.*erlangeri* (N Africa) is slenderer and with ssp.*tanypterus* (Middle East) is paler and much less heavily streaked, barred and spotted.

ark

white

juv

pale

grey

grey

grey

white
imm

grey

GYRFALCON; very variable. On the mainland Scandinavian
birds are the smallest and Siberian ones the whitest.
Adults' legs and feet can be blue-grey.

ark
nm

imm

juv

ad

pale

ad

SAKER

v dark

ad

juv

ad

juv

ad
feldeggii

LANNER

ad

calidus    brookei

♀

♂

♂

Sooty    Eleonora's

♀

♂    ♂

Cere and eye-ring yellow in male,
blue-grey in female.

**PEREGRINE** *Falco peregrinus.* Medium-sized, with a distinctive flight outline of long, pointed, broad-based wings and tapered, medium-length tail. Varies from dark to light grey above, with barred underparts whitish to buff; black moustachial streak conspicuous against white cheeks and chin. Juv dark brown above, streaked below; legs and bare face-skin blue-grey, not yellow. Hunting flight has fast, winnowing wing-beats; normal flight slower, with short glides; also soars, and power-dives steeply on prey. Voice harsh, deep and chattering. Open country, from tundra to semi-deserts, cliffed coasts, forests; breeds on crags and ledges, also in trees, on tall buildings; in winter also on other coasts and estuaries. L 36-48, WS 95-110 cm.        ⊙rW

Northern tundra ssp.*calidus* palest; Mediterranean ssp.*brookei* darkest, often more rufous below and with some rufous marks on nape.

**BARBARY FALCON** *Falco pelegrinoides.* Smaller and less heavily built than Peregrine (of which it may be only a ssp.), but much paler and more rufous, with longer wings and more rounded tail. Crown and nape largely rufous, but divided by a dark band, which the larger Lanner (p.104) lacks; moustache blackish-brown rather than black; underparts often not or only lightly marked. Flight even more vigorous than Peregrine. Dry, rocky areas inland, breeding on crags and cliff ledges (in N Africa Peregrine is coastal). L 34-40, WS 80-100 cm.

Ssp.*babilonicus* (Iraq deserts) is much paler, looking faded or washed out.

**SOOTY FALCON** *Falco concolor.* Medium-sized, slate-grey with black primaries; in some lights can seem much paler than slightly larger and longer-tailed Eleonora's. Lacks the rufous thighs of smaller and shorter-winged male Red-footed (p.108). Cere and eye-ring yellow; legs and feet red, orange or yellow. Juv browner, with cheeks whitish and underparts paler and streaked. In Eleonora-like flight two protruding central feathers of slightly wedge-shaped tail sometimes visible. Voice like Kestrel (p.108). Breeds in deserts with rocky outcrops. L 33-36, WS 85-110 cm.

**ELEONORA'S FALCON** *Falco eleonorae.* Between Peregrine and Hobby (p.108) in size, with a moustachial streak, but slenderer than Peregrine and longer-winged and longer-tailed than both. Has an almost parakeet-like jizz. Very variable, from pale to dark grey, rarely pale above and dark below. Paler birds resemble smaller Hobby, but greyer-brown above and more rufous on heavily streaked underparts. Darkest birds extremely like smaller Sooty, and differ from smaller male Red-footed (p.108) in dark grey thighs, yellow legs and feet, and yellow or pale blue eye-rings and cere. Sexes almost same size. Juv has tail barred and shows barred underwing in flight. Flight active; hangs in wind but never hovers. Gregarious, up to 50 birds sometimes hunting together. Chief call-note trisyllabic. Sea cliffs, rocky islands, also forages inland; breeds colonially in late summer, when young can be fed on migrant birds. L 36-40, WS 110-130 cm.        -V

**FALCONS**

juv

ad

peregrinus

juv

ad

ad

ad

**PEREGRINE**

ad

ad

juv

ad dark

juv

ad

juv

ad

ad grey

elegrinoides

**BARBARY FALCON**

ad

**SOOTY FALCON**

juv

ad light

juv

♂ light

♂ dark

♀ dark

dark

2nd year light

**ELEONORA'S FALCON**

**HOBBY** *Falco subbuteo*. Like a miniature Peregrine (p.106) in head pattern and outline, its long scythe-shaped wings and medium-length tail make it look like a giant Swift (p.216). Adult dark bluish- to slate-grey, with rufous thighs and under tail coverts, shared with male Red-footed Falcon; underparts boldly streaked. Female slightly and juv much browner above, best told from female Red-footed by behaviour and deep yellow underparts. Flight very active and agile. Chief call like Kestrel. Open country with scattered trees. L 30-36, WS 82-92 cm. ☉Sm

**MERLIN** *Falco columbarius*. Mistle-thrush-sized male is region's smallest raptor, with kestrel-like flight outline; wings narrower and more pointed than equally small male Sparrowhawk (p.92), shorter than other falcons; tail shorter than kestrels. Male grey above, with blackish primaries; markedly larger female brown above, tail grey; both have underparts streaked, tail barred, face pattern obscure. Flight dashing, often low over ground; may hover. Hills and moors; in winter also in lowlands, often on coast. L 25-30, WS 50-62 cm. ☉Rsmw

Ssp.*aesalon* (Britain to Russia), above; ssp.*subaesalon* (Iceland; winters Britain/Ireland) is paler and larger; ssp.*pallidus* (Siberia, winters S to Iraq) is much paler.

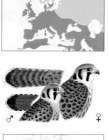

**KESTREL** *Falco tinnunculus*. One of the two commonest small raptors in W Europe, with long, pointed wings (blunter in female) and long tail, noted for its constant hovering. Male is region's only small raptor to combine blue-grey head and tail, dark-spotted (sparsely so in Canary Is) chestnut mantle, dark primaries and black tail bar. Rufous plumage speckled darker separates female/juv from other small raptors, except Lesser Kestrel. Call a loud, shrill 'kee-kee-kee'. Open country, sea cliffs, towns. L 32-35, WS 71-80 cm. ●Rsmw

**American Kestrel** *F.sparverius*. Rare transatlantic vagrant, smaller even than male Merlin, with diagnostic black-bordered white cheeks. Male like male Kestrel but chestnut crown-patch and blue-grey on wings. L 19-21 cm, WS 50-60 cm. -V

♂ ♀

**LESSER KESTREL** *Falco naumanni*. Differs from larger Kestrel in gregarious and noisy habits, more active flight, slenderer build and male's unspotted chestnut mantle, blue-grey inner wing and unmoustached face; both sexes have pale and much less spotted underparts. Female/juv very like Kestrel, but tail shorter and underwings paler. Hovers much less, with faster wing-beats, but often glides. Open country, nesting colonially on inland cliffs and ruins. L 29-32, WS 58-72 cm. -V

**RED-FOOTED FALCON** *Falco vespertinus*. Flight outline between Kestrel and longer-winged Hobby, but less robust and dashing; hovers; often in parties. Male dark grey with paler, almost silvery, primaries and chestnut thighs and under tail coverts (cf. Hobby); cere, legs and bill base orange-red, of female orange. Female orange-buff below and on head; imm tinged buff; juv much browner above, streaked below, cf. larger juv Hobby. Open country with scattered trees and small woods, nesting colonially in trees. L 29-31, WS 56-78 cm. -A

# SMALL FALCONS

juv

ad

ad

ad

juv

1st summer

**HOBBY**

♀

♂

♀

♂

pallidus

♀

aesalon

aesalon

♂

**MERLIN**

♂

♂

♀

♂

♀

**KESTREL**

♀

**LESSER KESTREL**

juv

♂

♂

♂

imm

♀

♀

juv

**RED-FOOTED FALCON**

● GROUSE *Phasianidae:* Tetraoninae. Gamebirds, with short, thick bill, short wings and whirring flight, differing from the pheasants and partridges (Phasianinae, p.114) especially in their feathered legs and nostrils, and in having no spurs.

Winter cock has black face patch ♂

W cock has no black line between eye and thicker bill. ♂ ♀

W male has red comb. w female/juv do not.

**PTARMIGAN** *Lagopus mutus.* The grouse of mountain tops and tundra and, with the Willow Grouse, the region's only bird to turn all-white in winter. Has three plumages. In summer upperparts greyish-buff, mottled darker in cock but more rufous in hen, with wings mainly white, especially in flight. In autumn both sexes, but especially cocks, become greyer above. In winter whole plumage white, except for black tail. Both sexes have wattle above eye, variable in size and redness. Differs from slightly larger Willow Grouse in less stout bill, toes more heavily feathered and winter cock's black mark between bill and eye. Calls a hoarse, croaking 'uk, uk' and a crackling 'karr, ikrikrrikrrrkrrr', also a brief crowing display song. Usually well above or beyond tree-line and in Britain mainly above 600 m. L 34-36 cm.                                              ⊙R

**WILLOW GROUSE** *Lagopus lagopus* ssp.*lagopus.* Like slightly smaller Ptarmigan has three plumages. In summer warm brown (Ptarmigan greyer), though wings and belly still mainly white, especially in flight. In autumn, when Ptarmigan greyer still, white patches appear. In winter all-white, except for black tail; for differences from Ptarmigan, see above. Adult has red comb above eye, variable in size and colour shade, and often obscure in hen. Calls a loud 'kok-kok-kok' and 'gobak, gobak'. Tundra, Arctic prairies with birch and willow scrub, heather moors and bogs, lower down than Ptarmigan; in winter also farmland. L 37-42 cm.

Willow Grouse from coastal Norway are intermediate with the all-dark Red Grouse of Britain and Ireland.

**Red Grouse** ssp.*scoticus.* An all-dark race of the Willow Grouse, never turning white in winter; confined to Britain and Ireland, and perhaps a separate species. Looks very dark in flight, when lack of white wing bar separates it from the larger Black Grouse (p.112), and dark, not rufous, tail from the paler partridges. 'Gobak, gobak' and other calls and habits as Willow Grouse. Heather moors and bogs, feeding on heather *Calluna*; in winter sometimes on farmland.        ●R

**HAZEL GROUSE** *Tetrastes bonasia.* A small, rather shy, grey-brown woodland grouse, both sexes readily identified in flight by black band at tip of grey tail. Crested male has distinctive white-bordered black throat; both sexes have small red wattle above eye. Song a high-pitched whistle; alarm call based on 'plitt' or 'pitt'. Flies more readily than other grouse, wings making a distinctive 'rrrrr' sound. Perches in trees. Mainly lowland conifer forest, but also mixed and pure broad-leaved woodland, usually with dense shrub layer, often near rivers. Aka Hazel Hen. L 35-37 cm.

There are several sspp. in the region. The northern ones tend to be more greyish and the southern ones more rufous.

# GROUSE

**PTARMIGAN**

autumn

♂

changing

♂ summer

♀ summer

courtship display

autumn

ost active in this plumage
spring, slowly changing
perparts to rufous.

♂ changing

juv

ad

summer

♀ summer

♀

♂ summer

♂ br

**RED GROUSE**

**WILLOW GROUSE**

greyish northern
sub sp. group

♀

♂

reddish
southern group

**HAZEL
GROUSE**

Courtship silent, cock flying up to show his white underwing; displays mostly on steep ground.

In spring and autumn Black Grouse gather, often daily and in numbers, at communal display grounds (leks). Male display is elaborate, with spread tail, drooped wings and red eye-wattles more prominent. Birds jump up and down, cooing, bubbling and crowing.

**BLACK GROUSE** *Tetrao tetrix*. Cock (Blackcock) much smaller than cock Capercaillie and the only large black bird with a lyre-shaped tail; white wing bar, under tail coverts and shoulder patch. Much smaller hen (Greyhen) and juv differ from both same-sized Willow/Red Grouse and much larger hen Capercaillie in forked tail and narrow pale wing bar; greyer and darker-legged than Willow/Red; lacking rufous breast-patch and white on flanks of hen Capercaillie. Flight alternates quick whirring and gliding on down-turned wings. Blackcock has several clucking and other notes, Greyhen a pheasant-like 'kok, kok'. Moors, steppes, wet heaths with woodland edges or scattered trees. See Rackelhahn below. L 40-55 cm.                ⊙R

**CAUCASIAN BLACK GROUSE** *Tetrao mlokosiewiczi*. Smaller than Black Grouse; cock tinged green and not glossy with no white wing bar or under tail coverts, the tail tips curving downwards rather than outwards. Hen and juv more uniformly vermiculated than Greyhen, and with tail square-ended. Hen calls like Greyhen; wings whistle in flight. Display less elaborate: fluttering jumps and wing-whistling but no calls. Alpine meadows and scrub. L 38-52 cm.

**CAPERCAILLIE** *Tetrao urogallus*. Much the largest game-bird of the region, turkey-sized. Cock largely dark grey, with brown wings, some white on flanks and long, broad, square-ended tail. Hen/juv differ from the two much smaller black grouse hens in their chestnut breast-patch, white marks on flanks, no wing bar and square-ended tail. When alarmed, both sexes may erect neck hackles to form prominent whiskers. Flight alternates quick whirring and gliding on down-turned wings; makes a great clatter when leaving trees, where perches and feeds. Cock has raucous, throat-clearing call, hen a pheasant-like 'kok, kok'. Remarkable song at lek (see above), starts with a resonant rattle and ends with a popping sound like drawing a cork and a gurgling, liquid call, with a crash as the wing quills scrape the ground. Coniferous forest, especially in hills and mountains. L 60-87 cm.                ⊙R

Sspp. *aquitanicus* (Pyrenees, N W Spain, in mountain hollywood) and *rudolfi* (Carpathians) are smaller and darker; ssp. *taczanowskii* (S Russia) is larger and paler.

Rackelhahn

**Rackelhahn** The occasional hybrid between Capercaillie and Black Grouse is usually male, and intermediate in both size and tail shape. Capercaillie may also hybridise with Pheasant (p.114).

# GROUSE

♂ in moult

BLACK
GROUSE

♂

♀

♂ br

♀

♂

CAUCASIAN
BLACK GROUSE

♀

♂ br

♀

northern
white bellied
courtship

♂

♀

♂ ad

♂ imm

CAPERCAILLIE

● GAMEBIRDS: *Phasianidae: Phasianinae* (pp.114-120). Birds mainly of open country, often in small parties (coveys) up to 20. Legs unfeathered (unlike grouse, p.110), often spurred. Bill short, thick, upper mandible longer; wings short, rounded, curved downwards in typical heavy whirring flight. Pheasants are large and usually long-tailed, partridges, francolins and snowcocks intermediate and quails the smallest.

**PHEASANT** *Phasianus colchicus*. The region's only native pheasant, large and long-tailed. Multi-coloured cock has head and neck usually metallic green and large red facial wattle. Hen/juv brown, mottled darker. Often rockets upwards when startled. Cock crows with a loud harsh 'kor-kok', often whirring its wings. Both sexes cackle 'kuttuc, kuttuc', when flushed. Juv has double bullfinch-like pipe with a creaking third note. Wooded mountain valleys, tamarisk and other scrub, reed-beds. L 53-89 cm.

**Introduced Gamebirds**. Due to over-shooting of native stocks, especially in central and W Europe, many alien gamebirds from Asia and N America have been introduced and managed in the region. The following have established themselves in at least one area.

**Game Pheasants.** Many subspecies of *P. colchicus* have been introduced in W Europe, beginning some 900 years ago with the dark-necked so-called 'old English' type *colchicus* (Transcaucasia, Azerbaijan), but latterly including several white-collared forms (ring-necks) from E Asia: the long-established *torquatus* (China) with lower back and rump mainly green; *principalis* (Transcaspia, Turkestan) with upperparts yellowish or orange-red and some white on wing coverts; *mongolicus* (Turkestan, not Mongolia) with upperparts coppery red glossed green, some white on the wings and a partial white collar; and the blue-rumped *formosanus* (Taiwan). These have interbred widely and may produce a dark form, the 'melanistic mutant', confusable with the less often introduced Japanese Pheasant *P. versicolor*. Another very distinct variety is the Bohemian Pheasant, buff or cream-coloured with blackish markings and dark head. Open country, with scattered woods and scrub, marshes, large reed-beds, often feeding on farmland.　　　●R

**Reeves's Pheasant** *Syrmaticus reevesii*. Cock's tail up to 2 m. Calls a twittering chuckle and a musical pipe. Wooded, hilly country, Austria. France. L 210 cm.　　　-E

Reeves's

**Lady Amherst's Pheasant** *Chrysolophus amherstiae*. Hen has shorter bill, longer and more strongly barred tail, and more rasping and higher-pitched call than Pheasant; legs, bill and bare face-skin blue-grey. England. L 60-120 cm.　　　○R

**Golden Pheasant** *C. pictus*. Hen differs from Lady Amherst's in having legs, bill and bare face-skin all yellowish. Call like Lady Amherst's. Prefers running to flying. Britain. L 60-115 cm.　　　○R

**California Quail** *Callipepla californica*. Between Grey Partridge (p.116) and Quail (p.120) in size; greyish, with a distinctive short black curved plume on the crown; cock with black throat outlined in white. Call a trisyllabic 'qua-quer-go'. Corsica. L 25 cm.

California

**Bobwhite** *Colinus virginianus*. Between California Quail and Quail (p.120) in size; mainly rufous, cock with dark brown and white eye-stripes and white throat, white areas buff in hen. Call a loud double whistle, 'bob-white'. France. L 25 cm.　　　-E

Bobwhite

**PHEASANTS**

♀

♂

PHEASANT

♀

small enough to use with Quail or juv ridges.

♀

melanistic

♂
Ring-neck
Game Pheasant

♀

♂
over
3 years
old

LADY AMHERST'S

♀

♂
1st
summer

♂
old

GOLDEN PHEASANT

**Partridges:** *Perdix* and *Alectoris*. Stoutly built, mainly brown, medium-sized, with rufous tail conspicuous in flight; sexes alike, male larger. *Alectoris* are mostly longer and more upright and so rather more pheasant-like than smaller *Perdix*, and have whitish chin and throat, conspicuous black barring on flanks and red bill and legs. *Alectoris* often, *Perdix* rarely, perch on rocks and other slight elevations.

**GREY PARTRIDGE** *Perdix perdix*. Much the most widespread partridge, differing from all *Alectoris* in large chestnut horseshoe on lower breast, chestnut cheeks and throat, bars on flanks and less conspicuous, greenish bill and grey legs; and from Red-legged in unspotted upper breast. Loud, high-pitched, creaky, grating 'keev' or 'keev-it' turns to a rapid cackling 'it-it-it ...' when bird flushed. Farmland, especially arable, downs, steppes, heaths, semi-deserts, shingle tracts, dunes. L 29-31 cm.　　　　　　　　　　　　　　　●R

Ssp.*hispaniensis* of slopes above 180 m in Pyrenees and Cantabrian Mountains is darker, with less chestnut.

**RED-LEGGED PARTRIDGE** *Alectoris rufa*. Distinguished from Grey and all chukar-type partridges by heavy black spotting below black band on upper breast; crown, nape and upperparts brownish. Call a loud, challenging 'chuka, chuka' or 'chik, chik, chikar'; also a reiterated, staccato, wheezing note. Habitat as Grey, but often drier and stonier. L 32-34 cm.　　　　●R

Hybrids with Rock Partridge are regular in the zone where the two meet in the Alps; flanks with a faint second bar and a distinctive call. Hybrid Red-legged x Chukar, especially in Britain, is similar.

**ROCK PARTRIDGE** *Alectoris graeca*. Larger, plumper and greyer above than Red-legged and with black line on breast sharply separating white throat from unspotted grey breast, and bill almost hooked. Call an abrupt, quadrisyllabic 'tchertsivitchi', a curiously nuthatch-like 'chwit, chwit, chwit', and a sharp 'pitchi-i'. Rocky, stony and thinly grassy hills and mountain slopes; vineyards. L 32-35 cm.

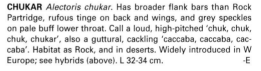

**CHUKAR** *Alectoris chukar*. Has broader flank bars than Rock Partridge, rufous tinge on back and wings, and grey speckles on pale buff lower throat. Call a loud, high-pitched 'chuk, chuk, chuk, chukar', also a guttural, cackling 'caccaba, caccaba, caccaba'. Habitat as Rock, and in deserts. Widely introduced in W Europe; see hybrids (above). L 32-34 cm.　　　　　-E

Several similar sspp, of which *cypriotes* (Crete to S Turkey) and pale pinkish ssp.*sinaica* (Syria to Sinai) are shown.

**BARBARY PARTRIDGE** *Alectoris barbara*. The most distinctive chukar-type partridge, generally pinker in tone, with chin and throat grey, small buff patch behind eye, no black line on neck and breast, and neck collar chestnut, speckled white. Call like Chukar, also a rapid 'kakelik'. Rocky or stony hillsides, deserts, scrub or open woodland. L 32-34 cm.

Rufous-tailed juv *Alectoris* are very hard to separate in the field. At 12-14 weeks they are like adult but with paler legs and bills and still some juv feathers in wing and breast.

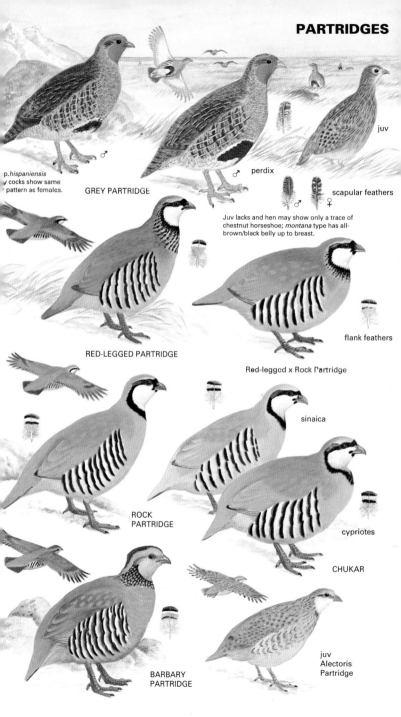

# PARTRIDGES

juv

p.*hispaniensis* y cocks show same pattern as females.

GREY PARTRIDGE

♂

perdix ♂

scapular feathers ♂ ♀

Juv lacks and hen may show only a trace of chestnut horseshoe; *montana* type has all-brown/black belly up to breast.

RED-LEGGED PARTRIDGE

flank feathers

Red-legged x Rock Partridge

sinaica

ROCK PARTRIDGE

cypriotes

CHUKAR

BARBARY PARTRIDGE

juv Alectoris Partridge

**CAUCASIAN SNOWCOCK** *Tetraogallus caucasicus*. Smaller and paler than Caspian Snowcock; more rufous, especially on flanks and hind neck, and less conspicuously white in the wing; at close range shows distinctive blackish vermiculations on upper breast. Has similar habit of running uphill or flying downhill. Utters several melodious and far-carrying whistling and fluty calls. Cliffs, stony slopes and alpine meadows up to the snow line; uproots plants by scraping in the ground with its very stout bill. L 54-56 cm.

**CASPIAN SNOWCOCK** *Tetraogallus caspicus*. Rather long-tailed and guineafowl-sized, suggesting an outsize Chukar (p.116). Male mottled grey and buff, with darker thighs and belly, white cheeks and foreneck and black moustachial stripe; female smaller and duller, with less white on head; juv duller still. A broad white patch on each wing makes it appear in flight as a large pale bird with white and grey wings. When flushed runs uphill or flies downhill, gliding on stiff wings and calling loudly. Most frequent call curlew-like, often uttered with head and neck thrown backwards. Alarm call a repeated 'chok, chok, chok'. High, steep, rocky screes and alpine and subalpine meadows and scrub, generally not below 1800-2000 m. L 58-62 cm.

◄ **Erckel's Francolin** *Francolinus erckelii*. A large and heavily built francolin from Ethiopia, introduced and now well established in Italy. Mainly olive-grey above, its head pattern of rufous crown with black forehead and cheeks and white throat distinguishes it from all other local game birds. Legs red, cock double-spurred, hen not spurred. Scrubby hillsides.

Now near extinction.

**DOUBLE-SPURRED FRANCOLIN** *Francolinus bicalcaratus*. A partridge-sized gamebird, with more uniform plumage than Barbary Partridge (p.116), chestnut crown and nape, white eye-stripe, chestnut, black and white flank stripes in rows of dark spots, yellowish bill and legs greenish or yellowish, spurred in cock. Calls include a loud, deep, repeated 'quair, quair' or 'coak, coak', often uttered from mound or tree stump at dawn or dusk; also 'cocoi'. Open woods and scrub, palm groves, clearings in cultivations. L 30-33 cm.

Well established introduction in Italy. Formerly bred Catalonia and Sicily, now extinct.

**BLACK FRANCOLIN** *Francolinus francolinus*. Spurred cock is one of the most distinctive partridge-sized gamebirds, with black face, throat and underparts; chestnut collar, belly and under tail coverts; white-spotted flanks and white patch behind ear. Unspurred hen differs from other brownish gamebirds in black-spotted appearance and chestnut patch on nape. As often heard as seen; far-carrying, loud, gratingly high-pitched call, 'che-chirree, chik, chiree' or 'chik-cheek-cheek-kkeraykek'. Dense vegetation in grasslands, crops, marshes and scrub, especially tamarisk. Formerly bred Spain, Balearics, Sardinia and Sicily, probably introduced; recently introduced Italy. Aka Black Partridge (India). L 33-36 cm.

CAUCASIAN
SNOWCOCK

Sexes of snowcocks very
hard to separate in field;
hens smaller and duller,
juvs duller still.

CASPIAN
SNOWCOCK

♀

♂

♀

ad

juv

BLACK
FRANCOLIN

DOUBLE-
SPURRED
FRANCOLIN

Good flier but prefers to run away among rocks, where well camouflaged; usually in pairs.

**SAND PARTRIDGE** *Ammoperdix heyi*. Between Quail and Grey Partridge (p.116) in size, and with the latter's rufous tail. Cock has predominantly pinkish-buff plumage with barred flanks, somewhat greyer on head, and distinctive head pattern (cf. same-sized See-see), with narrow white frontal band, no black eye-stripe, and cheeks and foreneck chestnut. bill orange, legs yellow. Hen vermiculated brown, virtually identical with See-see in the field. Double call resembles two stones grated together; wing quills make a rattling sound in flight. Broken rocky or stony and sparsely vegetated ground, semi-deserts. L 22-25 cm.

Adult males of sspp.*nicolli* (N E Egypt) and *cholmleyi* (S E Egypt) lack white frontal band; *nicolli* also more rufous.

**SEE-SEE PARTRIDGE** *Ammoperdix griseogularis*. Grey-brown cock differs from Sand Partridge especially in striking head pattern of black stripe above eye, white one below it, with grey cheeks and foreneck, and more boldly barred flanks. Hen very like Sand Partridge. Flight and habitat as Sand Partridge. Double, whistling 'see-see' call. L 22-25 cm.

**QUAIL** *Coturnix coturnix*. Much the smallest gamebird and the only migratory one. Mainly brown, cock with variable black or chestnut neck pattern; hen/juv with breast spotted; bill grey, legs pink. Juv differs from young Grey Partridge (p.116) in buff streaks on head and no chestnut in tail; and from Andalusian Hemipode (p.122) in paler breast and flanks streaked not spotted. Flying Corncrake (p.122) has chestnut in wings and legs dangling. Cf. also mainly rufous Bobwhite (p.114). Much more often heard than seen; chief call an unmistakable, far-carrying, liquid 'quic-ic-ic' or 'wet-mi-lips'; when flushed may call 'crwee-crwee' or 'crucc-crucc'. A curious growling 'row-ow-ow' heard only at very close range. Farmland, especially with crops, open grassland, steppes, semi-deserts. Numbers reaching N W Europe vary greatly from year to year. L 16-18 cm. ◯S

Japanese Quail *C. japonica* is larger, plumper and shorter-winged with distinctive 'brrr' or 'gwa-kuro' call; introduced S W France, escapes possible elsewhere. L 20 cm.

● GUINEAFOWLS: *Numididae*. Very large, plump, short-tailed and gregarious, with the short wings and whirring flight typical of gamebirds.

**HELMETED GUINEAFOWL** *Numida meleagris*. Most distinctive with conspicuous erect brown horny crest, and red wattles and bill. Grey, mottled with white spots, but neck dark purple; head featherless, with conspicuous bluish-white cheeks. Restless and noisy, with the squeaky cackle of the domestic bird. Wooded gullies in the hills, mainly on the ground but roosting in trees. Aka Tufted Guineafowl. The W African ssp.*galeata* is the origin of the domesticated guineafowl. L 60-65 cm.

Only on Middle Atlas, Morocco, and near extinction.

# PARTRIDGES, QUAIL, GUINEAFOWL

nicolli

heyi

♂

♀

juv

**SAND PARTRIDGE**

Juvs of both sexes are mostly of this male-like type, but some are female-like as in Sand Partridge.

♀

♂

**SEE-SEE PARTRIDGE**

pheasant
eeks

♂ brown throat

♀

♀

♂

**QUAIL**

juv Partridge
about 4 weeks

uv partridges and pheasants can fly when
few days old and so can be mistaken for
uv Quail, but have different head and flank
atterns.

ad

juv 12 weeks

**HELMETED GUINEAFOWL**

● **HEMIPODES** or **BUTTON QUAILS:** *Turnicidae.* Small quail-like ground birds, also known as hemipodes and more closely related to the rails and cranes than to the quails. Very shy and secretive in habits, keeping to cover; when flushed prefer to run like rodents rather than take to the air with their weak flight.

Long extinct in Sicily and Tunisia; near extinction in Algeria and Morocco. Very local in Iberia.

**ANDALUSIAN HEMIPODE** *Turnix sylvatica.* Smaller than Quail (p.120) and with diagnostic rufous breast and black-spotted flanks; bill slightly longer. Female larger and brighter than male; juv with rows of white spots on upperparts. Ground-living, shy, and very hard to flush as it zigzags about; often only detected by distinctive low mooing or crooning note. Flies low, with wings audibly whirring, and drops down, rarely rising again. Sandy plains and dry grassland with cover, such as dwarf palmetto scrub. Aka Small/Little Button Quail. L15-16 cm.

New-born hemipodes are tiny, weighing only 1.8 gm, but very agile on feet, fluttering when 10 days old and fully grown within 28 days; feet with no hind toe. Quails (p.120) weigh 5-6 gm when born, fluttering within 8 days; feet with hind toe.

● **RAILS** and **CRAKES:** *Rallidae.* Medium to small ground-dwellers; wings and tail rather short, legs and toes fairly long. Gait on land and water jerky, with tail often flirted, legs dangling in flight. All species in the region except Corncrake inhabit densely vegetated wetlands, swamps, bogs, fens, marshes, reed-beds and fresh waters and their margins. Unlike the aquatic Moorhen and Coot (p.126), the terrestrial species are shy and rarely seen in the open.

**CORNCRAKE** *Crex crex.* A bird whose loud rasping song, 'crex', 'crex', recalling a grated comb, is much more often heard than its slim brown form is seen. When flushed, legs dangle and shows much chestnut in wings, unlike Quail (p.120) and young partridges (p.116), whose legs do not dangle. Rough grassland, hayfields, decreasing towards extinction all over Europe and in both Britain and Ireland now almost confined to the extreme W, in the Hebrides and western Ireland. L 27-30 cm.  ○S

Long-legged new born Corncrakes can look rather helpless. They should be left alone, as the parents are never far away.

Juv rails are rather chicken-like with large long-toed feet and dark, mostly black, down; top of head red or blue, sparsely downy. The marsh-loving species prefer to hide in dense vegetation, but can swim and even dive when in danger, though they quickly become sodden and chilled in water.

**SORA** *Porzana carolina.* Transatlantic vagrant, differing from Spotted Crake (p.124) in its stouter, yellower bill, no white spots on neck and breast, and in breeding adults black face-mask and throat; winter adults still have some black on throat. Juvs have no black and differ from juv Spotted in black-centred rufous crown and fewer flank bars and white breast spots. Cocked tail reveals white/buffish coverts. Calls: a plaintive whistling 'ker-wee', a descending whinnying cry and a sharp 'keek'. L 20-23 cm.  -V

**Striped Crake** *P. marginalis.* Rare vagrant to N Africa, the size of a Little Crake (p.124), with stouter bill. Male has white-streaked olive-brown upperparts, paler, scarcely barred flanks, unbarred rufous under tail coverts and greenish legs; female greyer, juv browner. L 18-21 cm.

# HEMIPODES, CRAKES

**ANDALUSIAN HEMIPODE**

♀ calling

Very secretive and rarely seen. Best indication is distinctive mooing call, like a lowing cow, mostly heard at dawn, but also at night.

juv                    juv Quail

Juv hemipodes are especially quail-like, but have relatively longer bill.

Quail p.120

When flushed from cover, often taken for a Quail (p.120), but dangling legs and rufous wings are diagnostic.

♂ calling

Best field mark is the loud rasping 'crex, crex' call, mostly heard at night and in the early morning, several males often calling at once.

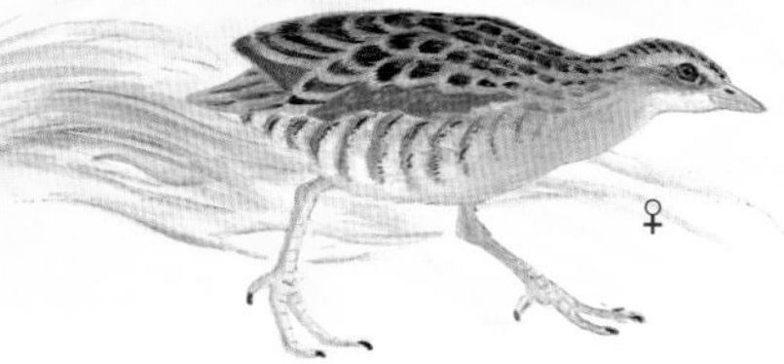

♀

**CORNCRAKE**

ad

▲
**SORA**
▼

juv

Spotted Crake (p.124) for comparison with similar Sora.

juv

**STRIPED CRAKE**

**Calls of Small Crakes**
- **Spotted Crake**: Chief calls, a rhythmical snipe-like 'tic-toc' and a loud, whiplash-like 'h'wit, h'wit' are usually heard at dusk.
- **Little Crake**: Call a repeated single note, ending in a yapping trill; also an explosive double note.
- **Baillon's Crake**: Main call a rasping sound like a grated comb.
- **Water Rail**: Clucking, grunting and miaouing calls include a loud harsh cry that begins as a grunt and ends as a squeal.

**SPOTTED CRAKE** *Porzana porzana*. Smaller and even shyer than Water Rail and has much shorter yellow-based green bill, olive-green legs, white-spotted upperparts and buff under tail coverts. Adults but not juvs are grey on face and neck. Larger than Little and Baillon's Crakes, differing from both in its completely white spotted or barred underparts. In flight shows a conspicuous white leading edge to primaries of short rounded wings. Most likely to be seen in the open when feeding on mud at edge of thick swampy cover. L 22-24 cm.          ○SM

**LITTLE CRAKE** *Porzana parva*. Much smaller than Water Rail, and with short green bill, flanks less conspicuously barred and under tail coverts barred. Male has grey face and underparts but otherwise differs from both sexes of slightly smaller Baillon's Crake in its longer wings and tail, olive-brown upperparts, unstreaked wing coverts, flanks barred only behind legs, red base of bill and brighter green legs. Female/juv have buff not grey face and underparts; juv's bill paler green. Swims, dives and walks on floating vegetation. In Britain and Ireland a rare vagrant. L 18-20 cm.          -V

**BAILLON'S CRAKE** *Porzana pusilla*. The region's smallest crake, both sexes differing from male Little Crake in their shorter wings and tail, darker reddish-brown upperparts, white-streaked wing coverts, flanks barred further forwards, duller olive-green legs and all-green bill. Juv has more conspicuously barred underparts and less conspicuously white throat than juv Little Crake; bill brown. All ages have distinctive greyish-pink legs. In Britain and Ireland a rare vagrant. L 17-18 cm.          -V

**WATER RAIL** *Rallus aquaticus*. When, as so often, seen dashing for cover, differs from larger Moorhen (p.126) in its barred flanks and greyer under tail coverts. Long red, black-tipped bill separates it from all crakes and rails of the region; legs pinkish-brown. Juv has buff underparts and white eye-stripe, throat and under tail coverts; bill mainly black, legs brownish. Much more often heard calling from dense vegetation than seen in the open, most often seen in hard weather, feeding on unfrozen patches. May also swim. L 23-28 cm.          ⊙RW

# CRAKES

**SPOTTED CRAKE**
Flight less agile than Baillon's and Spotted; a good climber up reed and other stems.

ad

juv

Little

Baillon's

**LITTLE CRAKE**
Like the other small crakes, often swims jerkily, when crossing short distances from one patch of cover to another.

juv

ad

juv

ad with brown cheeks

**BAILLON'S CRAKE**

1st w

1st w

ad

juv

**WATER RAIL**
Flight fluttering with dangling legs; more easily heard than seen, with pig-like grunts and squeals.

ad

ad

Size with bill and leg colour separate these two easily.

**MOORHEN** *Gallinula chloropus*. Red forehead, yellow-tipped red bill, green legs with red garter, white line along flank, no wing bar in flight and constant flirting of white undertail coverts all distinguish adult from larger Coot. Juv more olive-brown than juv Coot, and has white flank line. Downy young all-dark. Chief calls loud liquid croaks, 'curruc', 'kittic' and 'kaak'. Flight weak, with laboured, pattering take-off, legs straight out behind. Swims with jerky forward movement; dives to hide. Fresh water, even urban, swamps; may feed on grassland, but usually near water. L 32-35 cm. ●RW

**Allen's Gallinule** *Porphyrula alleni*. Vagrant from tropics, especially to Mediterranean. Like small Moorhen, but iridescent green above, purplish-blue below; bill and legs red, forehead pale greenish. Juv brown above, buff below; forehead reddish. L 22-24 cm.                    -V

**American Purple Gallinule** *Porphyrula martinica*. Rare moorhen-sized transatlantic vagrant. Larger than Allen's Gallinule and with yellow legs and bill tip; juv more olive, with white under tail coverts. L 30-36 cm.                    -V

**PURPLE GALLINULE** *Porphyrio porphyrio*. An outsize and uni-formly dark bluish-purple Moorhen, with long red legs and a massive all-red bill; juv greyish on head, neck and underparts. Calls include loud hooting, cackling, clucking and hoarse rip-pling notes, and a softer 'chuck-chuck' contact note. Shy where persecuted; elsewhere often in the open, flirting white under tail coverts; climbs reed stems; flight like Moorhen. Swamps, reed-beds, freshwater margins with thick cover. Aka Purple Swamp-hen. L 45-50 cm.

Ssp.*madagascariensis* (Egypt) has greenish back; sspp.*caspius* and *seistanicus* (Middle East) have greyish head and neck.

**COOT** *Fulica atra*. Dumpier and more rounded in shape than most ducks, coots are the only black waterfowl with white forehead and bill; in flight wing shows narrow white trailing edge; legs mainly green, toes lobed. Juv has whitish throat and breast, dark grey underparts. Downy young have rufous head and neck. Calls loud, high-pitched: 'kowk', 'kewk' and 'cut'. Gregarious in winter, large flocks making curious roar-ing sound on water surface when raptors appear. Much given to quarrelsome chases, dives much more than Moorhen, and has similar pattering take-off. Fresh water, even in towns, usually with vegetated margins; in winter also estuaries. L 36-38 cm. ●RW

**American Coot** *F. americana*. Slightly smaller rare transatlantic vagrant, with white under tail coverts and reddish-black band on bill and patch on forehead. L 31-37 cm.                    -V

**CRESTED COOT** *Fulica cristata*. Adult like Coot, but has no white in wing, blunter angle of black between bill and fore-head, bluish bill and feet, hooting call and (hard to see) two red knobs on forehead. Juv brownish; throat pale, underparts grey. Fresh water, usually with vegetated margins. L 38-42 cm.

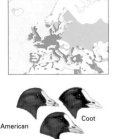

American

Coot

Crested

American has black band on bill. No red knobs on Crested in winter.

Now very rare in Spain; still common in Morocco but declining.

# GALLINULES, COOTS

Moorhen and gallinules swim with jerky forward movements.

juv

ad

**MOORHEN**

1st w

ad

**AMERICAN PURPLE GALLINULE**

juv

ad

**ALLEN'S GALLINULE**

juv

porphyrio
ad

caspius
ad

madagascariensis
**PURPLE
GANINULE**

ad

juv

**COOT**

ad

**AMERICAN COOT**

**CRESTED
COOT**

juv

ad br

stork

goose

crane

Cranes have strong, slow but direct flight on long broad wings, with both neck and legs stretched out, like storks (p.52) and geese (p.56), but unlike herons (p.48). On migration usually fly in lines or V-formation.

heron

● **CRANES: *Gruidae*.** Large gregarious land and marsh wading birds with long neck and legs and rather short tail; bill stout, straight, shorter than herons and storks. Adult grey, juv/imm browner. Voice loud, clanging or trumpeting. Many species have remarkable dancing displays.

**COMMON CRANE** *Grus grus*. Grey, with black head and wing-tips, broad white stripe from cheek down neck, red crown (only visible at close range), and large tuft of wing plumes obscuring tail at rest. Juv/imm darker, with brownish head and neck. Differs from herons (p.48) in pattern of head and neck, shorter bill and plumes, also in outstretched neck in flight. Call a harsh, clanging 'krooh' or 'krr'. When migrating usually flies in either V-formation or lines. Extensive marshes, bogs and wet heathland or tundra; in winter also frequents drier open country. In late autumn whole European population may concentrate at just two sites, at the Hortobagy, Hungary, and at Lac du Der, N E France. L 110-120, WS 220-245 cm.          ○Rm

Sandhill

Common

Both in first spring; Sandhill still brown and always smaller.

**Sandhill Crane** *G. canadensis*. Rare transatlantic vagrant. Head and neck grey with bare red skin on crown and forehead and white patch on cheek. Head and neck of juv/imm brown. Escaped Sarus Cranes *G. antigone* from Asia are much larger, with bare red skin on head and upper neck and reddish legs. L 88-95, WS 175-195 cm.          -V

**SIBERIAN WHITE CRANE** *Grus leucogeranus*. All-white except for black wing-tips that only show in flight; white wing plumes conspicuous. Legs, bill (shorter than White Stork, p.52) and bare skin on face red. (N American Whooping Crane *G. americana*, never recorded in region, differs in black face mask and greenish bill.) Juv tinged buff; rufous on neck and feathered head. Voice softer and more musical than Common Crane, 'krouk, krouk'. Marshes, very local and rare. L 120-140, WS 230-260 cm.

Now only a few individuals at S Caspian Sea wintering area.

**DEMOISELLE CRANE** *Anthropoides virgo*. Appreciably smaller and more graceful than Common Crane, and with conspicuous white ear-tufts, black lower neck and breast, ending in a plume, and much less obvious wing plumes. Juv grey on black parts with smaller grey ear tufts. Calls similar to Common Crane. Marshes and marshy valleys; in Morocco on a high plateau, perhaps now extinct. L 90-100, WS 165-185 cm.          -E

**CRANES**

juv

ad

COMMON CRANE

ad

juv

SANDHILL
CRANE

ad

imm

juv

SIBERIAN WHITE
CRANE

imm

ad

DEMOISELLE
CRANE

● BUSTARDS *Otidae*. Large long-necked, long-legged, long and broad-winged land birds; bill stout. Sexes alike; males larger. Juv like female. Flight strong, legs and neck stretched out, like cranes and storks.

Adult male in full courtship display

Male Great Bustards take six years to become fully adult and acquire the striking white plumes they use in courtship. They are always much larger and stouter than females. Juv/imm resembles non-breeding adults.

**GREAT BUSTARD** *Otis tarda*. One of the region's largest land birds, with largely white, black-tipped wings in flight. Head and neck grey, rufous barred black above and white beneath; legs grey. Breeding male has long white moustachial bristles and rufous breast-band. Has barking alarm note. Steppes and extensive, treeless farmland. L 75-105, WS 190-260 cm.          -V

**LITTLE BUSTARD** *Tetrax tetrax*. The region's smallest bustard; though mainly brown at rest, suggesting a large, long-legged gamebird, it shows a striking contrast in flight, with almost as much white as a flying Shelduck (p.62). Brown above and white below, but breeding male has grey cheeks and throat and white-bordered black neck. Flight note a short 'dahg'; display note a far-carrying, snorting 'ptrr'. Flight recalls both ducks and gamebirds, with whistling or clattering wing quills. Shy when breeding. Grassy and cultivated plains, sometimes with scattered trees and bushes. L 40-45, WS 105-115 cm.     -V

display

**ARABIAN BUSTARD** *Ardeotis arabs*. Between male and female Great Bustard in size; like non-breeding Great, but less rufous above, with backward-pointing black crest and yellow legs; in flight shows much less white in the wing than the region's other bustards. Calls a rasping croak and a drawn-out fluty whistle. Semi-deserts in S E Morocco, where now very rare. L 70-90, WS 205-250 cm.

**HOUBARA** *Chlamydotis undulata*. Between Little and Great Bustards in size, but always separable by conspicuous vertical black and white neck frill and backward-pointing crest. When crouching, sandy grey plumage blends well with sandy background. Prefers to run, but flies fairly fast, with shallow wingbeats, the wing-pattern black and white but less conspicuously so than Great and Little. Very rarely vocal. Dry open plains, semi-deserts, deserts, usually with little or no scrub. L 55-65, WS 135-170 cm.          -V

The smaller and darker Canary ssp.*fuertaventurae* no longer on Lanzarote; only on Fuerteventura, where visits grass- and cornfields.

# BUSTARDS

♂ n br

alert ♂ ♂

resting flock

♀ br

triking amount of hite in wing in agle-like flight.

old ♂ br

GREAT BUSTARD

30 day old chick

nbr

♂ nbr

♀

♀

duck-like flight

♂ br

LITTLE BUSTARD

fuertaventurae

♂

macqueenii

♂

Male larger than females, but less so than in Great Bustard.

ARABIAN BUSTARD

Male larger; juv less black on neck.

HOUBARA

● OYSTERCATCHERS *Haematopodidae*. Large long-legged, long-billed but rather short-necked, gregarious black and white waders. Sexes alike.

**OYSTERCATCHER** *Haematopus ostralegus*. Long orange bill and pink legs and short neck separate it from all other large black-and-white shore birds. White wing bar shows in flight; throat black in summer, white in winter. Juv has dark bill tip. Main call a penetrating shrill 'kleeep', also a shorter 'pic, pic', and a loud communal piping display. Seashores; also breeds inland in river valleys, by salt lakes and on sand steppes. L 40-45, WS 80-86 cm. ●RsmW

**Canarian Black Oystercatcher** *H. meadewaldoi* All-black, except for faint pale patch on underwing. Formerly on Fuerteventura and Lanzarote, Canary Is, but now almost certainly extinct. L 50 cm.

● STILTS, AVOCETS: *Recurvirostridae*. Large long-legged, long-necked and long-billed black-and-white waders.

**BLACK-WINGED STILT** *Himantopus himantopus*. Grotesquely long pink legs (12-16 cm) and long straight black bill diagnostic; trailing legs make flying bird look unexpectedly long; wings black beneath. Male's crown usually black, female's usually white; females have browner mantle. Juv like female but with greyish head and neck. Call a rather coot-like 'kik-kik-kik'. Fresh and brackish marshes and pools, also in saltmarshes and on shore. L 35-40, WS 67-85 cm. -A(b)

**AVOCET** *Recurvirostra avosetta*. Unmistakable with its strikingly upcurved bill, used with a side-to-side sweeping motion in feeding, and blue-grey legs. Juv browner. Swims readily and upends. Main call 'klooit', also a soft, grunting flight note; loud yelps when nest or young in danger. Salt and brackish marshes and pools, coastal and inland, estuaries; also by fresh water. L 42-45, WS 77-80 cm. ☉SrmW

● CRAB PLOVER: *Dromadidae*. A large long-legged tropical wader, the only member of its family. Sexes alike.

**CRAB PLOVER** *Dromas ardeola*. Stout, sharp bill, adapted to deal with the crabs on which it feeds, readily separates it from other large black-and-white waders. Long neck is hunched at rest, outstretched in flight. Juv has mantle and wing-tips grey. Coastal lagoons, sandy shores and estuaries with crabs. Never inland. L 33-36, WS 75-78 cm.

● PAINTED SNIPES: *Rostratulidae*. Medium-sized, long-billed, snipe-like waders of freshwater wetlands.

Freshwater swamps with dense vegetation, reedbeds; may feed in open fields.

**PAINTED SNIPE** *Rostratula benghalensis*. Shorter-legged than Snipe (p.152) and with white underparts and shorter decurved bill. White eye-stripe and stripe on lower breast, buff stripe on blackish crown; female has rufous neck and upper breast. In flight legs dangle and rounded wing-tips show large round buff spots. Flight call a low 'kek'. L 23-26 cm.

**PIED WADERS, PAINTED SNIPE**

w

ad

w

OYSTERCATCHER

juv

juv

CK-
GED STILT

♀

ad

AVOCET

ad ♂

ad ♂

ad

ad

♀

ad

juv

juv

PAINTED SNIPE

CRAB PLOVER

● STONE CURLEWS, THICK-KNEES: *Burhinidae*. Large, mainly terrestrial waders, with large head, stout bill, yellow legs and swollen 'knee joints'. Sexes alike.

**STONE CURLEW** *Burhinus oedicnemus*. Named from its curlew-like call, a wild, shrill, often nocturnal 'coo-leee'. Pale brown, with a short straight black yellow-based bill; large staring yellow eyes set in large rounded head; and whitish bar on closed wing showing as two white bars in flight in contrast to black trailing edge and tip. Flight slow and direct. Open dry, usually stony country, downs, heaths, semi-deserts, farmland; may flock in autumn. L 40-44, WS 77-85 cm.   ⊙S

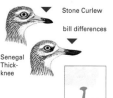

Stone Curlew

bill differences

Senegal Thick-knee

Ssp.*saharae* (N Africa, Middle East, Greece, Mediterranean islands) paler, sandier; in the Canary Is the smaller *insularum* in the E and *distinctus* in the W are darker and more heavily streaked.

**SENEGAL THICK-KNEE** *Burhinus senegalensis*. Smaller than Stone Curlew, with less yellow on longer bill and showing grey panel instead of bar on wing at rest and only one bar in flight. Call similar but more nasal or metallic. Habitat similar, but especially near rivers and sometimes in large orchards and gardens. L 32-38, WS 75-80 cm.

● COURSERS, PRATINCOLES: *Glareolidae*. Terrestrial, plover-like birds with pointed decurved bill, often appearing to stand on tiptoe, stretching neck. Sexes alike. Pratincoles are short-legged aerial feeders, swallow-like or tern-like in flight, with long pointed wings, forked tail and short bill.

**Egyptian Plover** *Pluvianus aegyptius*. Formerly bred upper Egypt; now rare vagrant. Uniquely patterned: black-and-white stripes on head, black stripe on breast. Strikingly black and white in flight. River banks and beds. Aka Crocodile Bird, Egyptian Courser. L 19-21 cm.

**CREAM-COLOURED COURSER** *Cursorius cursor*. A slender, sandy-coloured bird, longer-legged and with longer, more curved bill than pratincoles; head has black-and-white eye-stripes and grey rear crown. Juv speckled brown above. In jerky flight looks long-winged, with black wing-tips and under-wing conspicuous, but prefers to run and crouch alternately. Calls a liquid 'quit' and a harsher 'craak, craak'. Deserts, semi-deserts. L 19-21 cm.   -V

Also resident Canary Is.

**COLLARED PRATINCOLE** *Glareola pratincola*. In flight shows white rump, black forked tail and chestnut underwing. Throat and upper breast creamy, bordered black; secondaries pale-edged; bill black with red base. Juv has blackish streaks on throat and broader but incomplete black collar. Noisy flocks hawk for flying insects and perform aerobatics, chattering with tern-like 'kik-kik-kik'. Sometimes crepuscular. Open steppes and savannas, sun-baked mudflats, bare freshwater margins. L 23-26 cm.   -V

**BLACK-WINGED PRATINCOLE** *Glareola nordmanni*. Slightly darker and longer-legged than very similar Collared, differing especially in black underwing (best seen when birds lifts wings while at rest), lack of pale trailing edge to wing, and less red at base of bill. L 25 cm.   -V

# THICK-KNEES,
# COURSER,
# PRATINCOLES

saharae

ad

ad

female's dark wing bar
may be less prominent.

ad

ad

SENEGAL
THICK-KNEE

STONE CURLEW

ad

ad

EGYPTIAN
PLOVER

ad

juv

CREAM-COLOURED
COURSER

ad

ad

ad

ad

br

juv

ad

br

juv

ad nbr

ad nbr

COLLARED PRATINCOLE

BLACK-
WINGED
PRATINCOLE

● PLOVERS *Charadriidae* Small and medium-sized, short-billed, mainly terrestrial waders. Sexes usually alike. When feeding, characteristically run for a short distance and then stop, often bobbing head nervously or holding it up, as if listening, not down, like Knot and Dunlin (p.144). Gregarious when not breeding. *Charadrius* plovers are rather small, usually sandy or greyish-brown above and often have striking black-and-white patterns on head and neck. Cf. golden plovers (p.140) and lapwings (p.142).

**nbr**

**br** Ssp.*mongolus* has shorter bill.

**nbr**

**br** Ssp.*columbinus*, bill smaller.

**nbr**

**end of winter** In spring male's breast can be like female's.

**LESSER SANDPLOVER** *Charadrius mongolus*. Best told from slightly larger Greater by shorter, slenderer bill (but may overlap), more rounded head with steeper forehead and less obvious white eye-stripe, and shorter darker legs, not longer than tail in flight. Sexes alike in both winter and breeding season, when like male Greater. Rather silent in winter, but may fly off with a short, low double call. Feeds in closer flocks, at times also with Greater. On passage and in winter on shores of Gulf; rare vagrant elsewhere. L 19-21 cm.

Ssp.*atrifrons*, sometimes with white specks on forehead, winters in region. Ssp.*mongolus* with shorter bill, breeds C Asia, and is a possible vagrant.

**GREATER SANDPLOVER** *Charadrius leschenaultii*. The region's largest breeding *Charadrius* plover, with a heavy, stout bill, its best distinction; bill length exceeds distance from its base to behind the eye (cf. Lesser). Winter adult and breeding female pale grey-brown above, white below, with white wing bar in flight; eye appearing large, bill black, legs mainly grey. Breeding male has broad rufous breast-band extending to nape, and black face-mask. Call a turnstone-like trill. Deserts, semi-deserts; in winter on sandy or muddy shores, mainly coastal, often feeds in scattered flocks. L 22-25 cm.      -V

Ssp.*crassirostris*, Caspian eastwards, has largest bill. Ssp.*columbinus*, W of Caspian, has smaller bill, cf. Lesser Sandplover.

**CASPIAN PLOVER** *Charadrius asiaticus*. When breeding differs from larger Dotterel in rufous breast not underparts and much less conspicuous white eyestripe; and from both sand-plovers in black line under breast-band and no black face-mask. In winter tinged more buff than other *Charadrius* plovers; has eye-stripe more prominent than both sandplovers and less so than Dotterel; bill shorter and slenderer and wing-bar fainter than larger Greater Sandplover. Various soft piping and higher-pitched whistling double or triple calls. Grassy plains, semi-deserts, uncommon on freshwater or sea shores. L 18-20 cm.      -V

**DOTTEREL** *Charadrius morinellus*. Best distinctions from other *Charadrius* plovers are white eye-stripes meeting in V on nape, lack of wing bars in flight and diagnostic pattern of underparts (fainter in winter): throat white, white line separating grey upper breast from rufous lower breast, belly black and under tail coverts white. Numerous calls include a soft 'peep-peep-peep' flight call and a trilling 'wit-e-wee' alarm note. Mountain tops, tundra, rarely on arable; stopovers in open country on migration; in winter mainly in bare, semi-arid places inland. L 20-22 cm.      ⊙Sm

# PLOVERS

♀ br

nbr

♂ br
atrifrons

nbr

**LESSER SANDPLOVER**

♀ br

juv

nbr

nbr

♂ br

nbr

**GREATER SANDPLOVER**

nbr

nbr

♂ br          ♀ br

Quite tame; often
stands on stone or
earth clod.

**CASPIAN PLOVER**

♀ br

Breeding female; male
duller and has less black
on belly.

br

nbr

juv          nbr

**DOTTEREL**

**RINGED PLOVER** *Charadrius hiaticula*. One of the commonest northern shore birds, with distinctive black-and-white head and breast pattern, conspicuous pale wing bar, orange-yellow legs and black-tipped yellow bill. Juv has no black on head, and brownish breast-band often incomplete. Calls a liquid, musical 'too-i' and 'queep'; plangent song, delivered in bat-like display flight. Gregarious, but usually scatters to feed. Sandy and shingly seashores, less often similar fresh and brackish water shores and river beds, less often sandy flats inland; in winter also muddy seashores and estuaries. L 18-20 cm. ●RsMW

**Semipalmated Plover** *C. semipalmatus*. Transatlantic vagrant. Slightly smaller, shorter-billed and paler-legged than Ringed Plover, and with narrow yellow eye-ring; best distinguished by sharper, less fluty calls, 'kerwee' and 'chu-wit' and in hand by short webs between toes. L 17-19, WS 43-52 cm. -V

**LITTLE RINGED PLOVER** *Charadrius dubius*. Smaller and slimmer than Ringed, adult with conspicuous yellow orbital eye-ring (cf. Semipalmated Plover), no wing bar in flight, relatively smaller head, white line above black forehead, bill yellow only at base of lower mandible and legs dull yellowish. Juv has eye-ring obscure, yellowish forehead, no supercilium and breast-band often incomplete. Calls quite distinct and diagnostic: 'pee-oo', 'pip-pip-pip...' and a reedy note recalling Little Tern (p.184); song a trilling elaboration of calls. Much less gregarious. Freshwater margins, usually with sand or shingle. L 14-15 cm. ⊙S

**KENTISH PLOVER** *Charadrius alexandrinus*. Smaller, dumpier and paler than both ringed plovers, looking large-headed and short-tailed, with black bill and (usually) black legs and a wing bar (cf. Little Ringed). Breeding male has variably rufous crown, less black on cheeks and forehead than both and incomplete black breast-band. Breeding female, winter adults and juv have crown paler, no black on forehead and other black parts greyer; cf. the two juv ringed plovers. Calls weaker than both: 'wit', 'wee-it' and 'prr-ip', with a trilling song. Sand and shingle, mainly coastal. L 15-17 cm. ⊙Mw(b)

**KITTLITZ'S PLOVER** *Charadrius pecuarius*. The region's smallest *Charadrius*, 'large-headed' like Kentish, and with longer, often paler legs and bill, and upperparts dappled with well-marked feather centres. Adult differs from male Kentish in sandy crown, white nape, longer black line through eye, and no black on sides of pale rufous breast, but a dark shoulder-patch. Dappled upperparts distinguish juv from other juv *Charadrius*. Call a clear, plaintive 'pipip'. Freshwater or coastal margins, sand/mud flats. L 12-14 cm.

**Killdeer** *C. vociferus*. Transatlantic vagrant, easily recognised by its large size, long tail, conspicuous double breast-band, rufous rump, loud 'kill-dee' call and preference for grassland. L 23-26 cm. -V

Juv
Kittlitz's Plover

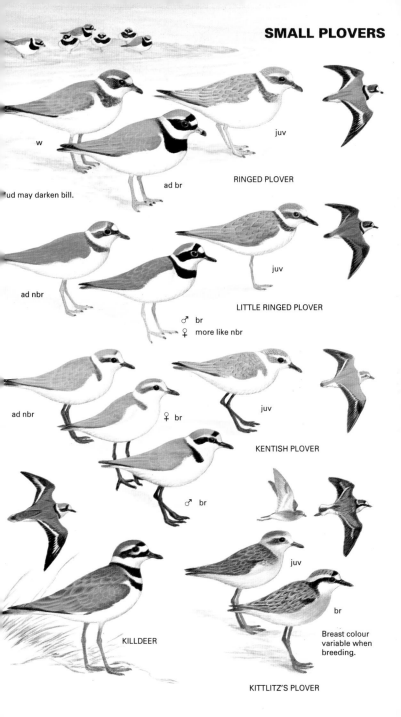

# SMALL PLOVERS

w

ud may darken bill.

ad br

juv

RINGED PLOVER

ad nbr

juv

♂ br
♀ more like nbr

LITTLE RINGED PLOVER

ad nbr

♀ br

juv

KENTISH PLOVER

♂ br

KILLDEER

juv

br

Breast colour
variable when
breeding.

KITTLITZ'S PLOVER

**Golden Plovers:** *Pluvialis*. Medium-sized waders with upperparts grey or yellowish spangled black, and underparts largely black when breeding.

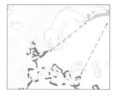

**GREY PLOVER** *Pluvialis squatarola*. In winter a large, rather plump, greyish plover with a whitish rump, easily told in flight from Golden Plover and smaller, longer-billed Knot (p.144) by black underwing and axillaries. When breeding, face and underparts strikingly black and white, upperparts spangled black and silver. Triple call, 'tee-oo-ee', with middle note lower, sounds like a human wolf-whistle. Feeds widely scattered on shore, not in compact flocks like Golden Plover and Knot. Breeds on tundra, otherwise inland only on migration; in winter on estuaries and muddy and sandy seashores. L 27-30 cm. ●MW

**GOLDEN PLOVER** *Pluvialis apricaria*. A large plover with yellowish-brown upperparts and white underwing and axillaries. Call a liquid piping 'tlui', and a mournful trilling song. When not breeding highly gregarious, both flying, with frequent aerial manoeuvres, and feeding in compact flocks, often together with Lapwings (p.142), when easily told by pointed wings. Moors, tundra marshes, arctic heaths; in winter on farmland, estuaries, muddy seashores. L 26-29 cm. ●RmW

♀ br
♂ br
intermediate
Southern
♀ b
Northern
♂ br

When breeding, northern populations have a broad pure white band on side of breast and underparts (cf. Grey Plover) that contrasts strikingly with black cheeks, throat, breast and belly. In southern populations this band is tinged yellowish, the cheeks are not black and the other black parts are less clear-cut and conspicuous.

▶ **American Golden Plover** *P. dominica*. Transatlantic vagrant, smaller, slimmer, longer-legged and greyer than Golden, and with longer, narrower wings, slightly longer bill, larger and more rounded head, and more marked eye-stripe - like a small Grey, but with whole underwing and axillaries grey. Calls a whistling, lapwing-like 'teeh' and a high-pitched, greenshank-like 'tu-ee' or 'tee-tew'. Usually inland. L 23-28 cm. -A

▶ **Pacific Golden Plover** *P. fulva*. Rare vagrant from E Asia, slightly smaller than American Golden, and with longer bill and legs, brighter, yellower (especially on face), and more contrasting winter plumage, so resembling a small Golden, but with eye-stripe yellowish and nape brown. May be hard to separate from American in field unless wing-length can be judged: Pacific shows (2-)3(-4) primary tips beyond tip of tertials, whereas American shows 4-(6). Calls similar. Usually coastal. L 23-26 cm. -V

# GOLDEN PLOVERS

♂ br

juv

♀ br

nbr

nbr

GREY PLOVER

juv

nbr

br

GOLDEN PLOVER

juv

nbr

AMERICAN GOLDEN PLOVER

juv

nbr

juv

PACIFIC GOLDEN PLOVER

**Lapwings:** A distinct group of larger plovers, with black wing-tips, and tail usually white-based and often black-tipped. Rather noisy, especially when breeding.

Flecking on throat

♀ br

**LAPWING** *Vanellus vanellus*. The region's most distinctive and most conspicuously crested plover, and the commonest inland over most of it. Generally appears black and white, though upperparts show green in bright sunlight and chestnut undertail coverts often prominent; easily recognised in flight by broad, rounded wings; throat black when breeding, white in winter. Calls and song are variations on 'pee-wit' (whence aka Peewit), usual ground call being 'peeet', flight call 'pee-wit' and aerial song, 'p'weet, p'weet, pee-wit, pee-wit'. In striking aerobatic display wings make a loud throbbing or 'lapping' sound (whence Lapwing name). In large flocks when not breeding. Farmland, grassland with short turf, marshy fields, heaths, moors, bogs; in winter also by fresh water and on estuarine and coastal mud and sandflats. L 28-31 cm.  ●RSMW

**SPUR-WINGED PLOVER** *Hoplopterus spinosus*. White cheeks, neck and wing panels contrast strongly with black crown, bib, primaries and underparts; upperparts greyish-buff, head slightly crested, tail all black and legs long and grey; named from small spur at angle of wing. Main call a loud shrieking cry, often rendered 'did he do it?'; alarm a high- pitched 'zit-zeet-zeet'. Often stands hunched; flies rather slowly. Wetlands: fresh and brackish lagoons, marshes, estuaries; flocks after breeding. L 25-27 cm.

**RED-WATTLED PLOVER** *Hoplopterus indicus*. Distinguished by bright red wattle around and in front of each eye and long yellow legs. Crown, nape, throat and breast black; sides of neck and nape and underparts white. Loud shrieking 'did-he-do-it' call and monotonous single note. Flight slow, deliberate. Not very gregarious. Open country near fresh or brackish water. L 32-35 cm.

**WHITE-TAILED PLOVER** *Vanellus leucura*. At rest is rather uniformly grey-brown, with pale face, dark wing-tips and long yellow legs. Most easily recognised in flight with its diagnostic all-white tail and striking contrast between black primaries and white secondaries. Rather silent when not breeding; some lapwing-like calls. Stands very upright; flight rather slow. Marshes, shallow lagoons, slow-flowing streams. L 26-29 cm.     -V

**SOCIABLE PLOVER** *Vanellus gregaria*. Mainly grey-brown, but when breeding has black crown, white forehead and eyestripes and dark chestnut belly, appearing superficially as a pale bird with a dark crown and belly. Always has dark line through eye, black legs, and black primaries contrasting with white secondaries. Calls a short, high-pitched whistle and a harsh, grating note. Breeds dry steppe; winters dry, open country, farmland, freshwater margins. L 27-30 cm.     -V

# LAPWINGS

juv

ad nbr

LAPWING

♂ br

juv

juv

SPUR-WINGED
PLOVER

ad

RED-WATTLED
PLOVER

ad br

w

juv

w

juv

br

WHITE-TAILED
PLOVER

br

SOCIABLE
PLOVER

Winter birds are similar;
some are paler in fresh
plumage.

In winter white belly,
mottled breast.

● WADERS: *Scolopacidae*, pp.144-163. Long-billed, long-necked, long-legged shorebirds, including the curlews, godwits, sandpipers, 'shanks, snipes and stints. Breed mainly on tundra and moorland, in winter mainly on coasts.

**Calidris Waders**, pp.144-149. Mostly rather small waders (the smallest called stints, or in N America 'peeps'), with only moderately long bill and legs and shortish neck and wings. All show white wing bar in flight. Calls piping or twittering, rather subdued, flocks often keeping up a conversational twitter.

**DUNLIN** *Calidris alpina.* The commonest small winter shorebird, identified by slightly decurved bill-tip, contrast between grey-brown above and whiter below, white sides of rump and tail, and flight-call, a weak 'treeep'. When breeding is only small wader with black lower breast and belly. Has a trilling song. Most females larger, with belly less black and more mottled. Juv has distinctive greyish spots on sides of lower breast. Breeds on moors, wet heaths, coastal marshes; winter flocks mainly on coastal mud. L 16-20 cm. ●rsMW

Northern ssp.*alpina* is generally larger and has a longer, distinctly more decurved bill than both southern ssp.*schinzii* and migrant and wintering ssp.*arctica* (N Greenland).

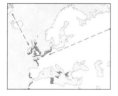

**CURLEW SANDPIPER** *Calidris ferruginea.* Combination of white rump (conspicuous and house-martin-like in flight) and markedly decurved bill distinguishes it from all other small waders. When breeding, brick-red plumage separates from all except larger Knot. Larger, more elegant and longer-legged than even large winter Dunlins and has more distinct white eye-stripe. Juv tinged buff and upperparts have distinctive scaly appearance. Flight note a soft 'chirrup'. L 18-19 cm. ⊙M

**KNOT** *Calidris canutus.* A dumpy wader, the region's largest commoner *Calidris.* In grey winter plumage differs from Dunlin and Sanderling in uniform grey tail, and from larger and much less gregarious Grey Plover (p.140) in longer bill and white axillaries. Brick-red breeding plumage distinctive, but cf. white-rumped, curve-billed Curlew Sandpiper. Juv slightly browner on more scaly back and tinged buff on underparts. Named from call, a low 'knut'. In large, closely packed winter flocks feeds with head well down. Uncommon inland. Aka Red Knot. L 23-25 cm. ●MW

**Great Knot** *C. tenuirostris.* Very rare vagrant from E Asia, darker above and slightly larger than Knot and with longer bill, dark-spotted breast contrasting with pale belly, and white rump. L 26-28 cm. -V

**SANDERLING** *Calidris alba.* Somewhat larger and more rotund than even large Dunlins, and with a shorter, straighter bill and broader white wing bar; in winter much paler and whiter than other same-sized shorebirds, with distinctive black shoulder-spot. Breeding plumage rufous above and on breast, but belly white. Juv's upperparts spangled black and white. Flight call 'twick, twick'. In winter almost confined to sandy shores, where patters fast and restlessly along edge of tide, running rather than flying when approached. L 20-21 cm. ●MW

144

# *CALIDRIS* WADERS

schinzii br

rctica

br alpina

nbr

nbr

juv

**DUNLIN**

ost females less contrastingly coloured
hind neck.

nbr

juv

nbr

moulting

**CURLEW SANDPIPER**

reeding female paler,
specially on belly, often
ith longer bill.

nbr

nbr

br, scapulars
chestnut.

juv

nbr

**GREAT
KNOT**

br
**KNOT**

nbr

juv

nbr

br

Some breeders may
be as bright rufous
as Red-necked Stint;
others, notably
females, are greyer.

br

nbr

**SANDERLING**

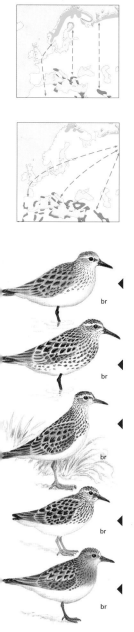

**TEMMINCK'S STINT** *Calidris temminckii*. The least typical small stint and the only one with white outer tail feathers. Plumper and shorter-legged than Little Stint, its uniformly grey-brown breast and longish wings and tail make it resemble a small Common Sandpiper (p.160). Breeding and winter plumages very similar; supercilium obscure; legs variably pale, often yellow. Juv like adult, but upperparts faintly scaly. Main call, a shrill spluttering 'pt-r-r-r-r', and habit of towering when flushed, both distinctive. Breeds in scrubby tundra; on passage mainly by vegetated fresh water. L 13-15 cm. ○sM

**LITTLE STINT** *Calidris minuta*. One of the smallest breeding waders; like a small, short- and straight-billed Dunlin (p.144), feeding more actively. Slimmer than Temminck's and differs in blackish legs, almost white breast and no white in tail. When breeding, upperparts and sides of breast boldly patterned with rufous and black, with two pale lines on mantle, and belly white; in winter grey-brown above, white below; may have faint breast-band. Juv like breeding adult but has distinct white V on back and breast often pale buff. Flight-note 'chik, chik', may be prolonged to a trill. L 12-14 cm. ⊙Mw

**Semipalmated Sandpiper** *C. pusilla*. Transatlantic vagrant, named from partially webbed toes, hard to see in field. Greyer and slightly larger than Little Stint in winter and juv plumages, with centre of breast white; bill heavier, thicker-based, blunt-tipped; legs dark. Juv has darker crown and marked white supercilium. Safest distinction is call, a soft 'chit' or 'chirrup'. Cf. Western Sandpiper. Feeds in plover-like stops and starts. L 13-15 cm. -V

**Western Sandpiper** *C. mauri*. Rare transatlantic vagrant. Slightly the largest small dark-legged stint; bill, especially of females, may be appreciably longer, narrower and more dunlin-like than Semipalmated and often slightly decurved at the tip; toes partly webbed. In winter extremely like a pale Semipalmated, except for bill, faint breast-band, and distinctive call, a high-pitched 'chi-et'. Juv duller than juv Little Stint, and pale V obscure; differs from juv Semipalmated in paler crown, less distinct supercilium and rufous-fringed upper scapulars. L 14-17 cm. -V

**Long-toed Stint** *C. subminuta*. Rare vagrant from Siberia. Longer neck and legs, upright posture, dark forehead, more marked supercilium and narrower wing bar are best distinctions from also yellow-legged Least Sandpiper in winter. Juv differs from juv Least in split eye-stripe and no distinct dark spot on ear coverts. Call a soft, house-sparrow-like 'chirrup'. In flight often towers. L 13-14 cm. -V

**Least Sandpiper** *C. minutilla*. Rare transatlantic vagrant, the smallest stint, appearing short-necked and dark-faced, with greenish-yellow legs (often dark when muddy); cf. Long-toed Stint. Bill short and slender for a stint and slightly decurved at tip; usually a faint pale V on back; breast densely streaked and sharply defined from white belly. Calls include a high-pitched 'weet' and a purring note. Often towers in flight. L 11-12 cm. -V

**Red-necked Stint** *C. ruficollis*. Rare vagrant from Siberia, the only stint with a reddish throat when breeding. Very similar to Little Stint; in winter best told by distinctive call, a single shrill 'chit', but somewhat greyer with longer wings, shorter and thicker bill and slightly shorter legs. Juv very like juv Little, but greyer on back and sides of breast, has plainer head markings and lacks prominent V on back. L 13-16 cm. -V

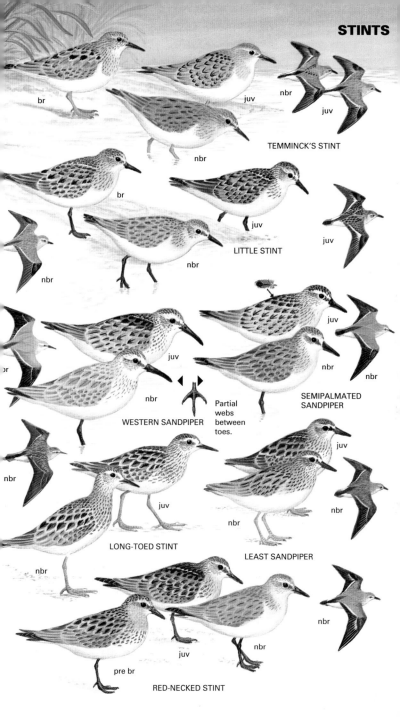

br

juv

nbr

juv

**TEMMINCK'S STINT**

nbr

br

juv

juv

nbr

**LITTLE STINT**

nbr

juv

nbr

nbr

**SEMIPALMATED
SANDPIPER**

r

nbr

Partial
webs
between
toes.

**WESTERN SANDPIPER**

juv

juv

nbr

nbr

nbr

juv

**LONG-TOED STINT**

nbr

**LEAST SANDPIPER**

nbr

juv

nbr

pre br

**RED-NECKED STINT**

**PURPLE SANDPIPER** *Calidris maritima.* Larger than Dunlin (p.144), and the only small wader of rocky shores looking all-dark above, with yellow legs, yellow base to bill and rather thick-set, round-shouldered appearance. Breeding adult and juv speckled paler, with spotted flanks; purple gloss on mantle often hard to detect. Call a low 'weet-wit', also a piping note. In winter in small parties on rocky shores, reefs, weed-covered groynes, breakwaters and patches of stones, often together with Turnstones (p.162). L 20-22.   ⊙mW(b)

**White-rumped Sandpiper** *C. fuscicollis.* Transatlantic vagrant, between stints (p.146) and Dunlin (p.144) in size. Has white rump like much larger Curlew Sandpiper (p.144), but bill shorter, pale-based and slightly decurved towards tip; wings longer, extending well beyond tertials and tail at rest, with less distinct pale bar in flight, and elongated dark spots on flanks; has conspicuous pale supercilium. Breeding adult and juv tinged rufous above; winter adult darker grey-brown than Curlew Sandpiper. Call a high-pitched, mouse-like 'jeet'. Freshwater margins. Aka Bonaparte's Sandpiper. L 15-17 cm.
                                                                                        -A

**Baird's Sandpiper** *C. bairdii.* Transatlantic vagrant, similar in size and elongated outline to White-rumped, but with blackish rump and centre of tail, and a straight black fine-tipped bill. Adult's conspicuous chequered (black-centred) scapulars are distinctive, as are juv's pale buff, scaly upperparts. Both have streaked breast band, pale supercilium and eye-ring and faint wing bar in flight. Main call a trilling 'kr-r-r-eep'. Freshwater margins, pastures. L 14-16 cm.   -A

**Sharp-tailed Sandpiper** *C. acuminata.* Rare vagrant from Siberia, differing from Pectoral in the heavy streaking of flanks and vent as well as breast, longer legs and shorter bill; rufous cap, especially when breeding; and prominent white supercilium, especially behind the eye. Juv has crown and upperparts rufous and breast warm brown. Call softer, more swallow-like. Freshwater margins, wet grassland. Aka Siberian Pectoral Sandpiper. L 17-20 cm.   -V

**Pectoral Sandpiper** *Calidris melanotos.* The most frequent transatlantic vagrant wader, several occurring annually in Britain, larger than Dunlin (p.144), and recalling small Reeve (p.150) when alarmed. Its best field mark is the sharp, bib-like division between the streaked breast and the white belly (cf. Sharp-tailed), coupled with yellowish legs and relatively short, very slightly curved bill, greenish or yellowish at base. Has two snipe-like pale lines down back. Main call a harsh single or double 'prrp'. In Europe mainly by fresh water, also estuarine/sea shores and wet grassland. L 19-23 cm.   -A

**BROAD-BILLED SANDPIPER** *Limicola falcinellus.* Smaller and darker than Dunlin (p.144), with longer bill and shorter legs; head conspicuously striped dark and white, with broad pale supercilium; narrower pale crown stripes almost meet the supercilia in front of the eye. Mantle snipe-like, warm brown (grey in winter), with scalloped appearance and a white line down each side; coppery edges of secondaries show at close range; wing bar often obscure; bill distinctly decurved at tip. Flight call a low-pitched trilling 'chr-r-eek', also a sharp 'tett' and a trilling song when breeding. Not gregarious, except on migration. Breeds in wet bogs. L 16-17 cm.   -A

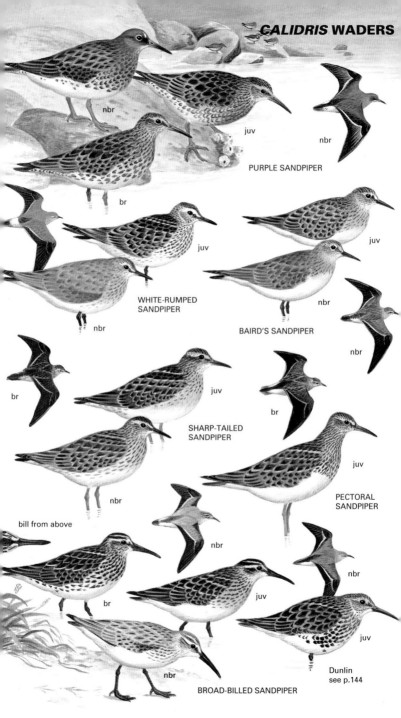

nbr

juv

nbr

PURPLE SANDPIPER

br

juv

juv

WHITE-RUMPED
SANDPIPER

nbr

nbr

BAIRD'S SANDPIPER

nbr

br

juv

SHARP-TAILED
SANDPIPER

br

nbr

juv

PECTORAL
SANDPIPER

bill from above

nbr

br

juv

nbr

juv

Dunlin
see p.144

nbr

BROAD-BILLED SANDPIPER

When breeding, male Ruffs assume fantastic neck-ruffs and ear-tufts, gathering on traditional display grounds for mock battles. Plumage may have almost any combination of black, white, rufous and buff, with bars and streaks, ruff usually differing from ear-tufts.

**RUFF** *Philomachus pugnax.* Breeding male unmistakable; winter male like same-sized Redshank (p.158), but has 'bottle-necked' appearance, only narrow white wing bar, unique white ovals on each side of dark-centred rump, distinctive mottled pattern on back, and often neither bill nor legs red. Female (Reeve) and juv markedly smaller and thinner-necked than winter male (Ruff), and also variable, with same basic pattern as males. Bill blackish-brown, but in breeding male varies red/yellow/brown; legs greenish-grey or orange-red. Puzzling ruff-sized waders much more likely to be Reeves than American vagrants. Rather silent, but has flight note 'too-i' and in spring a deep 'uk'. Marshes, swamps, damp meadows; in winter, often in small parties, at shallow freshwater and coastal margins. L Ruff 26-30, Reeve 20-24 cm.                    ●sMw

**Upland Sandpiper** *Bartramia longicauda.* Transatlantic vagrant: a ruff-sized, small-headed wader, plover-like in its gait, stance and short thin dark bill, and curlew-like in its mottled brown plumage. Long neck and tail and long yellow legs give it an almost Maltese-cross outline in flight. Call trisyllabic, mellow but loud. Short grasslands, usually away from water. Aka Bartram's Sandpiper. L 26-28 cm.                    -V

**Buff-breasted Sandpiper** *Tryngites subruficollis.* Scarce but regular transatlantic vagrant, the only small wader with whole underparts from face to under tail coverts buff. Not unlike a small juv Reeve with rounder head, shorter dark bill and bright yellow legs; no white wing bar or sides of tail, but white underwing conspicuous in flight. Calls a low trill and a sharp 'tik'. Freshwater margins, short grassland; often away from water. L 18-20 cm.                    -A

**Short-billed Dowitcher** *Limnodromus griseus.* Transatlantic vagrant, much rarer than very similar Long-billed, from which best told by flight call, a mellow 'tu-tu-tu', and pale markings in dark centres of juv/imm's wing feathers; also at close range in winter by shorter bill, lower breast not sharply demarcated from belly, and pale bars on tail broader than dark ones. Mainly coastal. L 23-25 cm.                    -V

**Long-billed Dowitcher** *L. scolopaceus.* Transatlantic vagrant, between snipes (p.152) and godwits (p.154) in size, very long-billed, with conspicuous white lower back and rump, barred flanks. In winter paler bars on tail narrower than dark ones. Juv/imm, most likely in Europe, lack Short-billed's pale markings in dark centres to tertials, scapulars and greater coverts. Diagnostic call a high-pitched 'keek' or 'keek-keek-keek'. Mainly by fresh water. L 24-26 cm.                    -A

150

# RUFF, SANDPIPERS, DOWITCHERS

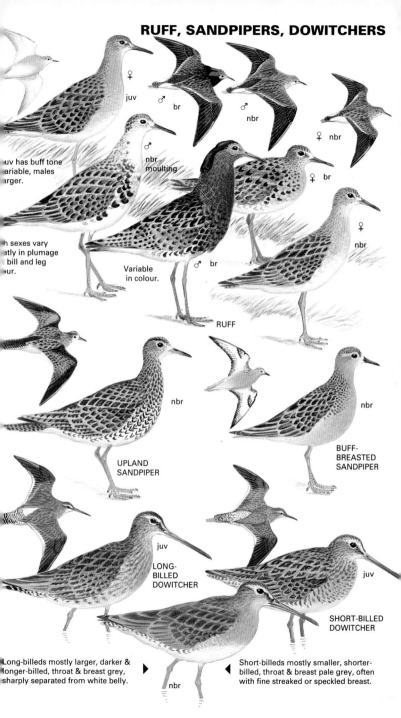

juv

♀ juv

br ♂

nbr ♂

♀ nbr

uv has buff tone
ariable, males
rger.

♂ nbr
moulting

♀ br

h sexes vary
tly in plumage
bill and leg
ur.

Variable
in colour.

♂ br

♀ nbr

RUFF

nbr

nbr

UPLAND
SANDPIPER

BUFF-
BREASTED
SANDPIPER

juv

LONG-
BILLED
DOWITCHER

juv

SHORT-BILLED
DOWITCHER

Long-billeds mostly larger, darker &
longer-billed, throat & breast grey,
sharply separated from white belly.

▶

nbr

◀ Short-billeds mostly smaller, shorter-
billed, throat & breast pale grey, often
with fine streaked or speckled breast.

**Snipes:** *Gallinago*. Medium-sized, very long-billed rather short-legged, pale-bellied brown waders, with striped head and rich patterning on back. Breeding in marshes, bogs and damp meadows, moors and heaths, and wintering mainly at freshwater margins with fairly thick vegetation, but also in drier places.

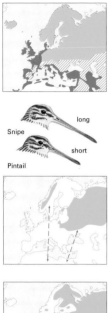

**SNIPE** *Gallinago gallinago*. The commonest snipe, with a 6-7 cm bill, the longest compared to its head of any bird in the region. This, together with its zigzag flight, showing prominent white trailing edges, and loud harsh 'creech' when flushed, is best distinction from all waders other than snipes. Perches on low objects, often uttering a persistent 'chip-per, chip-per', and has unique 'drumming' or 'bleating' display flight, diving at an angle of 45°. In winter small parties ('wisps') may perform aerial evolutions. L 25-27 cm.          ●RmW

Snipe — long

Pintail — short

**Pintail Snipe** *G. stenura*. Best identified in flight, less zigzag than Snipe's, with feet projecting further beyond shorter tail, and showing no white trailing edge to wing and no white on underwing. On ground lacks Snipe's broad pale back stripes, and slightly shorter, thicker-based bill also gives it a perceptibly different jizz. Call higher-pitched. More often on drier ground. L 25-27 cm. Local breeder European NE Russia; rare migrant Middle East.

**GREAT SNIPE** *Gallinago media*. Slightly larger, stouter and more woodcock-like than Snipe, with distinctly shorter bill, conspicuous white spots on wing coverts, much more white in tail, both belly and flanks barred, and no white on underwing. Flight slower, heavier and more direct, the bill held nearer the horizontal; usually drops down much nearer than most Snipe would. Silent, though may utter a low croak. Collective bubbling song on display grounds. More often on drier ground, especially in winter. L 27-29 cm.          -A

**JACK SNIPE** *Lymnocryptes minimus*. Much the smallest and shortest-billed snipe, with two narrow pale streaks on the crown, and no white in tail. Crake-like, prefers running to flying, often flushed from underfoot; has a slower and less erratic flight, dropping into cover much sooner, and often silent or with a low weak call. Drums like Snipe, but bobs and hovers in marionette-like display flight, with call likened to a distant galloping horse. Breeds in wet swamps and bogs; in winter more often in dry places than Snipe. L 17-19 cm.          ☉Mw

**WOODCOCK** *Scolopax rusticola*. Most often seen either as a long-winged rufous bird flying fast and twistingly out of sight in woodland, or in unmistakable 'roding' territorial flight. Roding male flies a circuit at dusk and dawn, with an owlish flight but interrupted wing-beats, uttering two distinct notes, a rather sibilant 'twisick' and a frog-like croak or grunting growl. On ground like a large, heavy, shorter-billed, rufous Snipe, with breast all barred and transverse bars on head. Woodland, heaths with scattered trees, feeding on marshy ground; on passage also in more open country. L 33-35 cm.          ●RsW

Melanistic form.

SNIPE

Snipe

Snipe    Pintail Snipe

tails from above

Great Snipe

PINTAIL SNIPE
Stockier, shorter bill,
very hard to tell in field.

GREAT SNIPE
Plump-bodied, shorter
bill, longer legs, more
contrasting wing pattern.

JACK SNIPE

n recent years shorter-
illed individuals more
egular in W Europe.

WOODCOCK

**Godwits**: *Limosa*. Medium large waders, rather variable in size, distinguished from all curlews (p.156) by their slightly upcurved long bills and quite different calls, also when breeding by handsome rufous plumage.

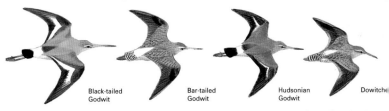

Black-tailed Godwit

Bar-tailed Godwit

Hudsonian Godwit

Dowitche

The region's three godwits are most easily identified in flight by the conspicuousness or absence of a white wing bar, and the distal end of the tail being either black or barred. The somewhat similar but smaller vagrant dowitchers (p.150) have a narrow white patch on back and lower rump.

**BLACK-TAILED GODWIT** *Limosa limosa*. In flight conspicuous white wing bar, coupled with black-banded white tail and white belly when breeding, makes it look almost as pied as an Oystercatcher (p.132), separating it at once from curlews (p.156) and the smaller Bar-tailed, from which also differs in almost straight bill, longer legs, more upright stance, and in winter greyer, more uniform upperparts. Flight call 'tuk' or 'kik', sometimes doubled, but not very vocal except on breeding grounds, where noisy, e.g. 'wicka, wicka, wicka', 'wik-ik-ik' and a lapwing-like 'pee-oo-ee'; song a repeated 'crweetuu'. Damp grassland, wet heaths; on migration and in winter mainly coastal, in flocks. L 40-44, WS 70-82 cm.                    ⊙smW

Ssp.*islandica* (Iceland), wintering mainly on estuaries in Britain and Ireland, has a slightly shorter bill, and the breeding plumage is a slightly darker rusty-red.

br

**Hudsonian Godwit** *L. haemastica*. Rare transatlantic vagrant, slightly shorter-legged and shorter-necked than Black-tailed and differing especially in black axillaries and underwing coverts, white wing bar being confined to inner half of wing and white on tail not extending to rump. L 37-42 cm.                    -V

**BAR-TAILED GODWIT** *Limosa lapponica*. Slightly smaller and shorter-legged than Black-tailed, and differs especially in having no white on upperwing or black on tail, in barred tail tip, in feet scarcely projecting beyond tail in flight, and in breeding male's whole underparts being rufous. In winter resembles same-sized Whimbrel (p.156) but with bill slightly upcurved, legs shorter and crown not striped. Flight notes 'kir-ruc, kurruc' and 'wik-wik-wik-wik-wik'. Has fast, direct flight, migrant and winter flocks sometimes performing dunlin-like aerobatics. Marshy parts of tundra; in winter mainly in estuaries. L 37-39, WS 70-80 cm.                    ●mW

br

**Willet** *Catoptrophorus semipalmatus*. A very rare transatlantic vagrant, half-way between godwits and Greenshank (p.158) in size and appearance. Resembles a small godwit, mottled grey-brown when breeding, paler grey in winter, with a shorter, stouter, straight bill and a striking black and white pattern on both wing surfaces; legs blue-grey. L 33-41 cm.

154

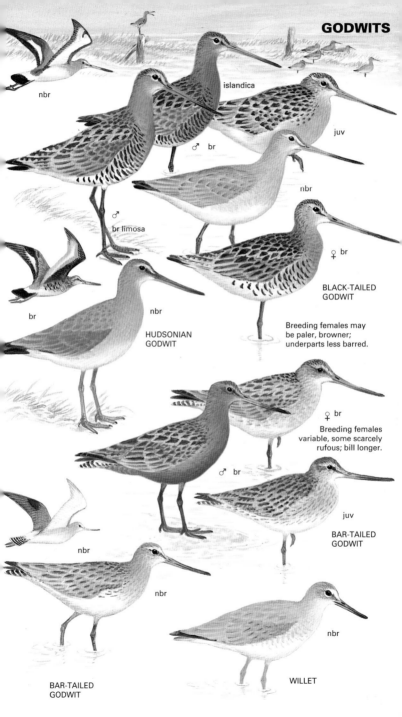

# GODWITS

nbr

islandica

juv

♂ br

nbr

♂ br limosa

♀ br

br

nbr

HUDSONIAN
GODWIT

**BLACK-TAILED
GODWIT**

Breeding females may
be paler, browner;
underparts less barred.

♀ br

Breeding females
variable, some scarcely
rufous; bill longer.

♂ br

juv

**BAR-TAILED
GODWIT**

nbr

nbr

nbr

**BAR-TAILED
GODWIT**

**WILLET**

**Curlews**: *Numenius*. Large waders, appearing uniformly brown at rest, most showing white rump and lower back in flight. Long to very long down-curved bill and long legs projecting beyond tail readily distinguish them in flight from superficially similar imm gulls (pp.166–179).

Upland Sandpiper    Little Whimbrel

**CURLEW** *Numenius arquata*. The region's largest and generally commonest white-rumped brown wader, very variable in size, but generally about as big as a Lesser Blackback (p.172). Juv shorter-billed and more buffish. Varied vocal repertoire includes well known loud 'cooorwee' or 'coor-loo' call from which it is named, and alarm call 'quee, quee, quee'; also a rarely heard whimbrel-like titter. Loud musical bubbling aerial song starts with more plangent 'quee'. Flight rather heavy and gull-like. Moors, bogs, wet heaths, dunes, moist grassland; in winter in flocks, mainly on intertidal area of coast. L 50-60, WS 80-100 cm.    ●RsmW

**Little Whimbrel** *Numenius minutus*. Rare vagrant from Siberia, a golden-plover-sized curlew. Crown uniformly brown with back. Crown striped like Whimbrel, but plumage warmer buff and bill much shorter; triple 'te-te-te' call diagnostic. L 28-30, WS 68-71 cm.    -V

**SLENDER-BILLED CURLEW** *Numenius tenuirostris*. An increasingly rare visitor from W Siberia, mainly to Morocco. A whimbrel-sized curlew, with no crown-stripes, and underwing, underparts and rump purer white; in adults greater contrast of large dark spots on flanks. Bill tip slenderer than Curlew and Whimbrel. 'Courlee' call higher-pitched and shorter than Curlew's; alarm-note 'kew-ee'. In winter on wet coastal grasslands, often with Curlews. L 36-41, WS 80-92 cm.

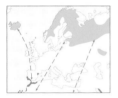

**WHIMBREL** *Numenius phaeopus*. Markedly smaller than smallest Curlews, from which also distinguished by faster wing-beats and at close range by two dark and one pale stripes on crown. Winter-plumaged Bar-tailed Godwits (p.154) look similar in flight, but have slightly up-curved bills. When breeding, rufous plumage distinctive. Song resembles Curlew, but flight call, a tittering trill, is distinctive, though Curlew's 'tyuyuyuyu' alarm call can be confusing. High northern sub-Arctic and Arctic moors and tundra; in migration further S; on migration and in winter mainly coastal. L 40-42, WS 76-89 cm.    ●sMw

with dark underwing

alboaxillaris

hudsonicus

phaeopus

S Ural breeding ssp.*alboaxillaris* is larger and paler, with stripes on crown and barring on flanks less distinct and rump, belly and underwing all whiter (cf. Slender-billed Curlew). N American ssp.*hudsonicus*, a rare vagrant, has darker underwing and lower back and rump grey-brown, uniform with rest of greyer-brown upperparts. Almost extinct little-whimbrel-sized **Eskimo Curlew** *N. borealis*, not recorded in region since 1887, has more heavily barred breast and distinctive Y-markings on flanks.

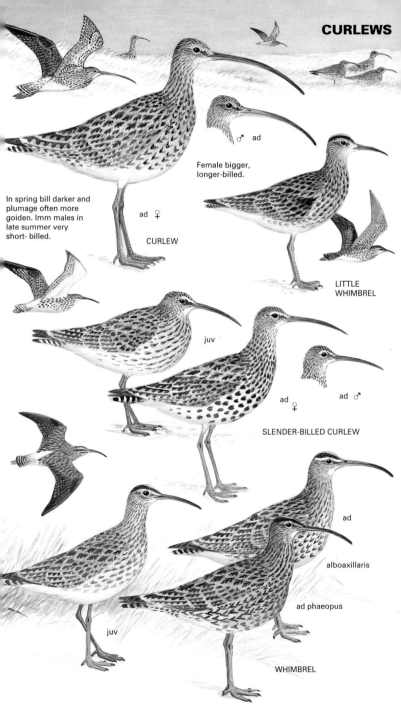

**CURLEWS**

♂ ad

Female bigger,
longer-billed.

In spring bill darker and
plumage often more
golden. Imm males in
late summer very
short- billed.

ad ♀

CURLEW

LITTLE
WHIMBREL

juv

ad ♀

ad ♂

SLENDER-BILLED CURLEW

ad

alboaxillaris

ad phaeopus

juv

WHIMBREL

**Shanks and Sandpipers**: *Tringa*. pp.158-161. Long-billed and usually long-legged medium and small waders, not forming large flocks. In winter by shallow fresh, brackish and salt water.

**SPOTTED REDSHANK** *Tringa erythropus*. When breeding all-dark (aka Dusky Redshank) except for wedge-shaped white rump, shared by no other all-dark wader breeding in region, and white underwing. Always separable from other shanks by long, straight, red-based bill; in winter also from slightly smaller Redshank by no white on wings, white supercilium in front of eye, whiter underparts and longer legs, trailing well behind in flight; and from slightly larger Greenshank by red legs. Call-note diagnostic, a clear disyllabic 'too-it' or 'tchu-eet', also a scolding 'chick'. Swampy places in forest, heath and tundra, in winter mainly by fresh and brackish water. L 29-31 cm.  ⊙Mw

**REDSHANK** *Tringa totanus*. Very noisy, the only wader with broad white hindwings, which with white rump conspicuous in flight. Grey-brown with no supercilium, paler beneath; bill and legs orange-red, cf. Ruff (p.150). Has many loud, yelping, often musical cries, mainly based on 'teu'; also a scolding 'teuk, teuk, teuk'. Musical song based on 'tyu', often ending with a repeated yodelling 'tahudi'. Fast, direct flight with quick clipped wing-beats; at rest often bobs head. Grassy fresh and coastal marshes, damp grassland, wet heaths, in winter mainly on estuaries, muddy shores. L 27-29 cm.  ●RmW

**MARSH SANDPIPER** *Tringa stagnatilis*. Like a small, graceful Greenshank, but with a thin straight bill and longer (occasionally yellow) legs, which project further beyond tail. When breeding, upperparts appear spotted darker; in winter greyer, with white face and forehead and distinct dark shoulder. White on rump more elongated than in Wood Sandpiper (p.160). Calls like but higher-pitched than other shanks, e.g. 'teu' and 'chik'. Marshy freshwater margins. L 22-24 cm.  -A

**Lesser Yellowlegs** *T. flavipes*. Vagrant, slightly smaller N American counterpart of Redshank, differing in yellow legs, dark grey bill and dark wings with white only on rump and tail. Recalls Wood Sandpiper (p.160), but legs longer and no supercilium. Call a single or double 'yew'. Mainly freshwater margins. L 23-25 cm.  -A

**Greater Yellowlegs** *T. melanoleuca*. Rare vagrant, slightly larger N American counterpart of Greenshank, differing in yellow legs and white on tail and rump not extending up the back; bill dark grey, slightly upturned. Call a loud, greenshank-like triple 'chew'; cf. Lesser Yellowlegs. L 29-31 cm.  -V

Both very similar, Greater has more powerful flight.

**GREENSHANK** *Tringa nebularia*. The region's largest breeding shank, paler than Redshank (especially in winter) and showing no white on upperwings in flight, but white of rump extending further up back; bill grey-blue, slightly upcurved, legs pale olive-green. Main call, diagnostic and almost always uttered when flushed, a clear, far-carrying triple or quadruple 'chu', also an insistent redshank-like 'chip'; song a fluty, repeated 'ru-tu'. Marshes, bogs, moors, swampy forest clearings; in winter by both fresh and salt water. L 30-33 cm.  ●sMw

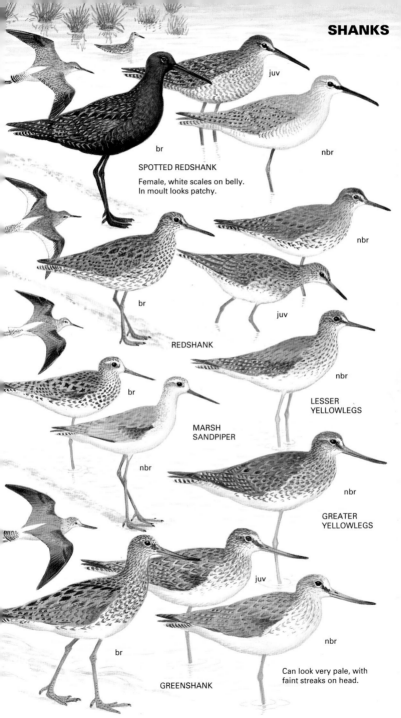

juv

br

nbr

**SPOTTED REDSHANK**

Female, white scales on belly.
In moult looks patchy.

nbr

br

juv

nbr

**REDSHANK**

br

**LESSER
YELLOWLEGS**

**MARSH
SANDPIPER**

nbr

nbr

**GREATER
YELLOWLEGS**

juv

br

nbr

**GREENSHANK**

Can look very pale, with
faint streaks on head.

**WOOD SANDPIPER** *Tringa glareola*. Smaller, slimmer, more elegant, paler, longer-necked and longer-legged than Green Sandpiper, and with less conspicuous white rump, more prominent white supercilium, greyish underwing and yellow or pale green legs, projecting further beyond tail in flight; has similar towering flight when flushed. Cf. larger Lesser Yellowlegs (p.158), which lacks supercilium. Calls distinctive, a rather flat 'wee-wee-wee' or 'wit-wit-wit' flight call, a more musical, greenshank-like 'chew-ew' and a shrill 'chip-chip-chip' alarm note; song liquid and musical, redshank-like. Swampy bogs, scrub and woodland; in winter mainly by fresh water. L 19-21 cm. ⊙sM

**GREEN SANDPIPER** *Tringa ochropus*. Larger and darker than Wood Sandpiper, its house-martin-like white rump contrasting strongly with the green-tinged blackish upperparts, dark underwing, more heavily barred tail-tip and dark green legs; larger and shorter-necked than Common Sandpiper, but without its bow-winged flight. When flushed dashes up and towers with a shrill 'weet-a-weet', much louder than Wood, before flying off with a rather snipe-like flight. Song liquid and musical. Swampy woodlands, nesting in old nests of other birds; in winter mainly by fresh water. L 21-24 cm. ●Mw(b)

**Solitary Sandpiper** *T. solitaria*. Rare vagrant, N American counterpart of Green Sandpiper; between Green and Wood in size, differing from both in black rump but white bars on sides of tail, and from Wood in dark underwing and slightly longer bill. Call like Green but quieter. L 18-21 cm. -V

**TEREK SANDPIPER** *Xenus cinereus*. The region's only small wader with a markedly upcurved bill; otherwise not unlike a small Redshank (p.158), especially in flight, but has longer bill, shorter yellow legs, two black lines along back, and white on wings only in narrow triangle along trailing edge. Calls include trills based on 'du', and, whimbrel-like, on 'wit' and an alarm note 'tu-li'; song a trisyllabic musical whistle. Active feeder, with forward-tripping gait; often bobs head like Common Sandpiper. Breeds by fresh water in forest and scrub, in winter on estuaries. L 22-24 cm. -V

**COMMON SANDPIPER** *Actitis hypoleucos*. Small and short-legged, best told from other grey-brown waders by flight and call notes and generally solitary habits. Typically flies low over the water with a shrill 'twee-wee-wee' call and flickering wings, which appear bowed on downward stroke; does not tower when flushed; in circular display flight song is based on call. Often perches on low objects, constantly bobbing tail and/or head. Freshwater streams and lakes and sheltered inlets of the sea; in winter mainly by fresh water. L 19-21 cm. ●Smw

**Spotted Sandpiper** *A. macularia*. Vagrant, the N American counterpart of Common Sandpiper; when breeding has black-spotted underparts. In winter best told by greyer, more uniform upperparts and sides of breast, shorter tail and wing bar, yellow legs and bill base, and flight call, based on 'weet'. Unspotted juv has bolder bars on coverts, less barring on mantle. L 18-20 cm. -A(b)

# SANDPIPERS

**WOOD SANDPIPER**

br

nbr

**GREEN SANDPIPER**

br

nbr

**SOLITARY SANDPIPER**

Flight often low over water.

**TEREK SANDPIPER**

br

juv

nbr

**COMMON SANDPIPER**

br

juv

Common

Spotted

**SPOTTED SANDPIPER**

br

juv

nbr

Feeding in deep water.

**Stilt Sandpiper** *Micropalama himantopus*. Transatlantic vagrant, shank-like in structure, *Calidris*-like in plumage, in winter like a large winter Curlew Sandpiper (p.144), but with longer yellow-green legs, projecting well beyond tail in flight; a longer bill, curved only at tip; more marked pale eye-stripe; and no pale wing bar. When breeding, underparts barred and ear coverts rufous. Calls a soft trill and a yellowlegs-like 'yew'. L 18-24 cm.                                                    -V

**Turnstones**: *Arenariinae*. Small short-billed, short-legged, plover-like, coastal waders, inland only on migration.

**TURNSTONE** *Arenaria interpres*. The only small, short-billed wader looking black and white both at rest and in flight; legs short, orange. When breeding, tortoiseshell appearance of mantle also distinctive. Calls a twittering 'kititit', a clear 'keeoo, keeoo' and a grunting 'tuk-a-tuk'. Coastal tundra; on small islands in Baltic. In winter in small flocks, mainly on rocky and weedy seashores, where turns over small stones and weed in foraging, often with Purple Sandpipers (p.148); non-breeders often summer well S of breeding range. L 22-24 cm.          ●MW

**Phalaropes**: *Phalaropodinae*. Small, rather tame and confiding aquatic waders, grey and white in winter, with some rufous when breeding; feet lobed. Males smaller and duller than females. Flight weak, but swim buoyantly, like tiny gulls, often spinning round in circles and picking insects off surface; much the smallest swimming birds, except for a few all-dark petrels. Moorland and tundra with shallow pools.

**GREY PHALAROPE** *Phalaropus fulicarius*. Easily identified when breeding by rufous underparts and sides of neck, with contrasting white face-patch; in winter has uniformly grey back. Always has clear white wing bar and black bill (yellow at tip in male, at base in female), broader and stouter than other phalaropes. Juv brown above and deep pink on neck and breast. Call a low 'twit'. Flight slower than Red-necked. Winters well out at sea. L 20-22 cm.                              ○Mw

**RED-NECKED PHALAROPE** *Phalaropus lobatus*. The smallest phalarope; when breeding orange-red throat and sides of neck contrast with dark grey head and white chin and underparts. Bill all-black, thin, almost needle-like, appearing longer than Grey Phalarope; in winter has more mottled back, but may be insepa-rable at sea. White wing bar shows in graceful, rather swallow-like flight. Juv as Grey. Calls 'twit', 'tirric, tirric' and a curious little pre-flight grunt. Winters well out at sea. L 18-19 cm.   ○sM

Looks like a rather pot-bellied shank.

**Wilson's Phalarope** *P. tricolor*. Almost annual transatlantic vagrant, the largest, longest-legged and longest-billed phalarope, with jizz somewhat like Lesser Yellowlegs (p.158) or large Wood Sandpiper (p.160); also has white rump, long needle-like bill, yellow legs and no wing bar. When breeding has bold blackish stripe from eye down neck. Swims less than other phalaropes, wintering on land and readily walking and running. L 22-24 cm.                    -A

# TURNSTONE, PHALAROPES

br

nbr

juv

nbr

**STILT SANDPIPER**

br

♂ br

♀ br

nbr

juv

**TURNSTONE**

♀ br

♂ br

nbr

juv

nbr

**GREY PHALAROPE**

r

♂ br

nbr

juv

nbr

**RED-NECKED PHALAROPE**

nbr

♀ br

♂ br

juv

nbr

**WILSON'S PHALAROPE**

● SKUAS: *Stercorariidae*. Slightly hook-billed gull-like seabirds; sexes alike. Piratical pursuit to make other birds disgorge their prey is much more persistent than that of imm gulls. Juv/imm very variable, like juv/imm larger gulls (p.178), but barred below, with pale fringes to mantle and tail feathers, white wing-patches, slightly projecting central tail feathers, and more angled wings. Barren moorlands, tundra; coastal on migration, well out to sea in winter. Aka Jaegers (N America).

**GREAT SKUA** *Catharacta skua*. The region's largest and heaviest skua, like a bulky imm Herring Gull (p.172), but usually rather darker and with shorter wings and tail and conspicuous white wing-flashes above and below, which are smaller in more rufous (especially below) juv/imm. Flight heavy, but remarkably agile when chasing other birds; also a harrier-like display flight, with wings raised. Calls 'a-er' in flight and a deep 'tuk, tuk' in nest defence. Aka Bonxie (Shetlands). L 53-58, WS 132-40 cm.                                                                    ⊙Sm

**South Polar Skua** *C. maccormicki*, a rare vagrant from southern oceans, is slightly smaller, slimmer and more agile, with bill smaller, forehead flatter, white wing-patch narrower and tail more wedge-shaped, the central feathers longer. Grey morph very like adult Great Skua, and dark morph very like juv. L 53, WS 127 cm.         [-V]

**ARCTIC SKUA** *Stercorarius parasiticus*. Generally the region's commonest skua, intermediate between Pomarine and Long-tailed, with size, head and bill as Common Gull (p.174); central tail feathers pointed, projecting 8-10 cm. Dark form more frequent southwards; pale form has cheeks, neck and underparts creamy white, but puzzling intermediates occur, e.g. brown with distinct dark cap and paler cheeks; and brown with yellow neck-ring. Bill and legs dark. Juv/imm usually much darker than imm gulls, juvs tinged rufous; bill dark-tipped. Flight graceful, buoyant, even shearwater-like. On breeding grounds has a wailing 'ka-aaow' and a deeper 'tuk, tuk'. L 41-46, WS 110-125 cm.                                                       ⊙SM

**POMARINE SKUA** *Stercorarius pomarinus*. Larger and heavier, the broader-based wings with larger white patches than Arctic; head and bill herring-gull-like. Diagnostic twisting of adult's blunt and elongated (to 10 cm) central tail feathers often hard to see. Pale form much more frequent than dark, usually with breast-band; intermediates rare. Juv/imm bulkier, and juv less rufous, than Arctic, with stouter bill and blunt central tail feathers. Flight like large gull, less active than Arctic, more so than Great. Call a sharp 'which-yew', also more gull-like notes. L 46-51, WS 125-138 cm.                                 ○M

**LONG-TAILED SKUA** *Stercorarius longicaudus*. The smallest and slimmest skua, adults with very long (12-25 cm) pointed central tail feathers, distinctive uniform dark underwing and dark lower belly and under tail coverts, and usually no breast-band; dark phase may not exist. Juv/imm dark or pale with many intermediates, and have contrasting pale hind neck, no rufous tinge and much less white in wings than other skuas; bill mainly dark. Flight the most graceful, tern-like and often shearwater-like of any skua. A high-pitched 'kreee' on breeding grounds. L 48-53, WS 105-117 cm.                        ○M

**SKUAS**

ad

South
Polar
Skua

ad

juv

GREAT SKUA

dark br

br light

juv

ARCTIC SKUA

br light

br dark

br light

juv

POMARINE SKUA

br light

br

br

juv

LONG-TAILED SKUA

● GULLS: *Laridae: Larinae*, pp.166-179. Gregarious, long-winged, web-footed seabirds; sexes alike. Larger and stouter than most terns (p.180), with broader, blunter wings (in flight and WS, pp.176-179), tail usually square-ended, and longer legs, and rarely diving. Some larger species have white heads flecked with grey-brown in winter. Juv/imm start brown with dark band near tail-tip, the larger ones taking 3-4 years to become fully adult; illustrated on pp.176-179. Many species are scavengers. Breeding colonies, often noisy, on cliffs or flat ground by the sea and inland.

**AUDOUIN'S GULL** *Larus audouinii*. Between Common and Herring Gull in size and appearance, differing from both in narrower wings, the white spots at the tip smaller, but obvious in flight and at rest; also in red eye-rim, dark green legs, and tricoloured bill, red with black band near drooping yellow tip, but looking all-black at a distance. Juv/imm pale brown with grey crown and hind neck; bill yellow. Calls a hoarse 'kiaou' and a quieter 'crick, crick'; alarm call a goose-like 'guggugguggugg'. Rocky islands, flat coasts; in winter sandy coasts or at sea. L 48-52 cm.

**SLENDER-BILLED GULL** *Larus genei*. White forewing blaze makes it like a large winter Black-headed (p.168), but has longer neck, less steep forehead, dark ear-spot fainter or absent and longer *not* especially slender, bill, drooping at tip, and sometimes looking blackish. When breeding, lower breast and belly strongly suffused pink, sometimes quite bright. Juv/imm have bill and legs orange-yellow. Calls lower-pitched than Black-headed, including 'kau, kau', recalling Gull-billed Tern (p.184). Fresh and brackish lakes, coastal lagoons, wintering mainly on coast. L 42-44 cm.                          -V

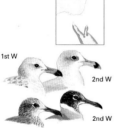

1st W

2nd W

**SOOTY GULL** *Larus hemprichii*. The size of a Common Gull, dark brown apart from white back of neck, tail and belly; eye dark with red ring; bill long, yellowish with dark band and slightly drooping red tip; and legs grey-green to yellowish. Cf. White-eyed Gull. 1st-year birds have brown back and breast band and paler legs like 2nd-year White-eyed. Juv lacks white collar and has black-tipped greyish bill. Call a herring-gull-like mewing whistle. Prefers perching on rocks or buoys to resting on water; has piratical habits. L 42-45 cm.

2nd W

1st W

**WHITE-EYED GULL** *Larus leucophthalmus*. Slightly smaller and slenderer than Sooty; adult with black head and throat, conspicuous white ring round brown eye, paler breast, dark grey upperparts, longer and slenderer black-tipped red bill, and yellow legs. In 2nd year back and wings brownish. Juv dark grey-brown; bill of juv black, of imm red-brown. Calls less high-pitched than Sooty. World range Red Sea and Gulf of Aden, vagrant to E Mediterranean. L 39-43 cm.

**GREAT BLACK-HEADED GULL** *Larus ichthyaetus*. The only large gull with a dark hood when breeding, and has distinctive white patch round dark red eye-ring. In winter like a large, rather dark, long-winged Herring Gull (p.172) with a blackish face-patch. At all times has distinctive tricoloured bill-tipped bill, heavy and slightly drooping at tip, and yellowish legs. Bill shape and usually a dark patch behind eye best distinctions from other imm gulls. Rather silent when not breeding, but has a loud harsh croak. Breeds by salt or brackish water, winters along coasts; by fresh water only on passage. L 57-61 cm.     -V

# GULLS

juv

br

AUDOUIN'S GULL

br

SLENDER-BILLED GULL

br

br

SOOTY GULL

WHITE-EYED GULL

ad nbr

br

GREAT BLACK-HEADED GULL

**BLACK-HEADED GULL** *Larus ridibundus*. The smaller of the region's two commonest gulls, with a chocolate-brown hood (not extending on to nape) when breeding, turning white with dark spot behind eye in winter. The region's only breeding gull (except Slender-billed, p.166) with conspicuous white flash on forewing, with no white spots on the black tip; bill and legs red. Juv richly mottled warm brown. 1st-winter still has brown-speckled wings; many 1st-year breeders do not develop complete hood. Calls harsh and varied; a raucous 'kraah' is frequent. Bogs, marshes, islands in lakes, dunes, shingle; in winter on coasts and estuaries, also widespread inland by fresh water and on farmland, short turf and waste ground; a typical urban bird in N W Europe. L 34-37 cm.  ●RsmW

**LITTLE GULL** *Larus minutus*. The smallest, most tern-like of all gulls, with rather rounded wings and diagnostic dark grey underwing. Breeding hood black, extending on to nape; no black on wing-tips, bill black, legs red. Diagonal wing bar separates brown-backed juv from all region's breeding gulls; grey-backed imm differs from imm Kittiwake (p.174) in dark crown and ear coverts. Calls a rather harsh, sharp 'kek-kek-kek' and 'ka-ka-ka'. Cf. marsh terns (p.186), which in winter plumage have hard-to-see shallowly forked grey tail, partly underwing and sharply defined white shoulder. Freshwater pools, marshes, bogs; on passage at fresh and coastal waters; in winter at sea. L 25-27 cm.  ⊙Mw(b)

**MEDITERRANEAN GULL** *Larus melanocephalus*. Slightly larger than Black-headed, and has whole head and upper neck black (not dark brown) when breeding. Smaller and stockier than Common (p.174), and with red bill and legs. Differs from both in white wing-tips and bill drooped at tip, and in winter more prominent dark patch behind eye. Juv has distinctive dark-chequered upperparts; 1st-year imm has a half-hood and central wing panel paler and more conspicuous than Common; 2nd-year has black wing-tips but no white spots. Calls higher-pitched than Common but deeper than Black-headed. Breeds on grassy marshes and other flat ground by coast; in winter in coastal waters. L 36-38 cm.  ○rmW

juv

Sabine's Gull

**Bonaparte's Gull** *L. philadelphia*. Transatlantic vagrant, very like a small Black-headed, but breeding hood greyish-black and covering nape, nape still grey in winter, underwing all-white except at tip, and a shorter slenderer black bill; imm has darker diagonal wing bar. Flight more tern-like, with faster wing-beats. L 28-30 cm.  -V

**SABINE'S GULL** *Larus sabini*. A small tern-like gull, the region's only one with an (often hard to see) forked tail and forewings strikingly black at all ages, with triangular white trailing edge (cf. distant imm Kittiwakes, p.174). Breeding adult has very dark grey hood, extending over nape; legs and yellow-tipped bill blackish. Juv has grey-brown head, mantle and wing coverts; tail-tip dark. Harsh, grating cry, like Arctic Tern (p.182), but briefer. Marshy tundra by fresh or coastal waters; winter at sea. L 27-32 cm.  ○M

st w

nbr

br

br

**BLACK-HEADED GULL**

nbr

br

br

nbr

**LITTLE GULL**

nbr

br

br

nbr

**MEDITERRANEAN GULL**

br

nbr

br

nbr

**BONAPARTE'S GULL**
see also next page

nbr

br

br

nbr

**SABINE'S GULL**

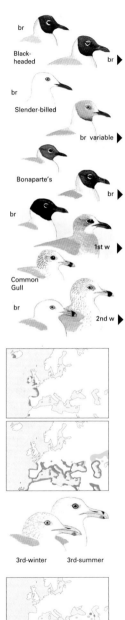

br

Black-headed — br

br

Slender-billed

br variable ▶

Bonaparte's

br ▶

br

1st w

Common Gull

br

2nd w ▶

3rd-winter    3rd-summer

**Brown-headed Gull** *L. brunnicephalus*. Increasing vagrant from C Asia to SE of region. Very like smaller Black-headed Gull (p.168), with which often associates and from which always best told by large white patch ('mirror') near wing-tip; also has paler brown head, bill stouter and eye whitish. L 41-46 cm.

**Grey-headed Gull** *L. cirrocephalus*. Rare vagrant from tropical Africa to S of region, with distinctive grey hood when breeding. In winter has red bill and legs like smaller Black-headed Gull (p.168), but white spots on black wing-tips like Common (p.174) and Brown-headed Gulls; forehead more sloping and underwing darker than Brown-headed. 1st winter may have dark ear spot, but if not can be separated from same-sized Slender-billed Gull (p.166) by darker mantle. Flight like Black-headed; regularly follows ships. L 39-42 cm.

**Franklin's Gull** *L. pipixcan*. Transatlantic vagrant, a rather small gull, broader-winged than Black-headed (p.168); darker grey than Common (p.174); and with shorter and rounder wings than Laughing Gull. Has white-black-white pattern at wing-tip, roundish head, slender bill, and breeding hood not extending to nape, white eye-patch conspicuous, and half-hood and cheeks dark grey in winter. L 32-36 cm.                                                                        -V

**Laughing Gull** *L. atricilla*. Transatlantic vagrant, larger than Black-headed Gull (p.168); blackish breeding hood extends on to nape, broken white eye-ring (also in 1st-winter); nape and cheeks grey in winter; upperparts dark grey, the trailing edge white, no white in black wing-tips; bill stout, drooped at tip, red to black, legs red-brown to black. L 36-41 cm.                                                        -V

**Ring-billed Gull** *L. delawarensis*. Rare transatlantic visitor to N W Europe. In winter like a large adult winter Common Gull (p.174) with longer legs, paler back, a narrower, squarer, white tertial fringe, and a heavier, duller yellow bill with a slightly better defined black band near bill tip; or a very small Herring Gull (p.172) with greenish-yellow legs and black band near tip but no red spot on bill; differs from both in pale eyes, smaller white spots near wing-tips and dark underside of primaries. Juv/imm Common (p.174) and Herring (p.172) are much less boldly spotted on breast and flanks. Pitch of calls and buoyancy of flight both between Common and Herring. L 43-47 cm.          -A

**YELLOW-LEGGED GULL** *Larus cacchinans*. Now regarded as distinct from Herring Gull (p.172), forming separate colonies in overlap zone in W France, and differing in its yellow legs, greyish-yellow eye, vermilion eye-ring, deeper yellow bill with larger red patch and darker (medium grey) mantle, and in winter no or fewer and paler head streaks. Imms' primaries usually uniformly dark, like Lesser Blackback (p.172). L 55-67 cm.    ○M

Ssp.*cacchinans* (Black Sea) described above; ssp.*michahellis* (W France to Morocco and Mediterranean), variable in size, interbreeds with ssp.*cacchinans* in Balkans; ssp.*atlantis* (Azores, Canaries), is smallest and darkest, most having only a small mirror at tip of outer primary.

**ARMENIAN GULL** *Larus armenicus*. Smaller and somewhat darker than Yellow-legged Gull, with more rounded head, neck appearing shorter in flight, and more black on wing tips. Especially in winter has distinctive black subterminal band on shorter blunter bill, often with a dark mark next to red patch on bill and dark eyes. Mountain lakes. L 55-60 cm.

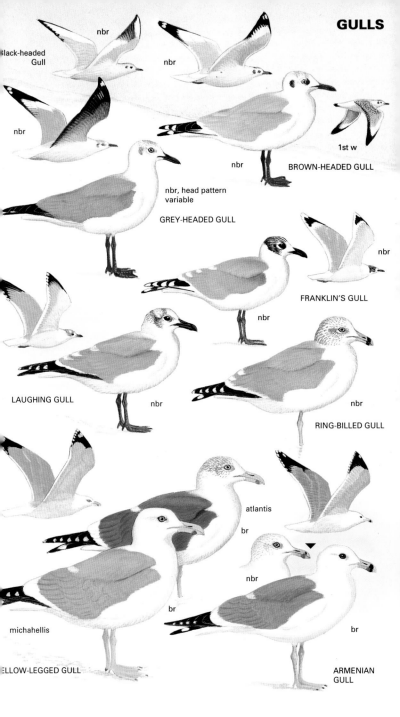

# GULLS

Black-headed Gull

nbr

nbr

nbr

nbr

1st w

BROWN-HEADED GULL

nbr

nbr, head pattern variable

GREY-HEADED GULL

FRANKLIN'S GULL

nbr

nbr

LAUGHING GULL

nbr

nbr

RING-BILLED GULL

atlantis

br

nbr

michahellis

br

br

YELLOW-LEGGED GULL

ARMENIAN GULL

**ad w**       **2nd w**

**HERRING GULL** *Larus argentatus*. The region's commonest large gull; variable in size (males larger) and mantle colour, pale to slate-grey; head streaked ash-grey in winter. Has yellow eye and yellow bill with red spot; most have pink legs; cf smaller Common Gull (p.174). Juv indistinguishable from juv Lesser Blackback; imm darker and smaller-billed than Great Blackback and unlike Lesser Blackback has inner primaries paler than outer. Has many wailing, yelping calls, especially 'kee-yow' and a loud echoing 'gah-gah-gah'. Breeds colonially on cliffs and flat ground by sea, also on moors and buildings; in winter on coasts and inland. L 52-60 cm. ●RW

Ssp.*argenteus* (Iceland, Britain, Ireland, W Germany) is silver grey on mantle and wings; slightly larger ssp.*argentatus* (Scandinavia) is a shade darker; ssp. *omissus* (E Baltic) is palest-backed and has yellow legs, as do some *argentatus* in Norway. Cf. Yellow-legged Gull (p.170).

Includes ssp.heuglini

**LESSER BLACKBACK** *Larus fuscus* The only gull with dark grey to black mantle and wings and white head and underparts, except for appreciably larger Great Blackback, from which differs in less stout bill, pale yellow eye and yellow legs, though most imms (cf Herring Gull) and all juvs have pinkish legs. Usually larger Herring has mantle always paler, legs and wings shorter and bill stouter, and calls distinctly less gruff. Habitat as Herring, but generally nests on flat ground, sometimes in same colonies. L 52-67 cm. ●Srmw

Sspp.*graellsii* and *intermedius* (N W Europe) have mantle less black than Great Blackback; ssp.*heuglini* (Arctic Russia; possibly a Herring Gull ssp.) paler still, with contrasting black wing-tips. Ssp.*fuscus* (Scandinavia) has back often as dark as Great Blackback and head less streaked in winter.

**GREAT BLACKBACK** *Larus marinus*. The region's largest gull, like a large Lesser Blackback, with very heavy bill, upperparts almost black, legs always pink and eye usually pale grey. Juv paler than Lesser Blackback and Herring, and with chequered upperparts. Voice lower-pitched than Herring, with a deep, goblin-like chuckle when breeding. Breeds, often singly, mainly on sea cliffs or marine islands; in winter mainly coastal, but some inland. L 64-78 cm. ●RW

**GLAUCOUS GULL** *Larus hyperboreus*. Like an outsize Herring Gull, but with the paler grey upperparts having no black wing-tips. Variable in size,from large Herring to small Great Blackback but always has larger head and neck and heavier bill than Iceland Gull, with wings not projecting far beyond tail at rest; adult's yellow eye-ring diagnostic. Juv/imm paler, more oatmeal-coloured than Herring and blackbacks, with dark bill-tip sharply demarcated from paler base. Calls like Herring. Breeds cliffed and rocky coasts; on flat coasts, harbours in winter; rare inland. L 62-68 cm. ○W

**ICELAND GULL** *Larus glaucoides*. Like a small, slenderer Glaucous Gull, with smaller head, shorter bill and longer wings projecting well beyond tail at rest; adult's narrow eye-ring brick-red. Dark bill-tip of juv/imm. not sharply demarcated from paler base. Cf. moulting Herrings with little black on wing-tips, also rare albinistic Herrings. Calls and habitat as Glaucous. Vagrant ssp.*kumlieni* (see p.179). L 52-60 cm. ○W

**GULLS**

ow-legged Gull

Armenian Gull

HERRING GULL

juv

fuscus

LESSER BLACKBACK

graellsii

GREAT BLACKBACK

juv

nbr

Iceland

br

aucous

br

GLAUCOUS GULL

br

br

ICELAND GULL

nbr

Common
winter

Kittiwake
winter

**COMMON GULL** *Larus canus*. Despite its name, not one of the two commonest W European gulls. Smaller than Herring Gull (p.172), with legs and less stout bill uniformly yellow-green; bill with dark band near tip in winter; cf. Ring-billed Gull (p.170). Winter Black-headed (p.168) has red bill and legs, white blaze on forewing and no white spots on black wing-tips. Cf. also Mediterranean (p.168) and Kittiwake. Winter adult has head streaked ash-brown like Herring, not smudged darker, like Black-headed. Juv/imm whiter on tail and underparts than Herring. Most frequent call, 'kee-ya', feebler and higher-pitched than Herring's; also a gobbling 'kak-kak-kak', often heard from migrating flocks in spring. Rocky, sandy and shingly coasts and islands, also inland by fresh water; in winter widespread on coasts, estuaries and farmland, often in towns. L 40-42 cm.     ●RmW

**KITTIWAKE** *Rissa tridactyla*. Slightly smaller and much daintier than Common Gull, with shorter, narrower, more pointed wings and no white spots on their black tips; bill thinner, legs black. In winter head and neck pale grey unstreaked, but with dusky eye-crescent and ear-spot, both variable in extent. Juv/imm (aka Tarrock) have dark collar and strikingly different wing-pattern, with one black bar across forewing and another diagonally from 'elbow' on to hindwing; but cf. Little (tail slightly cleft) and Sabine's Gulls (p.168). At breeding colonies deafening cries of 'kitt-ee-wayke'; also a wailing note and a low 'uk-uk-uk'. Breeds on ledges on sea cliffs and in sea caves, in some places also on coastal dunes, shingle and even buildings; in winter mainly well out at sea, often following ships, though flocks may come inshore. L 38-40 cm.     ●RSmw

**IVORY GULL** *Pagophila eburnea*. The region's only uniformly and strikingly pure white gull (but beware albinos of other gulls), with no streaks or smudges on head in winter; plump-bodied with shortish wings pointed and distinctively broad-based; bill short, yellow with red tip; eye-ring vermilion; legs short, black. Imm's 'ermine' plumage (p.177), unique among region's seabirds, has greyish face in front of eye and rows of black spots on wings; bill grey, with paler tip. Harsh 'krii-krii', 'keer' and 'karr' notes recall Arctic Tern (p.182). Nests on cliffs and rocky ground near sea; winters mainly near edge of pack ice. L 40-43 cm.     -V

**Ross's Gull** *Rhodostethia rosea*. The region's second smallest gull; breeding adult combines narrow black collar, strong suffusion of pink on underparts and small head, long wedge-shaped white tail, grey underwing, no black wing-tips, tiny black bill and red legs. In winter black collar goes, pink fades and creamy white head, tail and underparts contrast with pale grey mantle and wings. Imm like imm Little Gull (p.168), with similar 'W' wing pattern and black triangle at tip of wedge-shaped tail. Calls high-pitched, most frequent note 'e-vu, e-vu'. Breeds on grassy, wooded tundra; winters on Arctic coasts and at sea, vagrant on coasts further S. L 30-32 cm.     -V

1st W ▶

Little Gull 1st W

174

Common

br

COMMON GULL

Ring-billed
p.170

Ring-billed Gull
p.170

ad w

KITTIWAKE

br

juv

ad

ad

IVORY GULL

n br

juv

br

n br

ROSS'S GULL

GULLS in flight. Gulls (Larinae) usually have broader and less sharply pointed wings than terns, with flight buoyant, heavier and less graceful, and often soaring. Most species will swoop down to surface of water to seize food morsels. Most illustrations below are of imms and juvs, the adults being well illustrated on previous pages.

**Sabine's Gull** *Larus sabini*, WS 90-100 cm. Flight buoyant, graceful, comparatively tern-like, nearer Little Gull than Kittiwake.

**Kittiwake** *Rissa tridactyla*, WS 95-120 cm. Flight like Common Gull with faster wing-beats, buoyant and graceful, leisurely when calm, but more determined in strong winds, with sharply angled wings and shearwater-like glides.

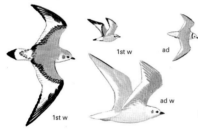

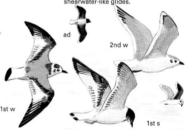

**Ross's Gull** *Rhodostethia rosea*, WS 90-100 cm. Flight rather slow but agile, similar to Little Gull, but long wings pointed and held angled like terns.

**Little Gull** *Larus minutus*, WS 75-80 cm. Flight hesitant, graceful and wavering, resembling the marsh terns in the way it habitually stoops to pick up food from water surface; wing-tips blunter than most gulls.

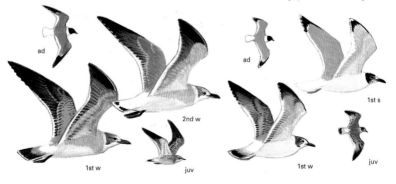

**Laughing Gull** *Larus atricilla*, WS 100-125 cm. Flight buoyant, similar to Black-headed Gull, but with rakish appearance due to longer wings.

**Franklin's Gull** *Larus pipixcan*, WS 85-95 cm. Flight almost dainty, sometimes with a distinctive fluttering action; wing-tips more rounded than Black-headed Gull.

1st w

ad

ad

1st w

1st s

1st s

juv

ad w

**Black-headed Gull** *Larus ridibundus*, WS 100-110 cm. Flight strong and buoyant over long distances, more wavering and almost tern-like at other times. Wing-beats noticeably faster than Common Gull. Occasionally dives from air.

**Bonaparte's Gull** *Larus philadelphia*, WS 90-100 cm. Flight more buoyant and tern-like than Black-headed Gull, with faster wing-beats. Underside of adults' primaries translucent in flight.

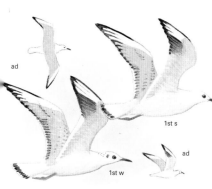

ad

1st s

1st w

ad

**Slender-billed Gull** *Larus genei*, WS 100-110 cm. Flight similar to Black-headed Gull, but wing-beats often slightly slower.

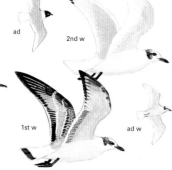

ad

2nd w

1st w

ad w

**Mediterranean Gull** *Larus melanocephalus*, WS 92-100 cm. Flight markedly buoyant, with shallower, more measured wing-beats, more frequent glides and wings less angled than Black-headed Gull.

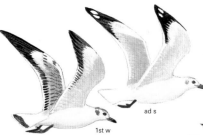

ad s

1st w

**Brown-headed Gull** *Larus brunnicephalus*. WS 41-43 cm. Similar to Black-headed Gull, regularly following ships.

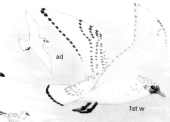

ad

1st w

**Ivory Gull** *Pagophila eburnea*, WS 108-120 cm. Flight buoyant, similar to Kittiwake, often with feet hanging down.

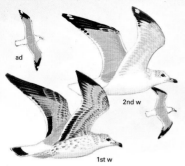

**Common Gull** *Larus canus*. WS 110-130 cm. Flight more graceful than Herring Gull, but less so than Black-headed, against which often makes skua-like piratical attacks.

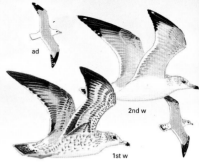

**Ring-billed Gull** *Larus delawarensis*. WS 120-135 cm. Flight more buoyant than Herring Gull, less so than Common Gull.

**Yellow-legged Gull** *Larus cacchinans*. WS 137-142 cm. Flight as Herring Gull.

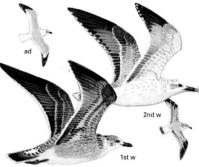

**Audouin's Gull** *Larus audouinii*. WS 115-140 cm. Flight buoyant, gannet-like.

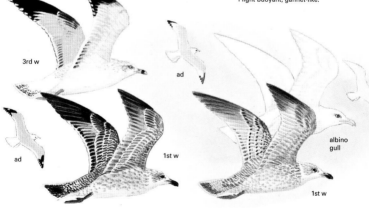

**Herring Gull** *Larus argentatus*. WS 138-155 cm. Flight strong, deliberate, often soaring and gliding.

**Herring x Glaucous Gull**. *Larus argentatus x L. hyperboreus*. Frequent and confusing in Iceland; also occasional in Britain.

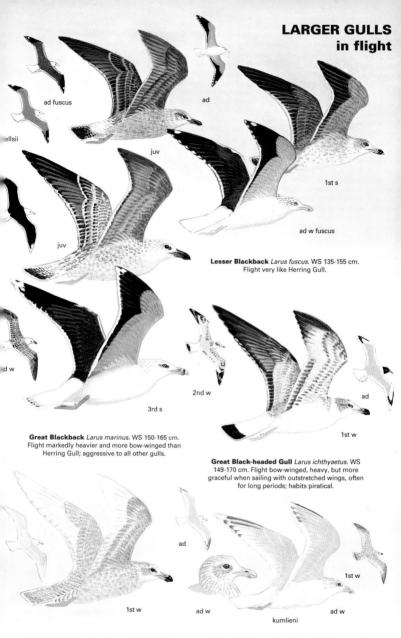

# LARGER GULLS
## in flight

ad fuscus

ellsii

ad

juv

juv

1st s

ad w fuscus

**Lesser Blackback** *Larus fuscus*. WS 135-155 cm.
Flight very like Herring Gull.

d w

2nd w

ad

3rd s

1st w

**Great Blackback** *Larus marinus*. WS 150-165 cm.
Flight markedly heavier and more bow-winged than
Herring Gull; aggressive to all other gulls.

**Great Black-headed Gull** *Larus ichthyaetus*. WS
149-170 cm. Flight bow-winged, heavy, but more
graceful when sailing with outstretched wings, often
for long periods; habits piratical.

ad

1st w

ad w

kumlieni

1st w

ad w

**Glaucous Gull** *Larus hyperboreus*. WS 150-165 cm.
Flight much heavier and more ponderous than
Iceland, like Great Blackback.

**Iceland Gull** *Larus glaucoides kumlieni*. Compared
with nominate ssp. (p.172), this vagrant ssp. from
Canada has grey markings in adult's wing tips.

● TERNS: *Sterninae*. Most terns are like graceful small gulls, with longer wings, held at an angle in their buoyant flight, well-forked tail, and thinner, more pointed bills, often held almost vertically downward as they hover and dive for small fish.

**Sea terns**: *Sterna*. Most species are pale to mid-grey above and white below, adults with black crown and nape, the forehead whitening in winter. Check size, bill colour and calls. Juvs speckled blackish or brown above. Flight often with more markedly up-and-down wing-beats than gulls. Very noisy when breeding; nest on ground, usually sand, shingle or rocky marine islands.

**CASPIAN TERN** *Sterna caspia*. The largest tern, readily told from same-sized gulls by black cap, very stout dagger-like red bill and shortly forked tail; legs black. Separable from somewhat smaller Royal by heavier, dark-tipped red (in winter sometimes orange-yellow) bill, shorter tail and dark undersides of wing-tips in flight; in winter also by whole forehead and crown streaked. Juv/imm like winter adult, but with dark patches on back (fewer in imm) and tail tipped black. Call a gruff 'kaah' or 'kaa-uh'. Flight heavy, like a large gull or a diminutive Gannet (p.36). Breeds by fresh and salt water; in winter mainly coastal. L 47-54, WS 130-145 cm.                    -A

nbr

The heads of all black-capped terns become whiter in winter with black remaining only towards the nape.

**ROYAL TERN** *Sterna maxima*. A vagrant, transatlantic or from tropical Africa. The region's second largest tern, less heavily built than Caspian, from which told by less heavy, uniformly orange-red bill, paler undersides of wing-tips, longer tail and more distinct crest; in winter by unstreaked white forehead, acquired before breeding ends. Cf. Swift Tern (yellow bill, white forehead, darker above) and smaller but similarly proportioned Lesser Crested (orange-yellow bill). Call higher-pitched than Caspian, a trilling 'kir'. L 45-50, WS 125-135 cm. -V

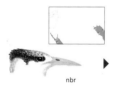

nbr

Black cap much reduced in winter; bill droops at tip.

**SWIFT TERN** *Sterna bergii*. A large tern, slimmer and slightly smaller than Royal, from which adult told by yellow bill, white forehead and much darker ash-grey upperparts, and in winter also by white forecrown (assumed before breeding finishes). Adult of appreciably smaller Lesser Crested has orange-yellow bill (yellow in winter), paler upperparts and usually much narrower white forehead. Juv/imm have dark wing-bar, unlike Royal, but cf. imm Lesser Crested. Calls a harsh 'kek-kek-kek' and a hoarse 'krow'. Aka Crested Tern. L 46-49, WS 125-130 cm.

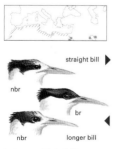

straight bill ▶

nbr

br

nbr            longer bill

Looks very white in field.

**LESSER CRESTED TERN** *Sterna bengalensis*. Much smaller, more graceful, shorter-winged and longer-tailed than Royal and Swift Terns and slightly smaller than both Sandwich and Gull-billed (p.184), from all of which told by orange or orange-yellow bill of breeding adult and white band on forehead (narrower than in Swift); and from latter two also by yellow bill of winter adult and imm. Imm has much less conspicuous blackish wing bar than imm Swift. Cf. Elegant Tern. L 35-37, WS 92-105 cm.                    -A(b)

**Elegant Tern** *Sterna elegans*. Rare vagrant from E Pacific, intermediate between Royal and Lesser Crested, differing from both in its longer slenderer curved bill, with usually shaggier crest than Lesser Crested; in winter from both in black on head extending forward to include eye; call harsher. L 43, WS 86 cm.          -V

# SEA TERNS

Same-aged Caspians all differ in mantle and wing colour; some get red bills sooner than others.

juv

juv

juv

br

**CASPIAN TERN**

ad br

In winter cap becomes only speckled, not reduced.

br

br

juv

juv

**ROYAL TERN**

In winter erect crest can look very 'brushy'.

juv

br

juv

**SWIFT TERN**

Erect crest makes head look different.

juv

juv

br

ad br

**LESSER CRESTED TERN**

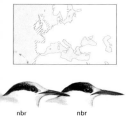

nbr       nbr

Winter head pattern can vary greatly; bill pattern changes during breeding.

**ROSEATE TERN** *Sterna dougallii.* Between larger Sandwich (p.184) and same-sized Common/Arctic in jizz, generally appearing whiter than Common/Arctic and differing in all-black bill (though base reddens from midsummer to early autumn), longer tail streamers, extending well beyond wing-tips at rest, and distinctive spotted-redshank-like 'chew-it' and harsh, grating 'aach, aach' calls. Also has longer bill and legs, pinkish flush on breast when breeding, and less black on wing-tips than Arctic. Juv differs from similar Common/Arctic in all-black bill, black legs and black markings on mantle, and from Common in white band on trailing edge of underwing and much paler shoulder mark and wing bar. Breeds mostly on marine rocks and islands; rare at fresh water, even on migration. L 33-38, WS 72-80 cm. ○S

**ARCTIC TERN** *Sterna paradisaea.* Differs from Common Tern in shorter blood-red bill, not dark-tipped when breeding; shorter legs when perched; shorter tail streamers; greyer neck and breast, contrasting less with grey upperparts and more with white face; and only outer primaries narrowly tipped black, with all bases translucent against light; *portlandica* type more frequent. Juv has all-black bill, grey-tinged head and mantle, less conspicuous black shoulder at rest and bar on forewing in flight, and blacker band on trailing edge of underwing. Calls higher-pitched. Often in same colonies; inland only on tundra; in winter mainly at sea. L 33-35, WS 75-85 cm. ●SM

**COMMON TERN** *Sterna hirundo.* Generally the region's commonest and most widespread tern, differing from Arctic Tern in longer vermilion bill, dark-tipped when breeding (blackish in both in winter); longer legs; neck, breast and underparts white, contrasting with upperparts but not with face; tips of all primaries blackish beneath, but bases of only innermost four showing translucent against the light. Uncommon *portlandica* type keeps white winter forehead when breeding. Juv has pale flesh-pink base of bill, orange legs, white forehead, brownish tinge on head and mantle, conspicuous black shoulder at rest and bar on forewing in flight, and dusky band on trailing edge of underwing. Main calls, shrill and strident, are 'keeerree', 'keeyah' and 'kik-kik-kik'. May breed by fresh water; in winter on southern coasts and at sea. L 31-35, WS 77-98 cm. ●SM

nbr

Common

Forster's       nbr

Forster's winter head with black mask very different from Common.

**Forster's Tern** *S. forsteri.* Transatlantic vagrant, with jizz of small Sandwich (p.184), differing from Common in grey primaries and inside of tail-fork, longer tail, heavier and more orange bill; winter adult and imm have a striking black patch behind eye. Call a diagnostic 'za-a-ap'. L 33-36, WS 73-82 cm. -V

**WHITE-CHEEKED TERN** *Sterna repressa.* Darker grey than Common Tern both above and below, making white cheeks conspicuous; bill blackish-red. In winter has reddish bill, darker grey upperwing and more uniformly grey rump and tail. Flight more hesitant, often recalling Whiskered Tern (p.186), but has more deeply forked tail as well as longer and thinner bill. Calls similar to Common. L 32-34, WS 75-83 cm.

White-cheeked

Whiskered

182

**SEA TERNS**

juv

juv

br

1st w

br

ROSEATE TERN

nbr

juv

autumn

juv

br

br

ARCTIC TERN

juv

juv

1st w

br

br

COMMON TERN

juv

nbr

br

br

FORSTER'S TERN

nbr

juv

nbr

br

br

WHITE-CHEEKED TERN

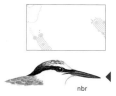

Little br    Saunders's br

br    nbr

Damara Tern *Sterna babaenarum*
possible vagrant from SW Africa.

**LITTLE TERN** *Sterna albifrons*. Much the smallest sea tern, readily told by unique combination of small size, white forehead when breeding, black-tipped yellow bill, orange-yellow legs and quicker, jerkier flight, hovering like a marionette. Longer bill and faster wing-beats than marsh terns (p.186). Juv's whole head and upperparts tinged brown; bill blackish with yellow base. Chief calls 'kik-kik', 'pee-e-eer' and trills. Frequents larger rivers as well as coasts, but uncommon on passage inland. L 22-24, W 48-55 cm. ●Sm

**Saunders's Tern** *Sterna saundersi*. Very similar to and often indistinguishable from Little Tern. Typical breeding individuals have three black (not two greyish) outer primaries, less white on forehead and above the eye, greyer rump and central tail, and darker red-brown legs, often hard to see. Arabian Gulf, where mainly summer visitor. L 23, WS 52 cm.

nbr

Bridled Tern head pattern similar
all year; paler edges to wing
feathers; grey back.

**BRIDLED TERN** *Sterna anaethetus*. Notably dark, with upperparts dark brown, except for white collar, forehead, extending as eyebrow behind eye, and sides of tail; bill and legs black. Cf. Sooty. In winter head mottled white, eye-stripe indistinct, upperparts sparingly marked white; juv/imm upperparts mottled buff. Flight graceful, slow, body moving up and down with each wing-beat; may soar high. Call 'kirk'. Coastal and at sea. L 30-32, WS 77-81 cm. -V

**Sooty Tern** *S. fuscata*. Rare vagrant to Red Sea and seas/coasts Canaries to Western Approaches. Larger and blacker than Bridled, with no white collar, white forehead extending only to eye, and only outer webs of tail feathers white. Imm all sooty black speckled white on upperparts. Flight less buoyant. Oceanic. L 33-36, WS 82-94 cm. -V

br    nbr

Cayenne Tern

**SANDWICH TERN** *Sterna sandvicensis*. Larger than Common (p.182) and Lesser Crested (p.180), and differing in whiter upperparts, yellow-tipped black bill and distinctive call, a rather harsh 'kirrick' or 'kirr-whit'; from Common in distinct crest, shorter tail, legs and feet black with yellow soles, heavier flight and plunge-diving from a greater height; and from Lesser Crested in black forehead. Cf. Gull-billed Tern. Juv/imm brown on head and nape, with dark tail tip and all-dark bill; black markings on juv's mantle and coverts soon lost. Almost entirely coastal. Cayenne Tern *S.s. eurygnatha* (S America) may occur in Europe. L 36-41, WS 95-105 cm. ●Sm

**GULL-BILLED TERN** *Sterna nilotica*. A strikingly white (especially winter adult's head), almost gull-like tern, with a distinctive short stout black bill. Has shorter neck, broader wings and heavier flight than Sandwich, also grey rump and tail and dark upper trailing edge to primaries. At rest in mixed flocks legs show longer. Juv/imm plainer above than similar Sandwich, with white forehead and small blackish ear patch. Call diagnostic, 'ger-vik' or 'cher-wuc'. Often breeds and feeds inland. L 35-38, WS 100-115 cm. -A(b)

**SEA TERNS**

juv

nbr

br

LITTLE TERN

br

1st w

SAUNDERS'S TERN

juv

br

BRIDLED TERN

br

nbr

juv

br

SOOTY TERN

1st w

br

nbr

1st w

juv

nbr

SANDWICH TERN

juv

nbr

br

1st w

nbr

GULL-BILLED TERN

**Marsh terns:** *Chlidonias*. Smaller than all sea terns, except Little Tern group (p.184); in winter similarly pale grey above with white forehead, and white below, but wings broader, tail less deeply forked and bill smaller; legs red. Cf. Little Gull (p.168). Flight most distinctive, graceful, dipping, often stooping to pick up insects from water, but rarely diving in. Fresh and brackish water and marshes; often in coastal waters in winter and on migration.

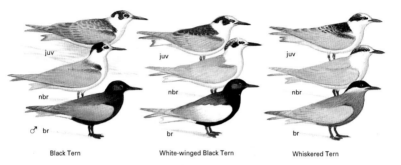

Black Tern     White-winged Black Tern     Whiskered Tern

**BLACK TERN** *Chlidonias niger*. The commonest marsh tern in Europe, and the only breeding water bird with whole head and body black or greyish-black, relieved only by marked contrast of white undertail coverts and paler grey of underwing; bill black, thinner than other marsh terns. Winter adults and some imms have more sharply defined white shoulders than any sea tern, offset by variable but diagnostic black mark on side of breast and by dark leading edge of inner wing; underwing pale with dark leading edge. Juv/imm similar but with darker mantle. Large flocks have a collective reedy cry; may also call 'kik, kik', 'keek' or 'krew'. Nest on floating vegetation in shallow water. L 22-24, WS 64-68 cm.                    ⊙M(b)

**WHITE-WINGED BLACK TERN** *Chlidonias leucopterus*. Conspicuous white forewing and black underwing coverts separate breeding adult from all other terns; also has shorter and stouter red-brown bill, longer and brighter red legs, slightly blunter wing-tips, and shorter and less forked tail than Black Tern. Winter adult and imm have less black on head, and no dark shoulder mark. Cf. Whiskered Tern. Juv's diagnostic all-dark mantle contrast with grey wings and white collar and rump. Calls hoarser; on passage a guttural 'kerr'. Breeds in drier marshes; also on coast in winter. L 20-23, WS 63-67 cm.     -A

**WHISKERED TERN** *Chlidonias hybridus*. Black cap and white cheeks make breeding adult look like a small Common/Arctic Tern, but underparts much darker grey with conspicuous white underwing and tail coverts. Winter adult and imm/juv differ from Black Tern in no black shoulder-patch, all-pale wings and less black on head; from White-winged Black in more forked tail and greyer rump; and from both in only obscure white collar and longer, stouter bill. Cf. *portlandica* type Common/Arctic Tern. Very noisy at breeding colonies; calls louder and harsher than black terns. L 23-25, WS 74-78 cm.     -V

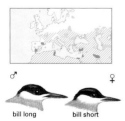

♂                    ♀

bill long     bill short

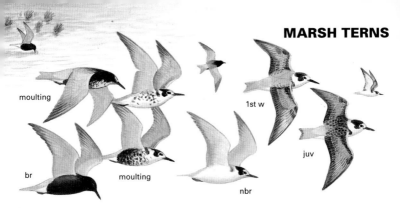

**Black Tern.** In flight breeding adult shows marked contrast of black body with white tail, under tail coverts and underwing. Female has greyer throat and underparts.

In winter tail and under tail coverts pale grey, other underparts white and underwing pale, wing with dark leading edge, which in juv makes T with dark upper back.

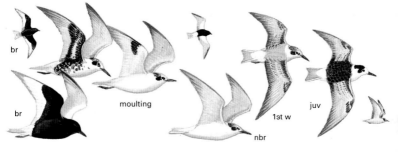

**White-winged Black Tern.** In flight conspicuous white forewing and black underwing coverts make breeding adult unmistakable. Winter adult and imm lack

Black Tern's dark shoulder mark, but have paler leading edge of forewing and rump. Juv has blackish back, grey wings and white collar and rump.

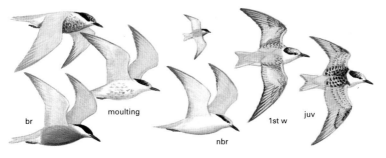

**Whiskered Tern.** Flight slower and less wavering than both black terns, with white underwing and tail coverts conspicuous in breeding adult.

Winter adult and imm/juv generally paler than black terns. Juv has distinctive mottled mantle.

● AUKS: *Alcidae*. Short-necked, short-tailed black-and-white diving seabirds; sexes alike. Wings rather short and narrow; legs set well back, giving upright stance at rest. Main call a harsh growling 'arrrr' or 'karrrr'. Flight whirring, fast and direct, low over water, legs and feet often outstretched. Auks swim and dive readily and constantly, but on land most can only shuffle awkwardly. In winter at sea.

Razorbill | Guillemot | Brünnich's Guillemot

In flight all show narrow white bar on trailing edge. Both guillemots appear more hunched than Razorbill, which shows more white at sides of rump.

**RAZORBILL** *Alca torda*. Bill, flattened in vertical plane, with vertical white bar, unique among seabirds; in imm less and in juv much less stout. When breeding, whole head and neck black, except for white line from bill to eye; cf. Guillemot. Winter adult and imm have white throat, lower cheeks and sides of neck; juv has head and neck dark brown. Juv has a shrill whistle. In flight appears less hunch-backed and has more white at sides of rump than Guillemot. Breeds on cliffs in loose colonies, not in rows, with single oval egg usually in a cavity. L 37-39 cm.                                        ●RSw

**GUILLEMOT** *Uria aalge*. Generally the commonest auk, with a long straight unmarked dagger-like bill, much shorter in juv. Head, neck and upper breast dark when breeding, but throat, sides of neck and upper breast are white in winter adult and juv/imm. Striking 'bridled' variety, more frequent in N of range, has narrow white eye-ring and white line back from eye (showing as an indented furrow in normal birds); cf. Razorbill. Juv has a shrill whistle. In flight, cf. Razorbill. Breeds in closely packed colonies on inaccessible narrow open ledges on sea cliffs; single egg markedly pear-shaped to prevent it falling off when disturbed. L 38-41 cm.                                        ●RSw

Arctic ssp.*hyperborea* and northern ssp.*aalge* have head and upper-parts very dark blackish-brown, less deeply black than Razorbill, head with a brownish tinge; bridled variety more frequent. Southern ssp.*albionis* has head and whole upperparts dark chocolate brown, tinged greyish in winter.

**BRÜNNICH'S GUILLEMOT** *Uria lomvia*. Very like northern Guillemot, but blacker, forehead steeper and bill shorter, stouter and when breeding with a pale line along base of upper mandible – beware some Guillemots, especially on Bear Is, with a much fainter white line, and even Guillemots carrying sand-eels can be confusing. In winter is darker above and black of crown extends well below eye, like Razorbill. In flight even more hump-backed than Guillemot, with as much white on sides of rump as Razorbill. Colonies less crowded. L 39-43 cm.                                        -V

nbr

1st s

RAZORBILL

bridled

br

bridled nbr

yperborea
r

aalge br

1st s

aalge nbr

albionis br

GUILLEMOT

nbr

br

1st s

BRÜNNICH'S
GUILLEMOT

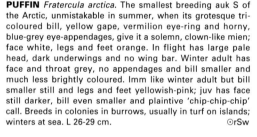

Swimming auks may be harder to identify, unless bill size and shape can be seen, especially Little Auk-sized juvs of the larger auks with their undeveloped bills; see Little Auk below. Black Guillemot is the smallest guillemot.

**PUFFIN** *Fratercula arctica*. The smallest breeding auk S of the Arctic, unmistakable in summer, when its grotesque tri-coloured bill, yellow gape, vermilion eye-ring and horny, blue-grey eye-appendages, give it a solemn, clown-like mien; face white, legs and feet orange. In flight has large pale head, dark underwings and no wing bar. Winter adult has face and throat grey, no appendages and bill smaller and much less brightly coloured. Imm like winter adult but bill smaller still and legs and feet yellowish-pink; juv has face still darker, bill even smaller and plaintive 'chip-chip-chip' call. Breeds in colonies in burrows, usually in turf on islands; winters at sea. L 26-29 cm. ⊙rSw

**BLACK GUILLEMOT** *Cepphus grylle*. The only all-black seabird with a large white wing-patch when breeding, and in winter, when face and underparts become white, is only seabird with barred black-and-white upperparts; bill black, inside of mouth, legs and feet red. Imm like winter adult with red-brown legs, but juv has dark parts brownish. Call a rather high-pitched whistle or whine. The region's least sociable auk, breeding in very loose colonies, in crevices of cliffs and rocks by shallower seas and much further up inlets than other auks; in winter mainly inshore. L 30-32 cm. ⊙R

Adults of ssp.*mandtii* (Jan Mayen, Bear Is, Spitsbergen) have much more white on underparts and juvs more mottled upperparts. Ssp. *islandicus* (Iceland) has brown line on white wing panel.

**LITTLE AUK** *Alle alle*. The region's smallest and shortest-billed auk and smallest diving seabird. Breeding adult has head and upper breast black; juv browner. Winter adult has throat, sides of neck and whole breast white; imm browner. In flight appears very short-necked, with blackish underwings and white trailing edges. Juv guillemots and Razorbills may have confusingly small bills, but also have pale underwing and less extensive white on cheeks; juv Puffin has larger head, grey face and dark trailing edges. Boulder-strown cliffs and slopes; winter at sea. L 17-19 cm. ⊙W

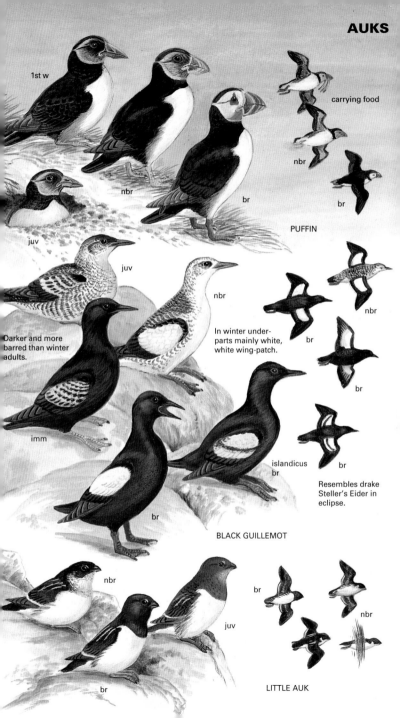

1st w

juv

nbr

br

carrying food

nbr

br

br

**PUFFIN**

juv

nbr

In winter under-
parts mainly white,
white wing-patch.

Darker and more
barred than winter
adults.

imm

br

islandicus
br

br

nbr

br

br

Resembles drake
Steller's Eider in
eclipse.

**BLACK GUILLEMOT**

nbr

juv

br

br

nbr

br

**LITTLE AUK**

● SANDGROUSE: *Pteroclididae*. Land birds, mainly sandy coloured and so hard to see in deserts. At rest like small long-tailed partridges, but in flight more like plump parakeets or long-tailed pigeons or golden plovers (p.140). Head small, neck and legs short, legs and toes feathered in front. Gait rather pigeon-like, tripping with short waddling steps. Often join flocks of other sandgrouse. Deserts, semi-deserts, other dry stony ground; nesting on ground. Flight fast, direct, flocks performing golden-plover-like aerobatics, and undertaking long, often noisy daily journeys - up to 40 miles and back - always in the morning, but sometimes in hot weather again in the evening, exact times varying regionally. Males soak their belly feathers in water and carry it for long distances for the chicks to suck out.

juv

**SPOTTED SANDGROUSE** *Pterocles senegallus*. Medium-sized and rather pale, with elongated, needle-like tail and narrow black band along centre of belly (cf. short-tailed Black-bellied and long-tailed Chestnut-bellied, p.194). Male largely uniform above, with blue-grey upper breast and eye-stripe; female's upperparts and upper breast dark-spotted (easily seen only at close range); both have throat and lower cheeks yellow. Differs from short-tailed Crowned in black-tipped primaries and black underwing secondaries. Has distinctive double liquid musical call, 'cuito, cuito', 'wittoo, wittoo' or 'waku, waku'; also a monosyllabic flight call. Flocks smallish. Sometimes in fairly thick scrub. L 30-35 cm.

juv

**CROWNED SANDGROUSE** *Pterocles coronatus*. Small, short-tailed and with no black on belly; male is region's only sandgrouse with black chin and white forehead bordered black (imm male lacks this), with rest of head and neck patterned pale rufous, pale blue-grey and pale yellow; upperparts largely uniform. Female uniformly and finely barred, above and below, except for yellow lower cheeks and throat, which smaller Lichtenstein's lacks; cf. females of larger dark-bellied Black-bellied (tail short) and Chestnut-bellied (tail long) (p.194). Both sexes differ from Spotted in contrast between white underwing coverts and black primaries. Call higher-pitched than other sandgrouse, and rising in pitch, a trisyllabic 'cla-cla-cla' or 'cha, chagarra'. Flies very fast to water, sometimes brackish. Stony deserts and mountainsides. L 27-29 cm.

Ssp.*vastitas* (Sinai, Israel, Jordan) darker, esp. female/juv, and more barred beneath, as are some Saharan populations.

**LICHTENSTEIN'S SANDGROUSE** *Pterocles lichtensteinii*. The region's smallest sandgrouse, no bigger than a Turtle Dove (p.198); short-tailed and appearing rather dark from its uniformly closely barred plumage, relieved only by pale bars on the wing and in the male by a distinctive black-and-white head pattern and a yellowish patch on the breast crossed by two black lines. Female is only sandgrouse uniformly barred both above and below; cf. female Crowned, which has yellow throat. Various whistling calls, including a wigeon-like double whistle, 'whittou', but often flies silently, and so escapes detection when flighting to water, usually before dawn and after dark. May descend into quite deep wells, their arrival and departure have been compared to wasps at a hole nest. Less gregarious than other sandgrouse; rocky and bushy desert areas. L 24-26 cm.

juv

# SANDGROUSE

♀

♂

♀

♂

SPOTTED
SANDGROUSE

♂ vastitas

♀

♂ coronatus

♂

CROWNED SANDGROUSE

♀

♂

♂

LICHTENSTEIN'S
SANDGROUSE

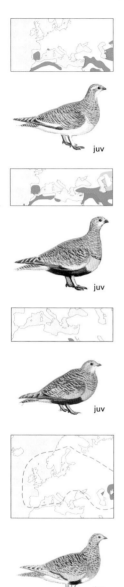

**PIN-TAILED SANDGROUSE** *Pterocles alchata*. One of the larger species, the only one breeding in the region that has a white belly, and the most distinctive of the four with needle-like elongated tail. Male is only sandgrouse with rufous throat and (when breeding) black chin and throat (Crowned (p.192) has black chin and Black-bellied has black throat, but both are short-tailed); female is only one with pure white throat and three dark breast-bands. In flight Pin-tailed shows distinctive white wing bar and black-tipped white underwing. Often in large, noisy flocks, flying in line and high overhead, when call, a loud, ringing 'kata, kata', can be very puzzling when light too bright to see birds. Avoids open desert; may nest in loose colonies. L 31-39 cm.

juv

**BLACK-BELLIED SANDGROUSE** *Pterocles orientalis*. The region's largest breeding sandgrouse, short-tailed and the only one with whole belly black (but cf. dark chestnut belly of much smaller long-tailed Chestnut-bellied) and the only short-tailed one with any black on the belly at all. In flight white forewings contrasting strongly with both black trailing edge of underwing and black belly are diagnostic. Male is region's only sandgrouse with throat but not chin black, and has pale grey head, yellow wings and dark bar on lower breast. Female has distinctive pale patch between spotted breast and black belly. Call rather gruff, variously rendered 'churr-rur-rur' or 'tchourou'. Avoids open desert. L 33-35 cm.

juv

**CHESTNUT-BELLIED SANDGROUSE** *Pterocles exustus*. A small species with needle-like elongated tail feathers, and the region's only one with whole underwing dark. Male is only long-tailed one with whole belly dark (chestnut) and is much smaller than short-tailed Black-bellied, which has white underwing; differs from smaller Spotted in having yellow head and wings as well as black line on breast. Female's dark belly barred paler, contrasting with pale lower breast is also distinctive (but cf. short-tailed Lichtenstein's, p.192) does not appear so spotted as female Spotted (p.192). Gathers in huge flocks to drink. Open deserts; Egypt only. L 31-33 cm.

juv

**PALLAS'S SANDGROUSE** *Syrrhaptes paradoxus*. The region's largest and longest-tailed sandgrouse, the only one that has an elongated primary, and the only one likely to be seen N of the Mediterranean region. Has a conspicuous and diagnostic black patch on the belly, very noticeable in flight in contrast to pale underwing and rest of body; wings are held distinctly down-curved, like a partridge, and quills may hum or whistle. Voice variously described as 'chack, chack', 'koecki, koecki' or 'koeckerik, koekerick'. Semi-deserts, steppes, dunes, arable fields and similar open habitats. Only occurs in W and C parts of region during and after one of its now very infrequent irruptions from C and E Asia. The largest such irruption was in 1888 and there has been no large-scale one since 1908. L 30-41 cm.                                                        -V

juv

# SANDGROUSE

♂

♀

♂ nbr

♂ br

**PIN-TAILED SANDGROUSE**

♂

♀

♀

**BLACK-BELLIED SANDGROUSE**

♀

♂

♀

♂

**CHESTNUT-BELLIED SANDGROUSE**

♂

♀

♂

**PALLAS'S SANDGROUSE**

● PIGEONS and DOVES: *Columbidae*. pp.196-199. Medium-sized land birds. Larger species usually called pigeons and smaller ones doves, but no real distinction. Soberly coloured, in pastel shades of grey or brown, *Columba* spp. with iridescent green/purple neck patches, smallish head, short bill, longish tail and crooning or cooing voice. Gait a walk. Tree or ledge nesters.

Includes Feral Pigeon.

**ROCK DOVE** *Columba livia*. Smaller and shorter-tailed than Woodpigeon, similar in outline to Stock Dove; rump white, eye red with yellow ring. Display flight circular. Voice the insistent coo of the Domestic Pigeon, 'coo-roo- coo'. Cliffs and rocks, mainly by the sea in the W, where many colonies are mixed with ferals and include some blue chequer variants, but in hills and mountains in the E, nesting on ledges and in caves. L 31-34 cm.          ⊙R

Sspp.*palaestinae* (Levant) and *gaddi* (E Med.) paler; *chimperi* (Nile) pale with pale grey rump; *canariensis* (Canary Is, Madeira) darker.

**Feral Pigeon** has range of plumages based on blue-grey, black, white and reddish cinnamon, e.g. blue rock, like wild Rock Dove; blue chequer with upperparts mottled grey-blue and black; red rock, cinnamon with white wing-tips and no black bars; and red chequer, similar but with wings and mantle mottled white.          ●R

**STOCK DOVE** *Columba oenas*. Like Rock Dove, but has black wing-tips, two short black bars on wing, grey underwing and grey rump uniform with mantle. Call a grunting double coo, with accent on second syllable. Display flight circular; may glide with raised wings. Open woodland, open country with sparse trees, inland cliffs, less often on coast. Nests in holes in trees, cliffs and ground. L 32-34 cm.          ●Rw

**Eastern Stock Dove** *C. eversmanni*. Vagrant from S Asia. Has shorter tail and longer wings than larger Stock Dove, but rump greyish-white, bases of primaries paler, so that wings appear grey with a dark trailing edge, underwing whiter and eye-ring yellow. Aka Yellow-eyed Stock Dove. L 29-31 cm.

**WOODPIGEON** *Columba palumbus*. Easily told by large size and white patch on wing, prominent in flight, when dark bar at tip of tail also shows. Adult also has white patch on each side of neck. Juv darker with no white neck patches. Usual song a soothing 'coo-cooo-coo, coo-coo'. In display flight flaps steeply upwards with loud wing-claps, gliding down with wings scarcely up-raised. Wooded country, farmland; also in W and C Europe in town parks and squares and large gardens. Nests in trees. L 40-42 cm.          ●Rw

**LONG-TAILED PIGEON** *Columba trocaz*. Darker and slightly smaller than Woodpigeon; no wing patches, much less conspicuous silvery neck patches, dark tail bar. Voice similar. Mountain laurel forests, Madeira. L 38-40 cm.

**BOLLE'S PIGEON** *C. bollii*. Smallest of the three island pigeons, large grey bar in middle of blackish tail. Voice more guttural. Higher forests, Canary Is. L 35-37 cm.

**LAUREL PIGEON** *C. junoniae*. Shorter, more rounded wings than the other two; no white on wings or neck, and paler tail with no dark tip. Lower wooded slopes, Canary Is. L 37-38 cm.

# PIGEONS

eral Pigeon, derived
om Rock Dove,
wns, ports,
iffs.

ROCK DOVE

white rumped

grey rumped

EASTERN
STOCK
DOVE

STOCK DOVE

WOODPIGEON

BOLLE'S
PIGEON

LONG-TAILED PIGEON

LAUREL PIGEON

**NAMAQUA DOVE** *Oena capensis*. The region's smallest and only long-tailed dove. Readily identified in flight by long black tail and chestnut underwings; male also has distinctive black face and upper breast. Call a weak 'coo, coo'. Flight fast, direct. Open bush country, palm groves. L 26-28 cm.

**Turtle doves:** *Streptopelia*. Smaller and slimmer than *Columba* doves, with faster flight, with quick, clipped jerks of the wings; also wing-clapping and gliding display flight. Tail pattern important as field mark. Tree nesters.

**COLLARED DOVE** *Streptopelia decaocto*. The region's largest and palest breeding wild *Streptopelia* dove, almost Rock Dove size. Ash-brown with blackish wing-tips and a black half-collar (obscure in juvs), the square-ended tail white beneath with a black base. Song an insistent triple 'coo-cooo-cuh', accented on middle syllable with last one somewhat truncated; also a strangled squawk. Flight slower, less clipped than Turtle Dove, often making a soft sibilant sound. In the E, areas with scattered trees and bushes, palm groves, oases, villages and towns; in the W as a colonist since 1950s, almost a commensal of man, especially in towns and villages, sometimes in large flocks where it can feed on loose grain. L 31-33 cm.　　　●R

**Barbary Dove** *S. 'risoria'*. A favourite cage bird, derived from the African Collared Dove *S. roseogrisea* (p.371); often escapes; breeds ferally in Canary Is, and perhaps elsewhere. Smaller and usually creamier than Collared Dove, and with much paler wing-tips and no blue-grey in tail. Call quite distinct, 'koo-krr-oo'. L 29-30 cm.　　-E

**TURTLE DOVE** *Streptopelia turtur*. Smaller and darker than Collared Dove, with upperparts mottled chestnut and black, and no black half-collar but two black-and-white neck patches. In faster flight best distinction is blackish fan-shaped tail, with white edges both above and beneath. Juv browner with no neck patches. Call a distinctive soothing 'turr, turr'. Open woodland, scrub, heaths, farmland with scattered trees, palm groves, large gardens and parks, often feeding on bare arable. L 26-28 cm.　　　●Sm

The desert-living sspp.*arenicola* (Balearic Is, N W Africa, Middle East) and *rufescens* (Nile valley), are generally paler, with less blue-grey on head and black on upperparts.

**Rufous Turtle Dove** *S.orientalis*. A rare vagrant from C and E Asia, larger, darker and more pigeon-like than Collared and Turtle Doves, differing from Turtle Dove in more heavily spotted wings, darker mantle, browner breast, 1-2 narrow white wing bars and blue-grey neck patches. Song a soporific 'cooo-cooo-kakoor'. Aka Oriental/Eastern Turtle Dove. L 33-35 cm.　　-V

Turtle

Rufous

When clearly seen, the adults' neck patches are a good field mark.

**PALM DOVE** *Streptopelia senegalensis*. Like a small dark round-winged Turtle Dove, with similar tail pattern, but upperparts unspotted, forewing more conspicuously blue-grey and no neck patches but a patch of small black spots on upper breast. Most distinctive song, a rising and falling 'oh-cook-cook-oo-oo'. Common in towns, villages and oases. Aka Laughing Dove; Little Brown Dove (India). L 25-27 cm.　　-E

**DOVES**

juv

ad

COLLARED DOVE

♀  ♂

juv

♀  ♂

NAMAQUA DOVE

juv

ad

rufescens

TURTLE DOVE

juv

ad

RUFOUS TURTLE DOVE

juv

ad

PALM DOVE

● PARROTS: *Psittacidae*. Short-necked, usually rather plump tropical land birds; bill stout, often with a cere, the curved upper mandible fitting over the lower. Often noisy in flight. None native, but several introduced to region.

**RING-NECKED PARAKEET** *Psittacula krameri*. The region's most frequently naturalised parrot, very long-tailed, with red bill and narrow rose-pink collar on hind neck; male has black throat. Cf. Alexandrine Parakeet. Juv like female, but bill paler and tail shorter. Flies strongly with fast, clipped wing-beats, constantly uttering shrill screech. In small parties in areas with trees in or near towns and villages. Hole-nester. From tropical Asia and Africa. L 38-42 cm. ⊙RE

In Europe most birds are a mixture of sspp.*borealis* and *manillensis* (both Indian sub-continent); in Britain most appear to be *borealis*. In France and perhaps Egypt some are ssp.*krameri* (Senegal to S Sudan).

**Alexandrine Parakeet** *P. eupatria*. Very like smaller Ring-necked, but with red shoulder patch and much heavier bill. Breeds Bushire (W Iran), Germany; from tropical Asia. L 53-58 cm. -E

**Masked Lovebird** *Agapornis personata*. Short-tailed, with blackish-brown head, yellow collar and breast-band and bright red bill. Calls twittering. Nests in rocks. Canary Is, from E Africa. L 15 cm.

**Peach-faced Lovebird** *A. roseicollis*. Short-tailed, with head dark pink except for red forehead, bill horn-coloured and rump blue. Noisy, with a high-pitched 'skreek'. Nests in trees and rocks. Gran Canaria; also non-breeding in France, Germany, Netherlands; from S W Africa. Aka Rosy Lovebird. L 16 cm.

**Budgerigar** *Melopsittacus undulatus*. The many attempts, especially in Britain, to naturalise this popular cage-bird from Australia have always failed. Yellow above, mainly barred black; green below, with wings and long tail blue; very variable, sometimes blue instead of green. Often joins flocks of House Sparrows (p.334), sometimes with Bee-eaters (p.222). L 18 cm. -E

**Black-hooded Parakeet** *Nandayus nenday*. Green to yellow-green, with head, underwings and tail black, breast bluish and thighs red. Very noisy with a loud harsh 'kree-ah' flight call and a high-pitched chatter. Breeds Canary Is, also at large in Italy and Spain; from S America. Aka Nanday Conure. L 35 cm.

**Monk Parakeet** *Myiopsitta monachus*. Long-tailed, with conspicuously blue wings, grey forehead, throat and breast, and buff belly. Flies fast, screeching noisily. Often perches on palms, TV aerials. Breeds France, Italy, Spain, Canary Is, also at large in Belgium, and Germany; from S America. L 29 cm.

# PARAKEETS

♀

♂ manillensis

♀

juv

RING-NECKED PARAKEET

♀

ALEXANDRINE
PARAKEET

ad

MASKED LOVEBIRD

juv

juv

PEACH-FACED
LOVEBIRD

ad

Budgie

MONK
PARAKEET

♂

BLACK-HOODED
PARAKEET

♀

juv

BUDGERIGAR

● CUCKOOS: *Cuculidae.* Medium to large, rather slender, solitary arboreal birds, with long, graduated tail and slightly decurved bill. *Clamator* and *Cuculus* cuckoos lay their eggs in other birds' nests.

Mainly found where Magpies are common.

**GREAT SPOTTED CUCKOO** *Clamator glandarius.* A large bird, adult unmistakable with conspicuous crest, long white-edged tail, white-spotted wings and cream-coloured under-parts. Juv with smaller crest on black crown, buffer underparts and rufous flash (retained in imm) in wings. Loud, harsh cries include a repeated grating 'keeow', a crow-like alarm note, 'cark, cark' and a tern-like chatter. Flight strong, direct. Open woodlands, olive groves, savannas and other areas with scattered trees. Parasitises crows, especially Magpie. L 38-40 cm.                                                                                    -V

**CUCKOO** *Cuculus canorus.* Grey adult superficially like male Sparrowhawk (p.92), but has graduated tail with white spots at tip, pointed wings, and bill not hooked. Rarely adult female can be rufous brown barred darker. Juv either grey or rufous brown, with conspicuous white nape patch, and at first very round-winged. Well known 'cooc-coo' call has variants such as 'cooc-cooc-coo'; hen has a 'water-bubbling' trill, and both utter coughing and choking notes when excited. In distinctive low-wing flight, wings scarcely raised above horizontal plane and depressed far below body at bottom of downstroke. Wide range of habitats includes tundra, moors, heaths, woodland, farmland, town parks, dunes and coastal marshes. Parasitises Meadow Pipit, Reed Warbler, Dunnock and other small song-birds. L 32-34 cm.                                                                                    ●Sm

▶ **ORIENTAL CUCKOO** *Cuculus saturatus.* Slightly larger and longer-winged than Cuckoo, but darker above and has stronger blackish bars below, deeper buff underwing and distinctive call: a muffled hoopoe-like 'du-du, du-du', repeated 6-8 times, and preceded by a more rapidly uttered 4-syllabic version of the same notes. Shy, keeping to tree tops in breeding season. Woodland, especially dense pine and spruce forests. Parasitises *Phylloscopus* warblers. L 30-32 cm.

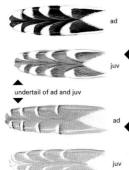

ad

juv

undertail of ad and juv

ad

juv

◀ **Yellow-billed Cuckoo** *Coccyzus americanus.* A slender transatlantic vagrant, dark grey-brown above, white below, with boldly white-spotted black tail, conspicuous rufous flash in open wings, and partly yellow bill. L 28-32 cm.                                                  -V

**Black-billed Cuckoo** *Coccyzus erythrophthalmus.* Another transat-lantic vagrant, slightly smaller than Yellow-billed, and with less or no rufous in wings, tail brown with much less conspicuous white spots, bill all-black and narrow red eye-ring. L 27-31 cm.                          -V

**SENEGAL COUCAL** *Centropus senegalensis.* The region's largest and bulkiest cuckoo, very distinctive with its black head, heavy bill, long black tail and rufous wings. Song a series of cooing and bubbling notes that run down and then up the scale. Shy and secretive, usually in thick cover or on the ground, but with a slow, rather clumsy flight. Marshes and swamps, often by fresh water. L 40-42 cm.

# CUCKOOS

ad

juv

ad

**GREAT SPOTTED CUCKOO**

♂

**CUCKOO**

♂

brown phase

♂

♀

**ORIENTAL CUCKOO**

♀

brown phase

**BLACK-BILLED CUCKOO**

**YELLOW-BILLED CUCKOO**

**SENEGAL COUCAL**

● OWLS: *Strigidae*. pp.204-213; for *Tytonidae* (Barn Owl), see p.212. Nocturnal birds of prey (some also hunt by day) with long rounded wings, short tail and (usually) feathered legs and feet. Head large, with large forward-looking eyes in a flattened facial disc, whose feathers usually hide the short hooked bill. A few have 'ear tufts', which are not true ears. Sexes alike, except Snowy Owl. Flight of larger owls slow and flapping, of smaller ones faster and bounding. Stance upright. Nest in hole in tree, rocks, building or old nest of other bird, or on ground.

Decreasing in much of Europe. Introduced England, late 19th century.

**LITTLE OWL** *Athene noctua*. Partly diurnal habits, open habitat and conspicuously bounding flight make this the most familiar of the region's six smaller owls. Greyer-brown and shorter-tailed than Tengmalm's. Call, a loud, ringing 'kiew, kiew' and song a remarkably curlew-like whistling hoot, both uttered by day. Juv has a shrill persistent wheeze. Often perches on posts and other prominent look-outs; bobs, waggles head, and may turn it through 180° when suspicious or curious. Often flies by night, and hovers for insects in dusk. Farmland, open country with scattered trees, open woodland, orchards, palm groves, dunes, semi-deserts, other treeless but rocky places. L 21-23 cm. ●R

Little Owls vary greatly in colour from one area to another, but not apparently due to climate or environment. In Europe birds may be dark, rufous or pale, from Sinai to Syria very pale, in S Iraq slightly darker, in N Africa darker still.

**SPOTTED LITTLE OWL** *Athene brama*. Rare vagrant to S Iraq, where once thought to breed; breeds S Iran, not overlapping with Little Owl. Differs from Little Owl in barred underparts and smaller, whiter spots on head. L 21-22 cm.

**PYGMY OWL** *Glaucidium passerinum*. Much the smallest owl of the region, with relatively small head, rather obscure facial disc and distinctive habit of flicking tail sideways and cocking it like a Wren (p.314). Calls a whistling 'tyu-tyu-tyu' and 'kuvitt'; song often likened to tree frog or Bullfinch's pipe. Flight bounding, hunting small birds and rodents, especially at dusk. Forests, usually coniferous and often dense, in taiga and on mountains. Nest usually in old woodpecker hole. L 16-17 cm.

**TENGMALM'S OWL** *Aegolius funereus*. The largest of the region's six smaller owls, fully nocturnal except in the Arctic. Browner than Little Owl, with more fully feathered feet and a more upright stance. Also has quite distinct facial expression: instead of Little's low-browed, frowning mien, Tengmalm's brows appear to be raised, as if slightly surprised, an effect accentuated by blacker edge of facial disc and broader white eyebrows. Juv uniformly rufous, including most of facial disc, except eyebrows. Song a hoopoe-like succession of hoots, rising at first and falling at the end, sometimes as a trill. Forests, usually coniferous, in the taiga and hill districts, roosting in a dense tree. Nest often in old Black Woodpecker hole. L 24-26 cm. -V

# SMALL OWLS

greyish

juv

Often flies by day for short distances, the alternation of folded wings and glides making deep undulations.

brownish

Cyprus, Levant

◀ LITTLE OWL. Moves easily on ground, hopping like a Robin with upright posture.

juv

◀ PYGMY OWL. Active by day, readily flying with rapid dipping woodpecker-like wing-beats, the wings folded in deep undulations interspersed with glides.

juv

TENGMALM'S OWL. Strictly nocturnal and hard to see. Best located at night by typical hoopoe-like call or when well grown young perch outside nest.

Striated Scops

Scops

grey phase

Often flies by day for short distances, with
bounding flight but undulations not quite so
marked as Little Owl.

brown phase

**SCOPS OWL** *Otus scops*. In Europe the only small owl with ear
tufts, not always easily seen, and unfeathered toes. Plumage
grey-brown, sometimes tinged rufous, streaked darker. Often
adopts slim, elongated posture. Largely nocturnal, so usually
detected by musical 'piu' call, not unlike tree frog or single note
of Redshank (p.158), monotonously repeated at short intervals,
sometimes duetting; many other calls. Areas with scattered
trees, open woodland, farmland, orchards, palm groves, parks,
ruins, villages, small towns, feeding mainly on large insects.
L 19-20 cm.

Ssp.*scops* (Europe) is very variable in colour, from grey to rufous;
ssp.*cyprius* (Cyprus) is dark grey and heavily streaked.

**STRIATED SCOPS OWL** *Otus brucei*. Egypt and Middle East
only, where best separated from very similar and only very
slightly smaller Scops Owl by quite different call, a softer,
dove-like single or multiple cooing hoot, repeated faster than
Scops; also utters a distinctive warbling 'tsirr-va-vaa'. Plumage
paler, especially on face, grey-brown or tinged yellow, never
rufous. Habitat as Scops, but often in semi-deserts. Aka Bruce's
Scops Owl. L 20-21 cm.

**EAGLE OWL** *Bubo bubo*. One of the region's largest owls, an
enormous brown bird, the size of a Bonelli's Eagle (p.96), the
prominent ear tufts and facial disc distinguishing it from all
diurnal raptors; eyes large, orange. Song a deep 'oo-hu'; other
calls include a harsh 'kveck, kveck'. Flight buzzard-like. Dense
coniferous and broad-leaved forests, also rocky mountain
gorges and (with paler plumage) deserts, hunting at dawn and
dusk for mammals and birds as large as roe deer and
Capercaillie (p.112). L 60-75, WS 160-188 cm.          -E(b)

Varies in size and colour from N to S. Ssp.*sibiricus* (W Urals) largest
and palest; ssp.*bubo* (Europe) described above; ssp.*hispanus* similar
but smaller; and ssp.*ascalaphus* (N Africa, Middle East) small, short-
tailed, long-legged and sometimes very pale.

**BROWN FISH OWL** *Ketupa zeylonensis*. Smaller than Eagle
Owl, and with more uniform plumage, more rufous underparts,
flatter head, much shorter, more spray-like ear tufts, yellow
eyes, unfeathered tarsi and feet, and more nocturnal habits.
Song a rather dismal moaning 'oomp-ooo-oo', accented on
middle syllable, also a single hoot. Forests, near fresh water,
feeding mainly on fish; spends much time on ground, even
trampling out trails along stream banks. L 54-57, WS 145 cm.

# EARED OWLS

bubo

ascalaphus

sibiricus

▲ EAGLE OWL. Unmistakable if well seen, heavy build with long ear tufts, but in restricted habitats.

In flight wings produce a slight singing noise.

▲ With fish, freshwater crabs are an important food, together with frogs, reptiles, birds and rodents.

BROWN FISH OWL

Short-eared

Marsh

Long-eared

Short-eared and Marsh Owls regularly fly by day, Long-eared Owl only rarely, when it can be distinguished from Short-eared by holding its wings more level, by the less prominent dark patch on the elbow of the wing and (hard to see) by the trailing edge of wing being darker. Marsh Owls when disturbed can, apparently out of curiosity, fly towards instead of away from the intruder.

**LONG-EARED OWL** *Asio otus*. The only medium-sized brown owl with long ear tufts. Slimmer and with more elongated face than Short-eared and Tawny (p.212) Owls. Hard to tell from usually paler Short-eared in flight, but has more rounded wings held more level, warmer buff patch at base of primaries, less black at wing-tips, less prominent dark elbow patch and darker trailing edge of wing (sometimes hard to see). Has longer wings than Tawny, together with ear tufts and orange-yellow eyes. Hooting call more long-drawn-out and moaning than Tawny; young birds have a similar unoiled-hinge call. Forests, especially coniferous, areas with scattered trees, heaths, marshes, dunes; communal day roosts frequent in winter; hunts small rodents, mainly over open country. Nest often in old crow's nest. L 35-37, WS 90-100 cm.  ⊙Rmw

with ears flattened

Geographical variation is slight, but ssp.*canariensis* (Canary Is) is smaller, male like ssp.*otus* (Europe; described above), but female distinctly darker and more heavily streaked below.

**SHORT-EARED OWL** *Asio flammeus*. Much the most likely medium-sized brown owl to be seen hunting in open country by day; short ear tufts rarely visible in field; eyes yellow. Wings conspicuously long, with blackish patch at elbow of both surfaces and blackish tips to underwing primaries. Cf. Long-eared and Tawny (p.212) Owls. In addition to normal slow, flapping, owl-like flight, can soar, wheel and glide like a harrier and has circular display flight, often uttering a deep triple hoot. Also has a harsh barking flight note. Open plains, moors, downs, rough hillsides, heaths, marshes, dunes. L 37-39, WS 95-110 cm.  ●RsmW

Decreasing in Morocco from habitat destruction.

**MARSH OWL** *Asio capensis*. N W Africa only. Markedly smaller and darker than Short-eared Owl, almost uniformly dark brown above, dark brown breast contrasting with pale underparts, and with brown eyes and eye-patches and rarely seen short ear tufts. Juv with less distinct face pattern and more uniform buff below. Call a single or multiple hoarse croak. Hunts at dusk and sometimes by day, often in small parties, quartering ground like a Short-eared. L 29-31, WS 82-99 cm.

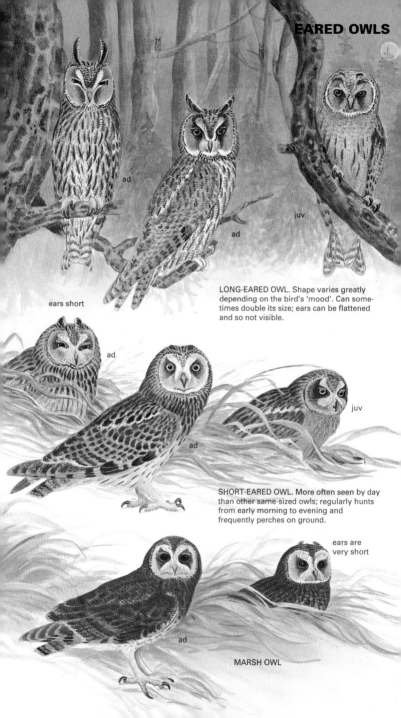

# EARED OWLS

**LONG-EARED OWL.** Shape varies greatly depending on the bird's 'mood'. Can sometimes double its size; ears can be flattened and so not visible.

ad

ad

juv

ears short

**SHORT-EARED OWL.** More often seen by day than other same-sized owls; regularly hunts from early morning to evening and frequently perches on ground.

ad

ad

juv

ears are very short

**MARSH OWL**

ad

**HAWK OWL** *Surnia ulula*. Short wings, more pointed than other owls, combine with smallish head and unusually long tail to give this medium-sized owl a strikingly hawk-like silhouette, recalling male Sparrowhawk (p.92); diurnal habits, fast flight, inclined attitude when perching and chattering 'ki-ki-ki' call also hawk-like. However, white facial disc, edged black to form distinctive sideburns is owl-like. White underparts barred darker are diagnostic. Flies low, often with a final upward sweep to a conspicuous perch; also hovers. Forests, especially coniferous, of northern taiga and mountains, and thickets on tundra. L 36-39, WS 74-81 cm.                              -V

Juv Hawk Owls grey with black face.

SNOWY OWL

♀

♂

1st-year plumage is like adult female, but 1st-year male is paler than 1st-year female.

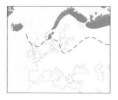

**SNOWY OWL** *Nyctea scandiaca*. Huge size and bulk and predominantly white plumage are unmistakable. Female appreciably larger and darker than male, and with much more numerous blackish or brownish bars on upperparts. Usually silent away from breeding grounds, where male has a loud harsh bark and a deep hoot, and female a higher-pitched bark. Flight more buzzard-like than owl-like, often gliding; frequently alights on ground. Tundra and high northern moorland, preying mainly on lemmings and birds as large as Ptarmigan (p.110) and Oystercatcher (p.132). Eruptions to S and W are linked with fluctuations in lemming stocks. L 55-66, WS 142-166 cm.                              -A(b)

HAWK OWL. Often perches conspicuously. Flight faster and more agile than other owls, low over trees.

URAL OWL

GREAT GREY OWL

**GREAT GREY OWL** *Strix nebulosa*. The region's second largest owl, after Eagle Owl, but predominantly grey, and with longer tail, rounder head with no ear tufts, black patch on chin, and smaller yellow eyes set in a facial disc with concentric dark rings. In flight shows large pale patch on upperwing and broad dark band at tail tip. Cf. smaller Ural Owl. Song and calls like Tawny Owl's (p.212), but hoot much deeper. Coniferous woodland, often hunting by day for mammals as large as squirrels and lemmings. Nest usually in old nest of other bird. L 65-70, WS 134-158 cm.

**URAL OWL** *Strix uralensis*. Only a little smaller than Great Grey Owl, differing chiefly in plumaged tinged yellowish, unlined facial disc, dark eyes and no black chin patch. From paler forms of much smaller Tawny Owl (p.212) differs in its long tail, which hangs down in flight, and relatively smaller eyes. Hoot more muffled and 'ke-wick' harsher than Tawny's, also a barking 'khau, khau'. Forests, both coniferous and deciduous, also in villages, towns and cities, often hunting by day for mammals up to squirrel size and birds as large as Hazel Grouse. L 60-62, WS 124-134 cm.

**TAWNY OWL** *Strix aluco*. The region's commonest medium-sized brown owl, mainly nocturnal or crepuscular and most often detected in daytime when loudly mobbed by smaller birds while hunched up in its tree roost, when can be told from Long-eared Owl (p.208) by its black eyes and lack of ear tufts. Larger-headed and stouter than Barn and Long-eared, and shorter-winged than Long-eared. Varies from rich tawny chestnut through buff, brown and grey-brown to greyish-white; juv barred. Most frequent calls, often heard by day, long quavering hoot and a sharp 'ke-wick'. Mainly deciduous woodland, also areas with scattered trees, such as farmland, parkland and large gardens; not uncommon in villages, towns and some cities, feeding on rodents, small birds. Nest usually in tree hole. L 37-39, WS 94-104 cm. ●R

◄ Do not approach juv Tawny Owls outside the nest hole as the female can attack and wound human 'predators'. At this stage they have a hunger cry likened to a gate on an unoiled hinge.

Ssp.*aluco* (C Europe) larger and greyer; *siberiae* (Urals) paler grey; *sylvatica* (Britain to Iberia) smaller and more rufous with a grey variant; *mauritanica* (N W Africa) larger and darker, with distinctive calls; also paler in Iraq.

Fledgling juv

**HUME'S TAWNY OWL** *Strix butleri*. So pale on underparts that almost looks like a Barn Owl with the same-sized Tawny's bulky jizz. At close range easily distinguished from both by its orange-yellow eyes; also has upper tail more boldly barred and toes unfeathered. Distinctive 5-syllabic hoot, 'hoooo huhu-huhu' recalls doves' coo rather than Tawny Owl's quaver. Very nocturnal in habits and always in or on the fringes of deserts, though may visit palm groves or villages and perch on rocks or posts. Does not overlap Tawny's range. L 37-38, WS 95-98 cm.

Distribution not well known, but seen increasingly in recent years.

● BARN OWLS *Tytonidae*. Owls that differ from the Strigidae especially in their heart-shaped face and usually shallowly V-shaped tail.

**BARN OWL** *Tyto alba*. The region's only owl which is golden-buff above and white below, though most often seen ghost-like in the dusk, or caught in car headlights, when it appears all-white. Call a prolonged, strangled, almost blood-curdling screech; also hisses, snores and barks. Farmland and other open, often arid country, with scattered trees, feeding mainly on small rodents. Often nests in barns, churches and other old buildings. It is found world-wide. L 33-35, WS 85-93 cm. ●R

Dark-breasted ssp.*guttata* (C, E and parts of N W Europe), deep buff below and strongly marked grey-blue above, can be told from Tawny Owl in flight by its longer and narrower wings and at rest by its longer legs. Ssp.*alba* (Scotland to N W Africa) is white below and darker above. On Madeira and eastern Canary Is is smaller and paler. In the Middle East more golden.

The heart-shaped facial disc is a good field mark.

**OWLS**

grey sylvatica

rufous aluco

▲
◀ TAWNY OWL

mauritanica

HUME'S TAWNY OWL

guttata

alba

BARN OWL. Buff-breasted individuals
may occur in white-breasted populations.

● NIGHTJARS: *Caprimulgidae*. Wholly nocturnal, seen by day only when flushed from ground or perched horizontally along a branch, well camouflaged by mottled brown plumage. Wings and tail long; flight very agile, gliding and wheeling, with sudden darts after prey. Feet small. Sexes largely alike.

**NIGHTJAR** *Caprimulgus europaeus*. The region's only widespread nightjar, most often detected by song, a far-carrying churr, sustained, but with abrupt changes of pitch; rarely heard till 45-60 minutes after sunset. When flushed, appears long-winged, long-tailed and hawk-like, but differs from all raptors in very short, straight bill, and from juv Cuckoo in unbarred underparts and no white nape patch. Male has white tips to outer tail feathers and three conspicuous white spots on outer primaries. Call a soft but insistent 'cu-ic'; also claps its wings with a whip-crack sound. Areas with scattered trees, open woodlands, forest edges, felled woodland, heaths, semideserts. L 26-28 cm.                                                ⊙S

Ssp.*meridionalis* (S Europe, Asia Minor, N Africa) is smaller and slightly paler; ssp.*unwini* (E Iraq) is greyer and still paler.

**RED-NECKED NIGHTJAR** *Caprimulgus ruficollis*. The region's largest nightjar, browner and somewhat stouter than Nightjar, and with stronger flight, larger head, conspicuous white throat and rufous collar, and more obvious white spots (smaller in female) on wings and tail. Song quite distinct, a rapid loud echoing repetition of 'kutuk'. Dry open country, semi-deserts, with scattered trees/shrubs. L 30-32 cm.        -V

**NUBIAN NIGHTJAR** *Caprimulgus nubicus*. The region's smallest nightjar, pale and greyish with a white throat patch, rufous collar, white spots on primaries and conspicuous white tips of outer tail feathers. Wings more rounded and wing-beats faster than Nightjar. Song a repeated echoing double 'koww' or 'kwua'. Tamarisk, thorn and other scrub, desert edges; roosts in shade of rocks or bushes. L 21-22 cm.

**EGYPTIAN NIGHTJAR** *Caprimulgus aegyptius*. The region's palest nightjar, in size between Nightjar and Nubian Nightjar. Plumage fairly uniformly sandy, with a white throat patch, but only rather obscure white spots on wings and tail and lacking Nightjar's dark band on forewing. Song a series of repeated 'kowrr' or 'purr' notes, often slower at the end; also calls rendered as 'kre-kre-kre', 'toc-toc' and 'tuki-tuki'. Deserts, semideserts, often with sparse scrub or scattered palms. L 24-26 cm.                                                -V

Ssp.*aegyptius* (Nile delta, Middle East) has more greyish, and ssp. *saharae* (N Africa) very pale, more pinkish, ground colour.

**Common Nighthawk** *Chordeiles minor*. Transatlantic vagrant, sometimes diurnal, slightly smaller than Nightjar, with longer, more pointed wings and shorter notched tail; also with conspicuous white patch (not spots) across primaries and, in male, a white throat patch and band near tail tip. Flight call a nasal 'peent' or 'peeik'. L 23-25 cm.                                                -V

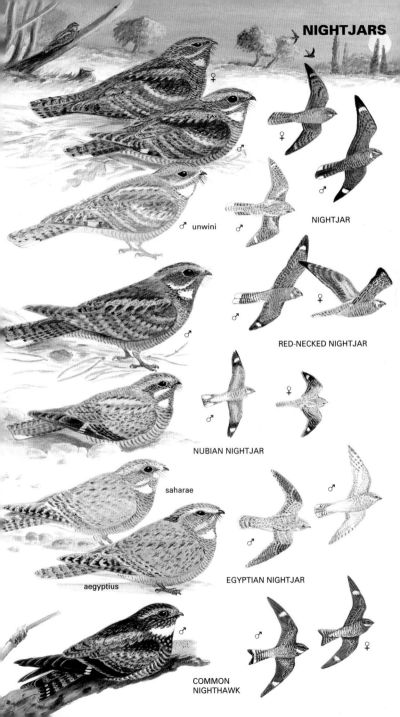

# NIGHTJARS

♀

♂ unwini    ♂    NIGHTJAR

RED-NECKED NIGHTJAR

♂    ♀

NUBIAN NIGHTJAR

♂    ♀

saharae

♂    ♂

aegyptius

EGYPTIAN NIGHTJAR

♂

COMMON
NIGHTHAWK

♂    ♀

● SWIFTS: *Apodidae*. The most aerial of birds, whose long narrow curved wings and short, usually forked, tail adapt them to very fast flight and feeding on flying insects. Basic plumage brown or blackish; sexes alike.

Pallid Swift

Rock Martin

Most swifts have much faster, bolder, more determined flight than swallows or martins (p.238), wheeling and gliding with no fluttering, and often in noisy parties. Their short-tailed, scimitar-winged flight outline is also quite different from the more Maltese-cross appearance of the hirundines. Some species feed very high up in morning and evening, often spending the night high aloft, sleeping on the wing. During the day, especially when it is cold or wet, they may feed lower down, alongside hirundines.

**Needle-tailed Swift** *Hirundapus caudacutus*. Rare vagrant from E Asia. Large, dark, broad-winged, glossed green or purple, with very short minutely spine-tipped square tail, white throat and forehead and conspicuous white horseshoe on underparts. L 19-20, WS 50-53 cm.                                                    -V

**LITTLE SWIFT** *Apus affinis*. The region's smallest swift, the only one with both a short square tail and a conspicuous broad square white rump; cf. larger White-rumped Swift, which has narrower white rump and forked tail. Juv paler, with white-tipped inner primaries. Same-sized House Martin (p.240) and larger Red-rumped Swallow (p.240) have forked tail, mostly pale underparts, and much less vigorous flight. Call a high-pitched twittering trill. Frequent in towns, sometimes in mountain gorges. Aka House Swift (India). L 12, WS 34-35 cm.    -V

Breeds in Africa S of Sahara. Since 1968 also Morocco and S Spain, May-Oct, sometimes over-wintering.

**WHITE-RUMPED SWIFT** *Apus caffer*. Larger than Little Swift and much more deeply forked tail, narrower white rump, plumage blue-black not brown-black, and pale underwing contrasting with black underwing coverts; both have pale throats. Much darker than either shorter House Martin (p.240) or longer Red-rumped Swallow (p.240). (NB Horus Swift *A. horus* breeding Sudan southwards, has larger white rump and shallowly forked tail.) Juv duller and has white tips to inner primaries. Less noisy than Little Swift, call more guttural. Flight like Swift (p.218). Uses old nests of Red-rumped and other swallows. L 14, WS 34-36 cm.

**ALPINE SWIFT** *Apus melba*. Much the largest breeding swift of the region, easily told by its dull, rather pale brown plumage, with distinctive white underparts crossed by a brown breast band, a feature not found in any of the region's other swifts. Flight fast, strong and determined, even more vigorous and powerful than Swift (p.218); wing beats slower, sometimes recalling a small falcon (p.108). Parties utter a distinctive loud trilling whistle, 'trihihihihi', rising and falling in pitch. L 20-22, WS 54-60 cm.                                                    -A

Southern birds paler, especially ssp.*tuneti* (N W Africa, except N Morocco, to Levant), and *archeri* (Dead Sea to Sinai).

Juv Alpine Swift has more extensive narrow white fringes to head and wing feathers than worn autumn adults.

**Pacific Swift** *A. pacificus*. Rare vagrant from E Asia. Larger and blacker than White-rumped Swift (slightly larger than Swift), with narrower swept-back wings, longer deep-forked tail, broader white rump and at close range grey body-scaling. L 17-18, WS 48-54 cm.                                                    -V

216

House Martin

Swift

Beware confusing partly albino Swifts (p.218) with white on rump, also House Martins (p.240).

ad

ad

juv

NEEDLE-TAILED SWIFT

LITTLE SWIFT

melba

WHITE-RUMPED SWIFT

tuneti

ALPINE SWIFT

PACIFIC SWIFT

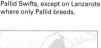

Swifts with their short legs never perch on the ground (except accidentally) or in trees, but cling to sides of cliffs or buildings. They spend both day and night on the wing, coming in only to roost at dusk when breeding.

Found on all Canary Is alongside
Pallid Swifts, except on Lanzarote
where only Pallid breeds.

**PLAIN SWIFT** *Apus unicolor*. Largely confined to Madeira throughout year and Canaries in breeding season. Extremely similar to both Swift and paler Pallid Swift, though distinctly smaller and greyer-brown and with slightly more deeply forked tail and hard-to-see grey chin and throat; can be best distinguished from below, by primaries appearing semi-translucent. Flight faster than Swift and Pallid Swift. Screams like Swift; has rapid trill. L 14-15, WS 38-39 cm.

**SWIFT** *Apus apus*. Distinguished from all swallows and martins (pp.238-241) of the region by long curved wings, short tail and all-dark plumage; throat whitish, but less obviously so than in juv. Has vigorous dashing flight, wheeling, winnowing and gliding; excited parties chase each other squealing round the houses in small towns and villages. Normal cry a harsh scream. Feeds over fresh water, open country and built-up areas. Nest in hole or crevice of cliff or building, often in towns and villages. L 16-17, WS 42-48 cm.　　　　　　　●Sm

Sspp. not separable in field, but paler, browner migrating *pekinensis* (Iran) with sometimes pale, almost off-white head and chin, could be mistaken for Pallid.

juv　　　　　　　　　　　ad

Juv browner than adult with larger throat patch and pale edges to body and wing feathers.

**PALLID SWIFT** *Apus pallidus*. Very similar to Swift, but somewhat paler and browner, with faint scaling on underparts, paler inner wings, contrasting dark mantle and primaries, very pale head and larger throat patch. Has distinctly different jizz, due to broader head, slightly broader and blunter wings, and slower, more deliberate wing-beats. Voice slightly deeper. Cf. smaller Plain Swift. Spends longer at breeding colonies; otherwise as Swift, with which it often flies. L 16-17, WS 42-48 cm.　　　-V

**Chimney Swift** *Chaetura pelagica*. Rare transatlantic vagrant. In bat-like outline resembles same-sized Little Swift (p.216), but has dark rump and differs from the region's three all-dark breeding swifts in its very short unforked tail with two tiny spines at tip.　　-V

# SWIFTS

Noisy evening flights of Swifts and/or Pallid Swifts over southern European towns can be spectacular, especially when the young birds join in.

PLAIN SWIFT

apus

pekinensis

SWIFT

brehmorum

Swallow (p.240)

PALLID SWIFT

p.*pallidus* (Middle East, Egypt)
allest and palest; ssp.*brehmorum*
'er in N Africa, Canaries and
deira than Spain and France;
.*illyricus* (Adriatic) largest, darkest.

CHIMNEY SWIFT

● KINGFISHERS: *Alcedinidae*. Small to large land or waterside birds, with large head; long, stout, sharply pointed, dagger-like bill; short neck and short legs; and feet with one backward and three forward toes, the forward ones joined towards their base. Sexes more or less alike. Normal flight usually fast and direct, with quick beats of the short, rounded wings. Perch upright. Hole nesters.

♂

♀

**KINGFISHER** *Alcedo atthis*. Both the smallest and the only widespread and common kingfisher of the region, brilliantly coloured and the region's only bird with plumage metallic blue-green above and rich chestnut below. Bill black, but female's lower mandible reddish; legs and feet red. Short tail gives distinctive flight outline and squat appearance when perched. Dives for fish either from perch or when hovering. Call, a loud shrill penetrating 'cheee' or 'chikeee', often draws attention to a bird speeding like a blue arrow up or downstream or across a riverside field. Song a whistling trill. Lowland fresh water, in winter also estuaries, sea coast. Nest in hole in river bank or sandpit, often marked by white splashes from droppings. L 16-17 cm.　　　　　　　　　　　　　　　　　　　　　　　●R

Ssp.*atthis* (Mediterranean, E Europe) has chin whiter than ssp.*ispida* (N Europe), contrasting more with chestnut breast.

**SMYRNA KINGFISHER** *Halcyon smyrnensis*. The region's largest breeding kingfisher, with striking combination of dark chestnut head and underparts, bright blue upperparts and tail, white chin, throat and breast, and massive red bill. In flight white bar on underwing. Very vocal, with a loud high-pitched whistle and raucous laughing cry. Swoops and dives for fish and, shrike-like, for large insects and other small animals. Farmland, town gardens, open plains, forests, fresh water coasts and estuaries. Aka White-breasted Kingfisher. L 26-28 cm.

♀

**LESSER PIED KINGFISHER** *Ceryle rudis*. Strikingly black and white, crested with a long black bill and longish tail. Male has two black bands on breast, female only one, not always complete, and juv a greyish band. Call a sharp penetrating 'keek, keek'; also a whistling note. Most often seen hovering, then plummeting into water for fish, also dives from a perch. Fresh and inland saline water, but not in forests or high on mountains, coasts and estuaries, often in small parties. L 24-26 cm.

**Belted Kingfisher** *C. alcyon*. Rare transatlantic vagrant. The only large blue-grey bird with a ragged crest at all likely to be seen in the region; bill blackish. Female has rufous band on belly and flanks. Call a raucous rattle, not unlike Mistle Thrush. Flight powerful and flapping. L 28-35 cm.　　　　　　　　　　　　　　　　　　-V

● HOOPOES *Upupidae*. A family with one species only. Hole nester.

**HOOPOE** *Upupa epops*. Quite unmistakable, with long curved bill and prominent black-tipped crest, either folded down or erected fan-wise. Plumage pinkish-cinnamon, with tail and rounded wings strongly barred black-and-white, in flight looking like a huge round-winged black-and-white moth. Chief call a rapid, far-carrying clipped 'hoo-hoo-hoo', less musical than Cuckoo (p.202) and less drawn-out and quavering than Tawny Owl (p.212). Grassy and wooded plains, farmland, orchards, vineyards, parks, gardens. L 26-28 cm.　　　　　　○M(b)

# KINGFISHERS, HOOPOE

LESSER PIED KINGFISHER

KINGFISHER
Bill black, but adult female has reddish lower mandible.

juv

ad

SMYRNA KINGFISHER

juv

ad

BELTED KINGFISHER

In flight like an outsize colourful butterfly.

HOOPOE

● BEE-EATERS: *Meropidae*. Brightly coloured, long-winged, long-tailed, gregarious land birds, with long, slightly curved bill; sexes alike. Adults have elongated central tail feathers. Perching on bushes or wires on look-out for flying insects; flight swallow-like, with long glides on sharply pointed, triangular wings and sharp acceleration to capture prey, then returning to perch with a graceful upward sweep to batter it to death before eating it. Open country with scattered trees and bushes, often near rivers. Nesting colonies in holes in sandy river banks and sand and gravel pits.

**BEE-EATER** *Merops apiaster*. The region's commonest and most widespread bee-eater, almost uniquely combining harlequin plumage with central tail feathers projecting from a long tail. Mainly blue-green (greener when not breeding), with chestnut head and mantle, yellow rump and throat, black breastband and broad eye-stripe. Juv duller and greener. Yellow rump and pale chestnut underwing with black trailing edge conspicuous in flight. Flight call a constantly uttered, liquid 'quilp'; also a throaty 'kroop, kroop'. L 27-29 cm.                    -A(b)

**BLUE-CHEEKED BEE-EATER** *Merops superciliosus*. Mainly green, fading to dull blue, with yellow chin, chestnut throat, no black breast-band, and pale blue cheeks and forehead separated by black eye-stripe; chestnut underwing shows in flight. Bill and central tail feathers longer and call rather higher-pitched and quieter than Bee-eater. Cf. blue-throated ssp.*cyanophrys* of much smaller Little Green Bee-eater. L 27-31 cm.            -V

Ssp.*persicus* (Egypt, Middle East) described above; ssp.*chrysocercus* (N W Africa) has slightly shorter wings and less white on forehead.

**LITTLE GREEN BEE-EATER** *Merops orientalis*. The region's smallest bee-eater, mainly green, with varying amount of blue on head and pale buff underwing. Throat colour, golden-green or blue, always separates from the two larger species, which can both look very green. Call a chattering 'tit, tit' or 'tree-tree-tree'. L 22-25 cm.

Ssp.*cleopatra* (Egypt) is mainly green tinged golden and has very long central tail feathers; ssp.*cyanophrys* (Israel) has most green parts tinged blue, bright blue head and throat, and shorter central tail feathers.

● ROLLERS: *Coraciidae*. Large, brightly coloured, crow-like birds, named from their somersaulting courtship display. Bill stout, slightly hooked; legs rather short. Sexes more or less alike. Hole nesters.

**ROLLER** *Coracias garrulus*. The region's only crow-like bird, apart from Indian Roller and Jay (p.320), to show a bright blue wing-patch in flight, but blue patch much larger than Jay's, wings appearing blue with black tips and edges. At rest like a smallish blue-green crow with a chestnut back; tail slightly forked. Winter adult/juv duller. Flight direct, recalling Woodpigeon (p.196). Call a harsh, rather crow-like 'rack, kack, kacker'. Open woodland, open country with scattered trees and scrub, parkland, orchards. L 30-32 cm.                    -A

**INDIAN ROLLER** *Coracias benghalensis*. Differs from Roller especially in chestnut breast, mantle and head except bluegreen crown, also in all-dark tip of square-ended tail, with blue only at sides. Voice croaking, heron-like, a loud quacking clatter and a staccato 'k'yow, k'yow'. L 32-34 cm.

**BEE-EATERS**

ad

BEE-EATER

juv

juv

ad

ersicus

ad

chrysocercus

BLUE-CHEEKED
BEE-EATER

cleopatra

ad

juv

ad

LITTLE GREEN
BEE-EATER

ad

cyanophrys

ad

ad

juv

ROLLER

ad

INDIAN ROLLER

● WOODPECKERS: *Picidae*. Land birds, highly adapted to climbing about trees, extracting insect prey from bark and rotten wood with long tongue and excavating nest holes with stout bill: tail square and stiff (except Wryneck, p.228) to act as support against vertical surfaces; feet with two toes pointing forwards and two (one vestigial) backwards. Some species also feed on ground. Flight markedly undulating; gait a hop. Most species drum in spring, a creaking mechanical sound made by resonance of dead branches under rapid blows from bill.

**BLACK WOODPECKER** *Dryocopus martius*. Much the largest (crow-sized) and most distinctive woodpecker of the region, male being the only large all-black bird with a red crown and crest; female/juv browner, female red on nape only. Holds head and neck in distinctive angular way, identifiable in profile at a distance. Flight strikingly but irregularly dipping, often straighter than other woodpeckers. Far-carrying voice a loud, clear, vibrant, fluty string of double notes; also a single repeated musical yelp; drums loudly. Coniferous, mixed and beech woodland. L 45-57 cm.

**GREY-HEADED WOODPECKER** *Picus canus*. Appreciably smaller than Green Woodpecker, with head and underparts predominantly grey and bill less stout. Male has red on forehead only, female no red at all, and black moustachial streaks are much narrower. Juv browner, with barred flanks. Main call more musical and slower than Green, falling away at the end; not often heard except when breeding; drums more often than Green. Woodland, especially larch, tree-lined rivers; often feeding on ground. L 25-26 cm.

Grey-headed

Green

Grey-headed Woodpecker has faster, more buoyant flight than Green, with slenderer body.

**GREEN WOODPECKER** *Picus viridis*. Combination of green plumage, conspicuous yellow-green rump in flight and red on head distinguishes from all birds of the region, except Grey-headed and Levaillant's. Both sexes have red crown and nape; moustachial stripe red and black in male, black in female, red in juv. Juv paler, speckled darker. Spring 'yaffling' call a far-carrying, loud, ringing 'plue-plue-plue'; also various loud yelping cries; drums rarely, with a light rattling sound. Deciduous/mixed woodland, open country with scattered trees; often on ground. Aka Yaffle. L 31-33 cm.                    ●R

♀ sharpei

Iberian race *sharpei* has grey cheeks, narrower black moustaches, and different voice.

Only in Atlas Mountains.

**LEVAILLANT'S WOODPECKER** *Picus vaillantii*. Differs from same-sized Green Woodpecker in face being grey (like Iberian race of Green), male having thick moustachial stripe black with no red, and female being red only on nape. Calls very similar to Green, but drums much more often. Open woodland in hill country, often feeding on ants on the ground, even above tree-line. L 30-32 cm.

# WOODPECKERS

Flight straighter, not undulating.

♀

♂

BLACK
WOODPECKER

♀

♂

Juv not
spotted like
juv Green.

GREY-HEADED
WOODPECKER

♀

♂

LEVAILLANT'S
WOODPECKER

♀

♂

viridis

GREEN
WOODPECKER

sharpei ♂

juv

**SYRIAN WOODPECKER** *Dendrocopos syriacus*. Adults differ from Great Spotted especially in whiter cheeks due to no black bar on side of neck (often hard to see), and by paler pink vent and flanks sometimes streaked. Juv differs from juv Great Spotted (which may have no black neck bar) in red breast band, and flanks always barred. Cf. Middle Spotted and White-backed (p.228). Drums and calls like Great Spotted, but 'chik' softer. Mainly lowland broad-leaved woodland and areas of scattered trees, Great Spotted being largely confined to mountain forests within its range. L 22-23 cm.

Syrian        Great

Besides face pattern and vent colour, amount of white in tail also differentiates Syrian from Great Spotted. Syrian has very little, some less than shown here, while some Great Spotted show more.

**GREAT SPOTTED WOODPECKER** *Dendrocopos major*. Generally the region's commonest black-and-white woodpecker, with prominent white wing-patches and red under tail coverts. Adults have black crown, male also red nape; juv has red crown. Flight conspicuously bounding, the wings folded in at the bottom of each bound. Usual call a sharp 'tchick', also trills and titters and a harsh churr like a Mistle Thrush (p.274) when excited. Drums frequently in spring, with 8-10 blows lasting one second only. Coniferous, mixed and broad-leaved woodland, also orchards, parks, large gardens and other areas with scattered trees. L 22-23 cm.          ●Rw

thanneri

canariensis

numidus

poelzami
N Iran

Sspp. *major* (N Europe) above; *pinetorum* (C & W Europe) smaller and a little darker; *anglicus* (Britain), *italiae* (Italy) and *hispanus* darker still with more buff on cheeks; *candidus* (Balkans) and *tenuirostris* (Crimea, Caucasus) have underparts white, creamy white or grey-buff; *parroti* (Corsica) and *harterti* (Sardinia) slightly larger; *numidus* (Algeria, Tunisia) has distinctive black and red breast-band, with both vent and lower belly red, so has *mauritanus* but with no black in mid breast; *canariensis* (Tenerife) is creamy buff below; and *thanneri* (Gran Canaria) is greyish buff below.

**MIDDLE SPOTTED WOODPECKER** *Dendrocopos medius*. Slightly the smallest of the three black-and-white species with a large white wing patch, with the white parts greyer or buffer, and the only one with red-crowned adults (female's hind crown golden brown) and the black moustache not reaching the bill; flanks more strongly barred than Syrian. Lacks red neck bar of juv Syrian and some juv Great Spotted. Restless, appearing very barred in flight. Has a repeated rattling 'kik' note and a 'wait, wait' song, uttered slowly on a rising or falling scale. Drums much less than Great Spotted, and habitat similar, but not in pure coniferous forests. L 20-22 cm.

226

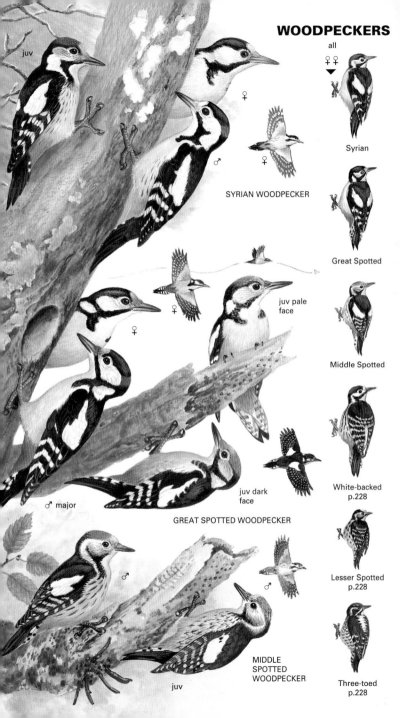

# WOODPECKERS

all
♀♀♀
▼

juv

Syrian

SYRIAN WOODPECKER
♀
♂

Great Spotted

♀

juv pale
face

Middle Spotted

♀

juv dark
face

♂ major

GREAT SPOTTED WOODPECKER

White-backed
p.228

♂

Lesser Spotted
p.228

MIDDLE
SPOTTED
WOODPECKER

juv

Three-toed
p.228

Prefers broad-leaved woodland, especially with plenty of rotten timber.

**WHITE-BACKED WOODPECKER** *Dendrocopos leucotos*. The region's largest, longest-necked and longest-billed black and white woodpecker, and the only larger one with white lower back and rump, and no large white patches but broad black-and-white bars on wings. Red-crowned male also differs from Middle Spotted in its Syrian-like face pattern, with both neck bar and complete moustache. Red of juv's crown and under tail coverts rather pale. Chief call, 'kjuk', softer than Great Spotted, but drumming louder, with single blows merging into a volley resembling a creaking branch. Woodland. L 24-26 cm.

Ssp.*lilfordi* (S Europe, Asia Minor) is paler with yellowish forehead and cheeks and has a black line behind ear coverts that is less distinct or absent in ssp.*leucotos* (N Europe, Carpathians) and always absent in ssp.*uralensis* (Urals).

**LESSER SPOTTED WOODPECKER** *Dendrocopos minor*. The region's smallest woodpecker, sparrow-sized, with short bill, streaked underparts and barred wings. Male's crown red; female and Three-toed are region's only black-and-white woodpeckers with no red at all. Most frequent note a rather weak, flat 'pee-pee-pee-pee-pee', lacking Wryneck's ringing quality; also 'tchik', weaker and more sibilant than Great Spotted. Drums in spring, fainter than Great Spotted, but for two seconds, with 10-30 blows. Flight more fluttering than other woodpeckers. Open broad-leaved and mixed woodland, areas with scattered trees, mainly in lowlands. L 14-15 cm.          ⊙R

**THREE-TOED WOODPECKER** *Picoides tridactylus*. The region's most distinctive black-and-white woodpecker: the only one with two black stripes on face and mainly black wings; the only one with a white rump, except White-backed; the only one with no red at all, except female Lesser Spotted; and the male's yellow crown is the only yellow plumage in any of them (cf. southern race of White-backed). Main call a soft 'ptuk' or 'ptik'; drums with loud machinegun-like 'takatakataka'. Coniferous forests; in far N also among birches and willows. L 21-22 cm.

Ssp.*alpinus* (C and SE Europe) is darker, with white back barred and flanks more heavily barred.

1st w

♀

♂

◄

**Yellow-bellied Sapsucker** *Sphyrapicus varius*. Rare transatlantic vagrant, barred above and pale yellow below, with large white wing patch and red fore-crown, male with red throat. L 18-20 cm.          -V

**WRYNECK** *Jynx torquilla*. The region's most songbird-like and only regular migrant woodpecker; barred and mottled brown, with a longish tail. Creeps about trees like much smaller Treecreeper (p.314), but has straight bill, longer tail and brown underparts. Flight less dipping than other woodpeckers; perches across branches like songbird; often feeds on ground, hopping with tail raised. Drums and utters loud, clear, rather musical 'kew-kew-kew-kew-kew', recalling Nuthatch (p.312), Lesser Spotted Woodpecker or even Kestrel (p.108). Open broad-leaved woodlands, other areas with scattered trees. Nest usually in tree hole. L 16-17 cm.          ⊙sM

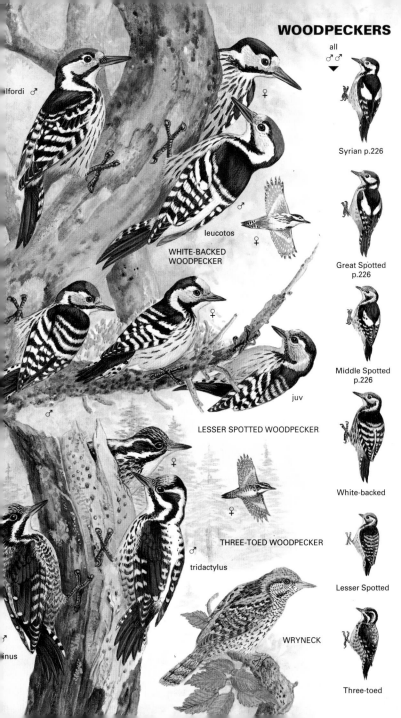

# WOODPECKERS

ilfordi ♂

leucotos

WHITE-BACKED
WOODPECKER

♀

♂

♀

♀

juv

♂

LESSER SPOTTED WOODPECKER

♀

THREE-TOED WOODPECKER

tridactylus

WRYNECK

inus

all
♂♂
▼

Syrian p.226

Great Spotted
p.226

Middle Spotted
p.226

White-backed

Lesser Spotted

Three-toed

● LARKS: *Alaudidae.* pp.230-237. Smallish ground-living songbirds, mostly with sober brown plumage, often darker in the N and paler in sandy desert areas; sexes usually alike. Hind claw usually long. Song usually well developed and delivered either when climbing steeply or when circling in the air. Flight typically direct and undulating. Gait normally walking or running, sometimes also hopping. Often in flocks when not breeding. Bill length and shape, outer tail feathers and voice all important in identification.

**WOODLARK** *Lullula arborea.* Smaller than Skylark, and with noticeably shorter wings and tail (but beware short-tailed juv Skylarks) making an almost bat-like flight outline. Has pale buff supercilia meeting on nape, black-and-white mark on leading edge of wing, tail with white tip but dark outer feathers, and small crest, often hard to see. Mellow, fluty song, often on interrupted descending scale, usually in circular song flight, sometimes at night. Flight and call note 'tit-looeet'. Open country with scattered trees, woodland verges, heaths, farmland, alpine meadows. L 15 cm. ⊙R

**SKYLARK** *Alauda arvensis.* A rather large brown lark, with an often obscure crest and white outer feathers in fairly long tail. Juv has no crest and shorter tail. Readily identified by sustained, high-pitched, musical, sometimes mimetic, aerial song, delivered ascending, hovering or descending (final plummet silent), often almost out of sight; sometimes at night. Call a liquid 'chirrup'. Crouches rather than runs when disturbed. Open, often treeless country, farmland, grassland, alpine meadows, heaths, moors, coastal dunes. L 18-19 cm. ●RmW

**SMALL SKYLARK** *Alauda gulgula.* Very like a small dumpy Skylark, woodlark-like in its shorter wings and tail, and with longer bill, rufous-tinged wings, tertials almost reaching wingtip, buffish outer tail feathers and often a small blackish spot at side of neck. Flight calls a buzzing 'pzeebz' (also in skylark-like song) and a softer 'pyup'. Aka Oriental Skylark. L 16 cm.

**CRESTED LARK** *Galerida cristata.* Like a Skylark, but with a longer, always conspicuously erect crest, short broad wings, buff outer feathers in shorter tail, and (in Europe) orange-buff underwing in flight. Song reedier and more plaintive, with shorter phrases and often mimetic; from ground or perch or in air, but never with soaring display. Flight call a liquid 'whee-whee-ooo', rising from first to second syllable and then falling; also a fluty 'too-hee'. L 17 cm. -V

Dry, bare stony and sandy ground, wadis, semi-deserts, dunes, farmland, waste ground in towns, e.g. railway sidings.

Some 15 sspp. in the region: In N Africa some much paler, e.g. *arenicola* (Tunisia); *cinnamomina* (Lebanon) rich cinnamon; others, e.g. *macrorhyncha* (Algerian Sahara), with stouter bill.

**THEKLA LARK** *Galerida theklae.* Hard to separate from Crested Lark, but very slightly smaller and has pale half-collar, more conspicuous dark spots, especially on breast, and (in Europe) greyish underwing and slightly shorter bill. Song rather similar, but variable and mimetic, delivered either in fluttering circular display flight or, oftener than Crested, from a bush top or tree. Flight call distinctive, more musical but 2-4-syllabic. L 17 cm.

Prefers more broken ground, often scrubby, higher in mountains and less cultivated, avoiding towns and villages.

Ssp.*theklae* (Iberia, S W France), above; 4 N African races, becoming larger, longer-winged, longer-billed, sandier, paler and less heavily streaked from N W Morocco E and S to the Atlas Mts and Algeria.

# LARKS

50-80 m high

50-100 m high

juv

ad

**WOODLARK**

**SMALL SKYLARK**

juv

ad

**SKYLARK**

juv

cristata ad

macrorhyncha

arenicole

**CRESTED LARK**

Crested Lark

Thekla Lark

juv

ad

superflua

thekla

**THEKLA LARK**

Tertials reaching tip of closed wing. Cf. longer primaries of Lesser Short-toed.

Dunn's

Bar-tailed

A rather stockily built lark.

**SHORT-TOED LARK** *Calandrella brachydactyla*. A small lark, streaked pale rufous or greyish above and uniformly whitish below (breast sometimes faintly streaked, usually with a small dark patch on each side); bill short, finch-like. Song sustained, musical, repetitive, in undulating circular display or on ground. Calls include a sparrow-like chirp and a short, dry, skylark-like rattle. Dry, treeless, bare or grassy steppes, cultivations, semi-deserts and dunes. L 13-14 cm.                                    -A

Becomes greyer and less rufous from W to E in Mediterranean, most rufous in ssp.*rubiginosa* (N W Africa), palest grey in ssp.*artemisiana* (Asia Minor, Caucasus).

**LESSER SHORT-TOED LARK** *Calandrella rufescens*. Very like Short-toed, but with well-streaked breast, no dark patches and tertials much shorter than wing tips. Song more musical, usually preceded by 'prrrit', often with mimicked phrases; uttered from ground, or in rising spiral or circular flight without undulations. Habitat stonier, more saline and less grassy, often at drier margins of marshes. L 13-14 cm.                                    -V

The 9 sspp. in the region vary in degrees of rufous and grey in their plumage, but with no east-west cline.

**BAR-TAILED LARK** *Ammomanes cincturus*. Smaller than Desert Lark, but with distinctive rounded head, shorter bill and well-defined dark bar at tip of shorter tail and blackish wing tips; and legs darker. Song weak, fluty, trisyllabic; flight call like Short-toed. Mainly in deserts with little vegetation and few rocks; often in small flocks. L 15 cm.

**DUNN'S LARK** *Eremalauda dunni*. Breeds locally Jordan, Israel, Sinai. Differs from desert larks in bolder face pattern, heavier and brighter bill, more streaked crown and upperparts and, in flight, black wedges in outer tail. Song recalls Bar-tailed Lark; calls 'chiup, chiup' and a liquid 'prrrp'. L 14 cm.

**DESERT LARK** *Ammomanes deserti*. Squat, round-winged and (except for dark brown lower tail) almost uniformly sandy, varying in shade with dominant ground colour. Call distinctive, a plaintive 'tweet'; song a repeated, far-carrying, musical 'too-too-wee'. Flight rather slow and weakly dipping. Deserts, semi-deserts, wadis and stony ground, sometimes with scattered trees; not normally flocking. L 16-17 cm.

Three of the region's 7-8 sspp. are illustrated here to show how plumage colour relates to soil colour, especially the very dark ssp.*annae* from the black lava deserts of Jordan.

**DUPONT'S LARK** *Chersophilus duponti*. A brown to rufous lark, with a long, slightly curved bill, patterned like Crested Lark (p.230) but with pale crown stripe instead of crest. Shy, flies reluctantly, and best located at dawn by its rather nasal, unlark-like song, uttered high in air; an even more nasal, main call a double whistle on a rising scale, 'hoo-hee'. Scrub, grassy steppes, dry farmland. L 18 cm.

Ssp.*duponti* (Iberia, N W Africa) above; ssp.*margaritae* (S Atlas Mts eastwards) is more rufous.

232

song flight

# LARKS

artemisiana

A rather variable species.
Some can be very greyish.

brachydactyla

**SHORT-TOED LARK**

♂

♀ Female often not or
less spotted on
breast than male.

rufescens

apetzii

**LESSER SHORT-TOED LARK**

**BAR-TAILED
LARK**

algeriensis

annae

payni

**DUNN'S LARK**

**DESERT LARK**

duponti

margaritae

**DUPONT'S LARK**

The normally rather stocky Dupont's
may look rather long-necked when alert.

**CALANDRA LARK** *Melanocorypha calandra*. A large lark, substantially more heavily built than Skylark, large-headed with no crest, pale supercilium, broad triangular wings, a conspicuous but variable black patch on each side of the neck and a very stout, seed-eating bill. Cf. Bimaculated Lark, female Black Lark. Skylark-like song, including both its own jangling 'kleetra' call and frequent notes mimicked from other birds, uttered either in high wide circular song flight, or lower down with curious slow wing action, or even on ground. Grassy steppes with low scrubby vegetation, dry stony ground, cultivations. L 18-19 cm. -V

Calandra          Bimaculated

Flocks are almost wader-like in flight, showing conspicuously white trailing edge of wing, contrasting with dark underside, and white outer tail feathers. Cf. Bimaculated, which has trailing edge of wing dark, underside paler, outer tail feathers buff and tail tip white.

**BIMACULATED LARK** *Melanocorypha bimaculata*. At rest very similar to Calandra Lark, but smaller, longer-winged and more rufous, with much smaller neck patches, dark lores and whiter supercilium; for differences in flight, see above. Song and calls similar to Calandra. Breeds higher up in the mountains and more often in semi-deserts and on barer ground. L 16-17 cm. -V

**BLACK LARK** *Melanocorypha yeltoniensis*. The largest thick-billed lark, the male very distinctive in its all black summer plumage (browner in winter). Female and juv have conspicuous dark underwing coverts and have neither dark neck patches nor any white in wings; female also has dark spots on lower breast and belly. Song like Calandra but in shorter bursts, uttered more often on ground than in low circular owl-like flight. Flight note skylark-like, also a piping call. Grassy, scrubby, and in winter also cultivated steppes. L 19-20 cm.

**WHITE-WINGED LARK** *Melanocorypha leucoptera*. Differs from other thick-billed larks most obviously in its broad white wing bar contrasting with rufous forewing and black tips, and rufous crown and ear coverts of male (less rufous, more streaked in female); outer tail feathers white. Song like Skylark (p.230), delivered either in high soaring flight or nearer the ground, or from low perch; flight call a tinny 'wed'. Dry grassy steppes, stony wastes, semi-deserts. L 18 cm. -V

**THICK-BILLED LARK** *Ramphocoris clotbey*. Much the stoutest-billed lark, with conspicuously dark-spotted breast, and black-and-white patches on sides of neck and on wings, obvious in flight. Song a medley of warbling notes, both in flight and on ground; calls varied, a low 'coo-ee' and 'sree', and a 'co-ep' flight note. Runs very fast and when stops does not crouch but stands with very erect carriage, holding head high or even slightly backwards. Breeds in deserts, mainly stony hammada; in winter also grassy wadis and marginal cultivations. L 17 cm.

# LARKS

CALANDRA LARK

BIMACULATED LARK
Smaller, shorter-tailed;
pure white supercilium.

♀

♀

♂
br

n br ♂
BLACK LARK

WHITE-WINGED LARK

THICK-BILLED
LARK

ad

juv

balcanica

bicornis

Since Shore Lark breeds on mountains and Temminck's in desert, they are completely separate in habitat.

Prefers flat arid areas and gently undulating lowlands. but also on high plateaus and sea shores.

**SHORE LARK** *Eremophila alpestris*. Looks just like many other larks at a distance, pinkish-brown mottled darker, and with tail black though outer feathers white-edged. At close range adult easily told by black-and-yellow head pattern, and when breeding by male's small black 'horns'. Cf. smaller Temminck's Lark. Commonest call is a quite unlark-like 'tsip' or 'tseep', recalling Rock Pipit (p.244) and Yellow Wagtail (p.248); also a thin, falling 'si-di-wi'. Song sometimes aerial, not unlike Skylark (p.230). Flight markedly undulating, and can run very fast. Breeds on tundra and rocky shores in high Arctic or in alpine zones of mountains, but winters on coast, often on dunes, or on nearby arable, sometimes with Snow or Lapland Buntings. Aka Horned Lark. L 14-17 cm.                  ○W

Northern ssp.*flava* is described above; ssp.*brandti* (S Russia) is paler and greyer and has face white not yellow; ssp.*atlas* (Atlas Mts) is paler brown, not pinkish, with longer 'horns'; sspp.*balcanica* (Balkans), *penicillata* (Asia Minor, Caucasus) and *bicornis* (Taurus to Israel) are slightly larger, with facial yellow paler and black on cheeks joining black on breast to make a bold black patch.

**TEMMINCK'S LARK** *Eremophila bilopha*. Smaller, paler and more uniformly coloured than Shore Lark, with warm buff upperparts, white underparts, white not yellow on the head and black on cheeks white not joining black on breast. Cf. Bar-tailed Lark (p.232). Call more disyllabic than Shore Lark, and song less vigorous, though more often in flight, with no final plumb drop. Sandy or stony, often bare deserts. Aka Temminck's Horned Lark. L 13-14 cm.

**BLACK-CROWNED FINCH LARK** *Eremopterix nigriceps*. The region's smallest lark, short-billed and more like a finch than a lark, though does not hop; male has distinctive black crown and underparts and white cheeks and forehead, but unstreaked sandy female best told from many other small desert passerines by black underwing in flight. Twittering song uttered in soaring display flight, followed by butterfly-like descent with wings raised and final plumb drop; when disturbed may fly round in a circle. Dry sandy wastes with very sparse vegetation. Aka Black-crowned Sparrow-lark. L 10-11 cm.

**HOOPOE LARK** *Alaemon alaudipes*. One of the largest and most distinctive larks, long-legged and long-tailed, with long, slightly curved bill and striking black-and-white wing pattern in flight both recalling Hoopoe (p.220). Unmistakable musical song, several loud clear notes followed by a long descending whistle, either on ground or during display flight, when male flies straight upwards and descends spirally on outstretched wings, with a final plumb drop. Looks like a small courser when running; when stops does not squat, but stands erect. Deserts, semi-deserts, wadis, sandy shores. Aka Bifasciated Lark. L 18-20 cm.

w

flava

dti

atlas

penicillata

1st s

♂ alpestris

**SHORE LARK**

juv

♀

♂

♂

♀

♂

**TEMMINCK'S LARK**

♀

♂

**BLACK-CROWNED FINCH LARK**

ad

ad

ad

juv

ad

**HOOPOE LARK**

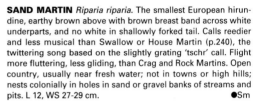

Swallows and martins regularly flock when they feed over open country or fresh water; also on migration, when they often gather on telephone wires beforehand.

● SWALLOWS, MARTINS: *Hirundinidae* (pp.238-241). Small, slender, short-necked aerial birds, with wings long (but relatively shorter than swifts, p.216), tail forked and bill short, flattened and wide-gaped. Sexes alike. Flight graceful, often fast.

**SAND MARTIN** *Riparia riparia*. The smallest European hirundine, earthy brown above with brown breast band across white underparts, and no white in shallowly forked tail. Calls reedier and less musical than Swallow or House Martin (p.240), the twittering song based on the slightly grating 'tschr' call. Flight more fluttering, less gliding, than Crag and Rock Martins. Open country, usually near fresh water; not in towns or high hills; nests colonially in holes in sand or gravel banks of streams and pits. L 12, WS 27-29 cm. ●Sm

The small greyish ssp.*shelleyi* (Nile valley) is paler with faint narrower breast band; *diluta* (Transcaspia, lower Ural River) is still paler with similar breast band. In all races juvs like adults but feathers with pale fringes so looking paler and less uniform.

**PLAIN MARTIN** *Riparia paludicola*. Differs from only slightly larger and less compact Sand Martin in its dingier, undistinguished plumage, the off-white underparts with no distinct breast band merging into a dull, pale brown breast, throat and chin. Differs from Crag and Rock Martins especially in no white in tail. Song twittering, chief call a high-pitched 'svee-svee' not unlike Sand Martin. Habits, habitat as Sand Martin. Aka Brown-throated Sand Martin. L 12, WS 26-27 cm.

**ROCK MARTIN** *Ptyonoprogne fuligula*. Smaller and greyer than Crag Martin and has both underwing and underparts paler, with uniform white throat. Differs from both Sand and Plain Martins in having white spots in tail and from Sand Martin also in having no breast band and in more gliding flight. Rather silent, but has liquid twittering song and calls include a clipped 'wik'. Desert regions, otherwise habitat and habits as Crag Martin. Includes Pale Crag Martin. L 12.5, WS 28-30 cm.

Ssp.*perpallida* (S Iraq) is very pale with throat almost white; ssp.*obsoleta* (Nile valley, Sinai) is darker, and ssp.*presaharica* (Algeria, Morocco) still darker.

The only hirundine which regularly overwinters in Europe; migratory in N of range.

**CRAG MARTIN** *Ptyonoprogne rupestris*. Larger and darker and with slower, more gliding flight than Sand and Plain Martins; also has blackish (not dusky brown) underwing, speckled throat, no breast band, no white on underparts and scarcely forked, white-spotted tail. Smaller Rock Martin has unspeckled white throat. Juv tinged rufous. Song and call-notes rather feeble and twittering, some recalling House Martin (p.240). Breeds cliffs, buildings, sometimes by sea and in towns. L 14.5, WS 32-34 cm.

# MARTINS

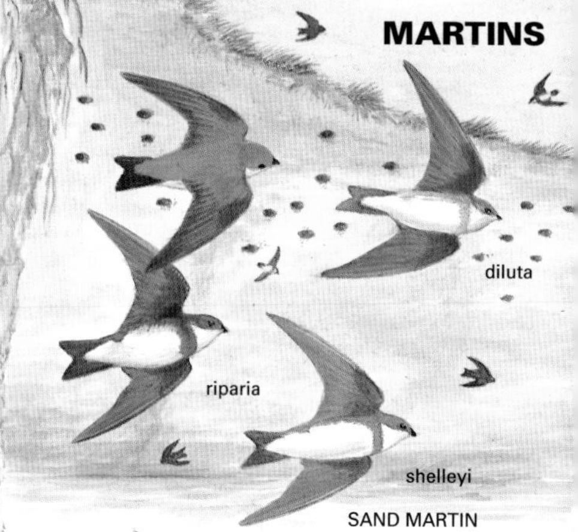

Nests from late April to August in colonies, with tunnels up to 100 cm, mostly in river banks and sandpits, also in sea cliffs and even man-made holes, such as drain-pipes.

diluta

riparia

shelleyi

**SAND MARTIN**

Nests from November to February, with tunnels up to 80 cm, mostly in river and road banks.

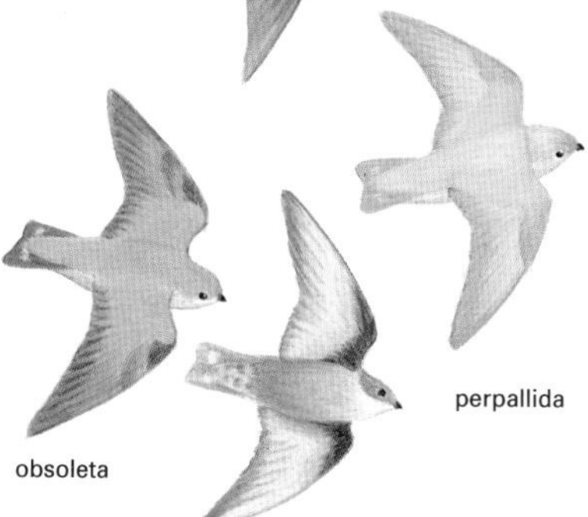

**PLAIN MARTIN**

Rock and Crag Martins make similar cup-like nests (from mud, like Swallow) under overhangs on vertical cliffs, under bridges, in tunnels and on ledges on houses or verandas.

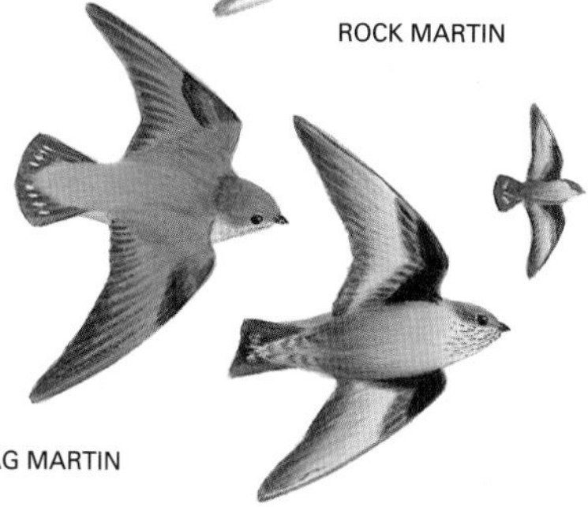

obsoleta

perpallida

**ROCK MARTIN**

**CRAG MARTIN**

see also on
next page
right.

**HOUSE MARTIN** *Delichon urbica*. The region's only hirundine with a prominent white rump (but beware the two white-rumped swifts (p.216) and Red-rumped Swallow) and whole underparts pure white. Upperparts blue-black, tinged brown in juv; tail only shortly forked. Usual call a brief flat 'prt' or 'pr-prt', also a spluttering 'chirrp' or 'chichirrp'; alarm note 'tseeep'. Gentle, twittering song. Breeds in or near farms, villages and small towns, also caves, cliffs, quarries; nest very often against wall under eaves of building, sometimes against cliff. L 12.5, WS 26-29 cm. ●Sm

**RED-RUMPED SWALLOW** *Hirundo daurica*. The region's only hirundine with rufous nape and rump; also lacks rufous forehead, dark breast band and white tail spots of larger but shorter-bodied Swallow and has slightly shorter (shorter still in juv) thicker incurved tail streamers, faintly streaked underparts and black under tail coverts. Flight note a long-drawn 'quitsch'. Song less musical, calls similar to, and flight slower than Swallow. When breeding, usually near cliffs, bridges or buildings, often in towns. L 16-17, WS 32-34 cm. -A

**Cliff Swallow** *Hirundo pyrrhonota*. Very rare transatlantic vagrant, all so far juvs, like a small Red-rumped Swallow, but has almost square tail, rufous face and throat, and a dark patch on lower throat which is lacking or obscure in dingier juv. L 14 cm. -V

**SWALLOW** *Hirundo rustica*. The region's commonest hirundine, blue-black above, with distinctive rufous throat and forehead and blue-black band on upper breast, contrasting with white to pinkish-cream rest of underparts; adult also has very long streamers to white-spotted tail. Rare hybrids with House Martin have interrupted breast band, dark forehead, buff rump, white under tail coverts and tail shorter than Swallow but not spotted. Most frequent call is twittering 'tswit, tswit, tswit'; alarm note a shrill 'tsink, tsink'. Pleasant, twittering song, 'feetafeet, feetafeetit'. Aka Barn Swallow. L 17-19, WS 32-34 cm. ●Sm

Sspp.*transitiva* (Levant) and *savignii* (Egypt) are both slightly larger, with underparts more rufous in *transitiva* and still deeper rufous in *savignii*, matching throat and making bird appear quite dark.

Juv Swallow has broader but much shorter tail streamers, and often appears paler about head.

Rare hybrid Swallow x House Martin has buff rump like Red-rumped Swallow, but lacks pale collar and streaks on belly.

# SWALLOWS

Mud nest like a half bowl, open side flat against wall, access by small slit at top on one side.

**HOUSE MARTIN**

juv

Nest like a whole bowl, open top beneath flat overhanging surface, with elongated entrance spout.

**RED-RUMPED SWALLOW**

**CLIFF SWALLOW**

s from ove

♀ shorter streamers

♂

rustica

**SWALLOW**

savignii

♂

transitiva

Nest an open saucer, of mud and dried grasses, resting on ledge or rafter inside building or cave.

● PIPITS, WAGTAILS: *Motacillidae*. Small, rather slim, long-tailed, thin-billed, ground-feeders, with distinctive habit of wagging tail up and down; sexes alike. They are divided into pipits *Anthus* (pp.242-247) and wagtails *Motacilla* (pp.248-251).

**Pipits** *Anthus* are brown, with paler underparts and usually streaked breast; tail shorter than wagtails, usually with white outer feathers. Habits like the shorter-legged, shorter-tailed larks (pp.230-237): dipping flight, aerial song flights, walking and running gait and restless activity. Call note often best initial field mark.

**TREE PIPIT** *Anthus trivialis*. Very like Meadow Pipit, but more robust, and with fewer and larger streaks on yellower breast, bill stouter and hind claw shorter. When breeding best clue is habitat – perches in trees – and voice, the trilling aerial song normally ending with a distinctive, far-carrying 'see-er, see-er, see-er', while flying up from a tree or bush. Call, a loud harsh 'teez', also diagnostic. Open woodland, heaths, scrub and other areas with scattered trees; rarely near villages; near coast on passage. L 15 cm. ●Sm

**MEADOW PIPIT** *Anthus pratensis*. The most widespread pipit of open country, with well-streaked breast and underparts tinged greyish or buff; juv tinged yellow-buff. Like Tree legs vary from pale brown to yellow and flesh-pink, but have a longer hind claw. Differs from Tree in voice, habitat and presence in winter: aerial song, starting from ground, lacks Tree's terminal 'see-er's; usual call a single or triple high-pitched 'pheet', like Rock Pipit. Breeds in open, usually treeless, uncultivated country, moors, bogs, heaths, grassy hills, alpine meadows, tundra, dunes. On passage and in winter damp grassland, freshwater margins, marshes and estuaries, often in small flocks. L 14.5 cm. ●SrMW

**RED-THROATED PIPIT** *Anthus cervinus*. Breeding adult unmistakable, with rufous face and throat (pinker in female/1st summer). Otherwise very like Meadow Pipit, but has more contrasting pattern on back and flanks, more heavily streaked rump and flanks, and white wing bar; hind claw long. Call distinctive, like Tree Pipit, but higher-pitched and more drawn-out, 'skee-eaz'; song more prolonged and musical than Meadow, taking off from ground and often delivered at greater height. Open or scrubby tundra, and its coasts. L 15 cm. ○M

**OLIVE-BACKED PIPIT** *Anthus hodgsoni*. Like Tree Pipit, but has almost unstreaked, more olive-brown upperparts, marked supercilium (orange-buff in front and white behind eye), smallish bill, a white and a black ear-spot, boldly marked breast and white underparts. Song like Tree; calls, a loud 'teaze', recalling Red-throated, and a less distinctive 'tsee' or 'tseet'. Wags tail more vigorously than other pipits. Coniferous forest; perches in trees. L 14.5 cm. -A

**PECHORA PIPIT** *Anthus gustavi*. A brightly patterned small pipit with two pale streaks down back, boldly streaked rump (cf. Red-throated), warm buff outer tail feathers and white belly; cf. also Tree. Call most distinctive, a loud 'pwit', softer and lower-pitched than Meadow and usually repeated 2-3 times; aerial song has a wood-warbler-like trill, followed by a low throaty warble. Wooded and scrubby tundra, fringes of coniferous forest. Vagrant in W Europe; skulks, hard to flush. L 14 cm. -V

**PIPITS**

Pipit's aerial song begins and ends tree or bush.

ow Pipit's aerial flight begins and on the ground.

Pink or rufous breeding plumage very variable. Some males as dull as females.

TREE PIPIT

MEADOW PIPIT

br

br

br

nbr

RED-THROATED PIPIT

OLIVE-BACKED PIPIT

PECHORA PIPIT

The only European passerine that winters N of its breeding areas.

Breast colour of breeding Water Pipits can vary, e.g. in Pyrenees often yellowish and slightly streaked.

Especially in spring, Water Pipits often forage on snowfields, mostly for frozen insects but also for wind-blown seeds, sometimes originating as far away as the Sahara.

**WATER PIPIT** Anthus spinoletta. Together with Rock Pipit, the region's only dark-legged and dark-billed breeding pipit; upperparts warm to grey-brown; conspicuous supercilium and outer tail feathers both white. When breeding, has pinkish-buff, often almost unstreaked, breast and grey head. In winter brown above, but not as dark as slightly smaller and less wagtail-like Rock Pipit, and dull white below, with obvious dark streaks on breast and flanks. Song louder, more musical than Meadow Pipit; high-pitched 'phist' call, usually uttered singly, very like Rock. Mountain tops, alpine meadows, with scattered small trees and scrub (unlike Rock perches in bushes); in winter lower down, often at cress-beds and other freshwater margins. L 17 cm.  ⊙W

Ssp.spinoletta (C & S Europe), above; the smaller ssp.coutellii (Turkey, Caucasus) is paler and more clearly streaked above and more buff below.

**Buff-bellied Pipit** A. rubescens. Differs from Water Pipits in usually pale legs, whiter outer tail feathers, more sharply defined black streaks on breast and flanks, buffer supercilium and underparts often warm buff. Ssp.japonicus (above), regular visitor to Middle East from E Asia; ssp.rubescens, rare autumn vagrant (aka American Pipit) from N America to W Europe, is smaller, dark-legged and even more buff, less heavily streaked, below. L 17 cm.          -V

**ROCK PIPIT** Anthus petrosus. Appreciably larger, darker and greyer than both Meadow and Tree Pipits, from which always separable both by dark legs and bill, and by the greyish, not white, outer tail feathers that also separate it from Water and Buff-bellied Pipits. Very distinct from Water Pipit in breeding season, when, as in winter, it is olive-brown, heavily streaked below, with only obscure supercilium. Song like Meadow Pipit, delivered in air, rising from and returning to either ground or a rock. Chief call a sharp 'phist', lower-pitched than Meadow Pipit's 'pheet' and rarely uttered in triplicate. Breeds only on rocky coasts, though may spread inland a short distance on islands with no Meadow Pipits; in winter on all coasts, less often at freshwater margins. L 17 cm.          ●Rw

Ssp.petrosus (Britain, Ireland, W France), above; ssp.littoralis (Denmark, Scandinavia, N W Russia) not distinguishable in autumn, but when breeding pinkish on both throat and often less heavily streaked breast, and darker and less olive above; sspp.meinertzhageni (Outer Hebrides) and kleinschmidti (Faeroe, Shetland, Orkney) are scarcely distinguishable.

**PIPITS**

w

br worn

br fresh

spinoletta

nbr

coutellii

**WATER PIPIT**

ad

ad

juv

spinoletta

petrosus

two outermost tail feathers

rubescens

japonicus

**BUFF-BELLIED PIPIT**

w

br worn

br fresh

petrosus

w

ad br

littoralis

**ROCK PIPIT**

**BERTHELOT'S PIPIT** *Anthus berthelotii*. The region's smallest pipit, greyish and with a very pale supercilium; appearance and habits recall both Rock and longer-tailed Tawny Pipits. Birds that look very reddish may be stained by the soil of their habitat. Mostly seen singing from a song-post, high or low, even in pine trees; song a repeated plangent 'tsiree'. Main call a low, rather hoarse 'tsik', with a louder 'chir-ee' alarm note. Ubiquitous in Canaries in all habitats from sea level to high mountain; in Madeira only in uplands. L 14 cm.

**TAWNY PIPIT** *Anthus campestris*. A large pale, mainly sandy brown pipit, with mantle and sides of breast faintly streaked, underparts mostly unstreaked, pale-edged dark median coverts and pale supercilium both conspicuous, lores dark, flanks whitish and legs yellowish to pale brown. Cf. slightly larger, longer-legged and more streaked Richard's Pipit; also Blyth's Pipit. Juv well streaked like juv Richard's, but lores darker. Song a metallic 'chivree-chivee-chivee', in high display flight, plummeting to ground. Calls varied, all softer than and distinct from Richard's, especially a yellow-wagtail-like 'tsweep' and a sparrow-like 'chup' or 'chirrup'; cf. Long-billed Pipit. Dry, open, sparsely grassy, sandy areas, heaths, dunes, arable. L 16.5 cm.          ○M

**LONG-BILLED PIPIT** *Anthus similis*. Slightly larger and greyer than Tawny Pipit, standing more upright and with faintly streaked mantle and breast, narrower but more distinct supercilium, slightly longer, stouter and paler bill, darker tail with outer feathers more buffish (but varying from pinkish to whitish), belly buff to deep buff, and shorter, redder legs. Juv more markedly streaked. Musical song uttered either on ground or in air; 'tchup' and 'che-vee' calls not unlike Tawny Pipit. Rocky mountain slopes, often with scattered scrub; lower down in winter. L 17-19 cm.

Local resident Lebanon, W Syria, Israel, Jordan.

**Richard's Pipit** *A. novaeseelandiae*. The region's largest pipit, warm brown, streaked above and below, with buffish breast, deep buff flanks and relatively long tail. Head with conspicuous pale supercilium, pale lores and rather long stout bill. Legs orange-red, rather long with long hind claw visible at close range. Cf. very similar Blyth's, also Tawny and dark-legged Water (p.244) Pipits. Has a most distinctive loud, harsh call, 'schreep'. Stance rather upright and thrush-like; often hovers before landing; gait can be almost strutting. Wanderer from Siberia, annually in some numbers W to W Europe, mainly in autumn. L 18 cm.          -A

**Blyth's Pipit** *A. godlewskii*. Rare vagrant from Siberia to N W Europe, adults differing from very similar but larger Richard's Pipit most reliably in paler tips and squarer shape of dark centres of median coverts, paler underparts, and short, clipped, hard 'chep' or 'choop' call, diagnostic especially when preceded by a 'psheeoo'; also never struts like Richard's. In the hand white on inner tail feathers can be seen to be more confined to the tips. The slightly smaller juv Tawny Pipit has the dark streaks on the upperparts crescentic and arranged in lines instead of linear and scattered haphazardly as in Blyth's. L 17 cm.          -V

| 28-32mm |

| 15mm |

Richard's

| 24-28mm |

| 13mm |

Blyth's

BERTHELOT'S PIPIT

Can look very reddish if stained by the local soil.

juv

TAWNY PIPIT

ad

ad

LONG-BILLED PIPIT

juv

ad

RICHARD'S PIPIT

ad

BLYTH'S PIPIT

**Wagtails** *Motacilla*. Wagtails are longer-tailed than pipits (p.242), with plumage in combinations of black, grey, white and yellow, and white outer tail feathers. They repeatedly wag their tail up and down. Flight notably bounding; gait a quick, often rather jerky, run. Some species flock after breeding season.

Most *yarrellii* resident, but some move S as far as Morocco.

**PIED WAGTAIL** *Motacilla alba*. The only small black-and-white bird of its size with such a long tail. Breeding plumage strikingly contrasted (less so in female): head black and white, breast black, tail black with white outer feathers, mantle and rump blackish or grey. Flight note a double high-pitched 'tschizzick', also a single 'tchik'; twittering song, based on calls, in flight, from a perch or on ground. Open country, tundra to semi-desert and farmland, often near fresh water and in or near villages and small towns. L 18 cm. ●RSm

Ssp. *yarrellii* (Britain, Ireland, coastal W Europe) has mantle and rump black in male, blackish in female; rump colour only absolutely reliable distinction from White Wagtail ssp. *alba*, whose mantle and rump are grey. Other sspp., p.250.

Seldom breeds far from fast-flowing water.

**GREY WAGTAIL** *Motacilla cinerea*. The region's largest and longest-tailed breeding wagtail, in outline and behaviour nearer Pied than Yellow. Blue-grey above, with yellow-green rump; underparts yellow, brighter in black-throated breeding male. Juv very pale yellow beneath, with breast speckled. Call more staccato and metallic than Pied, often only a single sharp 'tit'. Song, rather infrequent, a shrill 'tsee-tee-tee(-tee)'. Breeds by fast hill streams, lowland waterfalls and weirs; in winter at freshwater margins, even in towns. L 18-19 cm. ●Rs

Ssp. *canariensis* (the 5 western Canary Is) is richer yellow below, greenish on back; *schmitzi* (Madeira) and *patricia* (Azores) are darker with white supercilium only behind eye.

**YELLOW WAGTAIL** *Motacilla flava*. The region's smallest and most pipit-like wagtail, shorter-tailed than White and Grey, strikingly yellow beneath and dark or pale greenish-brown above. Flight note 'tsweep' quite distinct from other wagtails; brief, trilling, somewhat robin-like song, not often heard, uttered in bounding song flight or from perch. Grasslands, damp or dry, often associated with cattle, farmland, saltmarshes; on passage also by fresh water. L 17 cm. ●Sm

Has many races, whose breeding males have distinctive head patterns; see pp.250-251.

**CITRINE WAGTAIL** *Motacilla citreola*. Breeding male largely bright yellow, with dark grey mantle, diagnostic black base of nape and double white wing bar. Winter male/breeding female mainly grey on head and above, paler yellow below, nape marking obscure. Juv/imm largely pale grey with pale buff forehead and (unlike imm Yellow) complete pale ring round ear coverts. Tail, legs and bill longer than Yellow; stance and behaviour, e.g. more vigorous tail-wagging, more like Grey. Flight call 'drreeep' not unlike Tree Pipit (p.242). Tundra, marshes, wet moors, usually by fresh water. L 17 cm. -A(b)

248

# WAGTAILS

juv

♀ nbr

♂ nbr

♂ br

**PIED WAGTAIL.**
For sspp. see next page.

juv

♂ nbr

♂ br

**GREY WAGTAIL**
See also next page.

juv

nbr

br

white phase

♂ flava br

**YELLOW WAGTAIL.** For the
many sspp. in the region,
see next page.

juv

♀ nbr

♂ br

**CITRINE WAGTAIL**

# WAGTAILS

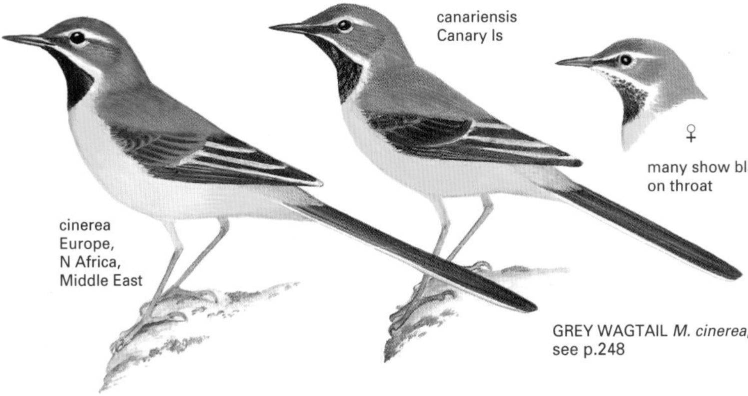

canariensis
Canary Is

♀

many show black
on throat

cinerea
Europe,
N Africa,
Middle East

GREY WAGTAIL *M. cinerea*,
see p.248

♀

alba

♂

alba
Europe,
Asia Minor

YELLOW WAGTAIL *M. flava* (opposite) has man
sspp., whose breeding males have distinctive
head patterns. Females' and winter males' head
patterns much less distinctive, and so harder to
distinguish; juvs, which have a blackish breast-
band, usually impossible to distinguish. The
different sspp. can be very hard to separate: the
ranges often overlap and they may also
hybridise, the hybrids sometimes mimicking
quite different races, e.g. *flava* x *flavissima*
mimics *beema*. Birds in migrating flocks, often
mixture of several races, need special attention.

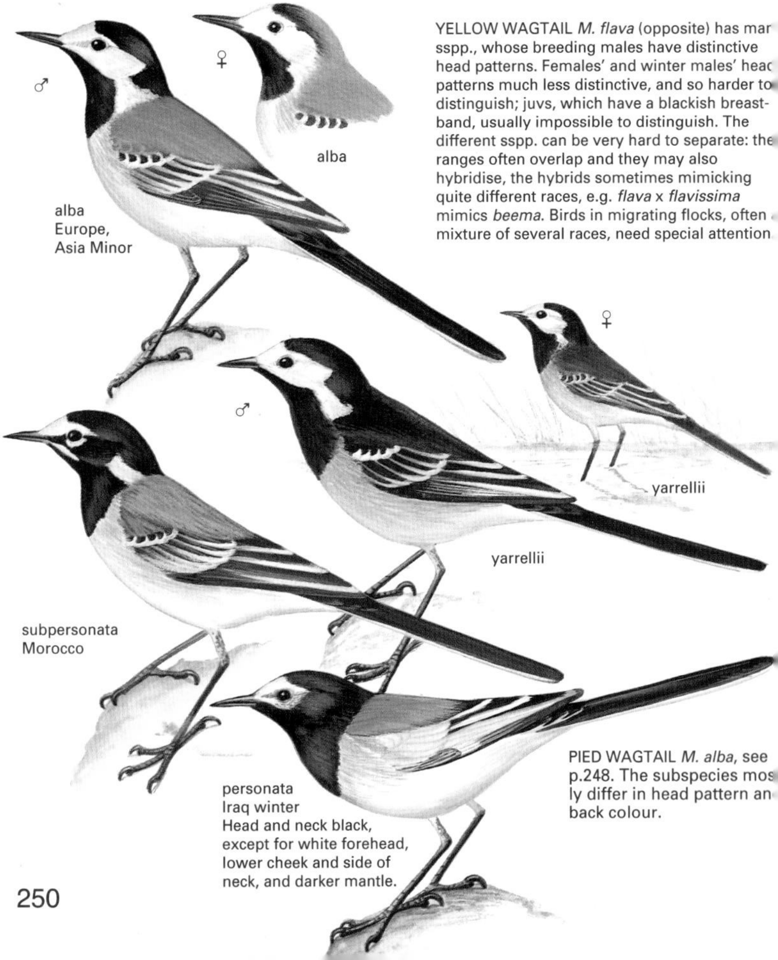

♀

♂

yarrellii

yarrellii

subpersonata
Morocco

personata
Iraq winter
Head and neck black,
except for white forehead,
lower cheek and side of
neck, and darker mantle.

PIED WAGTAIL *M. alba*, see
p.248. The subspecies most
ly differ in head pattern an
back colour.

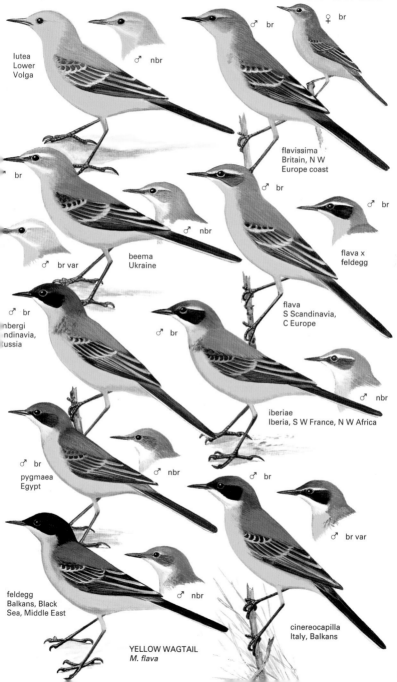

**WAGTAILS**

lutea
Lower
Volga

♂ nbr

♂ br

♀ br

flavissima
Britain, N W
Europe coast

br

♂ nbr

♂ br var

beema
Ukraine

♂ br

♂ br

flava x
feldegg

♂ br
nbergi
ndinavia,
ussia

♂ br

flava
S Scandinavia,
C Europe

♂ nbr

iberiae
Iberia, S W France, N W Africa

♂ br
pygmaea
Egypt

♂ nbr

♂ br

♂ br var

feldegg
Balkans, Black
Sea, Middle East

♂ nbr

YELLOW WAGTAIL
*M. flava*

cinereocapilla
Italy, Balkans

● WAXWINGS: *Bombycillidae*. Two birds with rather short thick beaks, one shrike-like, the other starling-like, perhaps not closely related.

Scrub in semi-desert, cultivations, gardens, date and other palm groves.

**GREY HYPOCOLIUS** *Hypocolius ampelinus*. Superficially like a slim Great Grey Shrike (p.316), with bill not hooked, tail longer and not graduated (but flicked like shrikes) and underparts pinkish-buff with conspicuous black cheeks (in male) and wing and tail tips; male grey above but female/juv all creamy-buff. Flight direct and whirring, not undulating, alighting in middle of tree or bush, where skulks and may utter a whistling, buzzard-like 'peeeooo'; also has a weak 'quee' flight note. L 23 cm.

**WAXWING** *Bombycilla garrulus*. The only crested pinkish-brown bird of the region that has 'waxy' red and yellow appendages markings on wings and broad yellow tail tip; adult has black bib. Jizz rather starling-like, but flight slower and shows distinctive grey rump. Song, a variant of chief call, a rather high-pitched trilling 'sirrrrr'. Open coniferous and birch forests, especially in the taiga, but during periodic westward eruptions usually seen at berried shrubs in parks and gardens or at *Sorbus* or hawthorn scrub. L 18 cm. ○Wm

● BULBULS: *Pycnonotidae*. Gregarious birds, with fairly slender bill, longish tail and rather weak flight. Sexes alike. Often in human settlements.

**WHITE-CHEEKED BULBUL** *Pycnonotus leucogenys*. Conspicuous white cheeks, contrasting with black head, together with white spots at tip of tail, distinguish from slightly larger Yellow-vented Bulbul. Juv's head browner. Noisy, chattering and common in town and villages gardens, orchards, palm groves, open bushy country, wadis, semi-deserts. L 18 cm.

Habitat like White-cheeked also large towns, villages.

**YELLOW-VENTED BULBUL** *Pycnonotus xanthopygos*. Differs from slightly smaller and also yellow-vented White-cheeked Bulbul, in uniformly blackish head and tail and conspicuous white eye-ring. Another chattering bird, with wide, mimetic vocabulary, including monotonous flute-like song. Town and village gardens, orchards, palm groves, open bushy country. Aka Black-headed Bulbul. L 19 cm.

From town gardens to remote desert wadis.

**COMMON BULBUL** *Pycnonotus barbatus*. A N African bird, very like same-sized Middle Eastern Yellow-vented Bulbul, but with a white vent and no whitish eye-ring. Song rich, fluty and staccato; otherwise noisy and gregarious, especially at roosts. Towns, villages, gardens, orchards, palm groves, open country with scrub. L 19 cm.

Prefers evergreen bushes.

**RED-VENTED BULBUL** *Pycnonotus cafer*. A widespread Asian species now breeding in Kuwait. Dark brown with peaked head and throat black, white rump, white-tipped black tail, and the region's only bulbul with a red vent. Noisy and vocal like other bulbuls, and also frequenting gardens, orchards and other bushy places. L 20 cm.

GREY
HYPOCOLIUS

juv

ad

WAXWING

WHITE-CHEEKED
BULBUL

YELLOW-
VENTED
BULBUL

RED-VENTED
BULBUL

COMMON BULBUL

● ACCENTORS: *Prunellidae*. Small terrestrial birds, sparrow-like in outline, but with thin, insect-eating bills and streaked flanks. Sexes alike. Generally solitary. Usual gait a hop or a shuffling walk, with characteristic intermittent wing-flicking. Most species inhabit mountains.

High mountain slopes and plateaus; stony, rocky areas. Winters lower down.

**ALPINE ACCENTOR** *Prunella collaris*. The region's largest accentor, paler, greyer and more brightly coloured than Dunnock, with white chin and throat speckled black, pale double wing bar enclosing conspicuous blackish panel, and flanks so strongly streaked as to show as a chestnut blaze at a distance. Often jerks pale-tipped tail, like a chat. Song much more musical than Dunnock, almost skylark-like; commonest call a rippling 'truiririp', also a more metallic, somewhat sparrow-like 'churrrp'. Sparsely vegetated mountains; a rare vagrant elsewhere. L 18 cm.                                                    -V

Scrub, especially juniper, on high mountain slopes.

**RADDE'S ACCENTOR** *Prunella ocularis*. Slightly larger and paler than Dunnock, and with striking head pattern of dark crown and cheeks divided by white supercilium, and creamy white throat and belly separated by warm buff breast and flanks. Secretive; most easily located by warbling song, and most frequent, high-pitched call, both similar to Dunnock. Scrub on mountains, winters lower down. L 15.5 cm.

Spruce/fir taiga with birch, rowan and willow, N Urals.

**SIBERIAN ACCENTOR** *Prunella montanella*. Differs from slightly larger Radde's Accentor mainly in darker, more rufous, less streaked upperparts, duller white supercilium and throat and more uniformly buff underparts. General behaviour skulking, with song recalling Dunnock, but louder; most frequent call a subdued 'dididi'. Taiga, N Urals; rare vagrant further S and W. L 14.5 cm.

**BLACK-THROATED ACCENTOR** *Prunella atrogularis*. The region's only accentor with a black throat (sometimes mottled paler in winter), differing also from slightly larger Radde's in its deep buff supercilium and more extensively buff underparts and from slightly smaller Siberian in its paler, more streaked upperparts. Rather secretive in thick birch scrub. Song recalls Dunnock and Siberian; calls include a quiet 'zee-zee-zee-zee'. L 15 cm.

**DUNNOCK** *Prunella modularis*. The region's only widespread accentor, at first glance not unlike the rear view of a Robin (p.258), but readily told by grey head and breast, well streaked rufous flanks and thin bill. Song, a rather flat little warble, has neither the sweetness of the Robin (p.258) nor the vehemence of the Wren (p.314). Commonest call, a high-pitched 'tseep', often first betrays the presence of this inconspicuous rather than actually skulking bird. Jerky gait also separates from other small brown birds. Bushy places of all kinds, scrub, heaths, hedgerows, parks, gardens, woodland, also mountain woods; a common suburban bird in W Europe. Aka Hedgesparrow, Hedge Accentor. L 14.5 cm.                                                ●Rm

Ssp.*hebridensis* (Ireland, W Scotland) darker and heavily streaked; *occidentalis* (England, Wales, E Scotland) intermediate with typical *modularis* (Europe); *obscura* (Crimea to Transcaucasia) browner, less grey, and mottled on breast.

juv

ad

ALPINE ACCENTOR

RADDE'S ACCENTOR

SIBERIAN ACCENTOR

BLACK-THROATED ACCENTOR

juv

ad

juv

ad

DUNNOCK

1st winter and females often browner, but individual variation marked. Worn birds can look very drab.

● THRUSHES, CHATS and ALLIES: *Turdidae*. A large family containing some of the finest European songsters, in two groups, the smaller robins, chats, wheatears and redstarts, and the larger thrushes (pp.272-275). They are all insect-eaters, and many eat fruits and berries. Gait a short run or hop.

**THRUSH NIGHTINGALE** *Luscinia luscinia*. Extremely like slightly smaller Nightingale, but has more pointed wings and slightly longer tail; in good light at close quarters usually appears darker and greyer olive-brown, with less rufous rump and tail, less obvious supercilium and lightly mottled breast. Juvs not separable in field. Song also very similar, usually louder and still richer, often lacking Nightingale's crescendo, but equally variable and sometimes almost confined to harsh notes. Calls rather higher-pitched, the croak more grating. More exclusively confined to damp thickets, especially by fresh water. Aka Sprosser (Germany). L 16.5 cm.          -A

**NIGHTINGALE** *Luscinia megarhynchos*. Like a large, all-brown Robin (p.258), with a conspicuously rufous tail, often all that can be seen as it dives for cover. Sexes alike. Cf. Thrush Nightingale. Juv like outsize juv Robin, but with rufous tail (less rufous than juv Redstart; p.262) and paler underparts. Song, as often by day as by night, outstandingly rich in volume and range of notes, with some, such as 'jug, jug' and 'chooc, chooc' that only Thrush Nightingale can emulate; also many harsh guttural and almost frog-like notes, recalling Great Reed Warbler (p.282). Song usually from thick cover, sometimes also from open perches. Calls include a soft, leaf-warbler-like 'hweet', a hard 'chat-like 'tacc, tacc', a scolding 'krrr' and a grating 'tchaaa'. Broad-leaved woodland, scrub, thickets. L 16.5 cm.          ●S

**WHITE-THROATED ROBIN** *Irania gutturalis*. Male has distinctive combination of blue-grey upperparts, whole underparts rufous, black cheeks, rump and tail and white throat and supercilium. Female much browner, with cheeks grey and no supercilium. Juv spotted. Aerial song of nightingale-like clear, bell-like notes; tail often fanned out in descending flight. Chief calls a wagtail-like 'tirric' and a hard, nightingale-like 'tec'. Scrub in ravines and other stony country; may skulk in bushes or perch on stones, tail often cocked. L 16.5 cm.          -V

**RUFOUS BUSHCHAT** *Cercotrichas galactotes*. Not unlike a slim long-billed Nightingale, but with pale supercilium and distinctive long, graduated rufous tail, conspicuously tipped black and white and often fanned and raised. Song varied and musical, but somewhat disjointed, like nightingales or larks; from open perch or in butterfly-like descending flight. Chief call a hard 'teck, teck'. Scrub, in oases, wadi-beds, semi-deserts, gardens, orchards, vineyards and olive and palm groves. Aka Rufous Bush Robin, Rufous Scrub Robin. L 15 cm.          -V

Ssp.*galactotes* (Iberia, N Africa, Israel) has upperparts largely rufous; ssp.*syriacus* (Balkans, Turkey) is mainly greyish brown and rufous only on rump and tail.

**Black Bushchat** *C. podobe*. Vagrant to Israel from Arabia and Algeria from S of Sahara. All-black except for broad white tips to outer feathers of very long graduated tail and wings showing pale rufous in flight. Aka Black Bush Robin. L 18 cm.

256

# NIGHTINGALES

**THRUSH NIGHTINGALE**

ad

**NIGHTINGALE**

ad

The two nightingales
hybridise where they overlap in C Europe.
Hybrids are intermediate in appearance, with
song mostly more like Thrush Nightingale.

♀

♂ br

♀

juv

**WHITE-THROATED ROBIN**

galactotes

syriacus

♂

**RUFOUS BUSHCHAT**

**RED-FLANKED BLUETAIL** *Tarsiger cyanurus*. Breeding male has head, tail and whole upperparts dark blue (tinged olive in winter), contrasting with white throat and orange-red flanks; female/imm olive-brown instead of blue, except rump and tail, with conspicuous white eye-ring. Speckled juv has only upper tail blue. Song clear, melodious, repetitive; chief calls, 'tic, tic' and 'peep'. Coniferous and mixed forests. L 14 cm.          -V

**ROBIN** *Erithacus rubecula*. One of the most familiar European birds: the only red-breasted one with a red face. Shows pale under tail coverts when flying away. Juv speckled like juv nightingales and some chats. Residents in Britain and Ireland especially tame and easy to approach. Pleasant, rather thin, warbling song heard almost throughout year; commonest call 'tic, tic', also a thin 'tsit' and, especially from juvs, a high-pitched 'tswee'. Forests, scrub, hedgerows, town parks, gardens; common in suburbs in W Europe. L 14 cm.          ●Rsmw

Ssp.*superbus* (Gran Canaria, Tenerife) darker above with red deeper; on western Canary Is as in Europe. In far E of region birds are paler.

**SIBERIAN RUBYTHROAT** *Luscinia calliope*. Jizz like Robin, but bulkier. Male has distinctive head pattern of two white stripes (supercilium greyish to pure white) and red chin and throat; female/imm have only buff supercilium and chin and throat usually white. Juv speckled. Song loud, melodious, nightingale-like, often mimetic. Chief calls a loud whistling 'tiuit, tiuit' and a rattling churr. Often cocks tail, like Bluethroat. Thickets in the taiga, often in damp valley bottoms; rare vagrant W of Urals. L 14-15 cm.          -V

**BLUETHROAT** *Luscinia svecica*. A shy, robin-like bird, both sexes with distinctive rufous tail base, pale supercilium and black breast-band. Breeding males have diagnostic blue throat and breast with red or white spot, above a red band; winter and imm males paler blue with no spot; juvs speckled with rufous tail base. Song loud, rich, varied and mimetic, with a distinctive metallic 'ting, ting, ting' and some nightingale-like notes. Chief calls also nightingale-like, 'hweet' and 'tacc, tacc'. Swampy and marshy thickets by fresh water and on tundra. L 14 cm.          ○M(b)

magna
variation

♂ br

♂ br

svecica

♂ w

1st w ♀

magna          ♂ br

Ssp.*svecica* (Scandinavia, N Russia) has red spot on blue breast; ssp.*pallidogularis* (Volga eastwards) has red bar or triangle; ssp.*cyanecula* (C & S Europe) has white spot; and ssp.*magna* (Caucasus, E Turkey), the largest race, has either no spot or a small white one.

258

♀

juv

RED-FLANKED BLUETAIL

superbus

ad

juv

ROBIN

Robins look slender and slim when alert, plumper
when resting or crouching in the rain.

♂

♀

juv

SIBERIAN RUBYTHROAT

Some females are partly red on throat; 1st winter
males like females with red throat.

juv

cyanecula

♂ br

♀

♂ nbr

BLUETHROAT

When freshly moulted, throat markings are
mostly hidden by paler fringes; some 1st-summer
males have little blue on breast.

**BLACKSTART** *Cercomela melanura*. The region's only chat that is uniformly grey, but with darker wings and a black rump and tail (female/juv Black Redstart have rufous tail); sexes alike. Juv brownish-grey but not speckled. Constantly lowers and spreads tail, often with wings also half-spread. Song a pleasant, but subdued and rather monotonous warble; chief call a soft 'cher-u'. Rocky hills and semi-deserts. L 14 cm.

**Chats:** *Saxicola*. Small and robin-like, with habit of perching upright on prominent lookout, often flicking tail jerkily and uttering harsh chacking note. Juv like females but speckled.

**CANARY ISLANDS CHAT** *Saxicola dacotiae*. Intermediate between Stonechat and Whinchat, male with dark head and all-dark tail of Stonechat but paler appearance of Whinchat, with white throat and supercilium; less chestnut on breast than either. Female duller. Song, sometimes aerial, and chief call resemble Stonechat. Sparsely vegetated rocky and stony ground, usually on slopes of small, steep-sided valleys. Canary Islands only. Aka Fuerteventura Chat. L 12.5 cm.

Now only on Fuerteventura; extinct on Alegranza.

**STONECHAT** *Saxicola torquata*. Male distinctively black, white and chestnut, with whole head, throat and upperparts black, breast chestnut, and shoulders, rump and wing bar white; black becomes brownish in winter male and even browner in breeding female. Lacks Whinchat's chestnut throat and white supercilium and sides to tail. Song a brief squeaky warble, often in dancing song flight; chief call a grating 'tsak, tsak' or 'hwee-tsak-tsak'. Moors, heaths, low scrub, gorsy sea cliffs, meadows, farmland, usually below 600 m. L 12.5 cm. ●Rs

Sspp.*maura* and *stejnegeri* (vagrants to W Europe) have unstreaked white rump, white at base of tail and distinct pale supercilium, both like Whinchat, and black axillaries. Sspp.*armenica* and *variegata* (on passage, Middle East; winter, N E Africa) have bold white areas on rump, shoulders and sides of neck; *variegata* also very pale with white also at base of tail. These eastern sspp. may form a full species 'Siberian Stonechat' *S. maura*.          -A

1st w

variegata

**Pied Stonechat** *S. caprata*. Rare vagrant to Middle East, slimmer and longer-tailed than the region's other *Saxicola* chats. Male all-black except for white rump, lower belly and patch on each wing. Female and speckled juv grey-brown with rufous rump, whitish under tail coverts and dark brown tail; cf. rufous-tailed female/juv Black Redstart and black-tailed female/juv Blackstart. Chief call a brief 'chuk', also a triple call, 'chek, chek, hee'. L 13.5 cm.

**WHINCHAT** *Saxicola rubetra*. A summer visitor, male distinguished from mainly resident Stonechat by paler plumage, pale supercilium, rufous throat and white sides to base of tail, but some eastern Stonechats (see opposite) also have supercilium and white tail sides. Female similar but duller; both sexes have white wing patches, conspicuous in flight. Song similar to Stonechat, but call a less grating 'tic-tic' or 'u-tic'. Habitat as Stonechat, but more often where grass is longer, e.g. riverside meadows, waste ground, railway embankments; up to 1800-2000 m in Alps, Caucasus. L 12.5 cm. ●Sm

# CHATS

**BLACKSTART**

juv

ad

**CANARY ISLANDS CHAT**

♀

♂

**STONECHAT** Ssp. *rubicola* (Europe, N Africa) has rusty orange breast, streaked, pale rufous rump and pale buff axillaries; ssp. *hibernans* (Britain, Ireland, Portugal coast) darker and more brownish red.

♀

juv

♂ nbr

♂ br

rubicola

hibernans

armenica

♂ br

♀

♂

**PIED STONECHAT**

nbr

♀

♂ br

**WHINCHAT**

**Redstarts:** *Phoenicurus*: Robin-like birds with rufous tail (both sexes, all ages); voice and behaviour generally chat-like. Juv like female but speckled. Make flycatching sallies and constantly quiver tail.

**BLACK REDSTART** *Phoenicurus ochruros*. Breeding male all black or dark grey (greyer in younger males and in winter) except for rufous tail and white wing patch, which is largest in older males. Female and speckled juv darker grey-brown than Redstart, especially beneath. Song a staccato, redstart-like warble, ending with a grinding sound; chief calls 'tsip', 'tic' and a redstart-like 'tucc, tucc'. Rocky hill slopes, cliffs, villages, towns. L 14.5 cm. ⊙sMw

This ssp. is very variable.

♂ br

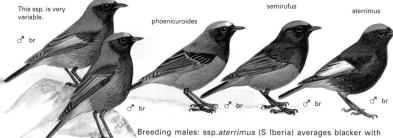

phoenicuroides

semirufus

aterrimus

♂ br    ♂ br    ♂ br

ochruros

Breeding males: ssp.*aterrimus* (S Iberia) averages blacker with whiter wing patch than ssp.*gibraltariensis* (Europe; above); ssp.*ochruros* (Caucasus area) variable, some with rufous beneath; ssp.*phoenicuroides* (N E Iran) chestnut below, sharply demarcated from black breast; ssp.*semirufus* (Levant) similar but blacker above.

**MOUSSIER'S REDSTART** *Phoenicurus moussieri*. The region's smallest redstart, endemic to N W Africa, where much more widespread than Redstart, from which male differs in black crown and upperparts, white forehead extending back to nape, conspicuous white wing patch and rufous throat; female has more rufous underparts. Song a brief, dunnock-like warble; chief call 'wheet', often followed by a rasping rattle. Forests, scrub, rocky hillsides. L 12 cm. -V

**REDSTART** *Phoenicurus phoenicurus*. Breeding male has grey upperparts, black cheeks and throat, white forehead and rufous underparts, rump and tail; female, winter male and speckled juv browner and duller. Song a rather squeaky, often mimetic, warble; chief calls a chat-like 'hwee-tucc-tucc' and loud, willow-warbler-like 'hooeet'. Woodland, rocky hills, parkland and river banks with scattered old trees, orchards, gardens. L 14 cm. ●Sm

**GÜLDENSTÄDT'S REDSTART** *Phoenicurus erythrogaster*. Much the largest redstart of the region, males with white crown, nape and wing-patch (conspicuous in aerial song flight), black back, wings, throat and breast, and rufous rump, tail and underparts; female/juv like Redstart. Quivers tail. Song a blackbird-like whistle; chief calls 'lik' and 'tek'. High rocky slopes, down to tree level in winter. L 18 cm.

**Eversmann's Redstart** *P. erythronotus*. Uncommon winter visitor to W Asia, the region's second largest redstart, breeding males like Redstart but with throat and back rufous and white wing bar. Female like Redstart but has two whitish wing bars. Tail flirted up, not quivered. Calls rather croaking. L 16 cm.

# REDSTARTS

BLACK REDSTART

gibraltariensis

♂ br

juv ♂

♀

MOUSSIER'S REDSTART

♂

♀ nbr

♀

REDSTART Ssp.*samamisicus* (Greece, Turkey) is like ssp.*semirufus* (Levant) of the Black Redstart, but has conspicuous white wing patch.

♂ br

samamiscus

♀

juv

♂

GÜLDENSTÄDT'S REDSTART

♂ br

♂ nbr

♂ br

EVERSMANN'S REDSTART

**Wheatears:** *Oenanthe.* Small songbirds, robin-like in appearance but chat-like in habits and open-country habitat, with pattern of rump (usually conspicuously white) and tail (often white with inverted black T at tip) very important in identification. Male usually distinctive, but female/imm often very like other species; juv speckled paler. Song usually a brief staccato warble, aerial or from a low perch. Often bob head and flick wings and tail; flight flitting, often flycatching.

**WHEATEAR** *Oenanthe oenanthe.* The only breeding wheatear in N and N W Europe. Breeding male has diagnostic head pattern (grey crown, white supercilium, black mask, pale throat), together with clear French grey mantle, conspicuous white rump and blackish wings; winter male browner, but retains black lores. Female/imm and speckled juv also browner, but lack other distinctive field marks, apart from white rump. Chief call a grating 'chack-chack' or 'weet-chack-chack'. Open treeless country, tundra, rocky slopes, moorland, heaths, grassland, dunes. Aka Northern Wheatear. L 14.5-15.5 cm. ●Sm

Greenland Wheatear ssp.*leucorrhoa*: many migrants through W Europe in spring are larger and brighter, but others not separable in field; cf. Isabelline Wheatear. Males and some females of ssp.*seebohmi* (N Africa) are paler and have black face, throat and underwing.

♂ br

**BLACK-EARED WHEATEAR** *Oenanthe hispanica.* Breeding male has striking contrast of creamy buff crown (darker in winter), back and underparts with black wings and underwing; mask always black but throat either black or white; rump and tail like Wheatear, not Desert Wheatear (p266). Female like Wheatear, also with black or white throat, but wings and mask blacker and supercilium usually fainter. Squeaky song preceded by 'plit' note; call rather rasping. Rocky slopes, steppes and other flat terrain, with maquis or other scrub. L 14.5 cm. -V

♂ br    ♀ 1st w    ♀ br    ♀ br

♀

melanoleuca    ♀ br    melanoleuca    ♀ br

hispanica
♀    ♀

Individual variation, especially of throat colour, considerable within both western ssp.*hispanica* and eastern ssp.*melanoleuca*, which is generally paler, often almost white, with larger black patches on cheeks and throat; cf. very similar Pied Wheatear (p.266).

**ISABELLINE WHEATEAR** *Oenanthe isabellina.* The region's longest-legged, palest and most uniformly plumaged larger wheatear, differing from the largest female Greenland Wheatears (above) in longer bill, paler wings and broader black band at tail tip with very short vertical limb of T. Sexes alike, but male's lores darker. Often stands upright. Loud mimetic song, sometimes aerial; chief calls a piping 'dweet' and higher-pitched 'wheet-wit'. Steppes, semi-deserts, stony wastes and hillsides. L 16.5 cm. -V

# WHEATEARS

oenanthe

♂ w

♂ seebohmi

♂ br

♀

♀

east colour varies: 1st-
nter male duller, brown-
more like old breeding
nales.

**WHEATEAR**
Some males are very pale
and some females almost
as bright as duller males,
especially in N Africa.

♂ br
leucorrhoa

♂

♂ w

♂ w

♂ w

♂ br
hispanica

♂ w

♂ br
1st w

melanoleuca

sexes alike

**ISABELLINE
WHEATEAR**

hispanica
black-throated
morph occurs in
both subspecies

♂

hispanica
pale-throated
morph

**BLACK-EARED WHEATEAR**

**DESERT WHEATEAR** *Oenanthe deserti*. Both male and female have diagnostic all-black tail; breeding male otherwise resembles black-throated form of Black-eared Wheatear (p.264), but differs in having white inner wing coverts. Female/imm lack any distinctive field marks, except for black tail; cf. Hooded Wheatear (p.268). Song a plaintive 'swee-you' or 'trutrutitu'; call fluty or piping. Semi-deserts, steppes, areas with scattered scrub; in winter also in cultivations. L 14-15 cm.                                                                   -V

♂ br

Ssp.*homochroa* (N Africa) is more pinkish-brown; ssp.*deserti* (Levant), above; ssp.*atrogularis* (Caucasus, Iran), darker with more white in wing; straggler Palestine and Egypt, accidental W Europe, including Britain.

**MOURNING WHEATEAR** *Oenanthe lugens*. Both sexes black and white with pale wing panel in flight and buffish under tail coverts; differs from pale and black-throated eastern forms of Black-eared Wheatear (p.264) in black mantle and black of wings being joined to black neck. Cf. also Finsch's, Red-rumped (both p.268) and Pied Wheatears. A striking black morph (N Jordan, S Syria), white only near vent resembles Eastern Pied Wheatear (p.270). Song variable, short and repetitive or longer and warbling. Chief call 'tchut, tchut'. Wadis, rocky hillsides and semi-deserts. L 14.5 cm.

♂ br

Ssp.*halophila* (N W Africa) has wing panel obscure; female/imm have mantle and sometimes also throat grey.

**CYPRUS WHEATEAR** *Oenanthe cypriaca*. Breeding adult resembles Pied Wheatear, of which it was once considered a ssp.; male and female often not separable in the field, though female has a greyer crown and a browner mantle. Especially when freshly moulted in autumn, both sexes with rufous-buff breast and belly, much darker than Pied Wheatear. Song a cicada-like 'bizz-bizz-bizz'. Open stony country with scrub, hillsides, low cliffs, cultivations, gardens. Breeds only in Cyprus, as a summer visitor. L 13-14 cm.

**PIED WHEATEAR** *Oenanthe pleschanka*. Male differs from Mourning Wheatear in its buff-tinged underparts and white under tail coverts; cf. also Finsch's Wheatear (p.268). In many ways very like black-throated form of Black-eared Wheatear (p.264), tail pattern and behaviour being identical, but has black mantle. Female/imm like female Wheatear (p.264), but with all-dark underwing, and even more like female Black-eared, but usually less warm buff. Song variable, mimetic, at times reminiscent of both Black-eared Wheatear and Black Redstart (p.262); chief call 'zack'. Open stony country with bushes, hillsides, low cliffs, also in cultivations and even gardens. L 14.5 cm.                                                                   -V

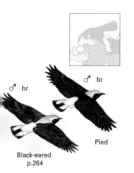

♂ br                    ♂ br

Pied

Black-eared
p.264

# WHEATEARS

♀ fresh

♂ br

♀

♂ nbr

**DESERT WHEATEAR**

ck ♂
rph.
Eastern
d p.270.

♂ br lugens
♀ similar

♀ br
halophila

♀

♂ nbr

**MOURNING WHEATEAR**

♂ 1st w ▶

sexes often
alike

♀ br

**CYPRUS WHEATEAR**

1st w
♂

♂ br

♂ nbr

♀ br

♀ br

**PIED WHEATEAR**

**FINSCH'S WHEATEAR** *Oenanthe finschii*. Male differs from Mourning and Pied (p.266) in having whole upperparts pale, except for wings, and from pale, black-throated forms of Black-eared (p.264) in black of wings joining black of neck. Winter male and female/imm less contrastingly black and white, but throat and cheeks usually blackish and upperparts silvery grey, separating them especially from buffer female Wheatear (p.264) and Pied Wheatear (p.266). Song a squeaky warble, with harsh monosyllabic calls. Shy, uncommon; rocky hillsides, semi-deserts, nearby cultivations. L 14 cm.

**RED-RUMPED WHEATEAR** *Oenanthe moesta*. Appreciably larger than the only other rufous-rumped wheatear, the Red-tailed, from which differs in its paler rufous rump and tail base, as well as paler crown, nape and wings with marked wing bar. Rufous rump, all-black tail and paler wings also separate from other pale-crowned wheatears. Rufous crown and all-black tail separate female/imm from other similar wheatears. Both sexes utter remarkable whirring song, on an ascending scale, through-out the year; chief call a hard 'prrt'. Sparsely vegetated desert edges. L 16 cm.

**RED-TAILED WHEATEAR** *Oenanthe xanthoprymna*. The region's only wheatear with a rufous rump, except for Red-rumped, whose breeding male has pale grey (not dark brown) crown and nape and rufous sides to tail base. Females either resemble males or have paler throat with rump slightly less rufous. Juv not speckled. Song strongly mimetic; has a 'thr, thr, thr' call. Rocky mountain slopes and hillsides; in winter in semi-deserts. L 14.5 cm.

Males of ssp.*xanthoprymna* (E Turkey), have black throat and face and white sides to base of black tail; males of ssp.*chrysopygia* (W Iran), have these brown and rufous respectively; all females like male *chrysopygia*, except for some *xanthoprymna*, which have paler throat; intermediates exist.

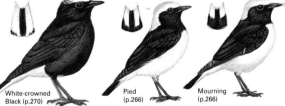

Hooded

White-crowned Black (p.270)

Pied (p.266)

Mourning (p.266)

**HOODED WHEATEAR** *Oenanthe monacha*. One of the larger wheatears; male mainly black, with white crown and belly, the only wheatear (except even blacker White-crowned Black, p.270) with outer tail feathers white to the tip. Cf. also white-breasted Mourning (p.266). Tail pattern best distinction of very pale female/imm. Flight buoyant, butterfly-like. Song a sweet subdued warble; chief call the usual harsh wheatear 'zack'. Unvegetated desert wadis and ravines, sometimes near human settlements. L 17 cm.

# WHEATEARS

♀ dark throat

♀ pale throat

♂ br
FINSCH'S
WHEATEAR

♀

♂

breeding
male in fresh
plumage

RED-RUMPED
WHEATEAR

♀ see text

♂

‹ sexes
alike ›

chrysopygia

xanthoprymna

RED-TAILED WHEATEAR
Main difference between races is in tail colour, with
very little white in the western race and rufous in the
eastern. All juvs like eastern females.

♀

♂ br

♂
1st autumn

HOODED WHEATEAR

**EASTERN PIED WHEATEAR** *Oenanthe picata*. Very like larger Hume's, but male has smaller head, less upright stance, more black on throat, white extending further up back to a square-cut (not rounded) end, buff under tail coverts, and pale flight feathers contrasting with black underwing coverts. Female's black parts browner and white ones duller or buffish. Iran: breeds N, rare winter visitor to S W. Aka Variable Wheatear. L 15 cm.

**HUME'S WHEATEAR** *Oenanthe alboniger*. A large and highly contrasted black-and-white wheatear, the region's only one (except smaller Eastern Pied) with whole upperparts black (except for long extension of white rump up back) and whole breast and underparts white; sexes alike. Song loud and fairly melodious; chief calls a short 3-4-syllabic whistle and a typical harsh 'chack' alarm note. Rocky, sparsely vegetated hillsides. L 17 cm.

**WHITE-CROWNED BLACK WHEATEAR** *Oenanthe leucopyga*. A large wheatear, the region's only one that is all-black except for white on crown as well as on rump, tail and under tail coverts; sexes alike. Imms (and confusingly some breeding adults) have black crown, but differ from larger Black Wheatear in outer tail feathers being white to the tip. Song loud, fairly musical; chief call a soft 'trip, trip'. Rocky desert country; near houses in oases. L 17 cm.                              -V

**BLACK WHEATEAR** *Oenanthe leucura*. The region's largest wheatear, and the only all-black one (though wings may appear paler), apart from white on rump, tail and under tail coverts (but some White-crowned Black have white-tipped outer tail feathers); female somewhat browner. Typical staccato chat song, with some musical warbling notes; chief call 'pee-pee-pee'. Cliffs, ravines and other dry, rocky places. L 18 cm.

**ROCK THRUSH** *Monticola saxatilis*. Breeding male is one of the most striking mountain birds, with unique combination of blue head and mantle, strongly contrasted with rufous underparts and short tail, with white patch on back most obvious in flight. Winter male and female/juv are brown, mottled and barred, with pale throat and rufous tail. A shy bird, as often heard as seen, with clear piping, often aerial, song, like a Wheatear's sung by a Blackbird, and grating, chat-like 'chack, chack'. Open rocky ground, ruins; in the W now only in mountains. L 18.5 cm.                              -V

**BLUE ROCK THRUSH** *Monticola solitarius*. Male is the region's only all-blue songbird, with darker wings and tail, though against the light can look nearly as dark as a Blackbird (p.272). Mottled female/juv darker than smaller Rock Thrush with both throat and tail dark grey-brown. Song repetitive, fluty, warbling, blackbird-like; chief calls a nuthatch-like 'uit, uit', a chat-like 'chuck, chuck' and a high-pitched 'tseee'. Cliffs, mountains, ruins, villages, towns, where often replaces Blackbird. L 20 cm.                              -V

# WHEATEARS

♀

picata

♂ br

EASTERN PIED WHEATEAR

HUME'S WHEATEAR

sexes alike

♀/juv ♂

♂

some
females
similar

WHITE-CROWNED
BLACK WHEATEAR

♀

♂

BLACK
WHEATEAR

♀

♂ br

♂ autumn

ROCK THRUSH

♀

♂ br

BLUE
ROCK
THRUSH

**Thrushes**: *Turdus*. Medium-sized songbirds with longish square tail and fairly thin bill adapted to diet of invertebrates, e.g. earthworms, molluscs; most also eat berries. Juv speckled paler. Song usually loud, often delivered high in tree. Nest usually in bush or tree.

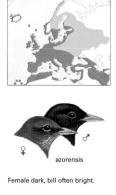

♀  azorensis  ♂

Female dark, bill often bright.

**BLACKBIRD** *Turdus merula*. One of the commonest European birds, longer-tailed than other thrushes. Adult male is region's only jet-black bird with a bright orange-yellow bill; smaller mottled and iridescent Starling (p.330) has paler yellow bill when breeding, also bustling gait and triangular flight outline due to much shorter tail. Female/imm darker brown and juv more rufous than other common thrushes, with breast much less distinctly spotted; bill blackish. Song mellow and fluty, not loud and ringing like Mistle Thrush or repetitive like Song Thrush (both p.274). Common calls include 'tchook, tchook', developing into a loud chattering scream in alarm; a persistent 'pink, pink' when going to roost or mobbing predators; and a high-pitched anxiety note, 'tsee'. Flight direct, impetuous, the tail flirted up on alighting; hops, runs and stands with head tilted listening for worms. Woodland, scrub, gardens, orchards, town parks; common in towns and villages in the W. Nest lined with dried grass over mud. L 24-25 cm. ●RmW

Females of sspp.*mauretanicus* (N W Africa), *cabrerae* (W Canary Is, Madeira) and *azorensis* (Azores) are smaller and darker, of *mauretanicus* also greyer.

**RING OUZEL** *Turdus torquatus*. Conspicuous white gorget distinguishes adult from Blackbird (but partially albino Blackbirds can have similar gorget), as do scaly underparts and pale fringes to wing feathers, which can make almost whole wing pale. Female browner and scalier; juv's underparts more distinctly spotted than Blackbird's. Song simple and fluty, with 2-3 notes, often based on clear piping call; also a harsh, grating 'tac, tac, tac', frequently running into a loud chatter. Mountains and moorlands, with rocks and scattered trees. L 23-24 cm. ●Sm

Ssp.*alpestris* (C & S Europe) is paler with more prominent pale fringes to wing and body feathers; ssp.*amicorum* (Caucasus to Transcaspia) has still more prominent pale feather fringes.

alpestris winter

**FIELDFARE** *Turdus pilaris*. Distinguished from all other thrushes of the region by combination of blue-grey head and rump and chestnut back and wings, the contrast greatest in adult males. Juvs duller than adults, with blue-grey only on rump, upperparts speckled whitish, and creamy-white supercilium and cheeks. In flight overhead best told by combination of white underwing flashes (shared only by Mistle Thrush, p.274) and distinctive chuckling 'chack, chack' call. Song a medley of chuckles, squeaks and whistles, sometimes in chorus from migrant flocks in spring. Open coniferous and broad-leaved woods, wooded moorland and tundra fringes, and in Scandinavia also town parks and gardens; in winter often on farmland and other grassland. L 25.5 cm. ●rMW

Has spread W as breeding bird.

**THRUSHES**

♂

♀

1st w ♂

juv

BLACKBIRD

torquatus

♂

♀

1st w ♂

juv

RING OUZEL

alpestris

♂

sexes similar
♀ often duller

FIELDFARE

Thrushes often feed in mixed flocks, especially in hard weather, when they may feed on haws in thorn bushes or on fallen apples.

**REDWING** *Turdus iliacus*. The smallest of the region's commoner thrushes, darker, slimmer and more streaked than most Song Thrushes, and readily told by white or creamy supercilium and under tail coverts, and conspicuous rufous flanks and underwing coverts; sexes alike, juv less rufous. Song rather stilted and repetitive, but briefer and flutier than Song Thrush, and often accompanied by warbling subsong, also from migrant parties in late winter. Flight note a very high-pitched 'see-ih', often from migrants overhead at night, also a soft 'chup' and a harsher 'chit-tic-tic' or 'chittuc'. Flight faster than Song Thrush. Woodland, especially birch, areas with scattered trees and scrub, and in Scandinavia and Iceland town parks and gardens; in winter often on grassland. L 21 cm.     ●rMW

**SONG THRUSH** *Turdus philomelos*. Generally the region's commonest spotted thrush; sexes alike, juv spotted buff above. Differs from larger Mistle Thrush in no white in tail; from smaller Redwing in no supercilium and pale flanks; from longer-tailed female/imm/juv Blackbirds (p.272) in much more distinct spotting on paler breast; and from all three in buff underwing. Loud, clear, sometimes mimetic song, has distinctive tendency to repeat each note. Chief calls a short soft 'sipp', a thin redwing-like 'seep' and a 'cheek' alarm note, higher-pitched than Blackbird's. Flight more direct than Mistle; hops, runs and stands with head on one side listening for worms. Woodland, scrub, farmland, orchards, town parks, gardens; frequent in suburbs in W and C Europe. Nest lined with bare mud. L 23 cm.     ●RmW

Upperparts of ssp.*philomelos* (Europe) tinged grey; of ssp.*clarkei* (Britain, Ireland, coastal W Europe) warm brown; of ssp.*hebridensis* (Outer Hebrides, Skye) darker brown.

**MISTLE THRUSH** *Turdus viscivorus*. The largest thrush over most of the region, greyer and with larger spots on underparts than Song Thrush, from which also separable in flight by flashes of white underwing (cf. Fieldfare, p.272) and whitish tips to outer tail feathers; sexes alike, juv spotted paler above. Loud ringing song, not fluty and mellow like Blackbird (p.272) or repetitive like Song Thrush. Harsh grating or churring flight note, like comb scraped against wood, quite distinct from other thrushes, except vagrant White's Thrush (p.276). Like Fieldfare (p.272), has distinctive flight, closing wings at regular intervals but with no marked dipping. Woodland, areas with scattered trees, town parks, gardens; mainly in mountains in S of range, elsewhere frequent in suburbs; after breeding frequents moors and open grasslands. Nest lined with dried grass over mud. L 27 cm.     ●Rs

**THRUSHES**

REDWING

SONG THRUSH

hebridensis

juv

ad

philomelos

ad

juv

MISTLE THRUSH

juv

juv

ad

Red-throated Thrush

1st w ♂

1st w ♂

ruficollis

♂ br

♂

BLACK-THROATED
THRUSH

♀

♂ br

WHITE'S THRUSH

**BLACK-THROATED THRUSH** *Turdus ruficollis* ssp.*atrogularis*, the western ssp; cf. Red-throated Thrush (opposite). Male has distinctive combination of dark grey-brown upperparts, black throat and upper breast and white belly; female browner with throat white and breast streaked or spotted darker. Both show rufous underwing flash in flight. Song simple, somewhat recalling Song Thrush (p.274); chief calls a redwing-like 'seee' and a softer blackbird-like chuckle. Taiga, open woodland, scattered subalpine scrub. Aka Dark-throated Thrush. L 24-25 cm.      -V

**WHITE'S THRUSH** *Zoothera dauma*. The region's bulkiest thrush; most likely to be confused with imm Mistle Thrush (p.274), but has heavier head and bill, shorter tail, golden brown plumage with crescentic black marks both above and below, and markedly dipping flight, when shows conspicuous black-and-white bands on underwing. Has a fluty, whistling song, a churring call like Mistle Thrush, a typical high-pitched thrush 'zieh' and a bullfinch-like pipe. Mainly on ground in thick cover; runs but does not hop. L 27 cm.      -V

Red-throated Thrush

1st br ♂

1st br ♀

♀

♀

var

♂

**Red-throated Thrush** *T. ruficollis* ssp.*ruficollis*, the eastern ssp. of the Black-throated Thrush (opposite) is a vagrant from Siberia. Male has breast, throat, cheeks, supercilium and sides of tail all rufous and rest of plumage browner; female similar but duller. Song simple, recalling Song Thrush (p.274); chief calls a redwing-like 'seee' and a softer blackbird-like chuckle. Taiga, open woodland, scattered subalpine scrub. L 24-25 cm.                        -V

**Dusky Thrush** *T. naumanni*. Vagrant from Siberia, distinguished especially by rufous rump and tail; also has white underparts and conspicuous pale supercilium. Female duller and browner than male; imms like adults but upperparts more scaly. Chief calls, see under ssp.*euonomus* . L 23 cm.        -V

Ssp.*euonomus* Dusky Thrush from N Siberia is the most likely ssp. to be seen in the N of the region. Adults have a more contrasting face pattern, with dark ear coverts and whiter supercilium, dark breast-band, rufous wings, rump more rufous than tail and black flecks on both mantle and underparts. Main call a loud high-pitched repetition of 'cheeh'; alarm note one or more 'chack's; also a high-pitched redwing-like 'shree'. Not infrequently hybridises with Naumann's Thrush.        -V

1st year

intermediate

Ssp.*naumanni* Naumann's Thrush from S E Siberia is the most likely ssp. to be seen in the S of the region. Adult males have rufous breast, with rump and tail more uniformly rufous, wings browner and mantle and underparts marked rufous; female slightly duller. Calls similar to Dusky Thrush. May hybridise with Dusky Thrush.        -V

♂ variable

**Eyebrowed Thrush** *Turdus obscurus*. Vagrant fr
Siberia, a small, slim thrush, the adult male differ
from same-sized Redwing (p.274) in grey head a
upper breast, throat with less conspicuous white sup
cilium, pale rufous lower breast as well as flanks, a
unspotted underparts. Female browner on head w
more extensive pale area on cheeks and throat; in
like female but with obscure pale wing bar. Cf. Du
Thrush (p.277). Calls include a thin, pipit-like 'zip-
and a soft 'tchuc'. L 23 cm.

**American Robin** *Turdus migratorius*. Transatlar
vagrant, confusingly named by first N American s
tlers from its red underparts as the nearest thing to
Robin (p.258) of Europe, with which it is in no way c
fusable. Generally resembles a Blackbird (p.272) w
conspicuously reddish underparts, grey-brown upp
parts, throat streaked black and white and lower be
white; sexes alike. Tail has white tips at corners,
Mistle Thrush (p.274). Calls 'kwik, kwik, kwik', lik
Blackbird and a softer, more song-thrush-like 'pit, pit
25 cm.

White's Thrush p

**Siberian Thrush** *Zoothera sibirica*. Vagrant from
Siberia. Both sexes identifiable by combination of
conspicuous supercilium (white in male, buff in
female) and broad black and white bars on underwing, but less bold than in larger White's Thrush
(p.276), like which it is a ground-dweller on forest
floors. Male all-dark, with head black, upperparts
slate black and underparts slate grey with paler
scaly markings; legs yellow. Female has upperparts brown like a Song Thrush (p.274), and underparts buff or whitish, with scaly markings. Calls
include a thin 'zit' and a gruffer note. L 22 cm.   -V

Nightingale
p.256

*Catharus*: four small vagrant North American thrushes, with spotted underparts like a Song Thrush (p.274); all rather secretive, skulking low down in cover.

◀ **Hermit Thrush** *C. guttatus*. One of the smaller species, nightingale-sized and readily recognised by rufous rump and tail contrasting with olive or greyish-brown head and rest of upperparts. Breast spots brownish and elongated, flanks uniformly buff and eye-rings narrow and buff. In flight at close range may show a faint pale wing bar. Has a most distinctive habit of cocking tail up and then slowly lowering it. Chief calls a low 'chuck', also a scolding 'tuk-tuk-tuk' and a grating 'pay'. L 17 cm.-V

◀ **Veery** *C. fuscescens*. Remarkably like a Nightingale or Thrush Nightingale (p.256), being only slightly larger and similarly rufous brown above and pale below; breast-spots grey-brown, much less conspicuous than the other *Catharus* thrushes; eye-rings greyish, obscure. Call a low whistling 'view', somewhat like Swainson's Thrush. L 18 cm.      -V

◀ **Swainson's Thrush** *C. ustulatus*. This and the Gray-cheeked Thrush are the two smaller *Catharus* thrushes whose uniformly greyish-olive-brown upperparts combined with their smallish brown-black breast spots make them look most like a diminutive Song Thrush (p.274). Swainson's is the browner of the two and is best distinguished by its broad buffish-yellow eye-rings, cheeks and upper breast. Call 'whit' or in flight a short 'heep'. L 18 cm.                          -V

◀ **Gray-cheeked Thrush** *C. minimus*. Somewhat greyer than the same-sized Swainson's Thrush, with similar close resemblance to a small, rather squat Song Thrush (p.274). Best distinguished by its grey cheeks, less buff breast and narrower and much less obvious off-white eye-rings. Chief call a rather high-pitched, descending 'quee-a' quite distinct from Swainson's but not unlike Veery. Ssp.*bicknelli* (Bicknell's Thrush, perhaps a full species) has tail slightly tinged rufous and more yellow at base and on lower mandible of blackish bill. L 18 cm.      -V

◀ **Wood Thrush** *Hylocichla mustelina*. The largest and plumpest of the five vagrant N American thrushes, but still much smaller than Song Thrush (p.274) in size, and much more boldly spotted on breast and whole underparts, but with most distinctively rufous head, mantle and wings, though rump and tail olive-brown; eye-rings broad, whitish. Call a rapid 'pit, pit, pit'. L 20 cm.                          -V

● WARBLERS: *Sylviidae.* Small, mainly migratory songbirds with thin, insect-eating bill. Sexes usually alike; juv usually like adult. Flight flitting. Voice often a key field character. Habitat requires some cover, from trees to low bushes or reeds; nest usually in bush or on or near ground.

**Grasshopper Warblers:** *Locustella.* Plain brown warblers, notable for their broad, graduated tail, which appears heavy when they do (rarely) fly, with long under tail coverts and for their reeling songs. These recall some stridulating crickets and sound louder or softer as the bird turns its head; usually uttered from thick cover, but sometimes from a perch. Extremely shy, usually skulking in dense scrub or tall marsh vegetation, or running through it rapidly like a mouse.

**GRASSHOPPER WARBLER** *Locustella naevia.* The most widespread of the group, olive-brown above, streaked darker (faintly on rump), obscure supercilium, and buffish-white below, streaked on long under tail coverts and faintly elsewhere; legs pinkish. Sustained, high-pitched, far-carrying, monotonous, trilling song recalls an angler's reel; chief call a short 'tchic'. Damp or dry scrubby or tussocky habitats: heaths, coarse grassland, fens, felled woodland. L 13 cm. ●S

**SAVI'S WARBLER** *Locustella luscinioides.* Not so shy as smaller Grasshopper, and unstreaked on warmer brown upperparts, paler underparts and warm buff flanks, so resembling a short-billed Reed (p.282). Eastern ssp.*fusca* is colder brown above with mottled breast. Buzzing song louder, faster, lower-pitched, in shorter bursts, recalling a bush cricket; calls a scolding 'tzwick' and a liquid 'puitt'. Marshes, swamps, fens, reedbeds. L 14 cm. ○S

**RIVER WARBLER** *Locustella fluviatilis.* Unstreaked earthbrown upperparts and mottled breast recall eastern Savi's, but bold whitish tips to very long brown under tail coverts are diagnostic. Song much shorter than Savi's and Grasshopper, and more rhythmic, with alternating pairs of grinding fast and slow 'derr-derr, derr derr, derr-derr' notes, recalling a bush cricket, often uttered from bush top; chief call rather harsh. Bushy swamps and freshwater margins, from woodland and steppes to town parks. L 13 cm. -V

**Pallas's Grasshopper Warbler** *L. certhiola.* A Siberian vagrant, smaller, shorter-tailed, drabber and even more skulking than Grasshopper Warbler, but is more reddish-brown, especially on rump, and has more heavily streaked crown and mantle, prominent pale supercilium and brown tail with diagnostic pale greyish feather tips. Imm yellower below with speckled breast. Chief call a sharp 'chi- chirr'. L 13.5 cm. -V

**LANCEOLATED WARBLER** *Locustella lanceolata.* The smallest of the group, darker and more heavily streaked above than Grasshopper, and with whitish throat and faint supercilium; well-streaked breast and flanks almost form a gorget. Song a trill like Grasshopper, but higher-pitched and more modulated, with rattling and whistling notes, often uttered from bush top; call like Pallas's but louder. L 11.5 cm. -V

**Gray's Grasshopper Warbler** *L. fasciolata.* A rare vagrant from Siberia, much the largest *Locustella*, uniform dull brown above, with marked pale supercilium and warm buff under tail coverts. Call a loud 'ruti-tuti'. L 18 cm.

# *LOCUSTELLA* WARBLERS

Skulks in thick cover, often near ground in marshes, where they move around like mice, but may sing from exposed perch.

**GRASSHOPPER WARBLER**

Monotonous, high-pitched, far-carrying song recalls angler's reel; mostly starts at dusk, continuing for hours.

**SAVI'S WARBLER**

Song like Grasshopper but louder, faster, lower-pitched, often in short bursts.

**RIVER WARBLER**

Slower and more rhythmic song than Grasshopper, often from top of low bush.

Unstreaked under tail coverts.

**PALLAS'S GRASSHOPPER WARBLER**

**LANCEOLATED WARBLER**

Almost as big as Great Reed Warbler (p.282), but with typical *Locustella* habits. Juv like adult with yellowish supercilium, throat and belly, and more olive on breast and flanks.

**GRAY'S GRASSHOPPER WARBLER**

**Reed Warblers** *Acrocephalus*. Brown above, paler below, with whitish throat and rounded tail. Scolding, churring calls rather similar, but mimetic, rather repetitive songs distinctive. Skulkers in thick marshy vegetation.

**REED WARBLER** *Acrocephalus scirpaceus*. Differs from Marsh and Blyth's Reed mainly by more rufous upperparts, especially of rump and in juv, also by dark alula. Best distinction is rather monotonous song, like two pebbles rubbed together, with general pattern 'churr-churr-churr...chirruc-chirruc-chirruc'; often mimetic, but normally lacks harsh interjections. Reedbeds, swamps, reed-lined freshwater margins. L 12.5 cm. ●Sm

**MARSH WARBLER** *Acrocephalus palustris*. Very hard to tell from Reed and Blyth's Reed, except by song, though adults more olive-brown with whiter throat and pinker legs; at short range evenly spaced pale tips of primaries conspicuous on closed wing. Typical song much jerkier and less uniform than Reed, with both harsh notes and much mimicry of other birds. Scrub and other tall dense vegetation, often near fresh water, also cornfields and gardens. L 12.5 cm. ○sM

**PADDYFIELD WARBLER** *Acrocephalus agricola*. The shortest-winged, longest-tailed and often most rufous of the smaller reed warblers, with prominent broad dark-bordered white supercilium, widest behind eyes, recalling Sedge Warbler (p.284). Song mimetic, like Marsh but with no harsh notes. Scrub, dense vegetation, in swamps or near fresh water. L 12.5 cm. -V

**BLYTH'S REED WARBLER** *Acrocephalus dumetorum*. Greyer than Marsh and has plainer upperparts (no pale fringes on wing feathers), paler supercilium in front of eyes, longer bill, greyer legs and shorter, more rounded wings, so that flight whirring. Song slower, more repetitive than Marsh, mimetic, with typical 'lo-li-lia' and 'tjec-tjec' phrases, almost continuous at night; 'chek-chek-(chek)' call distinctive. Habitat like Marsh, mainly scrub and tall plants. L 12.5 cm. -V

**GREAT REED WARBLER** *Acrocephalus arundinaceus*. A very large, almost redwing-sized, rufous-tinged warbler, like a giant Reed Warbler but lores blackish, supercilium buff and more conspicuous, and bill much stouter. Song loud, repetitive, 'karra-karra-karra, krik, krik' with froglike croaks, but less mimetic than Reed; calls a harsh 'chac' and a croaking 'gurk'. Reedbeds and other freshwater margins. L 19 cm. -A

Ssp. *orientalis* (China), probably a full species, is smaller with much more streaked throat and breast. Vagrant to Israel.

**BASRA REED WARBLER** *Acrocephalus griseldis*. Smaller and greyer than Great Reed, with longer, thinner bill, whitish supercilium, tail dark and legs greyish. Song, calls, nearer Reed Warbler. Marshes, Iraq. L c17 cm.

**CLAMOROUS REED WARBLER** *Acrocephalus stentoreus*. Paler and slimmer than Great Reed, with longer bill, obscurer whitish supercilium, shorter, rounder wings, and longer, more graduated tail. Song higher-pitched, more musical, less croaking, with frequent 'ro-do-pee-kis' theme; calls 'kchrr', 'chac', 'squark'. Reed beds, tall marsh vegetation. L 18 cm.

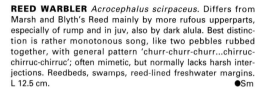

# UNSTREAKED REED WARBLERS

Rarely breeds away from reeds *Phragmites.*

**REED WARBLER**

Song often uttered from near top of reed stem, sometimes at night.

**MARSH WARBLER**

Much less often in reedbeds than Reed Warbler.

Sings from prominent perch more often than Reed, and more continuously at night.

**PADDYFIELD WARBLER**

**BASRA REED WARBLER**

Thick-billed Warbler p.372

**BLYTH'S REED WARBLER**

**GREAT REED WARBLER**

**CLAMOROUS REED WARBLER**

**MOUSTACHED WARBLER** *Acrocephalus melanopogon*. More rufous and darker-streaked above than Sedge Warbler and has plainer, blackish-brown crown, white supercilium, broader behind eyes, darker cheeks more contrasted with white throat, and whiter underparts. Juv has crown darker still. Song both musical like Nightingale (p.256) and scratchy and mimetic like Sedge; calls a soft 't-rrrt' and a louder 'tchuc'. Wetlands. L 13 cm.          -V(b)

**AQUATIC WARBLER** *Acrocephalus paludicola*. Has mantle more yellowish-buff and strongly streaked (dark 'tiger stripes', pale 'tramlines') than Sedge or Moustached, with both crown stripe and supercilium broad and buff (cf. juv Sedge), rump thinly streaked, diagnostic spiky tail, and pink legs. Song has more regular pattern of short distinct phrases than Sedge; calls as Sedge. Coarse wet sedgy grassland. L 13 cm.          -A

**SEDGE WARBLER** *Acrocephalus schoenobaenus*. The commonest of the region's three streaked *Acrocephalus*, with prominent creamy (buffer in juv) supercilium and narrow dark streaks on mid-brown upperparts; also has streaked brown crown, unstreaked deep buff rump and pale brown legs. Song a scratchy mimetic jumble of contrasting sweet and harsh notes; calls a harsh churr and a scolding 'tucc'. Scrub, reedbeds, coarse vegetation, rarely far from water. L 13 cm.    ●Sm

**CETTI'S WARBLER** *Cettia cetti*. A notable skulker, robust, uniformly dark rufous brown above and pale beneath, with narrow pale supercilium, short wings and rounded, often spread and cocked, tail. Song most distinctive, uttered from thick cover in loud staccato bursts 'chewee, chewee, chewee-wee-wee-wee' or 'pit, pit, pitipit, pitipit'. Calls include 'che', 'twic', 'huit' and a churr. Dense scrub and other tangled vegetation in marshes and by fresh water. L 14 cm.          ○R

**FAN-TAILED WARBLER** *Cisticola juncidis*. Like a tiny reed warbler, buff above with head heavily streaked blackish-brown, rump tinged rufous, short rounded tail and wings, tail tipped black and white. A skulker, most easily detected during its jerky high aerial song flight, when utters an insistent 'chip, chip, chip'; call 'tew'. Marshes, freshwater margins, dry grassland and farmland. L 10 cm.          -V

**SCRUB WARBLER** *Scotocerca inquieta*. Paler, sandier and less streaked above than Graceful, and with finely streaked breast, dark eye-stripe and bolder supercilium; tail never still, usually cocked, is less graduated, darker, unbarred. Song a high-pitched whistling 'psee-ee' or 'pseeyoo'; call a rapid 'pip-pip-pip'. Semi-deserts; often on ground. L 10 cm.

Ssp.*inquieta* (Middle East); ssp.*saharae* (N W Africa) paler, unstreaked.

**GRACEFUL WARBLER** *Prinia gracilis*. Tiny, short-winged; greyish and streaked above, paler and unstreaked below, with obscure pale supercilium; tail long, graduated, barred black with white tips, often cocked up and fanned out and sometimes twitched from side to side. Song a repeated, high-pitched, tinkling 'zer-wit'; calls include ticking and jitting notes, and triple wing-snapping 'brrp' in aerial display. Scrub, semi-deserts, palm groves, cultivations, gardens; rarely on ground. L 10 cm.

# STREAKED WARBLERS

Moustached mainly in reeds and reed-mace, also tamarisk; Aquatic in sedges and yellow iris.

MOUSTACHED WARBLER

AQUATIC WARBLER

song
explosive outburst

SEDGE WARBLER

CETTI'S WARBLER

FAN-TAILED WARBLER

harae

quieta

♀

♂

GRACEFUL WARBLER

SCRUB WARBLER

**Hippolais Warblers.** Uniformly coloured, with plain lores ('bland-faced'), separating them from the reed warblers (p.282), which have longer under tail coverts, the shorter-billed leaf warblers (p.294) and the stubby-billed Garden Warbler (p.288). Imms often greyer. Songs babbling, varied, sustained. Often raise crown feathers.

**OLIVACEOUS WARBLER** *Hippolais pallida*. Shares Melodious Warbler's structure and short wings but plumage pale grey-brown, lacking green or yellow; outer tail feathers edged whitish. Cf. Marsh Warbler (p.282), which has long under tail coverts, and Booted Warbler. Song low-pitched, repetitive, mimetic; call a hard 'tac', usually uttered with downward tail flick. Scrub, semi-deserts, farmland, gardens, town parks. L 12-14 cm.         -V

Western ssp.*opaca* noticeably longer-billed; smaller, paler, shorter-billed, shorter-tailed eastern ssp.*elaeica* is very like eastern ssp.*rama* of Booted and may interbreed where ranges overlap.

**BOOTED WARBLER** *Hippolais caligata*. Small size and rounded head recall leaf warbler (p.294); otherwise like small-billed, paler-legged, more buff-brown Olivaceous, with more marked, longer supercilium; outer tail feathers edged white. Song longer, faster, not repetitive or mimetic; call a constant 'chek-chek-chek'. Scrub, gardens. L 11.5-13 cm.         -A

Ssp.*rama* (S C Asia) has structure and coloration of Olivaceous and many are indistinguishable (see above). Vagrant to Britain, Sweden.

**UPCHER'S WARBLER** *Hippolais languida*. Like a large Olivaceous with browner wings, longer supercilium, and a long, dark brown, white-edged and white-tipped tail, which it constantly swings like a shrike (p.316). Cf. also Olive-tree Warbler. Song more musical than Olivaceous, recalling Whitethroat (p.288); call 'chuk'. Scrubby hillsides, gardens; perches on rocks. L 14-15 cm.

**OLIVE-TREE WARBLER** *Hippolais olivetorum*. The largest 'hippo', olive-grey with large yellow deep bill, dark blue-grey legs, peaked crown, very short supercilium, whitish-edged and tipped outer tail feathers, and (when breeding) pale wing panel. Song slower, deeper, more musical, less repetitive than Olivaceous; call 'tuc, tuc'. Scrub, open woodlands, olive groves, vineyards. L 14-16.5 cm.

World breeding range; winters in Africa.

**MELODIOUS WARBLER** *Hippolais polyglotta*. Very like slightly larger Icterine, but tail shorter and wings more rounded, without pale panels and not reaching tip of tail coverts. Song faster, more liquid, musical and mimetic, often including the bird's own diagnostic house-sparrow-like chatter; also a distinctive 'tit, tit' and an icterine-like 'hooeet'. Habitat as Icterine. L 13 cm.         -A

Spreading northwards.

**ICTERINE WARBLER** *Hippolais icterina*. Greenish-brown above with yellow underparts; imm and some adults greyer. Has longer tail than Melodious, and longer, more pointed wings, reaching tip of tail coverts and with diagnostic yellowish-white panel. Distinctive song, a vehement, repetitive, marsh-warbler-like medley of discordant and musical notes. Calls include a characteristic liquid 'dideroid', a hard blackcap-like 'tek, tek' and a softer chiffchaff-like 'hooeet'. Woodland edges, riversides, parks, orchards, gardens. L 13-15 cm.         ○M

# *HIPPOLAIS* WARBLERS

elaeica

worn ad

opaca

br ad

**OLIVACEOUS
WARBLER**

**BOOTED
WARBLER**

**UPCHER'S
WARBLER**

**OLIVE-TREE
WARBLER**

ad autumn

ad grey
autumn

**MELODIOUS
WARBLER**

spring

ad autumn

ad grey
autumn

spring

**ICTERINE
WARBLER**

**Sylvia Warblers.** Males usually brighter than females. Most have two characteristic notes, a harsh churr and a hard 'tacc'. Mainly in scrub and low bushes, tall vegetation, also woodland and tall vegetation.

**GARDEN WARBLER** *Sylvia borin.* Has roundish head and short, rather thick bill (cf. *Hippolais*, p.286), but most important visual field mark is uniform plumage, hair-brown above, pale buff below, with white belly, but no supercilium or other distinctive feature; legs grey-brown. Juv warmer buff, with rusty tinge on wings. Best identified by song, usually uttered from hidden perch, sometimes in snatches, but normally a very even musical warble, mellower, lower-pitched and more sustained than Blackcap (which may mimic it). Woodland with shrub understory, scrub, parks, large gardens. L 14 cm. ●Sm

**WHITETHROAT** *Sylvia communis.* Male Whitethroat and adult Spectacled (p.292) are the region's only warblers to combine a grey head (brown in female Whitethroat), rufous wings and a conspicuously white throat; both have white outer tail feathers. Juv like female, but throat duller white. Brief scratchy staccato song often uttered in short vertical song flight; also a 'wheet' or 'whit' call. Scrub, hedgerows, tall vegetation, also in gardens after breeding. L 14 cm. ●Sm

**LESSER WHITETHROAT** *Sylvia curruca.* Greyer than Whitethroat, with diagnostic dark ear coverts, grey legs and no rufous in wings (except in Siberian vagrant ssp.*blythi*, which is white below). Juv somewhat less grey. One of the more skulking warblers, with no song flight, the simple song, a tuneless rattle recalling Cirl Bunting (p.356), being uttered from a well-hidden perch; pleasant warbling subsong is more reminiscent of Whitethroat. Chief call a typical *Sylvia* 'tacc, tacc'. Open woodland, scrub, overgrown hedgerows, parks, large gardens. L 13.5 cm. ●Sm

**BARRED WARBLER** *Sylvia nisoria.* Large, stout, long-tailed; males greyish with barred underparts, females browner and less strongly barred, both with yellow eyes, two white wing bars and some white in outer tail feathers; in winter both have paler eyes and fainter barring on flanks. Juv not barred, like a rather large, greyish, long-tailed Garden Warbler with pale wing bars and a steeper forehead; eyes dark; cf. Olive-tree Warbler (p.286) and imm Orphean Warbler (p.290). Song like Garden Warbler, but in shorter bursts and interspersed with the loud harsh chattering call note 'charr-charr-charr'; delivered from perch or in dancing display flight. Scrub, woodland edges, thickets. L 15 cm. -A

**BLACKCAP** *Sylvia atricapilla.* Greyer-brown than Garden Warbler and readily identified by crown colour: black in adult male, blackish-brown in imm male, rufous brown in female/juv. Cf. much smaller, pale-cheeked Marsh and Willow Tits (p.308). Song much higher-pitched and less sustained than Garden Warbler, and often mimetic, with an especially confusing garden-warbler-like variant. Chief call a typical *Sylvia* 'tacc, tacc'. Woodland, scrub, parks, large gardens, with thick undergrowth. L 14 cm. ●Smw

# *SYLVIA* WARBLERS

juv

ad

♀

♂

WHITETHROAT

## GARDEN WARBLER

Ssp. *blythi* (Siberia) has
warmer brown upperparts.

fresh

curruca

althaea

minula

blythi

## LESSER WHITETHROAT

Hume's Lesser Whitethroat ssp. *althaea* (S W Asia) is much darker with
black ear coverts and stouter bill; Desert Lesser Whitethroat ssp.
*minula* (winter visitor from Iran) is paler with smaller or no dark cheek
patch and weaker bill; both often treated as species.

juv

song flight

♀

♂

ad

juv ♂

## BARRED WARBLER

Could be mistaken for a small shrike
(p.316); most seen in Britain are juvs.

♂ melanistic

BLACKCAP

**SARDINIAN WARBLER** *Sylvia melanocephala*. Generally the commonest and most widespread Mediterranean *Sylvia*. Adult male has whole head jet black, except for white chin and fore-neck, and conspicuous red eye and eye-ring; female/juv browner with crown grey-brown. Cf. also Orphean, Rüppell's and Ménétries's Warblers. Song more musical than Whitethroat (p.288), includes snatches of scolding, chittering, wren-like call; may be uttered in aerial display flight. Moves restlessly through scrub, maquis, open woodland, parks, gardens; very locally in towns. L 13.5 cm.                                                    -V

**MÉNÉTRIES'S WARBLER** *Sylvia mystacea*. Differs from Sardinian Warbler in its pale yellow eye-ring, greyer crown and pink underparts, with a moustache-like white line between black cheeks and pink throat. Voice and restless, skulking habits similar, but song softer with more rattling and hissing, and tail constantly waved about. Thickets, especially of tamarisk and along rivers, orchards, gardens. L 13.5 cm.

**CYPRUS WARBLER** *Sylvia melanothorax*. Male differs from male Sardinian Warbler in having its throat, breast and flanks heavily marked with usually crescentic black bars, a white moustache separating the throat from the black cheeks; female/juv browner, less strongly marked; legs often yellowish. Voice and habits as Sardinian. Scrub, maquis. L 13.5 cm.

World breeding range.

**RÜPPELL'S WARBLER** *Sylvia rueppelli*. Male is the region's only warbler with whole head, throat and upper breast black, relieved only by a broad white moustachial stripe; female/imm/juv greyer and browner, with throat variably streaked whitish or greyish and moustache often obscure. Both sexes have red eyes, variably reddish legs and conspicuous white outer tail feathers. Song like Sardinian Warbler, but interspersed note is a harder, more staccato rattle; may be uttered in greenfinch-like song flight. Scrub, maquis, on rocky hillsides. L 14 cm.                                                                           -V

**ARABIAN WARBLER** *Sylvia leucomelaena*. Differs from larger Orphean Warbler in dark eyes with white eye-ring, matt black nape and outer feathers of graduated tail much less conspicuously white, the inner ones with white tips beneath, visible when distinctively vibrating tail with a circular downward movement. Warbling song includes discordant notes and a babbler-like 'pift'; calls include a short churring rattle. Scrubby semi-deserts and wadis. L 14.5 cm.

**ORPHEAN WARBLER** *Sylvia hortensis*. The largest *Sylvia*, breeding male with forehead and cheeks black, crown dark, staring pale yellow eyes, white throat contrasting with both dark head and whitish underparts, and square-ended tail with conspicuous white outer feathers; cf. Arabian Warbler. Winter male and female/imm duller; imm's tail shorter than imm Barred Warbler (p.288) with no pale spots at base. Song a pleasant thrush-like (especially in the E) warble, repetitive (especially in the W) but with no discordant notes; also a loud rattling 'trrr' note. Open woods, scrub, parkland. L 15 cm.      -V

# SYLVIA WARBLERS

Females of both species similar; Ménétries's paler below. ◀ ▼

♀

♂

SARDINIAN WARBLER

w ♂

MÉNÉTRIES'S WARBLER

...ay have obscure ...hitish eye-ring. ▲

old ♀

♂

CYPRUS WARBLER

♀

♂

RÜPPELL'S WARBLER

♀

...ome males ...ave pale eyes.

♂

♀

juv

ARABIAN WARBLER

...Israel, often ...ave dark iris

♂

ORPHEAN WARBLER

♀

World range.

**MARMORA'S WARBLER** *Sylvia sarda*. At a distance grey underparts make male look like an almost all-black Dartford Warbler, but female browner above and paler beneath; eyes and eye-rings red. Ssp.*balearica* (Balearic Is) is paler. Juv greyer and paler above and whiter beneath than juv Dartford. Song clearer, faster and softer than Dartford; call a distinctive 'tsig', either singly or as a rattle. Open scrub, maquis. L 12 cm.      -V

World range.

**DARTFORD WARBLER** *Sylvia undata*. Usually seen only as a small dark long-tailed bird diving into cover, a close view shows unique combination of dark grey head, red eyes and eye-rings, dark brown upperparts, dark vinous underparts (throat spotted white), yellow legs and long, often cocked up, graduated, white-edged tail; female duller than male, juv whitish beneath. Cf. Tristram's and Marmora's Warblers. Whitethroat-like song often in dancing display flight; alarm a scolding 'jer-jit'. Dense scrub, especially of gorse, tall overgrown heather. L 12.5 cm.      ⊙R

World breeding and most of wintering range.

**TRISTRAM'S WARBLER** *Sylvia deserticola*. Male differs from darker Dartford and Sardinian Warblers in its rufous wings, obscure whitish moustachial streak and whitish eye-ring, and from Sardinian also in its vinous brown underparts. Female appreciably paler. Song like Dartford but call a distinctive sharp 'chit' or 'chit-it'. Open woodland and scrub in hills; in winter also in desert. L 12 cm.

World range; also breeds Cape Verde Is.

**SPECTACLED WARBLER** *Sylvia conspicillata*. Male like either a small Whitethroat (p.288) with darker head and back, whiter throat and pinkish breast, or a Subalpine with no moustachial stripe, but a white throat, paler breast and rufous wings; unlike both in its often yellow legs. Female/imm/juv paler, with strikingly rufous wings, but some less rufous imms confusable with Subalpine. Song a pleasantly musical whitethroat-like ditty, often in display flight; calls 'tac, tac' and a rattling 'kirrrr'. Dry open treeless country with low bushes. L 11-13 cm.      -V

**SUBALPINE WARBLER** *Sylvia cantillans*. Male like a Dartford Warbler, but paler and with a conspicuous white moustachial stripe (cf. black-throated Rüppell's (p.290)), but female more like a small, relatively longer-tailed female Lesser Whitethroat (p.288) with rufous wings or a darker female Spectacled, but with throat less white than both. Song like Sardinian, but more musical and with no harsh notes, often in dancing display flight. Calls a distinctive soft 'tec, tec' and a chattering note. Scrub, maquis. L 12-13 cm.      -A

**DESERT WARBLER** *Sylvia nana*. The smallest and palest *Sylvia*, with unique combination of greyish to golden buff plumage, rufous rump and tail, white outer tail feathers, and pale yellow eyes, legs and (dark-tipped) bill; sexes alike. Song simple and harmonious, like jingling of small silver bell; calls include a weak purring rattle and a high-pitched 'chee-chee-chee-chee'. Scattered bushes in deserts and semi-deserts and on dry hillsides. L 11.5 cm.      -V

Ssp.*nana* (S W Asia) greyish; ssp.*deserti* (N W Africa) golden buff.

# *SYLVIA* WARBLERS

♂

♀

juv

**MARMORA'S WARBLER**

♂

♀

juv

**DARTFORD WARBLER**

♀

1st w

♂

**TRISTRAM'S WARBLER**

♀

1st w

♂

**SPECTACLED WARBLER**

1st year ♂

1st year ♀

♀

♂ br

**SUBALPINE WARBLER**

nana

deserti

**DESERT WARBLER**

**Leaf Warblers**: *Phylloscopus*. Small greenish or yellowish warblers; sexes alike. Cf. generally larger *Hippolais* (p.286). Voice often diagnostic. Check presence/absence supercilium and wing bars. Active, with characteristic habit of flicking slightly notched tail.

**ARCTIC WARBLER** *Phylloscopus borealis*. Slightly larger than Willow Warbler (p.296), and differing in its whitish wing bar (some autumn birds show a faint second bar), whitish throat and underparts, dark eye-stripes and more marked long pale supercilium, up-turned towards nape; bill dark, legs pale. Smaller Greenish Warbler hard to separate in field except by voice. Cf. also much greener and yellower Green Warbler. Song a short, tuneless buzzing trill, usually preceded by a hard 'tzic'; calls 'tswee-ep', 'tzic' and a short rattling 'drrt'. Arctic and sub-Arctic woodland and scrub. L 12 cm.　　　　　-A

**GREEN WARBLER** *Phylloscopus trochiloides* ssp.*nitidus*. Like a small Wood Warbler (p.296), with bright yellow supercilium and underparts, but less bright olive-green upperparts; readily distinguished by yellow wing bar. Cf. Greenish Warbler (greyer above, whitish below, with cream supercilium) and North American vagrant Tennessee Warbler (pp.298 & 366); more prominent dark eye-stripe, less prominent wing bar). Song loud, with 5 notes recalling Cetti's Warbler (p.284), then 4-5 coal-tit-like notes; calls a cheerful 'chi-wee' and a pied-wagtail-like 'chirri-rip'. Mountain woods. L 11 cm.　　　　　-V

**GREENISH WARBLER** *Phylloscopus trochiloides* ssp.*trochiloides*. Differs from Chiffchaff (p.296) in its prominent but narrow pale wing bar (sometimes a trace of another, cf. eastern Chiffchaff races) more distinct supercilium, and whiter underparts. Very like slightly larger Arctic Warbler, but supercilium usually longer in front of eye but shorter behind it, and legs dark. Song a rapid, high-pitched, warbling, wren-like trill, often preceded by repeated 'tiss-yip' call. Open woodland, forest edges. L 11 cm.　　　　　-A

Ssp.*plumbeitarsus* Two-barred Greenish Warbler, a very rare vagrant from E Siberia, differs most notably in having two wing bars; also has darker and greener upperparts, whiter underparts with hardly any yellow, and both wings and tail slightly shorter. Lacks yellowish outer edges and tips to tertials of smaller Yellow-browed Warbler (p.298). L 11 cm.　　　　　-V

**BONELLI'S WARBLER** *Phylloscopus bonelli*. Greyer than same-sized Willow Warbler (p.296), especially on head, and with whiter underparts, wing and tail feathers conspicuously edged yellow-green and often a yellow rump patch; supercilium not prominent, no eye-stripes or wing bars, legs dark. Cf. Booted Warbler (p.286). Song a distinctive short, rather flat, single-note trill, recalling to some observers those of Wood Warbler (p.292), Lesser Whitethroat (p.288) or even Cirl Bunting (p.356); 'hoo-eeet' call more distinctly disyllabic than Willow Warbler. Woods and forests in the hills, often of pine or cork oak. L 11.5 cm.　　　　　-A

**Eastern Bonelli's Warbler** *P.b.*ssp.*orientalis* (often regarded as a full species) is slightly larger, longer-winged and greyer-brown above, with a shorter, quieter song and distinctly different 'chip' or 'chup' call-note.　　　　　-v

# LEAF WARBLERS

autumn

summer

**GREEN WARBLER**

autumn

summer

**ARCTIC WARBLER**

autumn

summer

**GREENISH WARBLER**

autumn

Two-barred Greenish Warbler

1st autumn bonelli

bonelli

orientalis

Chiffchaff

**BONELLI'S WARBLER**

Ssp. *orientalis* (Balkans to Levant) is confusable with a grey Chiffchaff (p.296).

**WOOD WARBLER** *Phylloscopus sibilatrix*. The region's largest breeding leaf warbler, with breast and supercilium bright yellow and underparts white; distinguished from Icterine and Melodious Warblers (p.286) by shorter bill, yellow legs and white belly. Has two quite different songs, a long quivering trill and a plangent repetition of its anxiety note, a mellow, plaintive, bullfinch-like 'dee-ur' or 'puu'. Forests and woodland, especially beech. L 12.5 cm. ●S

**PLAIN LEAF WARBLER** *Phylloscopus neglectus*. The smallest leaf warbler, like a dull olive-brown Goldcrest (p.300), thin-billed, dark-legged, short-tailed and paler beneath, with no green or yellow and supercilium obscure. Song brief and goldfinch-like, 'pt, toodla, toodla', sometimes uttered in flight; calls a distinctive harsh 'gyurr' and a quieter 'chic'. Actively flies from bush to bush in scattered low scrub in mountains. Aka Plain Willow Warbler. L 8.5 cm.

**MOUNTAIN CHIFFCHAFF** *Phylloscopus sindianus*. Very like *tristis* race of Chiffchaff (and may itself well only be a Chiffchaff race); mainly brown above and silvery white beneath, with no yellow (except beneath 'elbow' of wing) or greenish tinge, and sometimes a pale wing bar. Song 'more tinny' than Chiffchaff, but weaker with intervals between notes longer and less regular; calls 'tis-yip' and 'too-wit'. Mountain forests, sub-alpine scrub. L 11 cm.

**CHIFFCHAFF** *Phylloscopus collybita*. One of the region's two commonest leaf warblers, drabber olive-green above and greyer below, but less tinged with green and yellow than Willow Warbler (from which best distinguished by voice) and with legs always dark. Diagnostic song a repeated monotonic 'chiff-chaff' or 'zilp-zalp', often interspersed with a guttural 'chirr-chirr'; chief call, distinct from Willow Warbler, a monosyllabic 'hweet'. Woodland, scrub, large gardens. L 11 cm. ●Smw

Sspp.*abietinus/fulvescens/tristis* (N Europe to Far East, C Asia), rare autumn visitors to the W, are greyer/whiter above, becoming less olive eastwards, and whiter/less yellow below; some are brown above, white below and yellow only beneath the wing 'elbow'; some also show faint pale wing bars, especially in autumn (cf. Mountain Chiffchaff, Greenish Warbler, p.294); often uttering distinctive 'sad' 'sweeoo' call. **Iberian Chiffchaff** sp/ssp.*brehmii* is brighter with distinctive, more complex song; **Canary Islands Chiffchaff** sp/spp. *canariensis* (also ssp.*exsul*) is dark above, tawny buff below, with richer, louder song, recalling Cetti's Warbler's.

**WILLOW WARBLER** *Phylloscopus trochilus*. The commonest warbler over much of N Europe, olive-green above with underparts tinged yellow, especially in juv; legs usually pinkish (unlike Chiffchaff) but sometimes dark, supercilium more prominent than Chiffchaff and wings longer; no wing bars. Best distinguished from Chiffchaff by song, a fluent series of wistful descending notes, and call, a gentle disyllabic 'hoo-eet'. Woodland, scrub, areas with scattered trees and bushes, large gardens. L 11 cm. ●Sm

Ssp.*acredula* (N Europe, W Siberia) is either similar but paler, or mainly grey-brown above and white below, with almost no green or yellow tinge.

# LEAF WARBLERS

dull

bright

Wood Warbler song flight.

WOOD WARBLER

PLAIN LEAF WARBLER

MOUNTAIN CHIFFCHAFF

ad w

collybita summer

tristis summer

exsul E Canary Is.

juv

◀ CHIFFCHAFF ▶

canariensis W Canary Is.

juv

trochilus summer

acredula

WILLOW WARBLER

Willow Warbler (p.296) also has pale legs, but head and bill smaller than Radde's.

**Radde's Warbler** *Phylloscopus schwarzi*. A rather large, dark, long-legged, leaf warbler. Head brown, with white throat, long, broad, often dark-edged creamy supercilium, dark eyestripe; under tail coverts rufous and sturdy yellow or flesh-coloured legs; upperparts olive-brown. Imm often tinged green above and yellow below. Has stouter, stubbier bill than Dusky, with pinkish lower mandible. Chief calls a delicate, whistling 'twit', a low 'tuc' and a harder, sharper 'sok', similar to Dusky. Vagrant from Asia, usually skulking in low cover. L 12.5 cm.                                                    -A

**Dusky Warbler** *P. fuscatus*. Another Siberian vagrant, appreciably smaller, darker brown above and greyer below than Radde's Warbler, differing also in its darker brown upperparts with no greenish tinge, greyer underparts with under tail coverts usually buff, narrower, shorter, buffer and less conspicuous supercilium, thinner bill with duller lower mandible, and shorter legs. Compared with eastern races of Chiffchaff (p.296) has more conspicuous supercilium, pale legs and bill pale-based, not all-dark. Calls a hard, rather *Sylvia*-like 'tac' and a staccato, chattering 'tsek, tsek'. L 11 cm.         -A

**Pallas's Warbler** *P. proregulus*. Vagrant from Siberia. A very small leaf warbler, often even greener than slightly larger Yellow-browed Warbler, like which its tertials have conspicuous white fringes and tips, but has distinctive yellow crown stripe and supercilium, double yellow wing bars and yellow rump, most obvious when hovering to feed on flying insects. Cf. also smaller Goldcrest and Firecrest (p.300). Call a soft, rather high-pitched 'weesp' or 'wee-esp'. L 9 cm.        -A

**YELLOW-BROWED WARBLER** *Phylloscopus inornatus*. A small, pale greenish leaf warbler with long creamy supercilium, conspicuous creamy double wing bars and tertials with conspicuous white fringes and tips; cf. still smaller Pallas's Warbler, also Goldcrest and Firecrest (p.300) In autumn some unmoulted birds, especially of ssp.*humei*, may confusingly show only one wing bar. Call not unlike larger Chiffchaff's 'hweet', but louder. In autumn wanders westwards from Siberia to W Europe, where seen regularly in Britain, France, Germany and Scandinavia. L 10 cm.                               -A

Ssp.*humei* (C Asia), often regarded as a species, is greyer and less yellow, and has a less obvious upper wing bar; sometimes occurs in Middle East and as vagrant west to Britain.                              -V

Only breeding area in the region is on the W slopes of the Urals.

Golden-winged Warbler

♂ br

♀ w

Tennessee Warbler

1st w ♀

Yellow Warbler

**American Warblers** *Parulidae*, see p.366. Several parulid warblers, which are increasingly reported as vagrants from N America to Britain and elsewhere on the coastal fringe of W Europe, look remarkably like the Old World leaf warblers, notably the Tennessee *Vermivora peregrina* (p.366), Golden-winged *V. chrysoptera* and Yellow Warblers *Dendroica petechia* (p.373).

# LEAF WARBLERS

yellowish

Arctic Warbler (p.294) also has
supercilium, but has a small
wing bar.

buff

**RADDE'S WARBLER**

**DUSKY WARBLER**

tristis winter

Eastern races of Chiffchaff (p.296) very
like Dusky (see opposite).

**PALLAS'S WARBLER**

humei

**YELLOW-BROWED WARBLER**

inornatus

Firecrest (p.300) has different wing pattern, smaller
wing bars and whiter supercilium than Pallas's or
Yellow-browed.

♀

Firecrest

# KINGLETS

juv

♂

ad (♀)

inermis

GOLDCREST
Male's orange crown often
not visible in field.

juv

♂

madeirensis species
not fully known

TENERIFE KINGLET

ad (♀)

FIRECREST

**Kinglets**: *Regulus*. Very small 'large-eyed' greenish warblers, the region's smallest breeding birds, with a tiny needle-like bill.

**GOLDCREST** *Regulus regulus*. Differs from all leaf warblers in its tiny bill, black-bordered crest (orange in male, yellow in female, hard to see unless crown feathers raised in display) and dark mark below double whitish wing bar. Cf. Firecrest. Song very high-pitched, 'cedar-cedar-cedar-cedar-sissu-pee'. chief call a thin 'zi' or 'zi-zi-zi', confusable with Treecreeper (p.314) and tits (pp.308-311), except when intensified as 'zi-zi-zi-zeee-zeee-zeee-zi-zi-zi'. On or near conifers in woods, parkland, large gardens; in winter also in purely broad-leaved woods and scrub. L 9 cm.  ●RmW

Three sspp. in Azores: *inermis* (5 islands) is darker above and below; *azoricus* (S Miguel) is darker above, yellower below; *sanctae-mariae* (Sta Maria) is paler above, whitish below.

**TENERIFE KINGLET** *Regulus teneriffae*. Slightly darker, longer-billed and shorter-winged than Goldcrest (of which formerly considered a ssp.), and differing especially in having the black borders of the crest bolder and meeting across the forehead. Differs from Firecrest in having no white supercilium. Tree-heath scrub and nearby laurel forests. L 9 cm.

Ssp.*madeirensis* (Madeira), intermediate between Tenerife Kinglet and Firecrest, has shorter supercilium than latter.

**FIRECREST** *Regulus ignicapillus*. Greener above and whiter below than Goldcrest, and best distinguished by conspicuous white supercilium bordered above and below by black stripes, also by black forehead and bronzy patch on side of neck. Voice less high-pitched and intense, 'peep' rather than 'zi'. Broad-leaved and mixed woodland and scrub. L 9 cm.  ☉sMw

br ♂

br ♂

in moult

in moult ♂

♀

NILE VALLEY SUNBIRD

PURPLE SUNBIRD

br ♂

♀

Orange or yellow tufts seldom seen except in courtship.

PALESTINE SUNBIRD

● SUNBIRDS: *Nectariniidae*. The Old World analogues of the New World hummingbirds, brilliantly variegated jewels, darting from flower to flower, hovering to feed on nectar; bill usually long and decurved.

**NILE VALLEY SUNBIRD** *Anthreptes platurus*. Smaller than Palestine Sunbird and easily distinguished by short bill and breeding male's very long tail (one-third of total length) and bright green, violet and yellow plumage. Non-breeding male, female and juv are short-tailed, greyish above and yellow below, male sometimes with blackish throat. Voice and habitat similar to Palestine Sunbird. Aka Eastern Pygmy Sunbird. L 10-15 cm.

**Purple Sunbird** *Nectarinia asiatica*. Has shorter and less curved bill than Palestine Sunbird, male with a darker green sheen and sometimes a narrow rufous breast band, female with pale yellow, not grey, underparts. Scrub, dry forest, gardens; S Iran. L 10 cm.

**PALESTINE SUNBIRD** *Nectarinia osea*. Breeding male usually appears blackish, but has head, mantle and breast metallic blue (crown and mantle may appear green), and (not easily seen) orange and yellow tuft on each side of breast. Non-breeding adult/juv olive-green with pale supercilium and dark green tail. Song a high-pitched warbling trill; calls a repeated 'tchew' and 'twee'. Scrub, wadis, dry grassland, gardens. Aka Northern Orange-tufted Sunbird. L 11.5 cm.

● FLYCATCHERS *Muscicapidae*. Small songbirds, with rather broad, flattened bill for feeding on flying insects, caught in persistent to- and-fro sallies from perch. Rarely on ground except to fly down and pick up an insect. Chat-like alarm-note 'whee-tuc-tuc'. Nest in hole or on ledge.

**SPOTTED FLYCATCHER** *Muscicapa striata*. Uniformly mousy grey-brown above and paler below, except for some darker streaks on crown, forehead, throat, breast and flanks; sexes alike. Juv scaly from paler spots on upperparts. Song, some half-dozen shrill, rather grating notes, like two birds calling antiphonally; chief call a high-pitched robin-like 'tzee'. Perches upright and usually returns to same perch. Woodland edges, tree-lined stream-sides, orchards, parks, suburban and village gardens. L 14 cm. ●Sm

**RED-BREASTED FLYCATCHER** *Ficedula parva*. The region's smallest flycatcher. Male has red throat and breast; both sexes lack wing bars and are large-eyed with conspicuous whitish eye-rings and diagnostic white sides of tail base, revealed by frequent tail cocking. Much more secretive and inconspicuous than other flycatchers. Song variable, including some clear, bell-like and some wood-warbler-like notes; calls a sharp 'chic' and a wren-like chatter. Broad-leaved woodlands. L 11.5.cm.-A

**PIED FLYCATCHER** *Ficedula hypoleuca*. Breeding male Pied, Collared and Semi-collared Flycatchers are the region's only small black-and-white birds with flycatching habit. Winter male/female/juv Pied pale grey-brown above with distinctive broad white wing bars; winter male also has white forehead, and may breed in this plumage. Song, usually from a perch, rather varied, may recall Redstart (p.262), and has been rendered as 'tree, tree, tree, once more I come to thee'; chief call a sharp 'tchic'. Usually returns to different perch. Woodland, parks, orchards, large gardens. Males of sspp.*speculigera* (N Africa) and *iberiae* (Iberia) are like Semi-collared but without white half-collar. L 13 cm. ●SM

**SEMI-COLLARED FLYCATCHER** *Ficedula semitorquata*. Breeding male has white half-collar, intermediate between Pied and Collared, with smaller white forehead patch, greyer rump and more white on wing than Collared. Winter male/female/imm/juv more like Collared than Pied, with no half-collar. Voice and habitat as Collared, of which it may well be a ssp. L 12.5 cm.

**COLLARED FLYCATCHER** *Ficedula albicollis*. Breeding male told from both Pied and Semi-collared by conspicuous white collar from Pied also by whitish rump and more white on fore-head and wings, these markings fainter (but no white collar) in grey-brown/brown plumage of winter male/adult female/imm, but otherwise these and juv plumages almost identical to Pied. Voice and habitat as Pied, but song softer, more uniform. L 12.5 cm. -V

# FLYCATCHERS

♂ 1st br

Juv like female; 1st year male can breed with no red on throat.

SPOTTED FLYCATCHER

juv

ad

RED-BREASTED FLYCATCHER

♀

♂

Males' red throat at best at 2+ years.

♀

♂ br

juv

♂ br

♂ 1st w

PIED FLYCATCHER
Breeding males blacker in W than in E Europe; in N Africa have larger white spot on forehead; in Spain and Portugal intermediate.

♀

♀

♂ br

SEMI-COLLARED FLYCATCHER

♂ br

COLLARED FLYCATCHER

● BABBLERS: *Timaliidae*. The four species of *Turdoides* in the region are all super-ficially thrush-like, fairly uniformly brown above but paler below (sexes and most juvs alike), with a long, graduated, loosely hanging tail; legs, feet and slightly curved bill all strong. Their short rounded wings make them poor fliers, constantly on the move, in parties, both in trees and bushes and on the ground, with jerky movements and brief flights, usually one after another, like Long-tailed Tits (p.306). Noisy, often with a fairly loud musical song, but falling abruptly silent.

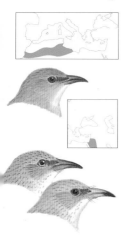

**FULVOUS BABBLER** *Turdoides fulvus*. The only N African babbler, uniformly sandy brown with paler underparts, some-what like a pale female/juv Blackbird (p.272), but with longer tail and slightly decurved bill; feet grey-green or yellow-brown. Song half a dozen drawn-out piping 'peeoo' notes; calls a soft trill and a short 'pip'. Scrub, especially acacia, in deserts, semi-deserts and oases. L 25 cm.

**ARABIAN BABBLER** *Turdoides squamiceps*. Uniformly earth-brown and paler beneath, with crown feathers tipped blackish and those of forehead stiff and scaly; separated geographically from all other babblers of the region. Highly sociable, parties performing curious evening dances, following each other round a bush, each bird hopping and then raising its tail and wagging it from side to side. Then they all fly off into a bush and preen noisily. Very inquisitive, they will fly down to inspect any strange object, and will torment it if proves to be alive and either smaller or less agile than themselves. Song a long hiss-ing trill 'tsee-tsse-trrr'; calls a ringing 'psee-oo' and a thin 'pseep'. Wadis, palm groves, dry scrub, scattered trees. L 26 cm.

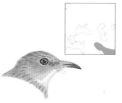

**COMMON BABBLER** *Turdoides caudatus*. Earth-brown tinged fulvous above, paler and streaked beneath, and looking not unlike a miniature hen Pheasant (p.114); legs yellowish. Juv heavily streaked darker and spotted paler. Cf. Iraq Babbler. On the ground hops with a bouncing gait, or scuttles along like a rodent, sometimes nervously twitching wings and trailing tail. Parties in flight utter a low rippling 'wich-wich-wich-ri-ri-riri', or a squeaky, partridge-like alarm note. Dry, open scrubby coun-try, cultivations, gardens. L 23 cm.

**IRAQ BABBLER** *Turdoides altirostris*. The region's smallest babbler, differing from Common Babbler in its unstreaked underparts, rufous buff breast, brown legs and shorter, stouter and more curved bill. Juv much paler above than juv Common Babbler, with cheeks and unstreaked underparts creamy buff and chin and vent white. Voice not recorded. Reed-beds, river-side thickets, palm groves and cultivations. L 22 cm.

**Pekin Robin** *Leiothrix luteus*. A well-known cage-bird, imported from the Far East in thousands to Europe every year, often escaping and now breeding in the wild on Gran Canaria and Tenerife, Canary Is. Throat and breast bright yellow, wings black with small orange patch and red and yellow edges (all yellow in female), and bill bright red. L 15 cm.

**BABBLERS**

FULVOUS BABBLER
sexes alike

Courtship display

ARABIAN BABBLER ♂

COMMON BABBLER

IRAQ BABBLER

PEKIN ROBIN

● REEDLINGS: *Panurinae*. A subfamily of the babblers (Timaliidae), superficially resembling the long-tailed tits (Aegithalidae).

Irrupts irregularly, especially Netherlands to S England and W France.

**BEARDED TIT** *Panurus biarmicus*. A rather small long-tailed reed-bed bird, predominantly tawny above, male with striking pattern of black 'moustaches' on grey head; under tail coverts black. Both sexes have yellow eyes and bill, black legs and black-and-white wing bars; female otherwise normally lacks black. Juv brown with whitish throat and black mantle; eye colour variable; bill yellow at tip and base. Chief call a metallic 'ching', also 'dzu-dzu'. Flight weak and undulating. Confined to extensive reed-beds. Aka Bearded Parrotbill, Bearded Reedling. L 16.5 cm. ⊙Rw

● LONG-TAILED TITS: *Aegithalidae*. Small, very short-billed tit-like birds whose very long tail occupies more than half their length.

**LONG-TAILED TIT** *Aegithalos caudatus*. A distinctive small black, white and pink bird: with a pure white head in N and E Europe; a black supercilium in the W; and mantle and supercilium both grey in the S. Chief calls a soft 'tupp' and a spluttering 'tsirrup'; rarely heard song based on call notes. Broad-leaved and mixed woods and scrub, less often in parks and larger gardens. When not breeding, usually in flocks, often with other tits. Domed egg-shaped nest, woven of moss and cobwebs and lined with more than a thousand feathers, is unmistakable. L 14 cm. ●R

Ssp.*caudatus* (N & E Europe) has head all white, whiter underparts and more white on darker ssp.*rosaceus* (Britain); ssp.*europaeus* (W Europe) has broad black supercilium extending on to nape; ssp.*taiti* (Iberia) is darker with broader stripes on side of crown; from S Denmark through N Germany and S Poland to N Romania birds are intermediate between *caudatus* and *europaeus*; ssp.*macedonicus* (W France and N Portugal to Greece) is like *rosaceus* but paler pink below; sspp.*irbii* (S Iberia), and the larger *italiae* (Italy), and *major* (Caucasus) have mantle and back grey; ssp.*siculus* (Sicily) is similar but with pale brown stripe on head; ssp.*tyrrhenicus* (Corsica) has upper back black, lower back grey; sspp.*tephronotus* (Asia Minor) and *alpina* (N W Iran) have crown buff blackish throat spot; and ssp.*passekii* (N W Iran) is paler with crown white and no black on throat.

Flight weak, dipping, often from tree to tree, one after another, like babblers (p.304).

● PENDULINE TITS: *Remizidae*. Small tit-like birds with a slightly longer and thinner bill than tits (p.308), and equally, if not more, active and acrobatic.

Has long been spreading N and W, but still sporadic at its breeding limits; makes irregular irruptions like Bearded Tit, breeding for a few years only.

**PENDULINE TIT** *Remiz pendulinus*. A small, long-tailed, grey and brown bird, less obviously long-tailed than Bearded Tit, with contrasting pale grey head and throat, black mask and chestnut mantle. Female paler, browner, with smaller mask; juv paler, duller, without black mask. Calls a low robin-like 'tsee' and a more tit-like 'tsi-tsi-tsi'. Marshes, fens, freshwater margins, with scrub or willow; nest domed, flask-shaped. L 11 cm. -A

Ssp.*pendulinus* (Europe, E to Volga, Turkey) described above; ssp. *menzbieri* (Asia Minor, Levant) is smaller; ssp.*caspius* (Caucasus, Volga plains) is chestnut on crown, sometimes joining with chestnut on mantle.

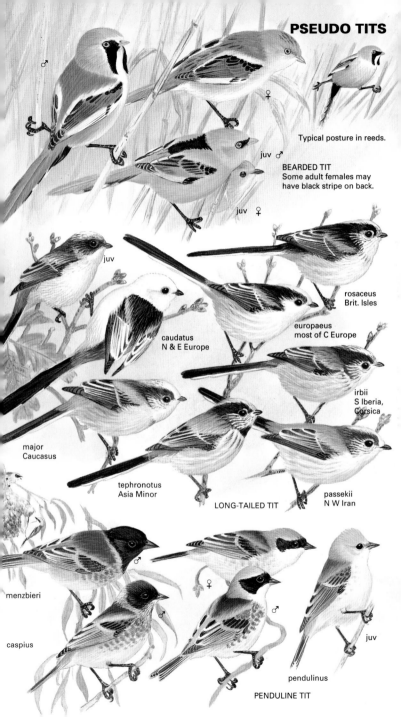

# PSEUDO TITS

Typical posture in reeds.

**BEARDED TIT**
Some adult females may
have black stripe on back.

juv ♂

juv ♀

juv

rosaceus
Brit. Isles

caudatus
N & E Europe

europaeus
most of C Europe

irbii
S Iberia,
Corsica

major
Caucasus

tephronotus
Asia Minor

LONG-TAILED TIT

passekii
N W Iran

menzbieri

caspius

♀

♂

pendulinus

juv

PENDULINE TIT

● TITS: *Paridae*. Small, active and acrobatic, insectivorous birds; sexes alike. Several species may flock together and with long-tailed tits (p.306), nuthatches (p.312) and leaf warblers (p.294). Nests usually in holes, including nestboxes; some species have explosive hissing threat display on nest.

**CRESTED TIT** *Parus cristatus*. The only tit, and indeed the region's only really small bird, with a crest. When crest cannot be seen, lack of wing bars and distinctive face pattern with black eye-stripe, no white on nape and much less black on head help to separate from Coal Tit (p.310). Chief call a rather soft purring trill, which also serves as 'song'; also the usual tit contact note, 'si-si-si...'. Forests, plantations, mainly coniferous, but also mixed. L 11.5 cm. ○R

**SIBERIAN TIT** *Parus cinctus*. Like a rather drab great-tit-sized Marsh or Willow Tit, but with more black on throat, crown and nape a browner black, cheeks whiter, and deep buff flanks. Song a repeated, high-pitched 'chee-urr'; chief call a rapid 'tee-tee, tay-ee, tay-ee', somewhat recalling Willow Tit. Coniferous and birch forests. L 13.5 cm.

**MARSH TIT** *Parus palustris*. The only small tit with nape as well as crown and chin black, apart from Willow, from which best told by voice. Also appears smaller-headed (like Blue Tit, p.310), with smaller black bib and no pale wing panel; adult's crown glossy black, juv's matt. Typical calls, 'pitchuu', often with a harsh 'tchaa', less grating and nasal than Willow, and scolding 'chicka-bee-bee-bee', both diagnostic. Frequent in broad-leaved woodland, tall scrub and rural gardens; no preference for marshes. L 11.5 cm. ●R

**WILLOW TIT** *Parus montanus*. Appears larger-headed and has larger black bib than Marsh Tit and crown sootier than adult Marsh; also has a pale wing panel. Typical call a grating 'tchay' or 'aig', sometimes preceded by 'chic' or 'chick-it', but never by Marsh's 'pitchuu' or followed by Marsh's scold; also a diagnostic high-pitched 'eez-eez-eez'. Coniferous and broad-leaved woods and tall scrub, with no preference for willows. L 11.5 cm. ●R

Ssp.*borealis* (N Europe) is slightly larger and greyer, with white cheeks; Ssp.*kleinschmidti* (Britain) tends to have buffer flanks than Marsh, especially in winter.

**SOMBRE TIT** *Parus lugubris*. The southern counterpart of the Siberian Tit, like which it resembles a Marsh or Willow Tit; as large as a Great Tit (p.310), but with a much browner crown and nape, whiter cheeks and a more extensive throat patch. Much of its vocabulary resembles other tits, especially Great and Coal, but has a distinctive, sparrow-like churr. Broad-leaved and mixed woodland, often rocky or mountainous; less gregarious than most tits. L 14 cm.

Ssp.*lugubris* (Balkans, Greece) described above; ssp.*anatoliae* (Asia Minor, Middle East) has crown and throat blacker; and ssp.*hyrcanus* (N Iran) has breast, belly and flanks tinged rufous.

CRESTED TIT

SIBERIAN TIT

In Lapland Willow Tit is always paler and greyer than Siberian Tit, with no rusty colour on flanks.

MARSH TIT

Song, a tuneless rattle, 'schip-schip-schip' or 'schuppi-schuppi-schuppi' is diagnostic.

montanus

leonbergi

borealis

WILLOW TIT

Two diagnostic songs: a ringing but rather sad 'piu-piu-piu' recalling Wood Warbler; a less frequent spasmodic liquid garden-warbler-like note.

anatoliae

lugubris

SOMBRE TIT

Blackcap
p.288

**COAL TIT** *Parus ater*. The region's smallest tit, readily distinguished by combination of black cap, white cheeks and conspicuous white nape, the cheeks and nape tinged yellow in juv. Many typical calls are similar to those of Great Tit, but higher-pitched, especially the frequent and characteristic 'ticha, ticha' and the so-called saw-sharpening song; also 'tsuu', 'tsui' and a goldcrest-like 'tsee'. Mainly in coniferous woodland, but locally also in mixed and even pure broad-leaved woods, town parks and gardens. L 11.5 cm.　　　　　　　　　　　　●Rw

Ssp.*ater* (Europe) has slate-grey upperparts; ssp.*britannicus* (Britain) has olive-grey upperparts; ssp.*hibernicus* (Ireland) has yellowish cheeks and nape patch; and ssp.*atlas* (Morocco) in holm-oak forest, never in conifers.

**GREAT TIT** *Parus major*. A large tit, easily recognised by combination of black-and-white head (with pale yellow-green nape) and black bib extending as black line (broadest in male) down centre of bright yellow underparts. Juv has black parts brownish and white parts yellowish. Large vocabulary includes a very chaffinch-like 'pink', various loud calls like other tits, and two 'songs' a loud 'teacher, teacher' and the so-called 'saw-sharpening' call. Common in woodland and among scattered trees in scrub, heathland, orchards, olive groves, town parks and gardens. L 14 cm.　　　　　　　　　　　　●Rw

Ssp.*aphrodite* (S Greece, Crete, Cyprus, Balearic Is) is paler; ssp.*excelsus* (N Africa) is brighter and yellower.

**AZURE TIT** *Parus cyanus*. The larger Asiatic counterpart of the Blue Tit, hybridising with it in Russia. Whiter than Blue Tit, with much less blue, no yellow, head all-white, a white V on each wing and longer tail; juv greyer, especially on head. Typical call a long-tailed-tit-like 'tsirrup'. Broad-leaved scrub, birchwoods, often by fresh water. L 13 cm.

Hybrid Azure x Blue Tit differs from Azure mainly in blue on crown and neck patch and less white in wing and tail. Most Azure Tits reported in W Europe may have been this hybrid, as was '*P.pleskei*'.

**BLUE TIT** *Parus caeruleus*. The region's only tit, indeed its only small bird, that appears mainly blue and yellow, the bright blue crown especially distinctive. Juv has white cheeks and nape tinged yellow. Most typical of many calls is a rather scolding 'tsee-tsee-tsee-tsit'; cheerful song can be rendered 'tsee-tseee-tsu-tsuhuhuhu'. Common in broad-leaved woodland (less so among conifers) and among scattered trees in hedgerows, orchards, palm and olive groves, town parks and gardens; in winter often in reed-beds. L 11.5 cm.　　　　　●Rw

In Mediterranean islands mostly paler, but palest and smaller in Zagros Mts, Iran. In Canary Is and N Africa head darker, mantle colour varies from grey through blue-grey to olive-green, and bill slightly longer and thinner. Ssp.*palmensis* (La Palma) has white belly; ssp.*ombriosus* (Hierro) has olive-green back; ssp.*teneriffae* (central Canaries) has hardly any white on wings; and *ultramarinus* (N Africa) has darker blue mantle. In Canaries feeds on tree trunks like Treecreeper.

TITS

ad

atlas
Morocco

juv

ad

ater
Europe

COAL TIT

ad

ledouci
Tunisia

ad

cypriotis
Cyprus

ad

hibernicus
Ireland

ad

aphrodite
Mallorca, Cyprus

juv

♂ ad

GREAT TIT

AZURE
TIT

ad

juv

ad

caeruleus
Europe

ad

ombriosus
W Canaries

BLUE TIT

persicus
SW Iran
ad

degener
E Canaries
ad

teneriffae
C Canaries
ad

ultramarinus
N W Africa
ad

● NUTHATCHES: *Sittidae*. Small, compact, short-tailed, active, birds, with jerky gait; sexes usually alike. No other birds habitually descend trees head downwards. They feed on invertebrates, nuts and seeds, the tougher items being wedged into cracks in bark and hammered open. Hole nesters.

The map shows the world distribution of this species.

**KRÜPER'S NUTHATCH** *Sitta krüperi*. Like a small Nuthatch with a black crown, grey nape, white supercilium and whitish underparts with rufous breast patch. Calls include a soft single 'pwit', recalling Great Spotted Woodpecker (p.226), a harsh jay-like 'schweee' and a rippling 'pip, pip, pip, pip ...'. Very active and feeding tit-like on outer branches of trees in coniferous forests. L 12.5 cm.

Discovered, 1975, at 2000 m in coniferous forest, Petite Kabylie, Algeria.

**ALGERIAN NUTHATCH** *Sitta ledanti*. Slightly larger than Corsican Nuthatch and with longer bill, grey nape and underparts often pinkish-buff; female may lack black crown and eyestripes. Has a loud ringing fluty cry of 7-8 notes, and a nasal jay-like call. Aka Kabylie Nuthatch. L 12 cm.

Confined to coniferous forests in Corsica.

**CORSICAN NUTHATCH** *Sitta whiteheadi*. Like a small Nuthatch with black crown and nape (grey in female), white supercilium above black eye-stripe, and whitish underparts; voice quieter and more nasal, including 'dew-dew-dew-did-di-di' song and a jay-like note. Habits tit-like. L 12 cm.

**NUTHATCH** *Sitta europaea*. Much the commonest and most widespread nuthatch, and over most of the region the only bird with longish straight bill that creeps about trees. No supercilium, underparts varying from white in N to deep orange-buff with white belly in S and W; juv duller. Songs loud piping repetitions of 'twee', 'chu' or 'pee'; numerous calls include loud ringing 'chwit-chwit' or 'chwit-it-it', and a sibilant 'tsirrup' recalling Long-tailed Tit (p.306). Unlike Rock Nuthatch, always associated with trees, in woodland, parkland, large gardens, where visits bird tables; often with winter tit parties; cracks hazel nuts wedged in bark. L 14 cm.                    ●R

Underparts are white in ssp.*europaea* (Scandinavia, N Russia); cream-coloured, ssp.*homeyeri* (Baltic); deep buff, sspp.*caesia* (C Europe) and *caucasica* (Caucasus); and pale buff, sspp.*britannica* (Britain), *hispanica* (Iberia, N W Africa) and *levantina* (Turkey, Palestine).

Mountains above 1000 m.

**EASTERN ROCK NUTHATCH** *Sitta tephronota*. Like ssp *tschitscherini* of Rock Nuthatch, but much larger and with a longer, stouter bill, a much longer, broader eye-stripe, and louder, lower-pitched and slower calls. Habitat similar, but usually above 1000 m. Aka Great Rock Nuthatch. L 19-20 cm.

**ROCK NUTHATCH** *Sitta neumayer*. Differs from Nuthatch especially in habitat, but is drabber, with underparts paler, flanks browner and no white in tail. Song has rising and falling scale of shrill 'zee-a' notes, recalling Tree Pipit (p.242) noisy, calls often nuthatch-like and include jay-like screams and rich fluty cadences. Inland cliffs, gorges, rocky hillsides, nesting in rock holes. L 14-15 cm.

Ssp.*tschitscherini* (Iran, Iraq) may be grey, not blue-grey, above, with black eye-stripes almost absent.

# NUTHATCHES

ALGERIAN
NUTHATCH

KRÜPER'S NUTHATCH

CORSICAN NUTHATCH

♂

♀

NUTHATCH

northern

Zagora Mt.

EASTERN ROCK
NUTHATCH

ROCK
NUTHATCH

**WALLCREEPER** *Tichodroma muraria*. Very distinctive with bright crimson wing patches constantly flicked in butterfly-like flight, but despite curved bill closer to nuthatches than treecreepers. Grey above with white spots on wings and tail, blackish-grey below but throat white in winter; juv as adult winter. Song like loud Treecreeper, on rising scale, habitually uttered while climbing. Inland cliffs, rocky gorges, to snow-line in mountains; lower down in winter, often on buildings. L 16.5 cm.                                                                  -V

● TREECREEPERS: *Certhiidae*. The region's only small brown land birds with curved beaks, and except for Wryneck (p.228) the only ones that habitually creep mouse-like about tree trunks and branches.

**TREECREEPER** *Certhia familiaris*. Brown above, white below, with rump rufous, but flanks buff in British ssp.*britannica*. Presence more often detected by ear than by eye; song, 'tee-tee-tee-titidooee' and chief call, a prolonged 'tseee', both very high-pitched. Rarely away from tree trunks and branches, except sometimes on stone walls or in bat-like display flight. Coniferous (mainly spruce and fir) and mixed woodlands, only on mountains in the S; in Britain and Ireland also broad-leaved woods, parks, gardens. L 12.5 cm.                                  ●R

**SHORT-TOED TREECREEPER** *Certhia brachydactyla*. Very hard to distinguish from Treecreeper in the field except by voice and habitat, but tends to be greyer above and duller white below, with pale brown flanks and supercilium not pure white and darker in front of eyes. Song shorter, louder and lower-pitched; 'tsee' call similar but has distinctive loud 'zeet' and 'chink' calls. Broad-leaved woods, olive groves, parks, gardens; also, in Mediterranean area, in coniferous forests. L 12.5 cm.                                                                  -V

● WRENS: *Troglodytidae*. Very small, short-tailed, dumpy birds. Sexes alike.

**WREN** *Troglodytes troglodytes*. The region's smallest warm brown bird, with distinctive barred plumage, whirring flight and tail-cocking habit. Vigorous clear warbling song is loud for so small a bird; chief call an irritable 'tic-tic-tic', often pro-longed into a scolding trill. Habitats varied, from rocky moun-tain tops, sea cliffs and moors to woodland scrub, heaths and suburban parks and gardens, May roost in domed nest after breeding season. L 9.5 cm.                                          ●Rw

● DIPPERS: *Cinclidae*. Dumpy, short-tailed aquatic birds, the only songbirds that not only swim on the surface but habitually dive, from either air or water, both swimming and walking underwater.

**DIPPER** *Cinclus cinclus*. Unmistakable with its conspicuous white throat and breast and habit of constantly bobbing on rock in midstream. Sexes alike; juv grey-brown above, whitish speckled darker below. Song loud, rather wren-like; calls 'zit-zit-zit' and a metallic 'clink, clink'. Only on fast streams in uplands, often wandering to lowland streams in winter. L 18 cm.    ●Rw

Belly black in N & S W Europe, dark rufous in C Europe, Britain and Ireland.

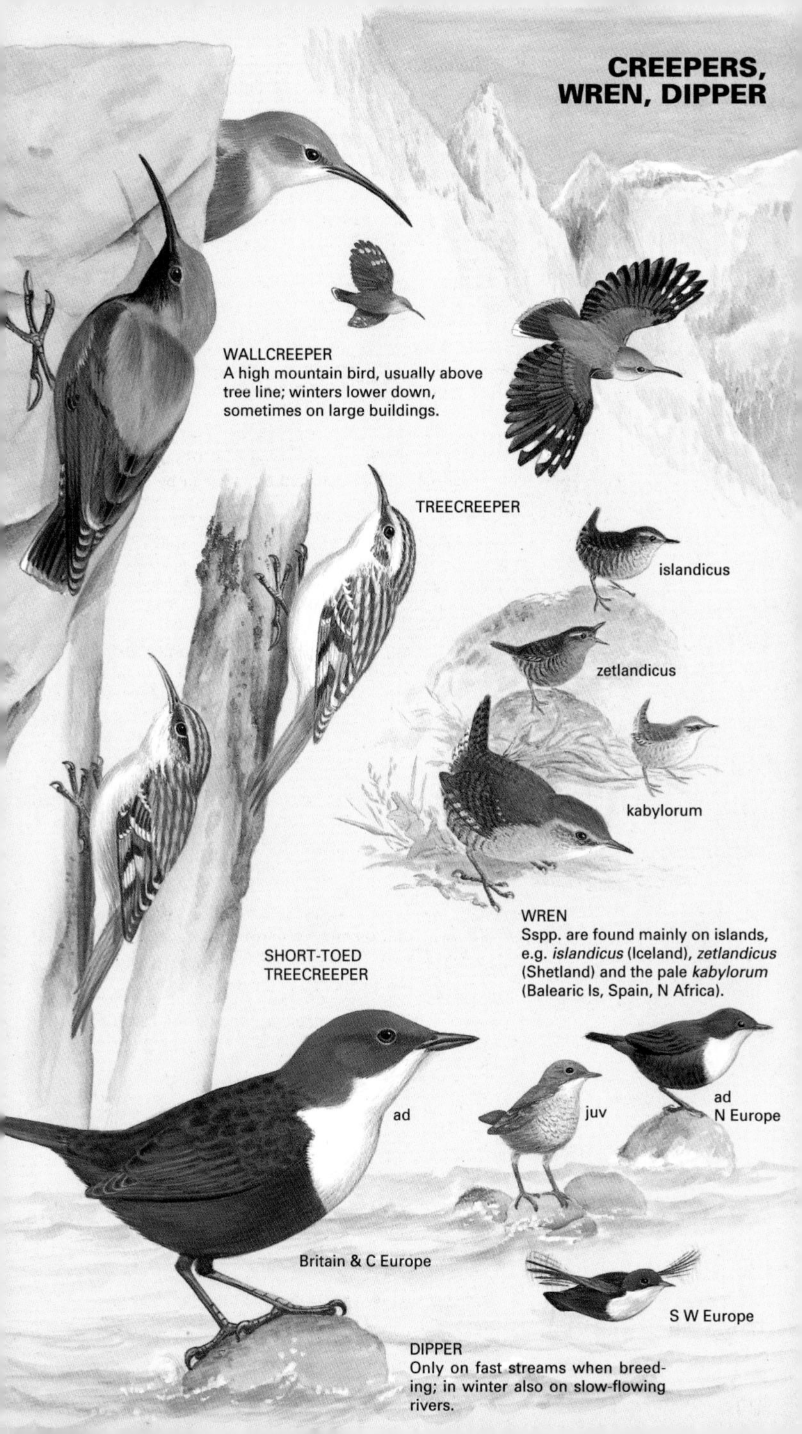

**WALLCREEPER**
A high mountain bird, usually above tree line; winters lower down, sometimes on large buildings.

**TREECREEPER**

islandicus

zetlandicus

kabylorum

**SHORT-TOED TREECREEPER**

**WREN**
Sspp. are found mainly on islands, e.g. *islandicus* (Iceland), *zetlandicus* (Shetland) and the pale *kabylorum* (Balearic Is, Spain, N Africa).

ad

juv

ad
N Europe

Britain & C Europe

S W Europe

**DIPPER**
Only on fast streams when breeding; in winter also on slow-flowing rivers.

● **SHRIKES:** *Laniidae*. Aggressive hook-billed birds with dipping flight, often impaling prey on thorns as 'larder'. Tail longish, rounded or graduated. *Lanius* shrikes have harsh chattering 'shek, shek' calls and rather subdued, often mimetic song, with both harsh and pleasing notes. They either hover or perch on prominent lookouts before swooping on large insect or small vertebrate prey. Woodland edges, scrub, hedgerows, olive groves, areas with scattered tall bushes.

**BLACK-CROWNED TCHAGRA** *Tchagra senegala*. Rufous wings, grey rump and white-tipped black tail are most conspicuous features as this strikingly plumaged but rather skulking bird dives for cover; also has black crown with broad white supercilium and black eye-stripe. Song a succession of vigorous but plaintive piping notes, rapid at first but later clear and bell-like, sometimes uttered in flight; alarm note churring. Display flight pigeon-like, rising with sharply flapping wings, sometimes 60-70 m into the air, before gliding or spiralling down to a bush. Thick scrub. Aka Black-crowned Bush-shrike. L 22 cm.

**GREAT GREY SHRIKE** *Lanius excubitor*. The largest shrike of the region, and in N Europe the only medium-sized black, white and grey bird that perches on prominent lookouts. Forehead grey, usually a white supercilium, eye-stripe broad and black and wing with one or two white bars; cf. Lesser Grey Shrike, which has black forehead and no supercilium. In N W Europe only, female and immature have faint grey bars on breast; juvenile brownish. L 24 cm.                    ⊙mW

meridionalis
(Iberia)

algeriensis
(NW Africa)

elegans
(N Sahara)

aucherii
(Middle East)

homeyeri
(Bulgaria to Urals)

Lesser Grey Shrike

Ssp. *homeyeri* has underparts and forehead whiter, and wing-bar larger than nominate *excubitor*. The first four pictured above now included in a separate sp., **Southern Grey Shrike** *L. meridionalis*. Ssp. *meridionalis* is darker than excubitor with a broader mask and less white in wing; ssp. *algeriensis* has greyer underparts and more white in wing; ssp. *aucherii* is like *elegans* but has greyish flanks, a narrow black forehead, and smaller wing-bar. Often treated as a third species, **Steppe Grey Shrike** *L. pallidirostris* (S Asia west to Caspian; vagrant to NW Europe) is longer-winged than Great Grey, with pale lores and bill and much white at base of primaries.

**LESSER GREY SHRIKE** *Lanius minor*. Appreciably smaller than Great Grey and with the black eye-stripe extending across the forehead as a broad black band (sometimes greyish in female and absent in imm), no white supercilium, underparts tinged pink, and relatively longer wings, shorter tail and shorter stouter bill; single white wing bar conspicuous in flight. Juv tinged pale yellowish-brown. Flight much less dipping than Great Grey, hovers more; erecter when perched. L 20 cm.    -A

# SHRIKES

**BLACK-CROWNED TCHAGRA**
Secretive, keeping to cover and first noted by song; hops on ground like a thrush.

*Lanius* shrikes often perch on an exposed branch or wire as a look-out.

pallidirostris
ppe Grey Shrike

GREAT GREY
SHRIKE

juv

excubitor

juv

♀ Narrow mask, often mottled.

♂ br

LESSER GREY SHRIKE

**ISABELLINE SHRIKE** *Lanius isabellinus*. Pale, mainly brown, with crown, rump and tail rufous, contrasting with greyish mantle and pinkish underparts, differing from female/imm Red-backed especially in its longer tail, white wing bar (especially conspicuous in male) and broad black eye-stripe (browner and only behind the eye in female/imm). Imm's mantle unbarred, unlike imm Red-backed. L 18 cm. Cf. also very rare vagrant Brown Shrike (p.373). -A

♂ with wing mirror

♂ pale

♂ pale

♂ dark

♂ dark

♂-like ♀    red-tailed ♀

Some male Red-backed have white wing patch; females vary in colour.

phoenicuroides    isabellinus    speculigerus

Migrant or vagrant races: ssp.*phoenicuroides*, most often seen in region; ssp.*isabellinus* paler, sandier above, creamier below, with eye-stripe brownish and often no wing patch; *speculigerus* intermediate between these two. Intermediates also occur where Isabelline and Red-backed meet.

**RED-BACKED SHRIKE** *Lanius collurio*. Male is the region's only shrike that combines blue-grey head and rump with rufous back; supercilium and chin white, eye-stripe black, underparts pinkish. Female/imm/juv mainly brown, with crescentic marks on underparts; tail sometimes rufous, cf. Isabelline. Juv also has crescentic marks on rufous upperparts; cf. paler juv Woodchat. In flight shows white on either side of base of black tail, but only exceptionally has white wing patch like Isabelline. Song slightly reminiscent of Garden Warbler (p.288). L 17-18 cm. ○sM

**WOODCHAT SHRIKE** *Lanius senator*. The region's only shrike with a rich chestnut crown and nape, also has black forehead extending as broad black bar well behind eye, and shows conspicuous white wing bars, shoulder patches and rump in flight. Female similar but duller. Juv resembles a pale juv Red-backed, but with only obscure wing bars and pale shoulder patches and rump. Song more musical than most shrikes; has a sparrow-like chatter. L 17 cm. -A

Ssp.*badius* (W Mediterranean islands) lacks white wing bars; ssp. *niloticus* (Cyprus to Iran) has basal third of tail feathers white.

**MASKED SHRIKE** *Lanius nubicus*. Has black-and-white flight pattern like Woodchat, but with black rump and most other plumage quite different: black crown and nape, white forehead, rufous flanks. Female greyer, juv very like juv Woodchat, but has longer, narrower tail and no brown in plumage above. Song rather scratchy, recalling Icterine and Olive-tree Warblers (p.286); most frequent call a harsh but shrill 'keer, keer, keer'. L 17 cm.

# SHRIKES

ISABELLINE SHRIKE

juv

ad

♀

RED-BACKED SHRIKE

juv

♀

♂

♂

juv

juv

♂ badius

♂ niloticus

senator

WOODCHAT
SHRIKE

♀

♂

♀

juv

juv

♂

MASKED
SHRIKE

♂

● CROWS: *Corvidae*. Large songbirds, mostly gregarious, with a high degree of intelligence and unmelodious song; most have a robust bill. Sexes alike; juvs rather similar. Nest in tree, on rock ledge, or in hole in tree or among rocks.

**NUTCRACKER** *Nucifraga caryocatactes*. The only crow-sized white-spotted grey-brown bird, with white on tail and under tail coverts very noticeable in flight. No song; warbling sub-song. Call a rather high-pitched and far-carrying caw; also a nightjar-like trilling alarm call and various harsh croaks. Flight markedly undulating and jay-like; often perches right at the top of a tree. Forests, especially coniferous: feeds on the seeds of Arolla pine *Pinus cembra*, especially in the Alps, and on hazel nuts, especially in Scandinavia and N Russia; stores food like jays. L 32 cm.                                                                      -V

**JAY** *Garrulus glandarius*. The region's only land bird that com-bines a white rump, very conspicuous in flight, with blue-and-white wing patches; tail black, often jerked. Usually located by harsh scolding screech, 'skaaak, skaaak', often when mobbing an owl; also makes loud crow-like screeches, a ringing 'kiew' and some curious creaking notes. Has no true song, but may utter, sometimes collectively, a crooning, warbling, mimetic subsong, together with harsher notes. Flight rather weak, markedly undulating; hops on ground. Usually singly or in small parties, but larger numbers gather for spring displays. Woodland, mainly broad-leaved, orchards, large gardens, sometimes in town parks. Collects and buries acorns in autumn. L 34 cm.                                                                      ●Rw

sewerzowii

Ssp.*glaszneri* (Cyprus) is dark-er with reddish forehead and smaller bill. Mountain pine and oak forests.

Ssp.*brandtii* (C Urals) is greyer, head rufous, crown streaked; ssp *sewerzowii* (N Russia) is intermediate between *brandtii* and *glandarius*.

Ssp.*krynicki* (Aegean, N Asia Minor, Caucasus) has crown black, forehead white, ear coverts pinkish.

**SIBERIAN JAY** *Perisoreus infaustus*. General outline jay-like, but tail relatively longer and bill less stout; dull grey-brown, with rufous on wings, rump and tail conspicuous in flight. Calls a harsh 'chair', a brisker 'kook, kook' and 'whisk-ee'. Taiga, mainly spruce, climbing out to tips of branches to feed tit-like on cones; also among birches, and in winter quite tame around towns and villages. L 30.5 cm.

**PLESKE'S GROUND JAY** *Podoces pleskei*. Like a short-billed Hoopoe (p.220), cinnamon-buff, with curved bill, black and white wings; adult with narrow black throat patch. 'Pee-pee-pee' call like Rock Nuthatch (p.312). Ground-living in steppes. L 24 cm.

**JAYS**

NUTCRACKER

Ssp. *macrorhynchos* (Siberia) has thinner bill.
Both sspp. erupt westwards at irregular intervals.

glandarius

hibernicus

Ssp. *glandarius* (Scandinavia,
C Europe) is pinkish-grey
with streaked crown.

Ssp. *hibernicus* (Ireland,
C Scotland) is slightly more
rufous and less grey on back.

JAY

atricapillus

cervicalis

whitakeri

minor

Ssp. *atricapillus* (S Turkey, Middle
East) has crown black, forehead white,
ear coverts whitish.

Ssp. *cervicalis* (N E Algeria, N Tunisia) crown all-black,
ear coverts pure white. Crown streaked black, mantle grey:
ssp. *minor* (Atlas Mts) rather dark, ear coverts pinkish; and
ssp. *whitakeri* (N Morocco, N W Algeria) ear coverts whitish.

juv

ad

SIBERIAN JAY

PLESKE'S
GROUND
JAY

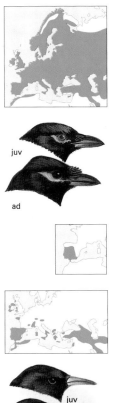

juv

ad

**MAGPIE** *Pica pica.* One of the region's most distinctive birds, the only large black-and-white land bird with a long graduated tail (much shorter in juv); purple-blue gloss on upperparts and green gloss on tail not always obvious. No true song; babbling subsong rare, but a musical 'chook, chook' during spring display. Chief call a loud harsh chatter or chuckle, but confusable with imitations by Jay (p.320) and with Grey Squirrel's rasping chatter. Flight weaker than typical crows, appearing slightly unbalanced by long tail; on ground walks, or hops sideways. Flocks small, except at roosts and in spring display. Scattered trees and scrub, from tundra and semi-desert to farmland and town parks and gardens; common in some towns. Nest large, domed. L 46 cm. ●Rw

Ssp.*mauretanica* (N Africa) is smaller with a very long tail, a more bronzy gloss. blue behind the eye, bristles above nostril and an all-black rump. In many ways almost a different species, living mostly in small groups up to 25.

**AZURE-WINGED MAGPIE** *Cyanopica cyanus.* Very distinctive, with head and nape jet black, wings and long graduated tail blue, and throat white. Gregarious and noisy, constantly uttering a rather peevish 'zhreee' on a rising scale. Flight and other behaviour similar to Magpie. Open woodland, orchards, olive groves, large gardens and other areas with scattered trees. L 34 cm.

**CHOUGH** *Pyrrhocorax pyrrhocorax.* The region's only all-black bird with red bill and legs (both orange-red in juv), which separate it at once from the yellow-billed Alpine Chough and the black-billed all-black *Corvus* crows and smaller grey-naped Jackdaw (p.324). No song; starling-like chattering subsong rare. One common call is like young jackdaw's 'kyow'; another is more like a gull than a crow; a third, 'k'chuf' provides its English name. Flight much more buoyant than other black corvids, raven-like aerobatics; both walks and hops. Flocks usually small. Steep, rugged cliffs, on coast and in mountains. Nest in rock crevice or sea cave. Aka Red-billed Chough. L 39-40 cm. ○R

juv

1st w

Chough

ad          ad

juv          1st w          ad

ad          Alpine Chough

**ALPINE CHOUGH** *Pyrrhocorax graculus.* The region's only all-black bird with yellow bill and red legs, its rounder head, shorter bill, shorter tail and less glossy plumage also separating it from Chough. Juv has yellow bill and blackish legs; cf. juv Chough. Flight and other behaviour very like Chough, but main call quite distinct, a musically metallic whistling 'chirrish', often uttered by flocks, e.g. when mobbing large predators; also a shorter, sharper 'tchiupp' comparable to Chough's 't'chuf'. High mountains with steep cliffs/crags, to snow line. L 38 cm.

mauretanica

pica

MAGPIE

juv

AZURE-WINGED MAGPIE

ad

CHOUGH

ALPINE CHOUGH

**ROOK** *Corvus frugilegus*. Adult is the region's only large black bird with a bare face patch. All ages can be told from Carrion Crow by purplish gloss and shaggy appearance, especially of thigh feathers, and more peaked head and 'pointy' face; and from smaller Jackdaw by no grey on nape; cf. also larger Raven (p.326). No song, but harsh 'caw' and 'caah' notes more deliberate and prolonged than Carrion Crow and not often repeated thrice; also raven-like croak and herring-gull-like 'ki-ook'. Flight rather heavy; walks sedately. In flocks throughout year, often with Jackdaws; nests colonially in trees; odd pairs may nest away from rookery. Farmlands and grasslands with scattered trees and small woods, feeding in more treeless country and on sea shore in winter. L 48 cm. ●Rw

**CARRION CROW** *Corvus corone*. Differs from same-sized Rook by its greenish gloss and tight-fitting thigh feathers and from adult also by feathered base of bill; from smaller Jackdaw by black nape; and from larger Raven (p.326) by less stout bill. Chief calls, often repeated three times, are an abrupt jerky rasping 'keerght' and 'kaaah' and a higher-pitched 'keeerk'. Flight and habitat see under Hooded Crow. Normally goes singly, in pairs or family parties, but also flocks, especially to roost. L 47 cm. ●Rw

Carrion and Hooded Crows meet in narrow zones (map above), where hybrids are frequent.

hybrids

**Hooded Crow** *C.c.cornix* (Ireland, N Scotland, N & E Europe, W Asia) differs from other black crows in its grey body, but intermediates with Carrion Crow *C.c.corone* occur where the two races meet. Voice and habits as Carrion Crow. Flight rather heavy; walks, and sidles with ungainly hops. All types of country except tundra, desert and bare mountain tops, but especially farmland, moorland, sea cliffs, town parks and suburbs. Nest in tree or on rock ledge. Ssp.*sardonius* (Corsica, Sardinia, Italy, Balkans, Asia Minor, Palestine, Egypt) is smaller and often paler; *sharpii* (Urals, Iran) is also paler and winters S to Iraq; much larger ssp.*capellanus* (N Iraq, Iran) has grey parts milky white. ●Rw

**JACKDAW** *Corvus monedula*. Both the smallest black crow and the region's only grey-naped black bird; eyes white. Typical calls higher-pitched than other black crows: a clipped metallic 'kow' or 'kyow' and a softer 'chack', both often repeated several times with an antiphonal effect. Flight and gait much quicker and jerkier than larger crows; walks, park-land, grassy and cultivated country, nesting in holes in old trees, rocks or crags; frequent in towns and villages, especially around cathedrals, castles and ruins. L 33 cm. ●Rw

**Daurian Jackdaw** *C. dauuricus*. Rare vagrant from Siberia. Two colour phases: one very like Jackdaw except for dark eyes and duller grey nape, the other strikingly patterned like Hooded Crow, with the grey parts white. L 33 cm.

# CROWS

ROOK

ad

juv

Juv/imm often hard to tell from Carrion Crow, which also has bristles at base of bill.

CARRION CROW

ad

House Crow p.326

HOODED CROW

ad

ad

soemmerringii
N E Europe

spermologus
Britain, C Europe

JACKDAW

DAURIAN JACKDAW

ad

ad

juv Raven      Raven      Crow p.324

Juv duller, less glossy, with no throat hackles, and eyes pale at first.

Formerly found all over Europe and in lowlands.

Nests on crags, old buildings and trees from sea level to high mountains.

Deserts, semi-deserts, on cliffs and crags from sea level to over 3000 m.

Raven's head and neck project further forward and wedge-shaped tail projects further behind than in Carrion Crow and Rook. Even juv shows this flight outline, which can give adult an almost Maltese-cross appearance on the wing. Raven's bill also much heavier, with a more distinct small hook at the tip.

**RAVEN** *Corvus corax*. The region's largest all-black bird, adult differing from all other crows in its massive size, as large as Buzzard (p.94), much stouter bill and distinctive flight outline and calls. Chief call a deep croaking 'pruk, pruk', but Rook may utter similar, less deep note. Normal flight rather heavy, but often soars like a Buzzard and in spring performs remarkable aerobatics, 'tumbling', flying upside down and nose-diving. Walking gait rather majestic. Will flock, especially to roost, but when breeding usually only in singles or families. Open and hilly country from tundra to sea coast and desert; frequent on sea cliffs and in woods and crags on hill and mountain sides. Nest on a rock ledge, sometimes in a tree. L 64 cm.   ●R

**BROWN-NECKED RAVEN** *Corvus ruficollis*. A desert crow resembling Raven in its longish wedge-shaped tail (but with central feathers protruding slightly) and Carrion Crow (p.324) in smaller size, voice, less stout bill, and longer, more pointed wings, often nearly reaching the tail at rest. Brownish tinge on nape and neck is hard to see in field, especially soon after moult, and is absent in juv. Cf. Fan-tailed Raven. Cawing calls include a bell-like note. Deserts, semi-deserts, savannas, wadis, in N Africa largely confined to wormwood *Artemisia* steppe, with scattered jujube *Zisyphus* trees. L 50 cm.

**FAN-TAILED RAVEN** *Corvus rhipidurus*. A strikingly short-tailed rook-sized all-black crow, with a distinctive bat-like flight outline; bill rather short and stout, upturned bristles at base visible only at close range. Plumage tinged bronzy-brown in good light, but short tail and stout bill always separate from Brown-necked. Calls still higher-pitched than Brown-necked, almost chough-like, with a varied repertoire. Often performs aerobatics, using thermals, and may walk with bill open as if panting. Cliffs and rocks in arid country, often in villages. L 47 cm.

**House Crow** *Corvus splendens*. A smallish, rather slender crow, with grey nape, neck and breast darker and less extensive than Hooded Crow's (p.324) and bill longer and deeper and crown more domed. Chief calls a high-pitched 'quah, quah' and more nasal 'kaan, kaan'. Around coastal towns and villages. Middle East, Egypt; a recent ship-borne colonist from India, also recorded near ports in W Europe. L 43 cm.

**RAVENS**

RAVEN

BROWN-NECKED RAVEN

ad

imm

HOUSE CROW

FAN-TAILED RAVEN

1st-year male Golden Orioles resemble females, but have yellower underparts and more contrast in tail, some breeding in this plumage. Some females are almost as yellow as males, but still have greyish, not black, lores.

● ORIOLES: *Oriolidae*. Medium-sized arboreal songbirds, with a fairly stout bill; juvs streaked darker below.

**GOLDEN ORIOLE** *Oriolus oriolus*. Male is region's only medium-sized black-and-yellow bird, but though often heard even its striking plumage is hard to see as it skulks among the foliage. Female/imm/juv mainly yellow-green streaked darker below, and confusable with juv Green Woodpecker (p.224), which lacks red on head, but though they have a woodpecker-like undulating flight, they never crouch on boles or branches and rarely feed on ground. Both sexes have stout, dark pink bill. Song a distinctive loud, fluty, mellow 'weela-weeo', also a cat-like squalling cry. Broad-leaved woodland, scattered trees, parks, large gardens. L 24 cm.                ○Sm

● STARLINGS: *Sturnidae*. Gregarious medium-sized land birds, with plumage often mainly blackish or iridescent and strong legs and bill; sexes alike. Flight fast and direct; on ground walk or run rather than hop. Hole nesters.

**TRISTRAM'S GRACKLE** *Onychognathus tristramii*. Blackbird-sized and fairly long-tailed, rufous primaries showing as a conspicuous patch on each wing in flight; adult male is otherwise black, with blue-violet sheen, female/juv duller with greyish head, neck and breast. Eyes red. Very gregarious and vocal, performing collective aerial manoeuvres, often while uttering sweet wild melancholy notes based on 'dee-oo-ee-o' theme. Wild rocky ravines, wadis, farmsteads, high mountains to sea level. L 25 cm.

Juv mynas have plumage and wattles duller than adult.

**COMMON MYNA** *Acridotheres tristis*. Dark brown with a black head, a large white wing patch conspicuous in flight, and bright yellow legs, bill and bare patch on face; sexes alike, juv duller with grey-brown head. Very like Starling (p.330) in noisy and gregarious habits, with an exceptionally wide vocabulary of notes, such as 'radio, radio', 'keek, keek' and 'kok, kok'. An Asian commensal of man, extending W to Aral Sea; introduced in Moscow, Kuwait. L 23 cm.

**Bank Myna** *A. gingianus*. Differs from slightly larger Common Myna in being mainly blue-grey, with wing-patches pinkish buff and bare skin round eye red; juv mainly brown. Voice, softer. An Asian commensal of man established in Kuwait; an escape elsewhere. L 21 cm.

328

GOLDEN ORIOLE

♂

♀

Green Woodpecker (p.224) with its yellow rump is often mistaken for Golden Oriole.

♀

♀

♂

TRISTRAM'S GRACKLE

♂

COMMON MYNA

BANK MYNA

moulting from juv to 1st winter

leucistic aberrant

ad early spring

worn ad

fresh     worn

Pale fringes and tips of feathers become worn towards spring, which makes birds look darker.

In summer Starlings can look just black in poor light, but in fresh winter plumage they can be so brightly spotted as to be mistaken for the much larger Nutcracker (p.320). The patchwork plumage of both dull grey-brown juvs moulting into adult plumage and adults moulting from winter to breeding plumage can be very confusing. A few juvs can appear almost as pale as juv Rose-coloured Starlings.

**STARLING** Sturnus vulgaris. One of the commonest European birds, like a short-tailed Blackbird (p.272) but with more bustling gait and triangular wings in flight. Adult blackish, iridescent with green and purple when breeding and spangled with pale spots, which are brighter in winter; bill yellow when breeding, brown in winter. Juv dull grey-brown with paler throat and unspotted breast. Chattering, whistling, mimetic song, like several birds in whispered conversation, often uttered in chorus; also many other clipped and often mimetic notes, and hunger cry of young an insistent 'cheeerr'. Open woods, scattered trees, farmland, parks, gardens, villages, suburbs, towns; after breeding often on hills and moors. Roosts communally in woods and reed-beds, and on trees and buildings in towns, often after spectacular mass aerial manoeuvres. L 21.5 cm.                                                                        ●RmW

Expanding its range in S; now breeds next to Spotless in Spain and has bred on Tenerife.

**SPOTLESS STARLING** Sturnus unicolor. Blue-tinged breeding adult completely unspotted, when green-tinged Starling's spots are rather subdued (a difference only detectable at close range), so appearing blacker than Starling; and only slightly spotted in winter, when Starling's spots are very conspicuous. Juv darker than juv Starling, especially on belly. Habits and habitat similar, but voice louder and song simpler, lacking Starling's confused multiple sounds. L 21 cm.

Expanding northwards, now breeding regularly in S France, often next to Starling.

**ROSE-COLOURED STARLING** Sturnus roseus. Crested adult is the region's only medium-sized black-and-pink land bird. Imm/juv differ from juv Starling in their paler sandy fawn plumage, pale rump, pink legs (red-brown in Starling) and yellow base of bill. Habits similar to Starling, with a similar harsh 'tschirr' call, a loud 'ki-ki-ki' flight note and rather more musical notes mixed with grating ones in song. Dry grass steppes, low rocky hills, farmland, often following locust swarms; erupts westwards at irregular intervals. Aka Rosy Pastor (India). L 21.5 cm.                    -A

Breeds irregularly in Hungary and S E Europe.

**Daurian Starling** S. sturninus. Escaped cage bird and possible rare vagrant from Siberia. Smaller than Starling, with grey head and underparts, violet-glossed back, rump, wing coverts and nape patch, a broad whitish wing bar and tail glossed green. Juv mainly brown, with darker brown wings and paler, streaked underparts. L 19 cm. -E

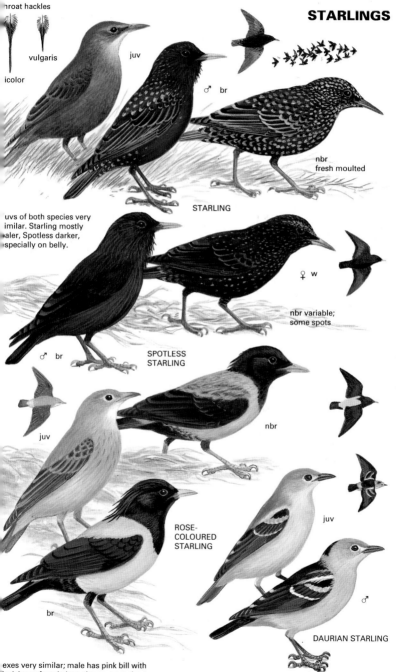

throat hackles

vulgaris

icolor

juv

♂ br

nbr
fresh moulted

STARLING

uvs of both species very
imilar. Starling mostly
aler, Spotless darker,
specially on belly.

♀ w

nbr variable;
some spots

♂ br

SPOTLESS
STARLING

juv

nbr

ROSE-
COLOURED
STARLING

juv

br

♂

DAURIAN STARLING

exes very similar; male has pink bill with
lack base; female less glossy, crest shorter.

**STARLINGS**

♂ br alpicola

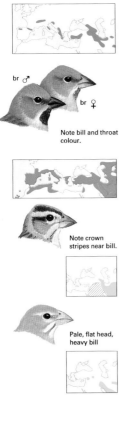

br ♂
br ♀

Note bill and throat colour.

Note crown stripes near bill.

Pale, flat head, heavy bill

● SPARROWS: *Passeridae.* Soberly plumaged songbirds, with a short, thick, seed-eating bill and rounded wings differing from the finches especially in having a shorter, square-tipped tail. Flight direct or bounding.

**SNOWFINCH** *Montifringilla nivalis.* A relatively large alpine sparrow, chocolate brown above. creamy white below, with grey head and black throat; black-and-white wings and tail, especially noticeable in flight; cf. Snow Bunting (p.360). Female has browner head and less white in wings and tail; juv duller still. Bill black, but yellow in winter. Perches erect, flicks tail. Song a monotonous 'sitticher, sitticher'; chief calls a grating 'tsweek' and a softer 'pitsch'. Rocky and stony mountains, where often hard to see when feeding; in winter lower down, even near buildings. L 18 cm.

Ssp.*alpicola* (Caucasus, Iran) looks paler in field, with head same colour as mantle, than ssp.*nivalis* (Europe) and birds from Zagros Mts, Iran, even paler than those from Caucasus and Turkey.

**ROCK SPARROW** *Petronia petronia.* Like a pale female House Sparrow (p.334), but with paler, more conspicuous supercilium and a pale crown stripe; pale yellow patch on upper breast (not in juv) and white spots at tip of tail. Various more or less sparrow-like notes, including a characteristic 'tut', a wheezy 'chwee' and a goldfinch-like 'pey-i'. Rocky mountain slopes, stony ground, desert edges, often unvegetated, sometimes near hollow trees; villages, especially with ruins. L 14 cm.          -V

**PALE ROCK SPARROW** *Petronia brachydactyla.* A plain, greyish-brown bird, not unlike an unstreaked female House Sparrow (p.334) with two whitish wing bars, white-tipped dark tail and orange-brown legs; sexes alike. Both musical whistling song 'tee-ze', ending in cicada-like trill, and distinctive 'twee-ou' call resemble cardueline finches; also a soft churring trill. Deserts or semi-deserts, with rocks or scrub; sometimes in large flocks among crops. L 14 cm.

**YELLOW-THROATED SPARROW** *Petronia xanthocollis.* Male differs from slightly larger Pale Rock Sparrow in its greyer head and mantle, yellow throat patch, chestnut shoulder patch, and less thick bill, black when breeding. Female/juv have paler chestnut patch and no yellow on throat. Song a monotonous 'chip-chip-choc', calls chirping and sparrow-like. Open woodland, farmland, gardens, areas with scattered trees, nesting in tree holes, nestboxes. L 12.5 cm.

**SPARROWS**

nbr

br

juv

SNOWFINCH

ad
sexes alike

juv

ROCK SPARROW

sexes alike

PALE
ROCK SPARROW

♀

br ♂

nbr ♂

YELLOW-THROATED
SPARROW

**SPANISH SPARROW** *Passer hispaniolensis*. Male differs from male House Sparrow in chestnut crown (but cf. hybrids and 'Italian Sparrow') and whiter cheeks; from Tree Sparrow in single white wing bar and no black patch on ear coverts; and from both in black breast, black streaks on flanks and darker streaks on back. Female/juv also have streaked flanks, white cheeks and darker back. Calls deeper than both, especially a contralto 'chup'. Scrub, olive groves, gardens, villages, scattered trees; in farmland may be hybrids. The common sparrow in Canary Is. L 14.5 cm. -V

Variation in Spanish Sparrow males and hybrids with House Sparrow.

Winter fresh

**HOUSE SPARROW** *Passer domesticus*. The classic small brown bird, male readily distinguished by chestnut mantle, grey crown and rump and black throat. Female/juv brown above, paler below, with a single pale wing bar. Numerous chirping and cheeping calls, and a double 'chissick', all sometimes strung together in a rudimentary song, often in chorus. Gregarious, rarely away from human settlements, from farms to city centres (where plumage often grubby), except to feed on nearby farmland. Nest on building or in hedge. L 14.5 cm. ●R

**House Sparrow Hybrids.** With Spanish Sparrow, scattered round Mediterranean. With Tree Sparrow, house-sparrow-sized, look more like Tree with dark ear patch.

**TREE SPARROW** *Passer montanus*. Chestnut crown, double white wing bar, yellowish-brown rump, smaller black throat bib and black patch on ear coverts distinguish both sexes from slightly larger male House Sparrow, but cf. chestnut-crowned 'Italian Sparrow' (opposite). Calls similar, but harder and higher-pitched, notably a quick 'chip, chip' and a 'tec, tec' flight note. Open woodland, river banks and areas with scattered trees, nesting in holes and nestboxes. Much less closely associated with man than House but more so than Spanish. L 14 cm. ●Rw

**DEAD SEA SPARROW** *Passer moabiticus*. Male differs from larger House Sparrow especially in lack of wing bar and in head pattern: white supercilium, grey cheek, yellow patch on side of neck. Female/juv paler than House. Call 'tri-rirp' or 'tlir', more rhythmical than House Sparrow. Very local in scrub near water, often flocking with Spanish Sparrows. L 12 cm.

**DESERT SPARROW** *Passer simplex*. Male has distinctive pale grey head and upperparts with two white and one black wing bars, black bib, paler underparts and when breeding a black bill. Female fairly uniformly sandy buff. Calls a multiple 'chu' and 'chip', higher-pitched than House Sparrow. Wadis, sandy and grassy areas and villages in deserts. L 13.5 cm.

# SPARROWS

juv

hispaniolensis

♀

♂ br

nbr

♂ br

italiae

SPANISH
SPARROW

Male Italian Sparrow *P.d.italiae* has chestnut crown, more black on breast, whiter cheeks and underparts.

♀

br

Hybrid House x Tree Sparrows occur where either species rare.

♂

br

HOUSE
SPARROW

sexes
alike

TREE SPARROW

♀

♀

♂ br

DESERT
SPARROW

♂ br

Male duller in winter, like House Sparrow.

DEAD SEA SPARROW

● **WEAVERS** *Ploceidae*. Tropical colonial finch-like birds with a typical stout conical seed-eating bill. Their most notable characteristic is, unlike finches, to build domed nests with the entrance at the top, bottom or side in trees and tall shrubs, remaining in flocks throughout the year.

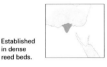

Established in dense reed beds.

**STREAKED WEAVER** *Ploceus manyar*. Breeding male with crown and nape yellow, throat and cheeks black, breast buff, streaked; female and non-breeding male shades of brown, streaked. Nile delta, introduced from India. 15 cm. Many other weavers have escaped, but have either failed to establish themselves or have been deliberately exterminated. Some, e.g. the Black-headed or Village Weaver *P. cucullatus* have bred several times in France and Germany.

● **WAXBILLS:** *Estrildidae*. Very small, gregarious tropical seed-eaters, frequenting reeds and other tall grasses. Introduced cage-birds that often escape. Besides those noted below the Zebra Finch *Poephila (Taeniopyga) guttata* (Australia) with a strikingly black-and-white barred tail has often been bred in small groups (two are currently established).

juv

Indian ad    African ad

The Silverbills will hybridise, the offspring having pinkish rumps.

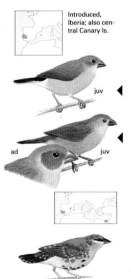

Introduced, Iberia; also central Canary Is.

juv

ad    juv

**Indian Silverbill** *Lonchura malabarica*. The Asiatic counterpart of the African Silverbill. A tiny brown bird with a pointed blackish tail, a white rump and a blue-grey bill. Introduced; breeds Wadi Araba, Israel/Jordan. Aka White-throated Munia. L 10 cm.          -E

**African Silverbill** *Lonchura cantans*. Slightly larger than Indian Silverbill and with black rump. S Egypt and W Arabia, spreading northwards; escapes have bred in Spain. L 10 cm.          -E

**COMMON WAXBILL** *Estrilda astrild*. A tiny African bird with broad red streak through eye, pale cheeks and black under tail coverts contrasting with red belly. Bill of adult coral-red, of duller imm blackish. Flight note 'tzep' or 'tjukup'. In reeds near vegetable fields, feeding in flocks, often large. L 9.5 cm.          -E

**Black-rumped Waxbill** *Estrilda troglodytes*. The first feral Common Waxbills in Portugal were mistaken for this species, but it is much paler and has a distinctive black rump and tail. Another escaped cage-bird that may be breeding in Spain. L 9.5 cm.          -E

**Orange-cheeked Waxbill** *Estrilda melpoda*. Differs from other waxbills mainly in its orange cheeks and red rump; crown and underparts grey, tail blackish. A frequent cage-bird, whose escapes have bred in Spain and France, but not yet established. L 9-10 cm. -E

**AVADAVAT** *Amandava amandava*. A tiny red-billed Asiatic seed-eater, the male strikingly all red except for brown wings, black tail and a few scattered white spots; female/juv brownish with red upper tail coverts and yellowish belly. Song a high-pitched twitter; call chirping. Reedbeds and other tall grasslands. Spain, N Egypt. Aka Red Munia. L 10 cm.          -E

**Senegal Firefinch** *Lagonosticta senegala*. Male is a tiny largely red bird with only wings and tail not crimson; female brown with red only on upper tail coverts and as a spot in front of eye. Has bred in Morocco and Egypt, perhaps as escapes. Aka Red-billed Finch. L 9-10 cm.          -E

Avadavat moulting from breeding to non-breeding; most males seen in this plumage.

♀ & nbr ♂

♂ br

STREAKED
WEAVER

ad

INDIAN SILVERBILL

juv

ad

COMMON WAXBILL

ad

AFRICAN SILVERBILL

ad

BLACK-RUMPED
WAXBILL

juv

♀

♂ full br

AVADAVAT

♀

♂

SENEGAL FIREFINCH

● FINCHES: *Fringillidae*. Small gregarious songbirds, with stout bills adapted to seed-eating, and with a characteristic bounding or dancing flight. Often better songsters than buntings. Breeding in habitats associated with trees and bushes, in which they nest.

**BRAMBLING** *Fringilla montifringilla*. Breeding male easily told by black head and mantle; in winter like brownish female/juv, and best told from Chaffinch, with which it often flocks, by white rump, conspicuous when flying away, and by orange-buff breast and shoulders. Song recalls Greenfinch's (p.344) 'dzhweee'; chief call a rather harsh 'tsweek', also a 'chuc-chuc' flight note. Birchwoods and willow scrub in northern taiga; in winter feeds on farmland and other open country, also under beeches and hornbeams. L 14.5 cm.          ●MW(b)

**CHAFFINCH** *Fringilla coelebs*. The commonest European finch, with white shoulder patch, conspicuous in flight, which is best distinction of female/juv from other brownish finches and sparrows. Male unmistakable with slate-blue head and nape, chestnut mantle, pinkish brown underparts and green rump. Rattling song varies widely by region, often ending in 'tic' like Great Spotted Woodpecker (p.226). Chief call 'pink, pink' very like Great Tit (p.310); also has a soft 'tsup' flight note, an insistent warning 'wheet' and a greenfinch-like 'tsweee'. Woodland, scrub, farmland, town parks, gardens; in winter often with other finches. L 15 cm.          ●RmW

palmae

tintillon

moreletti          spodiogenys

Males of island forms have black forehead and wings and variable mantle colour: slate-blue in ssp.*tintillon* (Canary Is) (also bright green rump) and ssp.*ombriosa* (Hierro, Canaries); greenish in ssp. *moreletti* (Azores) and *maderensis* (Madeira); and brighter green in ssp.*spodiogenys* (N Africa). Females/juvs rather dark.

maderensis

Still common on Tenerife in native pine forest, only marginally in alien pine plantations.

**BLUE CHAFFINCH** *Fringilla teydea*. The male of this large, strikingly slate-blue chaffinch is quite unmistakable, especially in lacking the pinkish breast of the Canary forms of Chaffinch. Female/juv mainly olive-brown, greyer beneath. Song and calls similar to Chaffinch, but has distinctive loud double chirp. Predominantly in natural forests of Canarian pine *Pinus canariensis* on the mountains. L 16.5 cm.

Ssp.*polatzeki* from the Pinars on Gran Canaria is now rather scarce

# FINCHES

♀ br

♂ br

nbr

br

♂ nbr

Breeding male variable,
some even with black
throat.

**BRAMBLING**

♂ nbr

♂ w

Chaffinch

♀ coelebs

Both species duller in winter.
Bill of male Chaffinch
changes from pale brown to
grey-blue when breeding; of
male Brambling yellow to
blue-black.

♂ br

**CHAFFINCH**

♂ br

♀ br

*olatzeki* looks brighter,
ith white belly and
ear white wing bar.

♂ br teydea

**BLUE
CHAFFINCH**

A European endemic closely related to the Corsican Finch.

All wooded habitats from sea level, but commoner higher up.

Nests in cypresses and other conifers. Also on Canary Is.

Endemic to the region.

From Turkey eastwards on high mountains; lower down in winter.

**CITRIL FINCH** *Serinus citrinella*. Grey nape, sides of neck and flanks of adult are best distinction from Serin and Siskin (p.344), also more greenish-yellow rump, unstreaked underparts, no yellow at sides of tail and noticeably thinner bill. Female duller; juv grey-brown, streaked below. Song recalls both Siskin and Goldfinch (p.344); call a twittering 'tsi-i' and a metallic 'chwic'. Mountain conifer forests, birch-holly woods (Spain) and in autumn and winter open rocky ground on lower slopes. L 12 cm.

**CORSICAN FINCH** *Serinus corsicanus*. Often treated as subspecies *corsicanus* of the Citril Finch. Male is brownish and more heavily streaked above than Citril Finch, with paler yellow, less greenish underparts. Breeds from sea level to mountains, in both deciduous and coniferous woods. L 12 cm.

**CANARY** *Serinus canaria*. The Atlantic Islands (Azores, W. Canaries, Madeira) counterpart of the Serin; slightly larger and with greyer back and yellower underparts, the yellow rump conspicuous in flight; female duller and browner, juv more streaked. Song is that of familiar cage bird, whose many, often all bright yellow, varieties derive from it. Woodland, cultivations, orchards, gardens. L 12.5 cm.

**SERIN** *Serinus serinus*. The smallest widespread European finch, yellow to yellowish-green above with darker streaks and bright yellow rump; male also has bright yellow head and breast. Differs from Siskin (p.344) in very stubby bill, more prominent yellow rump, and no yellow at sides of tail; also lacks male Siskin's black on head and chin. Juv heavily streaked; no yellow rump. Jingling song like a whispering Corn Bunting (p.354); calls like cardueline finches (p.344), a flight note 'tirrilillit' and an anxiety note 'tseooeet'. Woodland edges, clumps of trees, orchards, town parks, gardens, from mountains to suburbs. L 11.5 cm.                                    -A(b)

**SYRIAN SERIN** *Serinus syriacus*. Slightly larger and generally paler and less streaked than Serin, with bright golden-yellow forehead and mask round eye, yellow edges to feathers of longer tail, and uniformly yellow unstreaked underparts. Female greyer, juv browner. Song goldfinch-like; flight call 'tir-rrh'. Cedars and junipers in the mountains, also orchards. L 12.5 cm.

**RED-FRONTED SERIN** *Serinus pusillus*. A most distinctive finch, the fiery red forehead contrasting with the black head and breast, which are still quite dark in winter, and with yellow wing patches, rump and sides of tail; otherwise mostly rufous streaked darker, so appearing in flight to be dark in front and tawny behind. Females greyer; juv has head and breast pale orange-buff, with confusing mottling as it moults to adult plumage. Song recalls both Goldfinch (p.344) and Serin; call a descending trill 'tsirrup'. Scrubby and grassy mountains, with wild roses, junipers. L 12 cm.                                    -E

# FINCHES, SERINS

CITRIL FINCH

CORSICAN FINCH

CANARY

SERIN

SYRIAN SERIN

RED-FRONTED SERIN

**Redpolls, Linnets:** *Acanthis*. Gregarious small brown finches with stubby seed-eating bills, cleft tails, red or pink patches in plumage, a markedly dancing flight and a characteristic anxiety note 'tsooeet'.

**REDPOLL** *Acanthis flammea*. Distinguished from both Linnet and Twite by black chin and no white fringes to primaries, from Linnet and male Twite also by pink rump and from Twite by red forehead and male's red breast. Juv lacks black chin and any red plumage. Flight call 'chuch-uch-uch', alternating with 'err', also forms basis of song, often delivered in circular song flight. Coniferous and birch woods, willow scrub, locally in large gardens; in winter often on waterside alders with Siskins and Goldfinches (p.344). L 13-15 cm. ●RSMW

Redpolls vary both in size and in shade of brown. Smallest and darkest is Lesser Redpoll ssp.*cabaret* (Ireland, Britain, C Europe). Palest, with whiter wing bars and (sometimes unstreaked) rump is Mealy Redpoll ssp.*flammea* (N Europe). Largest is darker, large-billed Greenland Redpoll ssp.*rostrata*, a winter visitor.

**ARCTIC REDPOLL** *Acanthis hornemanni*. Paler than Redpoll, especially on head and neck, with pure white unstreaked rump (cf. often indistinguishable Mealy Redpoll), more conspicuous pale wing bars, whiter and less streaked underparts, and male's breast pale pink. Both song and calls similar to Redpoll, but 'chuch-uch-uch' slower. High Arctic tundra, wintering S to coasts of Scandinavia. L 13 cm. ○W

**TWITE** *Acanthis flavirostris*. The upland counterpart of the Linnet, sharing its whitish wing bar, but differing in its streaked brown plumage being featureless apart from tawny buff throat and male's pink rump. Also differs from Linnet and breeding Redpolls in yellow bill - grey when breeding. Male is only small bird with pink or red on rump but not on breast or chestnut above. Song a twittering medley, often in chorus; flight call both linnet-like, but nasal 'twa-it' call is distinctive. Rocky and heathery moors, from sea level to mountains; winters on open lower ground, especially coastal saltmarshes and grassland. L 13.5 cm. ●Rsw

Ssp.*pipilans* (Britain, Ireland) is darker than ssp.*flavirostris* (Scandinavia); paler ssp.*brevirostris* (Turkey to Caucasus) has brighter pink rump, much whiter wing and black spots on breast.

**LINNET** *Acanthis cannabina*. The commonest *Acanthis* in Europe, distinguished by prominent whitish wing patch and dark brown bill. Breeding male is only small brown bird with both grey head and red forehead and breast, and has much more chestnut above than Twite or Redpoll; red parts are pinkish in winter. Female/juv lack red or pink and are much less chestnut above. Song a twittering medley, often in chorus; flight call greenfinch-like but higher-pitched and less melodious. Areas with low trees or bushes, heaths, maquis, woodland edges, hedgerows, orchards, large gardens; may nest in loose colonies; in winter in more open habitats, such as farmland, saltmarshes and rough grassland near coast. L 13.5 cm. ●RSw

Ssp.*bella* (Asia Minor) is paler, especially on the head, and the rump is almost white; sspp.*harterti* (E Canaries), *meadewaldoi* (W Canaries) and *nana* (Madeira) are smaller and more richly coloured.

juv

♀

'Mealy
Redpoll'

♂ flammea

REDPOLL

♂

cabaret
reduced
like ♀

'Lesser Redpoll'

'holboellii'
long-billed

♂

1st w

♂

ARCTIC
REDPOLL

brevirostris

♂ br

♂ w

♀

♂

♂ w flavirostris

♂ br

flavirostris

♂
br
bella

♂
br cannabina

TWITE

♂

♀

♂ w

LINNET

**Cardueline Finches** *Carduelis*. Three related but very different specialised finches with yellow wing mirrors, the two smaller with an acrobatic feeding technique.

**SISKIN** *Carduelis spinus*. A small dark-streaked yellow-green finch with a yellow rump and (a good distinction from Serin, p.340) yellow patches at base of tail. Male's black crown and chin distinguish it from all other yellow-green finches; female/juv less yellow and more streaked, with no black on head. Sweet twittering goldfinch-like song often uttered in bat-like circular display flight; most frequent calls a distinctive 'tsuu' or 'tsyzing'. Usually among conifers, especially spruce, scattered or in pure or mixed woods; in winter often with Redpolls (p.342) on alders and birches. L 12 cm. ●RMW

**GOLDFINCH** *Carduelis carduelis*. A most distinctive finch, with unique combination of red face, yellow wing bars, whitish rump and black and white on head, wings and tail. Juv resembles larger juv Greenfinch, but without yellow in tail. Flight notably dancing. Song a series of tinkling variations on liquid 'tswitt-witt-witt' flight call; also has a rather harsh 'geez'. Habitat as Greenfinch, especially in orchards; in autumn often feeds on seed-heads of thistles and other tall plants. L 12 cm. ●RS

Goldfinches tend to be larger and whiter in the N E and smaller and greyer in the S: ssp.*carduelis* (Europe, Scandinavia) becomes larger and paler in Russia, where the large very pale ssp.*major* comes into the region from beyond the Urals in winter; ssp.*parva* (W Mediterranean, Canaries, Azores) is also paler; other sspp.in Middle East and Caucasus, some paler, others duller; ssp. *britannica* (Britain, Ireland) is darker, and more rufous, especially on back and flanks.

Goldfinches can be sexed, especially when a pair is seen together. Males are brighter with red reaching behind the eye.

**GREENFINCH** *Carduelis chloris*. The region's largest yellow-green finch, with distinctive bright yellow wing patches; also has yellow rump and patches at base of tail and stout, pale flesh-pink bill. Female duller; juv streaked darker. Song a twittering medley, often uttered in circular display flight; when breeding has distinctive nasal 'dzhwee'; also 'chi-chi-chi-chi-chi' flight call, softer and less metallic than Linnet, and canary-like 'tsooeet'. Woodland edges, scattered trees and shrubs, gardens, orchards, parks, villages, suburbs; in winter also farmland and flat coasts, often with other seed-eaters. L 14.5 cm. ●R

Greenfinches vary greatly in intensity of colour. Ssp.*aurantiiventris* (Mediterranean) is larger and brighter; ssp.*chlorotica* (Levant) is paler and more yellowish all over; ssp.*turkestanica* (Crimea, Caucasus) is much greyer.

Many European aviculturists breed Goldfinch x Canary hybrids, and release the females because they do not sing. These look like dull Goldfinches and in winter often appear at bird tables, where pure-bred Goldfinches are rarely seen.

# FINCHES

**SISKIN**

Males vary greatly in colour intensity and some have black in chin.

Breeds mostly in conifers; in winter often feeds on alders and birches.

♀

♀

♂  ♂

britannica

major

parva

juv

some
are
browner

♀

**GOLDFINCH**

juv

♂ br

chlorotica

**GREENFINCH**
All populations have two forms, one more grey-ish, the other more brownish.

rosskowi                    iberiae

pyrrhula

Bullfinches become smaller from N to S. The largest sspp. are the brighter *pyrrhula* (Scandinavia, N Russia) and the brighter, darker red and larger-beaked *rosskowi* (Caucasus, N E Turkey); *europoea* (Europe) and *pileata* (Britain, Ireland) are smaller and duller; *iberiae* (Pyrenees) is smaller and deeper red, with even some red on the back.

**BULLFINCH** *Pyrrhula pyrrhula*. Male is unmistakable with black crown and chin and red underparts; female pinkish-brown with black crown; juv brown with brown crown. White rump (more prominent than Brambling (p.338) and Goldfinch (p.344) and broad white wing bar conspicuous in flight. Generally rather shy, often only revealing presence by penetrating plangent low whistle 'deu', which also forms basis of feeble, creaky, often trisyllabic piping song. Mainly coniferous woodland, but in W Europe mainly in broad-leaved woods and in scrub, orchards and large gardens, but almost always near woodland cover. L 14.5-16 cm.                                                                                ●R

Restricted to Sao Miguel, Azores.

**AZORES BULLFINCH** *Pyrrhula murina*. Often treated as a ssp. of the Bullfinch, from which it is very different. Both sexes resemble a female Bullfinch, but with grey-brown rump and a larger bill. Inhabits impenetrable and largely self-sown woods of Japanese cedar *Cryptomeria japonica*; feared extinct for 40 years until recently rediscovered. L 16 cm.

The only species of a mainly Himalayan genus, which just overlaps into the region.

**WHITE-WINGED GROSBEAK** *Mycerobas carnipes*. Resembles a Hawfinch in its large head and stout grey bill, and a shrike in its long tail and upright posture, but is almost all black (dark grey in female) with yellow-green rump and belly (duller in female) and a conspicuous white wing patch. Has a loud far-carrying magpie-like chatter and a 'schweeup' note recalling Rock Sparrow (p.332). Mountain sides with junipers, on whose fruits it feeds. L 21 cm.

**HAWFINCH** *Coccothraustes coccothraustes*. The largest finch over most of Europe, unmistakable with its outsize bill (grey-blue when breeding, yellow in winter) used to crack nuts and fruit stones. Most often detected by hearing its clipped robin-like 'tic' note and seeing a dumpy form overhead in bounding flight, with conspicuous white in wings and short tail. Plumage mainly chestnut, with throat and wing-tips black. Sexes alike; juv has throat and bill yellow. Feeble bullfinch-like piping song rarely heard; also has a rather high-pitched sibilant 'tsip'. Broad-leaved woodland, scattered trees, large gardens and orchards. L 18 cm.
                                                                                              ☉R

# FINCHES

juv

♀

europoea
BULLFINCH

♀

♂

AZORES
BULLFINCH

♀

♂

WHITE-WINGED
GROSBEAK

juv

♂ w

♀ br

♂ br

nbr ♂

HAWFINCH
Male in winter only slightly duller
than when breeding. Some southern
birds are very pale; more greyish in
N Africa.

Hawfinch
p.346

**Evening Grosbeak** *Coccothraustes vespertina*. Rare vagrant from N America, with huge, hawfinch-like bill, short tail, even more striking black-and-white wing pattern, yellowish back and yellow forehead and supercilium. L 20 cm.                                                    -V

**Desert Finches** *Rhodospiza*. A group of four finches with a relatively short strong bill, frequenting dry, open habitats, often in mountains.

Nests in trees; often winters in fields.

**DESERT FINCH** *Rhodospiza obsoleta*. Not unlike a pale sandy-grey Greenfinch (p.344), with black and pale pink wings, showing a conspicuous white wing bar in flight and markedly cleft tail tip; male's lores black; female/juv duller. Bill black but brown in winter and yellow in juv; feet black. Song slightly recalls Song Thrush (p.274); distinctive call, a soft purring 'r-r-r-r-r-ee' falls in pitch and then rises. Open country with trees and bushes near fresh water; not especially in deserts, often by roadsides and in cultivations, orchards and gardens. L 14.5 cm.

**MONGOLIAN FINCH** *Bucanetes mongolicus*. Very like Trumpeter Finch, but male differs in yellow-brown bill, pink supercilium, white outer tail feathers and more sharply defined pink rump; female differs mainly in having more white in wings. Pleasant song 'do-mi-sol-mi', with delicate arpeggios; chief call 'djou-voud' or 'djoudjou-vou'. Rocky mountains, descending to plains in winter. L 13 cm.

Rocky, bare mountainous country, often with Crimson-winged and other finches.

**TRUMPETER FINCH** *Bucanetes githagineus*. Breeding adult pale brown with pinkish sheen (male variably pinker than female), red on wings, rump and flanks, grey crown, dark brown tail and orange legs; male's bill bright red when breeding. Cf. larger Sinai Rosefinch (p.350). Winter adult/imm/juv duller, mainly sandy grey, with contrasting darker wing tips, bill yellowish-brown and legs pinkish. Distinctive nasal buzzing or 'trumpeting' call, 'cheez', like a toy trumpet, also 'chee' and 'chit'. Stony deserts, rocky hills, never perching in trees. L 12.5 cm.                                                    -V

Eroded and semi-desert country, stony deserts and rocky hills; in Canaries on sea shore.

**CRIMSON-WINGED FINCH** *Rhodopechys sanguinea*. A high mountain finch, brownish speckled darker, with pink (paler in female) on tail, face and wings (conspicuous in flight, contrasting with white underwing); crown blackish-brown (only speckled black in female), nape pale, bill yellow when breeding, legs dark. Song a short sweet trill, often aerial; calls twittering and linnet-like, 'chee-rup' or 'dy-lit'. Rocky mountain tops and slopes with some scrub, not much below 2000 m; in winter on cultivations lower down. L 15 cm.

Dry, rocky mountains over 2000 m; in winter feeds on cultivated fields lower down.

Ssp.*aliena* (Morocco) is paler with less white in tail, greyish neck more prominent, white on throat, less pink on face and wings.

# DESERT FINCHES

juv/1st winter
how little pink
wing.

♀

♂ br

**DESERT FINCH**

juv

♂

♂ br

**MONGOLIAN FINCH**
Sexes alike, female duller, less
rosy, no pink supercilium.

♂ nbr

♂ br

♂ br

Very variable. On Canaries,
in E often deep pinkish breast
when breeding; in W often
silvery grey.

♀ br

**TRUMPETER FINCH**

♂ br
aliena

♂ br
sanguinea

♀

**CRIMSON-WINGED FINCH**

**Rosefinches**: *Carpodacus*. A mainly Asiatic genus of medium-sized to rather large, stout-billed seed-eaters, the males mainly red or pink, the females brownish and streaked; tail cleft. Undulating, finch-type flight.

**COMMON ROSEFINCH** *Carpodacus erythrinus*. The region's most widespread and frequent rosefinch, spreading westwards in N Europe. Older males have head, breast and rump with variable amounts of bright red, the tail and wings dark brown with a paler double wing bar. Female/imm/juv are rather plain brown birds, like a stouter-billed female House Sparrow (p.334) with two pale wing bars and whiter belly; some imm males breed in brown plumage. Song a clear piping 'tiu-tiu-fi-tiu'; chief call 'tweek', recalling both Chaffinch (p.338) and Twite (p.342). Woodland edges, thickets by rivers in taiga, scrub, orchards, farmland, gardens. Aka Scarlet Grosbeak. L 14.5 cm.          -A(b)

**GREAT ROSEFINCH** *Carpodacus rubicilla*. The region's largest (almost starling-sized) and reddest rosefinch, the male with head, rump and whole underparts dark red, all except rump streaked or flecked with white; female grey-brown with conspicuously streaked breast. Looks dark at any distance in its slow, undulating flight; hops on ground. High rocky and scrub-by slopes above the rhododendron zone in the Caucasus; in winter in scrub in higher valleys. L 20 cm.

An isolated population of this C Asian species in alpine meadows above 2000 m in the Caucasus.

**SINAI ROSEFINCH** *Carpodacus synoicus*. Larger and longer-tailed than Trumpeter Finch (p.348) and adult male redder (older ones strikingly so), especially on head, breast and rump, but has no pink in wings and bill grey not red. Female/juv grey-brown, some older females tinged pinkish. Song melodious, varied; chief calls 'chig' and a high-pitched 'tweet'. Very local among rocky hills and gorges. L 14.5 cm.

Dry barren rocky hills, dry stony wadis to 2000 m.

Two more rosefinches are imported from China in large numbers, so that birds seen in the region are more likely to be escapes than vagrants. **Pallas's Rosefinch** *C. roseus* is intermediate between Common and Great Rosefinches, male with redder underparts and browner back, wings and tail than Common and less conspicuous white marks on red parts than much larger Great; in flight appears bright pink with a longish tail. Female has pinkish rump. L 15 cm.

Pallas's

♀

♂

Long-tailed

**Long-tailed Rosefinch** *Uragus sibiricus* has a long tail, making it look like an outsize Tit (p.306) with white wing bars; male pinkish, female pale brown with pink rump. L 15 cm.

**PINE GROSBEAK** *Pinicola enucleator*. A very large, almost starling-sized finch, not unlike an outsize Crossbill (p.352), but with the stout bill not crossed. Adult variable, male mainly red, female/imm mainly bronzy yellow; juv browner; double white wing bars more conspicuous and bill much stouter than much smaller Common Rosefinch. Song a loud, whistling, twanging medley; calls a loud clear trisyllabic whistle, with a more musical alarm. High northern conifer forests, especially spruce and larch, also birch; very rarely erupting westwards. L 20 cm.

Winters further S than northern taiga belt, with irregular eruptions westwards.

COMMON ROSEFINCH

In all Rosefinches, bright males most often seen outside normal breeding areas. Males, looking like females, often sing and hold territory.

GREAT ROSEFINCH

SINAI ROSEFINCH

PINE GROSBEAK

**Crossbills**: *Loxia*. Large finches, unique among birds for the crossed mandibles with which, using a distinctive criss-cross motion of the head, they dexterously extract seeds from pine, spruce, fir or larch cones, their almost exclusive diet. Periodically erupting westwards to Atlantic fringes.

**TWO-BARRED CROSSBILL** *Loxia leucoptera*. The smallest crossbill, distinguished by usually conspicuous double white wing bars, paler in juv. Male pinker red and female paler olive-brown than Crossbill, and bill rather less heavy. Song a series of loud, almost canary-like, undulating trills of varying pitch; flight call a redpoll-like 'chif, chif' less metallic than Crossbill, also a more musical 'peet'. Coniferous forests with a marked prefer-ence for larches. Aka White-winged Crossbill. L 14.5 cm.     -V

Some Crossbills, especially juvs, show faint pale, sometimes pink-ish, wing bars, but never as broad and white as in Two-barred. though some of these can have rather small wing bars. However, size and voice always separate the two species.

**CROSSBILL** *Loxia curvirostra*. Much the commonest and most widespread crossbill, erupting irregularly far to W and S of main breeding area. Adult male bright red to orange-red, even yellow or olive-tinged; imm male orange-red, female olive-brown with yellower rump and underparts, juv brown streaked darker; all with wings and deeply cleft tail dark brown. Song a staccato series of bell-like notes, based on distinctive metallic 'jip, jip' call, which together with feeding motion is good field mark in poor light. Coniferous forest, especially spruce and fir; during irruptions also at isolated conifer clumps or trees, even in towns. L 16.5 cm.                                    ⊙Rw

Pyrenean                          poliogyna           guillemardi

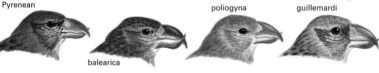

balearica

Crossbills in Pyrenean and Iberian pine forests have slightly stouter bills, but the populations are not isolated like the various island ones.

Isolated populations like sspp.*balearica* (Balearic Is), *corsicana* (Corsica), *poliogyna* (N Africa) and *guillemardi* (Cyprus) have stout bills like Scottish Crossbill, like which they all live in pine forests and do not migrate. Most males are seldom very red, more orange, and females are less yellowish, often very grey, but colour varies and some Balearic males are bright red. In the Crimean pine forests males of ssp.*mariae* are paler red and females greyer.

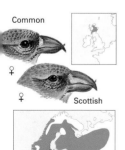

Common

♀

♀                  Scottish

**SCOTTISH CROSSBILL** *Loxia scotica*. So intermediate between Crossbill and Parrot Crossbill that taxonomists con-stantly debate whether it is a ssp. of either or (as is the fashion now) a full species. Closer to Crossbill, but separable from both only by habitat (confined to native pinewoods), with extreme dif-ficulty by bill, stouter and blunter-tipped than Crossbill but less so than Parrot Crossbill, and by deep 'toop' call. L 16.5 cm.   ○R

**PARROT CROSSBILL** *Loxia pytyopsittacus*. Slightly larger and bulkier than Crossbill, distinguishable at close range by larger head, flatter crown and forehead, much stouter bill (needed to feed on pine cones) with pale cutting edges, and somewhat greyish head and mantle. Calls lower, louder and harsher. Forests of Scots pine *Pinus sylvestris*, rare away from northern conifer belt. L 17 cm.                               -V(b)

juv

♂

♀

juv

TWO-BARRED CROSSBILL. Besides wing bars and size, males differ from Crossbill in being more carmine red.

♀
grey

♂

♀

♂

♂

♂

CROSSBILL. Colours vary greatly. Males may be very bright red, orange or even yellow, and females either olive-brown or dull greyish.

♂

♂

Female like Crossbill, but usually greyer

PARROT CROSSBILL

SCOTTISH CROSSBILL. Female usually duller than Crossbill.

● BUNTINGS: *Emberizidae*. Seed-eaters, most of which (especially *Emberiza*, differ from most finches and sparrows by smaller head; smaller, conical bill; and longer, only shallowly cleft tail. Mostly rather indifferent songsters. Flight bounding, fairly fast. Mainly ground-living, usually avoiding human settlements.

Farmland; in S also dry open steppes with well-scattered bushes. Mostly seen on telephone wires or isolated bushes.

**CORN BUNTING** *Miliaria calandra*. The largest, plumpest and stoutest-billed bunting, uniformly brown above; paler beneath with darker streaks, heaviest and forming dark patch on breast. Differs from all similar brown seed-eaters in having no wing bars, white outer tail feathers or other distinctive features. Also has unique habit, for a small songbird, of flying with dangling legs. Most distinctive field character is high-pitched song, like jangling of a bunch of keys, delivered in the air or from a perch, or even just a clod of earth; equally distinctive flight call is a rather liquid 'quit' or 'quit-it-it'. Open country with scattered trees or bushes, farmland, dry grassland, steppes, hillsides, rough ground near the sea. L 18 cm.     ●R

In N Africa in human settlements, very tame and entering houses. In Middle East also in remote rocky hills and wadis.

**HOUSE BUNTING** *Emberiza striolata*. Male is the only seed-eater with head, neck and upper breast uniform grey with variable white-striped head pattern; otherwise pale rufous or warm brown with outer tail feathers rufous (white in Rock Bunting); bill has upper mandible black, lower yellow. Female more or less uniformly warm brown. Song somewhat redstart-like; call a nasal 'tzswee', often when crouching on rock, window ledge or house roof. In N Africa a town and village bird, often as commensal with man as House Sparrow (p.334); in S W Asia also in deserts and rocky wadis, sometimes with sheep and goat flocks. L 13.5 cm.

Ssp.*striolata* (S W Asia) has marked black-and-white head pattern like Rock Bunting; cf. also African Rock Bunting *E.tahapisi* (p.375); ssp.*saharae* (N Africa) is less streaked above and has two faint pale stripes on head.

Sunny rocky and stony hillsides, vineyards, gardens. Winters lower down.

**ROCK BUNTING** *Emberiza cia*. Male has striking head pattern of three black stripes, separated by white supercilium and grey cheeks; grey throat separates from all seed-eaters except House Bunting and much smaller Syrian Serin (p.340). Female browner, duller, more streaked. Both have unstreaked chestnut rump, pale rufous underparts and grey tail, which also separate imm/juv from young Ortolan and Cretzschmar's Bunting (p.358). Song a typical high-pitched bunting buzz, 'zi-zi-zi-zirr', often from a rock with fluttering wings; call a sharp 'tzit', like Cirl Bunting (p.356) and a bubbling twitter 'tootootooc'. L 16 cm.                                                    -V

**PINE BUNTING** *Emberiza leucocephala*. Breeding male has unique head pattern of white crown, cheek, collar and breast patch with chestnut supercilium and throat, and rump and lower breast unstreaked chestnut; winter male duller with dark streaks on crown. Female greyer than female Yellowhammer (p.356) with no yellow and white belly and fringes to primaries. Song like Chaffinch (p.338). Open woodland, scrub, farmland, along roads and near fresh water. L 17 cm.          -V

In a narrow zone in W Siberia Pine Bunting and Yellowhammer (p.356) interbreed. Such hybrids have been seen in Europe, and females may be impossible to separate from their parents in the field.

# BUNTINGS

CORN BUNTING

♀ var

♂

striolata

♀

♂

saharae

HOUSE BUNTING

juv

♀

♂

ROCK BUNTING

♀ var

♀ s

♂ s

♂ w var

PINE BUNTING

**YELLOWHAMMER** *Emberiza citrinella*. Male is one of the region's yellowest song birds and the only mainly yellow one with chestnut back and rump; female/juv browner and less yellow, chestnut rump being best distinction from female/juv Cirl Bunting. White outer tail feathers conspicuous in flight at all ages. High-pitched song has unmistakable pattern, often rendered 'a little bit of bread and no cheeese', the 'cheeese' sometimes omitted; calls a sibilantly liquid 'twit-up' and a more grating 'twink' or 'twit'. Farmland, hedgerows, scrub, woodland edges. Hybridises with Pine Bunting (p.354). L 16.5 cm.　　●R

**CIRL BUNTING** *Emberiza cirlus*. Male easily told from male Yellowhammer by head pattern (grey crown, black throat), greyish-green breast-band and olive rump. Female/juv more buffish than female/juv Yellowhammer, but always differ in olive rump. Song quite distinct, a brief rattling trill like a rather flat Lesser Whitethroat's (p.288), and unlike Yellowhammer (which prefers a lower perch) usually from a tree; a rare variant is like Yellowhammer with no final 'cheeese'. Call 'zit', higher-pitched than Yellowhammer, also a wren-like churring alarm note. Farmland and other open areas with scattered trees, hedges and bushes. L 16.5 cm.　　○R

Endemic W Palaearctic species, replacing Yellowhammer in Mediterranean region.

**YELLOW-BREASTED BUNTING** *Emberiza aureola*. Breeding male very distinctive with dark head and yellow underparts, narrow chestnut breast-band and conspicuous double white wing bars; duller in winter. Female/juv differ from larger female/juv Yellowhammer chiefly in brown forehead, dark stripes separating creamy white supercilia and crown stripe, unstreaked underparts (except flanks) and prominent double wing bars. Loud musical song, like Ortolan (p.358) but higher-pitched and faster; calls a short 'zipp' and a soft 'trssit'. Open woodland, scrub. L 14 cm.　　-A

Migrates to S E Asia, returning in June.

**RED-HEADED BUNTING** *Emberiza bruniceps*. Striking plumage of male, with chestnut face, throat and upper breast and bright yellow underparts. Female very like female Black-headed Bunting, but tinged grey-green above and may have yellow-green underparts. Juvs not separable. Song a loud pleasant ortolan-like whistle; chief call a musical 'tweet'. Scrub in steppes and semi-deserts and by fresh water; in winter mainly on farmland. A frequent cage-bird, so most males in the W are presumed escapes. L 16.5 cm.　　-E/V

Migrates to India, flocking in plains with Black-headed in winter.

Red-headed and Black-headed Buntings may be conspecific and interbreed where they meet. Such hybrids are hard to distinguish.

**BLACK-HEADED BUNTING** *Emberiza melanocephala*. Contrast of black head with unstreaked yellow throat and underparts (duller in winter) separates breeding male from males of other yellow buntings. Female like a large female House Sparrow (p.334), but with upperparts tinged rufous, rump pale chestnut and belly and under tail coverts pale yellow. Juv has rump and underparts buff or yellowish-buff. Cf. Red-headed Bunting. Song melodious for a bunting, beginning with a rather grating 'chit, chit, chit'; calls 'chup', 'chit', 'zee'. Scrub, olive groves, vineyards, gardens. L 16.5 cm.　　-E/V

Migrates S E from August, returning to European breeding grounds in late April.

# BUNTINGS

YELLOWHAMMER

CIRL BUNTING

YELLOW-BREASTED
BUNTING

RED-HEADED BUNTING

BLACK-HEADED BUNTING

Ortolan's distinctive circular display flight, singing both in flight and from tree.

Ortolan and other buntings on this page are all migratory, arriving relatively late on their breeding grounds and returning early to tropical Africa, especially the Sahelian or sub-Saharan zone.

Often near wetlands, but prefers well-drained sandy soil to heavy clays.

**ORTOLAN** *Emberiza hortulana*. Soberly coloured, mainly pinkish-brown with greenish-grey head and breast, yellow throat and underwing, and pinkish bill and legs; identified at close range by its white eye-ring. Female/juv successively duller and browner than male, with dark streaks on breast. Cf. Cretzschmar's, which has blue-grey head and pinkish-brown throat, and Rock Buntings (p.354). Rather mournful song of 6-8 'zeu' and 'zeee' notes, usually with a change of pitch; call a weak cirl-bunting-like 'zit', also a piping 'tseu' and a liquid 'pwit' flight note. Woodland and scrub, sparsely vegetated stony ground on mountains, farmland, vineyards, gardens, in both hills and plains; in winter mainly in cultivations. L 16.5 cm. ○M

Sparsely vegetated rocky hillsides, semi-deserts; usually perches on ground.

**CRETZSCHMAR'S BUNTING** *Emberiza caesia*. Male resembles male Ortolan but with blue-grey head, pinkish-brown throat and whitish underwing; duller in winter. Juv more buffish-chestnut than juv Ortolan and with whitish underwing; pink bill and less rufous rump separate from juv Rock Bunting (p.354). Song similar to Ortolan but briefer, only 3-4 notes; call a loud insistent 'styip'. Can be remarkably tame on migration. L 16 cm. -V

Dry open stony country with sparse vegetation above 2000 m.

**GREY-NECKED BUNTING** *Emberiza buchanani*. Male differs from Ortolan and Cretzschmar's in having whole head and mantle pale blue-grey and underparts reddish; female duller. Juv less boldly streaked on mantle and breast than juv Ortolan and Cretzschmar's, with no rufous on rump. Song longer than Ortolan's, 'dze dze dze dzee-oo', inflection rising then falling on last note; calls include 'sip' and 'choup'. Bare stony slopes with rocky outcrops above 2000 m. L 16 cm.

Grassy, rocky slopes, rare and local; on migration also in deserts.

**CINEREOUS BUNTING** *Emberiza cineracea*. Greyish-brown, the breeding male with yellowish-green head, yellow throat pale yellow eye-ring and bluish or greyish bill; belly white or yellowish. Winter male/female/juv duller with throat streaked; juv's rump grey-brown. Brief typical bunting song has three long and two short notes; call 'kip'. Uncommon on high rocky slopes up to the tree limit and on Corfu and Mytilene in the Aegean; in deserts on migration. L 16.5 cm.

Belly is whitish in ssp.*cineracea* (Turkey), but yellow in ssp. *semenowi* (Iran; also migrates to and winters in Iraq and Syria).

juv

♀ s

♂ s

ORTOLAN

juv

♀

♂ s

CRETZSCHMAR'S
BUNTING

juv

♂

♂

GREY-NECKED BUNTING

semenowi

♂

juv

♂

♀

cineracea

CINEREOUS BUNTING

winter

Little winter

Rustic winter

**REED BUNTING** *Emberiza schoeniclus*. Breeding male has whole head and upper breast black (browner in winter) offset by white nape and moustachial streak; female/juv streaky brown, with full buff supercilium, young males moulting into adult plumage having triangular brown breast-patch. All have white feathers in tail and dark brown legs. Cf. Little, Rustic and Lapland Buntings. Staccato, squeaky song, 'tweek, tweek, tweek, tititic'; chief call a yellow-wagtail-like 'tsweep', also 'ching' and 'tsip'. Fens, marshes, rushy fields, by fresh water, less often in drier habitats; in winter also farmland., L 15 cm.                ●Rmw

Mediterranean and S Russian races, e.g. *intermedia* (Caucasus to Sicily) and *pyrrhuloides* (S W Asia), have much stouter bills than the typical N and W European ssp.*schoeniclus*.

**LITTLE BUNTING** *Emberiza pusilla*. Like a small short-tailed female Reed Bunting with rufous cheeks and crown, marked buff supercilium behind eye, paler eye-ring, dull brown (not chestnut) lesser wing coverts, whiter underparts and flesh-pink legs. Song brief, twittering, almost robin-like; call a reed-bunting-like 'tsew', but alarm call 'pwick' or 'tip, tip', quite distinct. Tundra scrub; on migration in W Europe mainly coastal. L 13.5 cm.                -A

**RUSTIC BUNTING** *Emberiza rustica*. Breeding male differs from male Reed Bunting in its white throat and supercilium, purer white lower breast and belly and chestnut breast-band; both sexes differ in pale patch on nape, rufous rump and flank streaks, more prominent whitish wing bars and shorter tail; winter adults have chest parts browner. May raise crest feathers. Song brief and warbling, recalling Robin (p.258) or Dunnock (p.254); call a shrill 'tsip, tsip, tsip', like Little Bunting but louder. High northern forests, usually swampy. L 14.5 cm.                -A

**SNOW BUNTING** *Plectrophenax nivalis*. Breeding male strikingly black and white, with increasing admixtures of brown in winter male/female/imm/juv, all having long wings and white wing patches and underparts. Cf. Snowfinch (p.332). Loud, sweet, rather repetitive song uttered from low song post or in aerial display; flight call a silvery rippling 'tirrirrirrip', mostly from flocks, other notes including a soft 'twee' or 'tweet', a rather mournful whistling 'tew' and a disyllabic 'chis-ic'. Barren tundra, remote rocky sea shores and mountain tops; in winter in 'snowflake' flocks, on coasts and on inland hilltops. L 16.5 cm.                ⊙rmW

**LAPLAND BUNTING** *Calcarius lapponicus*. Heavier and longer-winged than Reed Bunting, breeding male differing in buff stripe back from eye, chestnut nape, more black on sides of breast and whiter underparts; winter adults differ from female Reed in two dark patches behind ear coverts and yellow bill; imm has broad pale crown stripe. Song brief, melodious, recalling Skylark (p.230); chief call a distinctive flat little trill, 'ticky-tic-tic', also 'teeu'. Tundra; in winter in small flocks on coast and moors, often with Snow Buntings. Aka Lapland Longspur. L 15 cm.                ⊙MW(b)

**BUNTINGS**

REED BUNTING

♀

♂ w

intermedia group

pyrrhuloides group

w

♂ s

RUSTIC
BUNTING

♀ w

♀

LITTLE
BUNTING

s

♂ s

1st w

juv

♀ w

♂ s

SNOW BUNTING

♂ w

♀ s

♂ w

LAPLAND BUNTING

♀ s

**Vagrant Asian and N American Buntings** *Emberizidae*. An increasing number of buntings which breed in Siberia and winter in S E Asia, including the four species on this page, are being recorded in W Europe. Although a few may be genuine vagrants, the majority are escapes from the many thousands imported as cage-birds. However, most of the N American *Emberizidae*, generally known as `sparrows' (opposite), reach Europe as genuine transatlantic vagrants.

**Pallas's Reed Bunting** *Emberiza pallasi*. A small population breeds in N E European Russia; otherwise rare vagrant from Siberia. Smaller, paler, greyer and less rufous above and much less streaked below than Reed Bunting (p.360), male with a pale slate-blue (not rufous) patch on lesser wing coverts (best certain field character, with voice) and underparts streaked on flanks only; female/imm with grey-brown lesser wing coverts and paler, more uniform ear coverts; in winter pale crown stripes are faint or absent. Main calls are a distinctive tree-sparrow-like 'tseeep' and a Richard's-pipit-like (but fainter) 'r-r-reep'. L 13-14 cm. -V

**Chestnut Bunting** *Emberiza rutila*. Rare vagrant from E Siberia. Breeding male unmistakable with rufous chestnut head, breast, mantle and upper tail coverts, and yellow underparts with streaked flanks; in winter rufous parts become mottled. Lack of white in tail distinguishes female from females of both Yellowhammer (p.356), which has yellow, not white, throat, and Yellow-breasted Bunting (p.356), which has brown, not chestnut, rump. Imm/juv like female, but more heavily streaked. L 14-15 cm. -E

**Yellow-browed Bunting** *Emberiza chrysophrys*. Rare vagrant from Siberia. Breeding male has a most striking black-and-white head pattern, with white crown-stripe, broad yellow supercilium and black ear coverts, and white underparts streaked darker on throat, upper breast and flanks. Female has brown instead of black on head with supercilium less bright yellow. Winter adult/imm very like breeding female, some with supercilium yellow in front, white behind, recalling White-throated Sparrow, which has grey, not brown, ear coverts; cf. also Rustic Bunting (p.360). Call a high-pitched metallic 'tic', not unlike Little Bunting (p.360). L 15.5 cm. -V

**Black-faced Bunting** *Emberiza spodocephala*. Rare vagrant from Siberia. Breeding male has dark grey head and breast with black face, brown rump and faintly streaked buff underparts, all duller in winter. Female generally dull greyish-brown, dunnock-like, with supercilium and crown stripe often obscure; imm varies between female and winter male. Call a metallic 'tzit' or 'tzee'. L 16 cm. -V/E

**Dark-eyed Junco** *Junco hyemalis*. Transatlantic vagrant. All dark grey, males often almost blackish, except for white belly and broad white outer tail feathers, especially conspicuous in flight. Female brownish; juv even more so, streaked above and below, on breast. Bill of adults pinkish-yellow. Calls variously described as a sharp 'dit' and a light 'smack'; also a twittering flight note. Includes Slate-colored Junco. L 15-16 cm.                   -V

**White-crowned Sparrow** *Zonotrichia leuco-phrys*. Transatlantic vagrant. Adult shares striking black-and-white head pattern with White-throated Sparrow, but differs in having white supercilium extending forwards only to eye, with upper lores black; bill pale, usually pink; throat much duller white; and face below eye with whole underparts unstreaked pale grey. Imm is plainer with similar but less distinct head pattern. Call a loud 'pink' or 'chink' and a sharper 'chip'. L 17-19 cm.        -V

**White-throated Sparrow** *Zonotrichia albicollis*. Transatlantic vagrant. Adult has striking black-and-white head pattern, shared with no other N American seed-eater than White-crowned Sparrow, from which differs in darker bill, longer white supercili-um (the fore part bright yellow), conspicuously white throat contrasting with and darker grey cheeks and upper breast, and underparts diffusely streaked. Imms (and some adults) have whole supercilium buff; otherwise like adult with less distinct head pattern. Cf. Yellow-browed Bunting, which has similar head pattern, but white crown stripe narrower, ear coverts brown, and under-parts with heavier, more clear-cut streaking. Most frequent call a slurred 'tseet', also a hard 'chink'. L 17-18 cm.                                     -V

**Song Sparrow** *Melospiza melodia*. Transatlantic vagrant. The archetypal small brown North Ameri-can sparrow, not unlike a female Reed Bunting (p.360) but with no white in tail; heavily streaked on the underparts, the streaks converging on a diagnostic large dark spot on the breast (some-times absent in imm); striped head pattern, with grey supercilium, but without the yellow usually present in the similar Savanna Sparrow (p.374). Characteristically pumps tail in flight. Call a nasal 'chimp' or 'tchep', song, comparatively musical for a N American bird, starts with a melodious 'sweet' uttered 3-4 times, followed by some buzzy notes and ending with a short trill, but unlikely to be heard in the region. L 14-16 cm.                  -V

**Fox Sparrow** *Passerella iliaca*. Transatlantic vagrant, Corn Bunting-sized, between a rather large female House Sparrow (p.334) and a same-sized Hermit Thrush (p.279) in appearance, with 'foxy' rufous tail, rump and wings; breast heavily marked with large rufous triangular spots and a song-sparrow-like larger spot in the middle. Calls a loud 'tchek' and a high-pitched 'tseep'. Tends to skulk in undergrowth. L 17-19 cm.               -V

**Vagrant American Passerines.** Every year a few vagrant N American songbirds arrive in Europe. Many are carried across the Atlantic in the strong westerly airstream of a large depression. Others come on ocean-going ships, where lost migrants alight and stay till they see land, which is often a windswept island off the coast of W Europe, especially Ireland or Britain, or reach port. Some then penetrate well inland.

**Rose-breasted Grosbeak** *Pheucticus ludovicianus*. Strikingly plumaged breeding male is unmistakable, but all so far recorded in the region have been imms. Broadly striped head and heavy hawfinch-like bill make female/imm look much more like other streaked brown seed-eaters, but are easily distinguised by large size; imm male has pink underwings (yellow in female) and may show white wing bars and a pink tinge on breast. Call, a sharp 'eek'. L 18-21 cm.                                    -V

**Indigo Bunting** *Passerina ciris*. Has the size and shape of a Linnet (p.342). Breeding male, bright blue all over except for some blackish on face, wings and tail is completely unmistakable (though against the light, may appear all-black), but also likely to be an escaped cage-bird. Winter male like brown female/juv, but usually still has some blue, at least on rump. Absence of any obvious spots, streaks or bars is best field mark of female, brown all over but paler beneath and with two obscure wing bars. Call a short wood-warbler-like 'tsick'. Has reached Azores, where unlikely to be an escape. L 14 cm.                                    -V

● AMERICAN ORIOLES *Icteridae*. A rather diverse family of New World songbirds much more closely related to the buntings than to the superficially similar Old World orioles (p.328). They include the grackles and North American blackbirds, but few have so far been reported on the E side of the Atlantic. Most species have a strong direct flight, not undulating.

**Bobolink** *Dolichonyx oryzivorus*. Breeding male mainly black, but white on wings, rump and base of tail, showing up strikingly in flight, and buff on nape, becoming in winter very like female/imm, which recalls a yellow-buff Corn Bunting (p.354), heavily streaked on the head and upperparts and with pale mantle 'braces' Tail feathers distinctively pointed at all ages. Flight note, a repeated 'pink'. L 15-20 cm.    -V

**Yellow-headed Blackbird** *Xanthocephalus xanthocephalus*. Breeding male is one of the most strikingly plumaged N American birds, the whole head, nape and breast, except for the black lores and chin, being bright yellow, in contrast to the black of the rest of the body, which is offset only by the white wing-patch, which shows well in flight. Female/imm is smaller with yellow mainly on throat and breast, the rest of the plumage being blackish brown, with no wing bars but some white streaks on the lower breast. Call a croaking 'kruk'. L 20-28 cm. -V/E

**Baltimore Oriole** *Icterus galbula*. Starling-sized with similar pointed bill. Breeding male is the only black-and-orange bird at all likely to be seen in the region; head, throat, mantle, wings and most of tail are black, with white in the wings, while rump outer tail feathers and rest of underparts are deep orange; imm male has the black parts blackish-brown and the orange parts more yellowish. Female mainly dull yellow, somewhat like larger female Golden Oriole (p.328) but with double white wing bars. Call a rich, whistling, 'hew-li'. L 18-20 cm. -V

● TANAGERS *Thraupidae*. A family of arboreal New World songbirds, closely related to the buntings, and noted in the tropics for the brilliance of their plumage. Only four species breed in N America and so are likely to become transatlantic vagrants. The name derives from 'tangara', used by the Tupi Indians of Brazil. See also p.374.

**Scarlet Tanager** *Piranga olivacea*. Breeding male (unlikely to occur in the region) is an unmistakable scarlet with black wings and tail. Winter male/female/imm resemble a large finch, with large pale bill and greenfinch-like colouration, greenish-olive on head and upperparts and greenish-yellow below; imm male has some black in wings. Distinguished from similar Summer Tanager (p.374) by smaller bill, darker wings and whitish (not pink) underwing coverts. Call a low 'chip-burr'. L 18-19 cm. -A

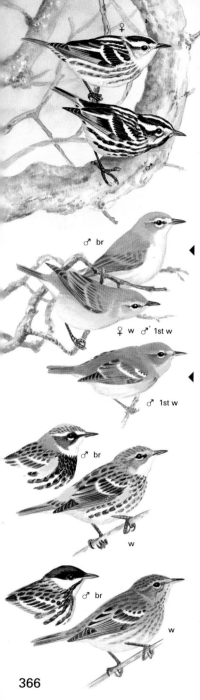

♀

♂ br

♀ w   ♂ 1st w

♂ 1st w

♂ br

w

♂ br

w

● **AMERICAN WOOD WARBLERS** *Parulidae*. A large family of small migratory insectivorous songbirds, inhabiting broad-leaved and deciduous woodland; bill sharply pointed. Calls of most species varied and very similar, often a short 'tsik'. Most males and many females are distinctive, but many winter adults and almost all imms, especially on autumn migration when they are most likely to stray to Europe can be hard to separate; American field guides call them 'confusing fall warblers'. See also pp.373-374.

**Black-and-white Warbler** *Mniotilta varia*. A most distinctive wood warbler, the only one that creeps along branches and up and down tree trunks like a Nuthatch (p.312); head and upperparts black with white stripes, underparts white with dark stripes; females have whiter and imms largely buff underparts. Call usually buzzing or chattering, but may be 'chip' or 'seek', like Treecreeper (p.314). L 11-14 cm.-V

**Tennessee Warbler** *Vermivora peregrina*. Superficially resembles a Willow Warbler (p.296), but very pointed bill distinguishes at once. Adults/imms both mainly yellow-green and unstreaked with white under tail coverts; breeding male with grey head and white supercilium; winter male and female with head less grey and underparts yellower; imm with supercilium yellow and faint wing bar. Cf. Red-eyed Vireo. L 12 cm.                                    -V

**Northern Parula** *Parula americana*. Small, chiffchaff-sized, dainty, mainly blue-grey, with yellow throat and breast, white belly, double wing bar, white eye-ring, and distinctive yellow-green patch on back. Male has dark and rufous bands between throat and breast, also present but obscure in some females; imm like female. Aka Parula Warbler. L 11 cm.                                    -V

**Yellow-rumped Warbler** *Dendroica coronata*. Yellow crown (sometimes absent), rump and flank patches, coupled with white patches near tip of outer tail and pale throat and eye-ring are best field marks at all ages and in all seasons. Breeding male is blue-grey above with black patch on breast. Winter male/female/imm duller and browner with no black patch on streaked underparts. Calls a distinctive loud hoarse 'chep' or 'tchik' and a somewhat fainter 'tseet' or 'tsit'. Includes Myrtle Warbler. L 13-15 cm.                                    -V

**Blackpoll Warbler** *Dendroica striata*. Recorded as a vagrant only in autumn, so distinctive black-and-white breeding male with its all-black crown contrasting with white cheeks unlikely to be seen. Winter adult/imm larger and heavier than Willow Warbler (p.296), dull olive-brown above, dull yellowish below, both faintly streaked, with conspicuous white double wing bars, white under tail coverts and whitish patches at tip of tail sides; legs usually pale orange or yellowish but may be dark brown. Call 'chip', but usually silent in autumn. L 13-14 cm.                                    -V

**American Redstart** *Setophaga ruticilla*. A small bird and a great flycatcher; distinctive black-and-orange breeding male unrecorded in region, where all records have been of female/imms in autumn. These have a large tail, usually fanned, dark with conspicuous bright yellow patches at base; grey-green upperparts, most showing conspicuous yellow wing patches; head bluish-grey; underparts off-white with pure white undertail and yellow patches on sides of breast. L 13 cm.                    -V

**Ovenbird** *Seiurus aurocapillus*. One of three larger terrestrial wood warblers that resemble a diminutive Song Thrush (p.274) or a rather short-tailed Meadow Pipit (p.242), with olive-brown upperparts and underparts streaked with rows of blackish spots; legs pinkish. Distinguished by rufous centre of crown, bordered by two dark stripes, and conspicuous white eye-ring. In natural habitat forages on woodland floor. Call a high-pitched 'tseet' and alarm note a loud 'tzik'. L 15 cm.          -V

**Northern Waterthrush** *Seiurus noveboracensis*. Differs from Ovenbird especially in head pattern, crown being all-brown like upperparts, with pale buff supercilium and no eye-ring, and in its underparts being more buffish and more clearly striped. Walks bobbingly, on seashore or at edge of streams, like Common Sandpiper (p.160). Call a sharp 'chink' or 'chip'. L 15 cm. NB Louisiana Waterthrush *S. motacilla*, the third of the genus, not yet seen in Europe, is very like Northern, but with a slightly longer, heavier bill, and underparts and supercilium both white.   -V

**Common Yellowthroat** *Geothlypis trichas*. Male has highly distinctive white-bordered black face mask, with yellow throat and breast and white belly. Female similar but with no face mask; imms may have the shadow of a face mask, and imm male a white eye-ring. Has wren-like habit of cocking up tail. Call, a hoarse 'chep'. L 11-14 cm.     -V

● VIREOS Vireonidae. Vireos resemble somewhat heavier wood warblers, with stouter bills slightly hooked at the tip, and generally with olive, brownish or yellowish plumage. Some species have a supercilium and no wing bars, others have both eye-rings and wing bars. See also p.373.

**Red-eyed Vireo** *Vireo olivaceus*. The most frequent transatlantic vagrant songbird, now annual in S W England in October. Olive-brown with paler underparts, somewhat resembling a stocky *Hippolais* warbler (p.286), but with a blue-grey crown, conspicuous black-bordered white supercilium, plain green upperparts, silky white underparts, strong bill and stout blue legs; eyes dark red or brown. Has a petulant nasal call, variously rendered as 'queee', 'mew' or 'tchway'. L 15 cm.                    -V

**Accidentals and Rare Vagrants.** These are birds which have been recorded only as accidental vagrants in the region, and are either not described or mentioned only marginally in the main text. They all originate from areas beyond, and sometimes well beyond, the region. Most are simply lost migrants, blown off course by adverse winds. The part of the region where they are seen often provides a clue to the normal range of these vagrants. Thus birds from N America or the Caribbean are most likely to turn up in the Azores or W Europe, while those originating in S Asia or E Africa are more likely to appear in Kuwait, Israel or Egypt. Vagrant seabirds mostly come from the S Atlantic and S Indian Oceans.

Almost any bird that is kept in captivity may escape, so obvious escaped cage-birds, for instance, are omitted unless they are fairly frequent.

\* indicates birds that may have escaped or been released from captivity, or else are recent and still unconfirmed.

For more detailed information than can be given in these thumbnail sketches, consult Harrison *Seabirds*; Madge and Burn *Wildfowl*; Hayman, Marchant & Prater *Shorebirds*; Turner & Rose *Swallows and Martins*; Clement, Harris & Davis *Finches and Sparrows* (these five all Helm); Peterson's field guides for North America (Houghton Mifflin); National Geographic Society's *Field Guide to the Birds of North America*; and Lewington, Alström & Colston's *Field Guide to the Rare Birds of Britain & Europe* (HarperCollins).

**Yellow-nosed Albatross** *Diomedea chlororhynchos*. Like a smaller Black-browed Albatross (p.28), with narrower black margins to underwing and yellow-ridged black bill. L 71-81, WS 200-256 cm. \*Britain, Norway.

**Wandering Albatross** *D. exulans*. Much larger than Black-browed Albatross, adult mainly white with dark tip and trailing edge to wing and huge pale bill. L 107-135, WS 254-351 cm. Portugal, Sicily.

**Southern Giant Petrel** *Macronectes giganteus*. Like a huge dark heavy-bodied Fulmar (p.30). Imm told from *M. halli* only by pale (not dark) tip to bill. L 86-99, WS 185-205 cm. \*Britain, \*France.

**Cape Petrel** *Daption capense*. Like a small Fulmar, with dark head and upperparts mottled black and white. L 38-40, WS 81-91 cm. Aka Cape Pigeon. \*E Atlantic, \*Mediterranean.

**Schlegel's Petrel** *Pterodroma incerta*. Distinctive, large (almost fulmar-sized) gadfly petrel; dark brown except for white underbody. L 43, WS 104 cm. \*Israel.

**Streaked Shearwater** *Calonectris leucomelas*. Similar to Cory's Shearwater (p.30) but white face and streaked nape diagnostic. L 48. WS 122 cm. Israel.

**Wedge-tailed Shearwater** *Puffinus pacificus*. Slightly smaller than Flesh-footed Shearwater (p.30), with dark bill, pointed tail and broader-based wings. Two morphs. L 38-46, WS 97-105 cm. \*Red Sea.

**Red-footed Booby** *Sula sula*. Two morphs: one white, like small Masked Booby (p.36), the other grey-brown, including underwing; all adults have white tail, but imms and intermediates confusable with other boobies. L 66-77, WS 91-101 cm. Red Sea, Norway.

**Schrenk's Bittern** *Ixobrychus eurhythmus*. Like Little Bittern (p.42) with chestnut upperparts, adult with chestnut face and female/juv with wing coverts conspicuously white-spotted. L 33-39, WS 55-59 cm. Italy.

**Dwarf Bittern** *I. (Ardeirallus) sturmii*. Like Little Bittern but with upperparts dark slate-grey; female paler with rufous belly. L 27-30 cm. Canary Is.

**Chinese Pond Heron** *Ardeola bacchus*. Unmistakable when breeding. Winter adult/imm probably inseparable from Squacco and Indian Pond Herons (p.44). L 45 cm. Norway.

**Little Blue Heron** *Egretta caerulea*. Adult slate-blue; imm white, like Little Egret (p.46) but wings usually dark-tipped, bill thicker, pinkish and dark-tipped and legs greenish-pink. L 51-76 cm. Azores.

**Tricolored Heron** *E. tricolor*. Unmistakable: mainly dark blue with white underwings, belly and rump and long slender bill; juv has chestnut neck and wing coverts. L 50-76, WS 90 cm. Azores.

**Snowy Egret** *E. thula*. Very like slightly larger, longer-billed Little Egret but lores are bright yellow; and has pale yellow of feet extending up back of legs. L 48-68, WS 96 cm. Azores, Iceland.

**White-faced Whistling Duck** *Dendrocygna viduata*. Adult unmistakable; juv duller with grey face. L 38-48 cm. *Spain.

**Ross's Goose** *Anser rossii*. Smaller, shorter-necked and shorter-billed than Snow Goose, with head rounder and 'gentle' expression. L 53-66 cm. Netherlands, *Belgium, *Britain, *Faeroe, *Germany, *Sweden.

**Spur-winged Goose** *Plectopterus gambensis*. An unmistakable large, ungainly black-and-white goose with long reddish bill and legs; imm browner, duller and lacks bare facial skin. L 73-100 cm. Morocco.

**Red-billed Teal** *Anas erythrorhyncha*. Combination of dark crown, white face and all-red bill are diagnostic. L 43-48 cm. *Israel.

**Cape Shoveler** *A. smithii*. Differs from Shoveler (p.68) at all times by contrast between dark body and small pale head, which makes black bill appear longer. L 51-53 cm. *Morocco.

**Canvasback** *Aythya valisineria*. Like a large Pochard (p.70) with long triangular black bill and steep sloping forehead; demarcation line between dark breast and pale flanks slopes forward (perpendicular in Pochard). L 48-61 cm. Iceland, *Britain, *Germany.

br

nbr

juv

ad

imm

juv

ad

juv

Little Egret
p.46

ad

Snow p.54

exes alike

Cape

eler ♀

Pochard p.70

**369**

**Swainson's Hawk** *Buteo swainsoni*. Wings more pointed and flight feathers darker than Buzzard (p.94); pale morph confusable with Booted Eagle but upperwing lacks pale wing bar. L 48-55 cm. Norway.

**Black Crake** *Limnocorax (Porzana) flavirostra*. Small, all-black, with yellow bill and pink legs; bill dark and legs duller in juv. L 23 cm. Madeira.

**Oriental Pratincole** *Glareola maldivarum*. Darker brown above and shorter-tailed than Collared or Black-winged Pratincoles (p.134); underwing rufous but no white trailing edge. L 25 cm. Britain, Cyprus, Egypt.

**Three-banded Plover** *Charadrius tricollaris*. Freshwater plover, smaller but longer-tailed than Ringed Plover (p.138); white forehead separates it from similar Forbe's Plover *C. forbesi*, not recorded in region. L 18 cm. *Egypt.

**Chestnut-banded Sandplover** *C. pallidus*. Small, long-legged, grey-backed, with chestnut breast band (incomplete and grey in juv), recalling a long-tailed Kentish Plover (p.138); in Africa on alkaline lakes. L 15 cm. *Israel.

**Black-headed Plover** *Hoplopterus tectus*. Unmistakable with lapwing-like crest. Slimmer but longer-tailed than Spur-winged Plover (p.142) with longish slender pink legs and staring yellow eyes. Dry grasslands. L 25 cm. Israel, Jordan.

**Swinhoe's Snipe** *Gallinago megala*. Very like Pintail Snipe, but on ground tail extends obviously beyond folded wing-tips and in flight tail corners show more white. L 28 cm. Caucasus.

**Grey-tailed Tattler** *Heteroscelus brevipes*. Knot-sized, *Tringa*-like, with uniform grey upperparts and underwing and shortish yellow legs; call a ringed plover-like 'tu-weet'. Estuaries. L 25 cm. Britain.

**Aleutian Tern** *Sterna aleutica*. Smaller than Common Tern (p.182), darker above and below, with white forehead, and black bar near trailing edge of wings, black legs and bill, L 33-38, WS 76-81 cm. Britain.

**Least Tern** *S. antillarum*. Distinguishable from Little Tern (p.184) only by greyer back and centre tail, and squeaky call, reminiscent of Oystercatcher (p.131). L 20-28, WS 50-55 cm. *Britain.

**Brown Noddy** *Anous stolidus*. Sandwich-tern-sized, all dark brown with white cap and wedge-shaped tail. L 40-45, WS 79-86 cm. Germany, Norway.

**African Skimmer** *Rynchops flavirostris*. Resembles a large tern. Black above and white below, with knife-like orange bill, the lower mandible much longer than the upper and immersed as birds fly low over water in characteristic feeding action. L 38, WS 106 cm. Israel, Morocco.

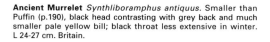

**Ancient Murrelet** *Synthliboramphus antiquus*. Smaller than Puffin (p.190), black head contrasting with grey back and much smaller pale yellow bill; black throat less extensive in winter. L 24-27 cm. Britain.

**Crested Auklet** *Aethia cristatella*. Sooty grey above and below, bill red (brown in winter), and adult with prominent crest. L 23 cm. Iceland.

**Parakeet Auklet** *Cyclorrhynchus psittacula*. Upperparts and throat slate grey, underparts white, bill distinctively stout and red. L 23-25 cm. Sweden.

**African Collared Dove** *Streptopelia roseogrisea*. Slightly smaller and shorter-tailed than Collared Dove, with white vent and tail darker than mantle; song distinctive, consisting mainly of descending cooing notes. L 28 cm. Sinai, Israel.

**Mourning Dove** *Zenaida macroura*. In plumage rather like a slender juv Palm Dove (p.198) with large black spots on wings, but has long tail tapering to a point like Namaqua Dove. L 31 cm. Britain, Iceland.

**Didric Cuckoo** *Chrysococcyx caprius*. A small shrike-like African cuckoo, male green shot with rufous above (female more rufous), with barred whitish underparts. Named from its call. L 19 cm. Cyprus, Israel.

**Northern Flicker** *Colaptes auratus*. A fairly large brownish N American woodpecker barred above and dark-spotted below, with conspicuous white rump in flight; male has black moustache. L 32 cm. Denmark, Ireland.

PASSERINES. A surprising number of these included here are of North American origin – the majority lost immature migrants carried to Western Europe by autumnal gales.

**Eastern Phoebe** *Sayornis phoebe*. Large, longish-tailed N American flycatcher, grey-brown above, darkest on head; whitish below, washed olive/yellow, perches upright, often pumping tail. L 18 cm. Britain.

**Acadian Flycatcher** *Empidonax virescens*. Spotted-flycatcher-sized, olive-green above, whitish below, tinged grey on breast and yellow on belly, with conspicuous pale wing bars and eye-ring. Emphatic 'wee-see' call is best distinction from other notoriously extremely similar N American *Empidonax* flycatchers. L 15 cm. Iceland.

**Hume's Short-toed Lark** *Calandrella acutirostris*. Inseparable in field from grey race of Short-toed Lark (p.232); in hand has less white in outer tail feathers and longest 4 (not 3) primaries equal in length; Asian steppes, uplands. L 13 cm. Israel.

**Tree Swallow** *Tachycineta bicolor*. Small N American swallow with shallow-forked tail; adult green-blue above, white below; grey-brown/white juv confusable with smaller Sand Martin (p.238). L 15 cm. Britain.

**Ethiopian Swallow** *Hirundo aethiopica*. Much smaller than Swallow (p.240), with rufous forehead, pale buff chin and throat, and incomplete breast band; juv with browner back. L 14 cm. Israel.

371

**African Pied Wagtail** *Motacilla aguimp.* Easily separated from smaller and shorter-tailed Pied Wagtail (p.248) by broad white wing patches. L 20 cm. Israel.

**Cedar Waxwing** *Bombycilla cedrorum.* Smaller, browner and plainer winged than Waxwing (p.252); belly yellow, undertail coverts white. L 18 cm. *Britain, Iceland.

**Northern Mockingbird** *Mimus polyglottos.* Differs from same-sized Great Grey Shrike (p.316), in longer legs and lack of hooked bill and face mask. Juv duller, streaked below. L 25 cm. Britain, Netherlands.

**Brown Thrasher** *Toxostoma rufum.* An unmistakable skulking N American bird like a long-tailed, short-winged rufous thrush with longer bill and streaked underparts. L 29 cm. Britain, Germany.

**Grey Catbird** *Dumetella carolinensis.* A starling-sized N American skulker, all sooty grey except for black cap and tail and rufous under tail coverts; imm brown-winged. L 22 cm. Germany, Ireland, Jersey.

**Siberian Blue Robin** *Luscinia cyane.* Blue/white male unmistakable; female somewhat like slim dull Red-flanked Bluetail (p.258), but lacks orange flanks and white throat and has less blue on short, often quivered tail. L 15 cm. *Sark, Channel Is.

**Varied Thrush** *Zoothera naevia.* Unmistakable fieldfare-sized blue-grey and orange N W American thrush; female browner above with fainter breast band. L 24 cm. Britain.

**Tickell's Thrush** *Turdus unicolor.* Male like a small, pale grey female Blackbird (p.272) with a white belly; female browner with streaked white throat and duller yellow bill and eye-ring. L 21 cm. Heligoland.

**Thick-billed Warbler** *Acrocephalus aedon.* Differs from Great Reed Warbler (p.282) in plainer face (lacks pale supercilium and dark lores) and shorter thicker bill with all-pale lower mandible; longer, graduated tail and upright stance recall a shrike; bushes (not reeds); Asia. L 18-19 cm. Britain, Finland.

**Ruby-crowned Kinglet** *Regulus calendula.* North American equivalent of Goldcrest (p.300) differing in having distinctive white crescents in front and behind eye; male's red crown patch rarely visible. L 11 cm. Iceland.

**Brown Flycatcher** *Muscicapa dauurica.* Plumage grey-brown, unstreaked, pale eye-ring and patch on lores; imm has pale wing bar and tertial fringes. (Beware possible **Sooty Flycatcher** *M. sibirica*, browner with brown sides to breast, shorter bill and darker lores.) L 13 cm. Denmark, Sweden.

**Red-breasted Nuthatch** *Sitta canadensis*. Like Corsican Nuthatch (p.312), but smaller, with dark corners to tail, and male especially has more colourful underparts. L 11 cm. Britain.

**Rufous-backed Shrike** *Lanius schach*. Like a same-sized Great Grey Shrike (p.316) with rufous upperparts and long graduated buff-edged black tail; juv duller, browner, barred above and below. Aka Black-headed Shrike. L 24 cm. Hungary, Israel, Turkey.

**Brown Shrike** *L. cristatus*. Very like distinctly smaller Isabelline Shrike (p.318), but has heavier bill, longer, more graduated tail, pale forehead and rufous underparts (barred brown in imm). L 19 cm. Britain, Denmark. See also p.318.

Hooded Crow
p.324 in Iraq/Egypt

**Pied Crow** *Corvus albus*. Carrion-crow-sized, with white belly and neck collar. L 46 cm. Libya.

**Amethyst Starling** *Cinnyricinclus leucogaster*. Starling-sized; male unmistakably purple above and white below; female/juv dark brown above, speckled brown on breast and flanks. L 18-19 cm. Israel.

**Yellow-throated Vireo** *Vireo flavifrons*. Distinctive with bright yellow breast, throat and spectacles, white belly and broad white tertial fringes and double wing bars. L 14 cm. Britain.

**Philadelphia Vireo** *V. philadelphicus*. Rather small, with grey head, white supercilia and yellow underparts; typical robust, slightly hooked vireo bill distinguishes from Tennessee Warbler (pp.298, 366). L 13 cm. Britain, Ireland.

**North American Wood Warblers** *Parulidae*, see also p.366.

**Golden-winged Warbler** *Vermivora chrysoptera*. Yellow wing patches with striking black-and-white head pattern make adult male one of the easiest wood warblers to identify; female greyer on head. L 12 cm. Britain.

**Yellow Warbler** *Dendroica petechia*. Plump, short-tailed; breeding male yellow streaked rufous beneath; other plumages duller, unstreaked, dark eye prominent in pale face. L 13 cm. Britain, Denmark.

**Chestnut-sided Warbler** *D. pensylvanica*. Chestnut flank stripe when breeding unmistakable, but mostly lost in autumn, when greenish above with pale greyish underparts; double yellow wing bars and white eye-rings at all times. L 11-14 cm. Britain.

**Black-throated Blue Warbler** *D. caerulescens*. Male unmistakably blue-grey above with black face, throat and flanks and white underparts; female mainly brownish-green with darker cheeks, narrow white supercilia and eye-rings and often a small white wing patch. L 13-14 cm. Iceland.

**Black-throated Green Warbler** *D. virens*. Breeding male has distinctive yellow face and black throat and breast (female black on upper breast only, imm no black); all ages have double white wing bars and streaked flanks. L 11-13 cm. Heligoland, Iceland.

**Blackburnian Warbler** *D. fusca*. Breeding male's orange throat (yellow in female) and crown stripe and white wing panel distinctive. Other plumages mainly brownish above and yellowish below, with streaked flanks and yellow supercilia; white wing bars and lines on mantle at all times. L 13 cm. Britain, Iceland.

**Cape May Warbler** *D. tigrina*. Breeding male's chestnut cheeks unique among wood warblers. Other plumages have yellowish rump, broad double wing bars, and yellow on face and sides of neck, but head pattern and streaking on underparts less prominent; bill thin, tail short. L 13 cm. Britain.

**Magnolia Warbler** *D. magnolia*. Black of cheeks and upperparts of distinctive breeding male mostly absent from other plumages, and broad double wing bars much less so; head grey, upperparts grey-green, rump yellow, underparts yellow, streaked on flanks. L 12 cm. Britain, Iceland.

**Palm Warbler** *D. palmarum*. Breeding adults have distinctive chestnut cap. Other plumages duller, browner above with yellowish double wing bars and supercilia less distinct and yellow underparts with streaked flanks paler. Ground dweller, constantly pumps tail. L 11-14 cm. *Britain.

**Hooded Warbler** *Wilsonia citrina*. Black hood with yellow face identifies all males; female black only on lores; both olive above, yellow below, with white undertail coverts and outer tail feathers. Skulks near ground. L 13 cm. Britain.

**Wilson's Warbler** *W. pusilla*. Differs from larger female Hooded Warbler in yellow lores, making dark eye more prominent, dark under tail coverts and no white in tail; male has small black cap. L 12 cm. Britain.

**Canada Warbler** *W. canadensis*. Another skulker, blue-grey above, yellow below with white undertail coverts, male with yellow eye-ring and lores, and blackish streaks on breast; female's eye-ring white and streaks greyish. L 13 cm. Iceland.

Scarlet Tanager p.3

Scarlet Tanager p.365

**Summer Tanager** *Piranga rubra*. Adult male all red with black wing-tips; female/imm less olive than similar Scarlet Tanager (p.365), and differ in stouter, often paler bill and pinkish-buff, not whitish, underwing coverts. L 20 cm. Britain.

**Rufous-sided Towhee** *Pipilo erythrophthalmus*. Unmistakable black N American woodland bunting with chestnut flanks and white belly and tips to outer tail feathers; female browner, juv streaked. L 22 cm. Britain.

**Lark Sparrow** *Chondestes grammacus*. Large, deep-bellied N American bunting with distinctive chestnut, black-and-white head pattern, and (also in much duller juv) conspicuously white corners to longish tail. L 17 cm. Britain.

**Savannah Sparrow** *Passerculus sandwichensis*. Undistinguished and somewhat like a female Yellow-browed Bunting (p.362), but with no white in tail; yellowish lores often absent in greyish ssp.*princeps* (Nova Scotia), which has occurred in Britain. L 14 cm.

princeps

**Meadow Bunting** *Emberiza cioides*. Striking black, white and chestnut head pattern of mainly chestnut breeding male diagnostic; winter male duller, female duller still. L 16.5 cm. *Finland.

**African Rock Bunting** *E. tahapisi*. Like slightly smaller House Bunting from S W Asia (p.354), but less rufous above, streaking on mantle blacker and male's throat blacker. Not in region; previous Sinai record now deleted. L 14 cm.

**Dickcissel** *Spiza americana*. A large-billed bunting with conspicuous broad yellow supercilia, yellow breast and rusty wing coverts; female/imm are duller and lack male's black bib. L 16 cm. Norway.

House Bunting p. 354

juv moulting

Starling p.330; juv moulting

**Brown-headed Cowbird** *Molothrus ater*. Like a smaller and much shorter-billed Starling (p.330); male all-black glossed green, but head brown; female sooty brown, paler and streaked below. L 19 cm. Norway, Britain.

juv

Blackbird p.272; 1st w

**Common Grackle** *Quiscalus quiscula*. Between a small crow and a large Starling (p.330) with a strikingly long keel-shaped tail; male all black, glossed purple or bronze; female/juv smaller, duller. L 28-34 cm. Denmark.

**Late Additions.** Ever increasing observation by experienced birdwatchers continues to produce new birds for the region, especially its southeastern and southwestern corners. The following are a selection of the most recent reports. Most of the records have yet to be confirmed and some, as for other 'Accidentals', might refer to birds that have escaped from captivity.

**Roseate Spoonbill** *Ajaia ajaja*. Told from Spoonbill by its pink plumage. *Azores.

**Lesser Whistling Duck** *Dendrocygna javanica*. Smaller than similar Fulvous Whistling Duck with a chestnut upper tail. *Israel.

**Crested Honey Buzzard** *Pernis ptilorhynchus*. Larger, broader-winged than Honey Buzzard, lacking prominent dark carpal patch on underwing. Turkey, Israel, Egypt.

**Tufted Puffin** *Lunda cirrhata*. Like Puffin but plumage entirely blackish except for white face (grey in winter) with long yellow plumes behind eyes. *Sweden.

**Grey-backed Finch Lark** *Eremopterix verticalis*. Similar to Black-crowned Finch Lark, but male with more black on head and white nape patch. Female with black belly. *Israel.

**Familiar Chat** *Cercomela familiaris*. Resembles an elongated, large-billed, brown-plumaged Blackstart with a reddish-brown tail, dark-centred and dark-banded near tip. *Canaries.

**Pale Thrush** *Turdus pallidus*. Larger and browner backed than similar Tickell's Thrush with white-cornered tail and yellow, dark-tipped bill. *Germany.

**Wattled Starling** *Creatophora cineracea*. Like a pale grey Starling with dark wings and tail, breeding male with yellow skin on head and black wattles. *Israel.

**Waterfowl Escapes**. Besides the escaped waterfowl which have established feral breeding populations, many more which are seen quite often have not yet established themselves. Some of the most frequent of these are illustrated below.

Domestic Chinese Goose

Swan Goose

ad
juv
Snow

Ross's

Blue Snow
juv

ad

**Swan Goose** *Anser cygnoides*. The wild ancestor of the domesticated Chinese Goose, which it closely resembles, but lacks the knob at the base of the bill. L 81-94 cm.

**Other Geese. Snow Goose** (p.54) is one of the most frequent escapes, both in its pure white form and in the darker Blue Goose morph. It also hybridises with other geese, making for even greater confusion. **Ross's Goose** (p.369) also escapes and together with Snow Goose is more likely to be seen as an escape than as a genuine wild vagrant.

**Emperor Goose** *Anser canagicus*. Not unlike Blue Snow Goose (p.54), but has only head and hind neck white, throat and foreneck being black; also differs in having dark ventral region and small bill. The only goose with yellow legs, except for Bar-headed (p.58). L 66-89 cm.

♂
♀
juv
ad    see also p.62

**Cape Shelduck** *Tadorna cana*. Drake differs from drake Ruddy Shelduck (p.62) in having head and neck grey; duck has forehead, cheeks and throat white and rest of head and neck grey. Aka South African Shelduck. Bill and legs black. L 61-66 cm.

**Other Shelducks. Paradise Shelduck** *T. variegata* drake is like an all-dark Ruddy Shelduck (p.62) with white and chestnut wing-patches. Duck differs from ducks of both Ruddy and Cape Shelducks in having whole head and upper neck white and body much darker. Aka New Zealand Shelduck. L 63-71 cm. **Australian Shelduck** *T. tadornoides*. Both sexes resemble drake Paradise Shelduck, but with whole breast rufous and narrow white neck-ring; duck also has white eye-ring. L 56-72, WS 94-132 cm.

**White-faced Whistling Duck** *Dendrocygna viduata*. Like other members of this mainly tropical genus, a long-legged, long-necked duck, the adult with an unmistakable white face, the imm duller, grey-faced. L 38-48 cm.

376

**Chiloe Wigeon** *Anas sibilatrix*. Wigeon-like (p.64) in general appearance, but differs from all other likely same-sized ducks in white face, rest of head and neck black (with dark green patch behind eye) and rufous flanks; duck duller. L 43-54 cm.

**Bahama Pintail** *Anus bahamensis*. A small duck, more like a Teal (p.66) than a Pintail (p.68), readily identified by strikingly white face, cheeks and neck, red patches at base of bill and pointed tail. Aka White-cheeked Pintail. L 38-51 cm.

**Red-billed Teal** *Anas erythrorhyncha*. A Shoveler-sized African duck, whose combination of dark brown crown and white face recall Bahama Pintail, but the whole bill is red not just the base. L 43-48 cm.

**Silver Teal** *Anas versicolor*. A South American teal with a yellow-based blue bill, the drake with a strikingly dark-capped head. One of its subspecies is known as the Puna Teal. L 38-43 cm.

**Cinnamon Teal** *Anus cyanoptera*. The tropical counterpart of Blue-winged Teal (p.66), the drake readily told by its bright rufous plumage, but the duck best told from duck Blue-winged by plumage being tinged rufous, not greyish. L 35-48 cm.

**Ringed Teal** *Callonetta leucophrys*. Drake has strikingly diverse plumage with pale face and cheeks outlined by black crown and neck-ring; duck's face is patchily white. Both sexes show white wing patch and green speculum in flight. Aka Ring-necked Teal. L 35-38 cm.

**Brazilian Teal** *Amazonetta brasiliensis*. A rather undistinguished brown duck with a more rufous breast; ducks always and drakes sometimes have a white face patch; bill and legs red. Aka Brazilian Duck. L 35-40 cm.

**Muscovy Duck** *Cairina moschata*. The wild bird is black, with a prominent white wing bar, a crest, bare red skin round the eye and a red knob on the pinkish bill; legs black. The more often seen domesticated birds are generally white or black and white. but can also be black or blue-grey. L 66-84 cm.

# Index of Common Names

## Index of Scientific Names

**383**